Advance English Grammar

Grammar

Class V Part 1

Suitable for Students of Class V of National Curriculum

Chandan Sukumar Sengupta

Creative Learning Series

English Grammar and Composition Class V Part 1

Chandan Sukumar Sengupta

This Activity Book is developed to meet the increasing demand of aspirants of High School standards having eagerness to develop themselves in terms of acquisition of basic competencies related to Communicative English. Some of the key areas of English Communicative curriculum is addressed through combinations of different content areas and other relevant study materials.

Major coverage is there on following topics:

Tenses	Modals	Subject-verb Agreement		Reported Speech	Commands
Statements		Questions	Determiners	Voice Change	Relative Clause

Prepositions

This workbook will provide an ample scope to students of high School standard and continuing education to improve their skills related to language and interpersonal communication. Communication process in modern world should be digitally sound also. We aspire for higher scope of progress as students involving in active communication process gains a lot.

Font size of some of the practice papers are kept small for ensuring accommodation of the material of large volume. Students of higher class can explore them with some easiness. They may not feel any specific problem while moving through content areas.

Resource Centre: Arabinda Nagar, Bankura, PIN – 722101 (W.B.) Attn: Chandan Sukumar Sengupta.

This Handbook is prepared for students of class V.

Contents

CONTENTS

Foreword

There are millions of books available in market which can introduce a learner to English language and English grammar. More discussed theme of language learning is the English Grammar. This effort came in focus due to the increasing demand of people from different walks of life regarding the type of workbook which can equip a student in a specific way in terms of the enhancement of language related skills.

This workbook is designed to provide additional study materials to fellow students of High School standards. They equip themselves differently by making them fit for forthcoming examination. Learning by doing is the best way of acquiring such kinds of skills in stipulated time frame.

A language stands upon its rules of grammar and compositions. Similar mechanism is applicable to English also. It has such kinds of sets of rules through which one can aspire for the attainment of a perfectness in writing and expressions.

English as a language is not so difficult for any non-English person. The basic structure of English language is user friendly and is also of a comprehensive type. Modern instruments are also much friendly with this language. Because of this reason and some other, English as a user friendly language is becoming popular day by day. Number of people from non-English community who can read, write and speak English quite fluently are growing in number day by day. They are also taking different roles assigned to them in the cosmopolitan environment.

Non-English learners and aspirants often feel difficulties in pronunciation English words properly with needful tunings. These difficulties often become a serious obstacle while some English people go on trying to establish communication with them. Due to such difficulties also they often become disqualified in proving their capabilities of doing something fruitful.

This workbook and practice manual will provide an ample scope of gaining adequate skill and competence in linguistic communication. Stress is implied in the portions related to grammar and composition of the language so as to enhance the related skills and competences of the fellow learner.

It is also recommended that one should go on practicing related exercises alongside the referral readings for the purpose of gaining proficiency. A discussion on the common mistakes related to the grammar and composition of this language is also included for the purpose of drawing attention of fellow students and aspirants towards the content areas of the communication techniques. English as a language came to India along with the colonial rule. They people felt it necessary to educate a considerable part of Indian as well as Asian communities in English for ensuring their service lines in the colonies. It was more perfectly pitched in through religious propagations.

People of India accepted the language gladly and started getting adjusted with the cultural bands of English orientation. This West Germanic language is developed from Anglo-Frician dialects.[1] This dialect is brought to Britain during 6th to 7th Century by Anglo-Saxon[2] Migrants. In due course of time this language developed considerably and transformed into the dialect of modern time.[3] Anglo –Saxon dialect was more commonly known as old-English.[4] Near

---

[1] *The Anglo-Frisian languages are the Anglic and Frisian varieties of West Germanic languages. The Northumbrian Language Society also considers Northumbrian a separate Anglic language.*
[2] *The Anglo-Saxon settlement of Britain is the process which changed the language and culture of most of what became England from Romano-British to Germanic. The Germanic-speakers in Britain, themselves of diverse origins, eventually developed a common cultural identity as Anglo-Saxons.*
[3] *Burke, Susan E (1998). ESL: Creating a quality English as a second language program: A guide for churches. Grand Rapids, Michigan: CRC Publications. ISBN 9781562123437.*
[4] *Shore, Thomas William (1906), Origin of the Anglo-Saxon Race - A Study of the Settlement of England and*

about 400 Latin loan Words[5] were introduced in English alongside the advent of Christianity. During the development Middle English near about 10,000 loan words from French origin[6] entered the English dialect and made it an enriched one. Fully developed English dictionary, the Dictionary of the English Language, was published by Samuel Johnson in 1755. English Grammar by Pristle[7] was an added contribution in the line of development of English Language. In modern time the total English speaking community worldwide may exceed 1.5 billion mark![8] There are several other instances to ascertain the fact regarding the ever increasing popularity of the International Language. It has also secured a prominent position in the international arena as a common dialect that people can opt with an ease.

After becoming assured about the ever increasing popularity of this language we can now imply adequate focus on the development of skills and competence of our fellow students and aspirants through exposing them to the horizon of interactive areas related to perfect and advanced English dialect. We also expect a timely participation of fellow scholars in this effort. They can continue evaluating their own skills through learning continuity supplemented with self paced evaluations. Evolution of English Pronoun is another additional advantage of the modern English. Conflated forms of pronouns are also called an objective case. Development of such name is

---

the Tribal Origin of the Old English People (1st ed.), London, pp. 3, 393

[5] English is a Germanic language, with a grammar and a core vocabulary inherited from Proto-Germanic. However, a significant portion of the English vocabulary comes from Romance and Latinate sources. A portion of these borrowings come directly from Latin,

[6] Baugh, Albert and Cable, Thomas. 2002. The History of the English Language. Upper Saddle River, New Jersey: Prentice Hall. pp. 158-178.

[7] Joseph Priestley was an English chemist, natural philosopher, separatist theologian, grammarian, multi-subject educator, and liberal political theorist who published over 150 works.

[8] Algeo, John. 2010. The Origins and Development of the English Language. Boston, MA: Wadsworth. pp. 182-187.

only because it is used only for objects of verbs. Once in old English there was distinct case system for both accusative and dative purposes. Later on such system collapsed into a single system of object (oblique) case having utility for objects of either a verb or a preposition. Studies in English were introduced in different universities during 19th and 20th Century because of its continuous developments in non-European continents. Development of such study was remarkably high in USA during 1970s. [9] It was also due to incorporation of English as another official language in most of the countries in the world.

Different courses in English are meant for different purposes. Studies in English are further accelerated with the advent of Informatics and allied fields. We consider English as a second language (a language study meant for non-English person). Errors in English are mainly observed from the field of syntax error, vocabulary error and error related to punctuations. Rules in English are periodically introduced by different scholars time to time. Not to terminate a sentence by preposition, for an example, was the another rule introduced by *Robert Lowth*[10] .

Chandan Sukumar Sengupta

---

[9] *National Center for Education Statistics (January 1993). "120 Years of American Education: A Statistical Portrait" (PDF). National Center for Education Statistics. Retrieved September 12, 2018.*

[10] *Robert Lowth (26 March 1794). A Short Introduction to English Grammar: With Critical Notes. Printed for J.J . Tourneisin – via Internet Archive.*

Preface

It is not so easy to generalise uses of materials and references related to English Grammar and Communication for making all the aspirants equally competent in best use of English as a language. Sharpness and aptness in phases of communication, especially communications of inter-personal types, are solely the subject matter of personality and affinity of aspirants.

On the basis of the problem related to the development of Social Media it would be better if we start by considering some examples of academic communications from our daily life. Some of desired changes which brought in our surrounding were related to alignment of text while writing any kind of conventional or non-conventional writings. Writing Email, formal letter, informal letter changed considerably after introduction of digital tools in the field of writing and editing text materials. Here we will consider some of such examples while discussing on Communicative English. The knowledge of Networking and E Learning tools is another pre-requisite for gaining mastery over the communication skills in modern context. We also confer ourselves for the type of interaction people often come across while attending any interview. The type of communication and interaction which is expected from a fellow job seeker is actually come in the form of the dimension with which the group of employers wants the job seeker to work for the team. In that context the approaches of different interview may differ in terms of composition of questions and interactions. But during most of instances they always want a job seeker to appear along with confidence, will power and courageous blend of mind. We also want aspirants to maintain a positive mental attitude in life and also want them to come forward with an ardent will to accept challenges.

You can also sort out a list of reference materials for gaining needful points to be incorporated in the proposed format of writing. Maintenance of vocabulary is the other way out for gaining mastery. One should maintain such list while moving across different types of composition. Because of that reason also side reading is most important on the way of enhancing communication skills of desired types. One should also take part in different types of competitive examinations and contests to develop a wider grasp on the language and related activities of composition. We will also move through different important parts of effective and conventional writing for which students put maximum effort and collect voluminous data. Here a sketch of conventional writing is placed as an example. One can have adequate freedom of considering different points to be incorporated in the writing as per wish and will. One cannot generalise such kind of writing at any instance simply on the basis of any pre-defined format.

Development in the field of Information and Communication Technology has also opened up a horizon of effective participation in the networks of Social Media. We also want people to go through the bands of short signals as such signals are extensively used in the platforms of different Social Media. We also intend to bring forth our feelings with such short signals which are used these days to remain linked up in the field of interactive social and community level platforms. We also aspire for a medium which can accept our such approaches and allow us to link up with millions. Academic English cannot allow use of such short signals in any kind of conventional witting. We also cannot allow use of other such short messages merely for linking up with socially active people at different horizon. Our apprehension of making ourselves enriched depends solely on the way we use academically enriched compositions of different types for keeping us effectively linked up.

1. Revision Works

Collected from previously conducted examinations.

Direct and Indirect Speech

In the Indirect speech, no inverted commas are used. The conjunctions that, if, whether, are generally used after the reporting verb. The first word of the reported speech begins with a capital letter. The tense of the reporting verb is never changed. The reporting verb changes according to sense: it may be told, asked, inquired.

Change in Tenses:
If the reporting verb is in the present or the future tense, the tense of the reported speech is not changed:
Satish says, "I am flying a kite."
Satish says that he is flying a kite.
Satish will say, "I want a glass of milk."
Satish will say that he wants a glass of milk.

If the reporting verb is in the past tense, then the tense of the reported speech will change as follows:

Direct	Indirect
Simple Present	Simle Past
Present Progressive	Past Progressive
Present Perfect	Past Perfect
Simple Past	Past Perfect
Past Progressive	Past Perfect Progressive

If the direct speech expresses a historical fact, universal truth, or a habitual fact, then the tense of the direct speech will not change:
Direct: He said, "Honesty is the best policy."
Indirect: He said that honesty is the best policy.
Direct: He said, "The sun rises in the east."
Indirect: He said that the sun rises in the east.
Direct: Rakesh said, "I am an early riser."
Indirect : Rakesh said that he is an early riser.
Direct: She said, "God is omnipresent."
Indirect: She said that God is omnipresent.

Direct: The teacher said, "The First World War started in 1914."

Indirect: The teacher said that the First World War started in 1914.

Changing Statements into Indirect Speech:

The reporting verb 'said to' is changed-to 'told', 'replied', 'remarked',

The reporting verb is not followed by an object, it is not changed.

The inverted commas are removed. The conjunction is used to connect the reporting clause with the reported speech.

The rules for the change of pronouns, tenses, etc. are followed.

Direct: Ramu said, "I saw a lion in the forest."

Indirect: Ramu said that he had seen a lion in the forest.

Direct: Satish said to me, "I am very happy here."

Indirect: Satish told me that he was very happy there.

Direct: He said, "I can do this work."

Indirect: He said that he could do that work.

Direct: Renu said to me, "I was washing the clothes."

Indirect: Renu told me that she had been washing the clothes.

Direct: She said, "I am not well."

Indirect: She said that she was not well.

Direct: He said to Sita, "I have passed the test."

Indirect: He told Sita that he had passed the test.

Direct: I said to my friend, "He has been working very hard."

Indirect: I told my friend that he had been working very hard.

Direct: My friend said to me, "I shall go to Delhi tomorrow."

Indirect: My friend told me that he would go to Delhi the next day.

Direct: I said, "I agree to what he said."

Indirect: I said that I agreed to what he had said.

Direct: The student said to the teacher, "I am sorry that I am late."

Indirect: The student told the teacher that he was sorry that he was late.

Rules for the Change of Interrogative (Questions) sentences:

The reporting verb "say' is changed into ask, inquire,

The interrogative sentence is changed into a statement by placing the subject before the verb and the full stop is put at the end of the sentence.

If the interrogative sentence has a wh-word (who, when, where, how, why, etc) the wh-word is repeated in the sentence. It serves as conjunction.

If the interrogative sentence is a yes-no answer type sentence (with auxiliary verbs am, are, was, were, do, did, have, shall, etc), then 'if or 'whether' is used as a conjunction.

The auxiliaries do, does, did in a positive question in the reported speech are dropped.

The conjunction is not used after the reporting clause.

Direct: I said to him, "Where are you going?"

Indirect: I asked him where he was going.

Direct: He said to me, "Will you go there?"

Indirect: He asked me if I would go there.

Direct: My friend said to Deepak, "Have you ever been to Agra?"

Indirect: My friend asked Deepak if he had ever been to Agra.

Direct: I said to him, "Did you enjoy the movie?"

Indirect: I asked him if he had enjoyed the movie.

Direct: I said to her, "Do you know him?"

Indirect: I asked her if she knew him.

Direct: He said to me, "Will you listen to me?"

Indirect: He asked me if I would listen to him.

Direct: I said to him, "When will you go there?"

Indirect: I asked him when he would go there.

Direct: He said to me, "How is your father?"

Indirect: He asked me how my father was.

Direct: I said to him, "Are you happy?"

Indirect: I asked him if he was happy.

Direct: He said to her, "Do you like apples?"

Indirect: He asked her if she liked apples.

In imperative sentences having commands, the reporting verb is changed into command, order, tell, allow, request,etc.

The imperative mood is changed into the infinitive mood by putting 'to', before the verb. In case of negative sentences, the auxiliary 'do' is dropped and 'to' is placed after 'not':

Direct: She said to me, "Open the window."

Indirect: She ordered me to open the window.

Direct: The captain said to the soldiers, "Attack the enemy."

Indirect: The captain commanded the soldiers to attack the enemy.

Direct: I said to him, "Leave this place at once."

Indirect: I told him to leave that place at once.

Direct: The teacher said to the students, "Listen to me attentively."

Indirect: The teacher asked the students to listen to him attentively.

Direct: The Principal said to the peon, "Ring the bell."

Indirect: The Principal ordered the peon to ring the bell.

Direct: The master said to the servant, "Fetch me a glass of water."

Indirect: The master ordered the servant to fetch him a glass of water.

Direct: I said to him, "Please bring me a glass of water."

Indirect: I requested him to bring me a glass of water.

Direct: I said to my friend, "Please lend me your book."

Indirect: I requested my friend to lend me his book.

'Let' is used in various meanings.

(i) 'Let' is used to make a proposal.

First change the reporting verb into 'proposed' or 'suggested'.

Use 'should' instead of 'let'.

Example:

Direct: He said to me, "Let us go home."

Indirect: He suggested to me that we should go home.

(ii) 'Let' is used as 'to allow'.

In Indirect Speech, we change the reporting verb to 'requested' or 'ordered'.

We start Reported Speech with 'to'.

Direct: Ram said to Mohan, "Let him do it."

Indirect: Ram ordered Mohan to let him do that.

Or

Ram told Mohan that he might be allowed to do that.

Question tags

(i) In the indirect speech the question-tag is usually left.

(ii) In indirect speech these words are removed and the word 'respectfully' is used in the reporting clause.

Direct: Mahesh said, "Sir, may I go home?"

Indirect: Mahesh respectfully asked his sir if he might go home.

Sentences containing 'Yes' or 'No'[11]

Direct : He said, "Can you dance?" And I said, "No."

Indirect: He asked me if I could dance and I replied that I couldn't.

Direct : My mother said, "Will you come home on time?" And I said, "Yes."

Indirect: My mother asked me if I would come home on time and I replied that I would.

Direct : She said to me, "You didn't break the window, did you?"

Indirect: She asked me if/whether I had broken the window.

Direct : He said to Geeta, "You are going to the station, aren't you?"

Indirect: He asked Geeta if/ whether she was going to the station.

12. Sentences with 'have to' or 'had to'

(i) Change 'have to' according to the rules.

(ii) But change 'had to' into 'had had to' in the indirect speech.

Direct : Hari said, "I have to work a lot."

Indirect: Hari said that he had to work a lot.

Direct : Hari said, "I had to work a lot."

Indirect: Hari said that he had had to work a lot.

13. Sentences with 'Sir', 'Madam' or 'Your Honour' etc. Generally such words are used to show respect to the person concerned.

Exclamations and Wishes[12]

Examples:

Direct : Rohan said, "Hurrah! We won the match."

Indirect: Rohan exclaimed with joy that they had won the match.

Direct : Reema said, "Alas! Karina's mother is suffering from cancer."

Indirect: Reema exclaimed with sorrow that Karina's mother was suffering from cancer.

Direct : The captain said to Kapil, "Bravo! You scored 89 runs."

---

[11] *'Yes' of 'No' hides a complete sentence. Therefore, change yes/no into a short answer.*

[12] *Sometimes Exclamatory sentences contain exclamations like Hurrah!, Alas!, Oh!, Heavens!, Bravo, etc. Such exclamatory words are removed in the indirect speech and we use 'exclaimed with sorrow', exclaimed with joy, exclaimed with surprise, etc. instead of 'said'.*

Indirect: The captain exclaimed with praise that he (Kapil) had scored 89 runs.

(a) Look at these sentences.

Direct : My mother said, "May God bless you!"

Indirect: My mother prayed to God for my well being.

Direct : She said, "May God save the country!"

Indirect: She prayed to God to save the country.

Direct : They said to the king, "Long live!"

Indirect: They blessed the king for his long life.

(b) Look at these sentences.

Direct : Mohan said, "What a pity!"

Indirect: Mohan exclaimed that it was a great pity.

Direct : I said, "How stupid he is!"

Indirect: I exclaimed that it was a very stupid of him.

Direct : "What a terrible sight it is!" said the traveller.

Indirect: The traveller exclaimed that it was a very terrible sight.

All the sentences in inverted commas are exclamatory sentences.

(i) Use 'exclaimed' in place of 'said' in the reporting verb in the indirect speech.

(ii) In Indirect sentences, we use exclamatory sentences as statements.

(iii) Indirect speech begins with that and full stop ($\bullet$) is used instead of the exclamation mark (!).

Exercise (Solved)

Change the following sentences into Indirect Speech:

(i) He said, "I will do it now."

Answer: He said that he would do it then.

(ii) He says, "Honesty is the best policy."

Answer: He says that honesty is the best policy.

(iii) Ramesh says, "I have written a letter."

Answer: Ramesh says that he has written a letter.

(iv) She said, "Mahesh will be reading a book."

Answer: She said that Mahesh would be reading a book.

(v) She said, "Where is your father?"

Answer: She inquired where his father was.

(vi) He said to me, "Please take your book."

Answer: He requested me to take my book.

(vii) The Principal said to the peon, "Let this boy go out."
Answer: The Principal ordered the peon to let that boy go out.

(viii) He said to me, "May you live long!"
Answer: He prayed that I might live long.

(ix) She said, "Goodbye friends!"
Answer: She bade goodbye to her friends.

(ix) The student said, "Alas! I wasted my time last year."
Answer: The student regretted that he had wasted his time the previous year.

Exercise (Unsolved)
Change the following sentences into Indirect Speech:
The captain said, "Bravo! well done, my boys."
He said to her, "Why do you read this book?"
He said to her, "Does your cow not kick?"
He said to his brother, "Shailesh has broken my glass."
Our teacher said, "The earth revolves around the sun."

He said to me, "Why have you come here?"
Usha said, "Father, you are very kind to me."
The teacher said to the boys, "Do not make a noise."
He said to his friend, "May you prosper in business!"
The officer said to the peon, "Let the visitor come into my office."

Reported Speech Continues

Reported Speech
Reported Speech (3 marks each)
Question 1.
Read the conversation given below and complete the paragraph that follows: (3 marks) (Board 2014, Set PRE2N18)
Principal: Why were you absent last week?
Student: I was absent because I was not well.
Principal: What will happen to your studies now?
Student: I will work hard to complete them.
The Principal asked the student (a)............. The student replied (b)............... The Principal was concerned and asked (c)........... The student replied that he would study hard to complete them.

Answer:
(a) why he had been absent the previous week.
(b) that he had been absent because he had not been well.
(c) what would happen to his studies then?
You can master in English Grammar of various classes by our articles like Tenses, Clauses, Prepositions, Story writing, Unseen Passage, Notice Writing, etc.
Question 2.
Read the conversations given below. Based on your reading, fill in the blanks appropriately. (3 marks) (Board Term-1 2013, Set 8SRR)
Julie: When is the fancy- dress competition in your school?
Mona: It is after two weeks.
Julie: Are you taking part in it?
Mona: Yes, I am taking part as an engine driver.
Julie: Why have you chosen that?
Mona: So that I can reach late.
Julie asked Mona when the fancy dress competition in her school was. To that Mona replied that (a) ______________ Julie enquired whether (b) ______________
Mona said that she was taking part as an engine driver. Julie asked why (c) ______________
She answered (d)

______________.

Answer:
(a) it was after two weeks.
(b) whether/if she was taking part in it.
(c) she had chosen that.
(d) then/so that she could reach late.

Question 3.
Read the conversation given below and complete the paragraph that follows : (3 marks) (Board Term-1 2013, Set 5007)
Haiku: The landlord has come. Take out the money you have set aside.
Wife: But there are only three' hundred rupees. If you give them to him, where is the blanket going to come from?

Haiku: Don't worry. I will figure out some other plan.
Haiku told his wife that the landlord had come, she should take out (a) .... His wife said that (b)............and asked him if he gave them to him (c)..............
Answer:
(a) the money she had set aside.
(b) that there were only three hundred rupees.
(c) where the blanket was going to come from.
Question 4.
Read the conversation given below and complete the passage that follows : (3 marks) (Board Term-1 2012, Set EC2,039)
Ali: Omar, why don't you leave this place? I can drop you on my way back home.
Omar: I have no home.
Ali: Where have you come from?
Omar: From Tunisia.
Ali asked Omar (a)...................and offered to (b)................... Omar replied that he had no home.

Then Ali asked
(c).................... Omar told
him that he had come from
Tunisia.
Answer:
(a) why he didn't leave that
place.
(b) drop him on his way back
home.
(c) where he had come from.
Question 5.
Read the following
conversation between a mother
and son and then complete the
paragraph that follows : (3
marks) (Board Term-1 2012,
Set EC2,043)
Mother: You seem so tired.
Take some rest.
Suraj: I can't even think of
relaxing. I have lots of
homework to do.
Mother: You should not take
so much of stress.
Suraj: Don't worry. Please
give me a hot cup of tea.
Mother said to Suraj that
(a)...................... Suraj
replied that
(b)...................... The
mother advised him not to take
so much of stress. Suraj told
his mother
(c)......................
Answer:
(a) he seemed so tired and
advised him to take a rest.
(b) he could not even think of
relaxing as he had lots of
homework to do.
(c) not to worry and requested
her to give him a hot cup of
tea.
Question 6.
Given below are instructions
for making soup. Use these to

complete the blanks in the
paragraph that follows. (3
marks) (Board Tenn-I 2012,
Set EC2,042)

Mix the soup powder with 750
ml of water without allowing it
to form lumps.

Pour the mixture into a heavy-
bottomed vessel.

Bring it to a boil, stirring
continuously.

Simmer the soup for five
minutes.

Pour the soup into soup bowls
and serve garnished with fried
croutons.
The packet containing the soup
powder (a) ______________
opened and the contents are
mixed with 750 ml of water
without allowing it to form
lumps. The mixture (b)
______________ into a heavy-
bottomed vessel. It is stirred
continuously and brought to
boil. The soup (c)
______________ on a slow flame
for five minutes. Finally after
the soup is ready, it is (d)

______________.

Answer:
(a) is opened
(b) is poured
(c) is simmered
(d) is poured into the soup
bowls and served
Question 7.
Read the conversation given
below and complete the
paragraph that follows: (3

marks) (Board Term-1 2012, Set EC2,0401)

Raju: Do you know Varun was hit by a two-wheeler yesterday?

Arun: Oh no! When did it happen?

Raju: He was hit by a scooter on his way back from school.

Arun: Is he badly hurt?

Raju asked Arun (a)…………………….. Arun was shocked and wanted to know when (b)………………….. Raju replied that (c)………………….. Arun enquired if he was badly hurt.

Answer: (a) if he knew that Varun had been hit by a two-wheeler the previous day.

(b) it had happened. .

(c) he had been hit by a scooter on his way back from school.

Question 8.

Read the conversation given below and complete the paragraph that follows: (3 marks) (Board Term-1 2012, Set EC2,064)

Vani: Harika, are you going to join the Dramatics Club with me?

Harika: No, I am going to join the Adventure Club.

Vani: I too would have joined the Adventure Club, but I am very scared of heights.

Harika: If that is the case, join the Dramatics Club.

Vani asked Harika (a)…………………….. Harika said that (b)…………………… Adventure Club. To this Vani replied (c)

…………………………

Adventure Club, but she was very scared of heights. Harika advised her to join the Dramatics Club.

Answer:

(a) if she was going to join the Dramatics Club with her.

(b) she was going to join the

(c) she too would have joined the

Question 9.

Read the conversation given below and complete the paragraph that follows: (Board Term-1 2012, Set EC2,039)

Pig: See how strong and hefty I am. Even the Jumbo was afraid of me.

Animals: Jumbo, was it out of horror?

Jumbo: I could have happily crushed the dirty pig under my heels but I avoided it so that I do not become dirty.

The jaunty pig said (a)………………………….. He further added (b)…………………………. All the animals enquired of Jumbo if that had been out of horror. Jumbo replied that he could have happily crushed the dirty pig under his heels but he (c)…………………………..

Answer:

(a) that he was very strong and hefty

(b) that even the Jumbo had been afraid of him.

(c) had avoided it so that he did not become dirty.

Question 10.

Read the conversation given below and complete the

paragraph that follows: (3 marks)
Rohan: When is the fancy dress competition at your school?
Seema: It is after two weeks.
Rohan: Are you taking part in it?
Seema: Yes, I am taking part as a caterpillar.
Rohan: Why have you chosen that?
Seema: So that I can reach late.
Rohan asked Seema
(a)…………………………..
Seema replied
(b)…………………………..
Rohan enquired
(c)………………………. Seema said that she was taking part as a caterpillar. Rohan asked why she had chosen that. Seema answered so that she could reach late. (Board Term-12012, Set EC2,048)
Answer:
(a) when the fancy dress competition in her school was.
(b) that it was after two weeks.
(c) whether she was taking part in that
Question 11.
Read the conversation given below and complete the paragraph that follows : (3 marks) (Board Term-1 2012, Set EC2,061)
Customer: Why is the meal so sour?
Waiter: Nobody has complained for five days sir, about the meal.
Customer: What! Where is the Manager?
Waiter: He has gone to some other hotel to take dinner, sir.

One day a customer was taking dinner in a hotel. He asked the waiter why
(a)……………………… The waiter told him (b)
………………………….. At this, the customer was shocked and wanted to know where the Manager was. The waiter replied (c)
…………………………..
Answer:
(a) the meal was so sour.
(b) that nobody had complained for five days about the meal.
(c) that he had gone to some other hotel to take dinner.
Question 12.
Read the conversation given below and complete the paragraph that follows : (3 marks) (Board Term-1 2012, Set EC2,049)
Teacher: Did you brush your hair this morning?
Asha: Yes, I did, but the wind blew it about while I was coming to school.
Teacher: Wear a hairband tomorrow.
The teacher asked Asha
(a)……………………… Asha replied that she had, but the wind
(b)………………………while she had been coming to school. The teacher instructed her
(c)………………………
Answer:
(a) if she had brushed her hair that morning.
(b) had blown it about.
(c) to wear a hairband the next day.

Question 13.

Read the following conversation and complete the paragraph that follows : (3 marks)

Mother: Rita, finish your food.

Rita: I don't want to have this food. You never give me a pizza or burger.

Mother: They are not good for health. You had pizza at your friend's birthday party last evening.

Rita: OK, then give me French fries and shake. '

Mother: If you live only on junk food, you will spoil your health.

Mother told Rita (a)........................... Rita replied that (b)...........................and told her mother that she never gave her a pizza or burger. Mother said that they were not good for health and reminded her (c)....................... Rita then asked her mother to give her french fries and a shake. Mother warned her that if she lived only on junk food, she would spoil her health.

Answer:

(a) to finish her food.

(b) she did not want to have that food

(c) that she had pizza at her friend's birthday party the evening before.

Question 14.

Read the conversation/dialogue given below and complete the paragraph that follows: (3 marks)

Patient: I want an appointment with the doctor for this evening.

Receptionist: I'm sorry, I can't give you an appointment before the 20th.

Patient: But I could be dead by then!

Receptionist: That's all right. I'll ring up your wife and cancel the appointment in that case.

The patient (a)......................evening. The receptionist (b)......................an appointment before the 20th. The patient (c)....................... The receptionist replied that it was all right as she would ring up his wife and cancel the appointment in that case.

Answer:

told the receptionist that he wanted an appointment with the doctor for that

(b) replied that she was sorry but she could not give him

(c) exclaimed that he could be dead by then

Question 15.

Read the conversation given below and complete the paragraph that follows: (3 marks)

Patient: Good afternoon. I need to get an E.C.G. done. .

Receptionist: Sorry. Our machine is not working. You can come tomorrow.

Patient: What! But I think I'm having a heart attack now.

Receptionist: Oh! In that case, 1 will book you for a bypass and inform our Senior Cardiologist.

A patient went to the doctor's clinic, greeted the receptionist, and said that (a)………………………. The receptionist apologized and told him (b) ……………………… She also added that (c) ……………………….. The patient reacted angrily and said he thought he was having a heart attack. To this, the receptionist replied that in that case she could book him for a bypass and inform their Senior Cardiologist.

Answer:

(a) he needed to get an E.C.G. done.

(b) that their machine was not working.

(c) he could come the next day.

2. Process Writing (3 marks each)

Question 1.

Given below are instructions on how to make cold coffee. Refer to the given notes and complete the paragraph : (3 marks) (Board Term-12012, Set EC2,046)

Pour 3/4 of a glass of cold milk in the mixer.

Add one teaspoonful of sugar and half a teaspoonful coffee powder to it.

Add a few ice cubes.

Switch on the mixer.

Coffee and sugar would blend with the milk and froth would appear on top.

Switch off the mixer.

Pour cold coffee in a tall glass.

Serve it cold.

To prepare cold coffee 3/4 of a glass of cold milk (a)………………… One teaspoonful of sugar and half a teaspoonful of coffee powder (b)…………………to it. A few ice cubes are also added to this. The mixer (c)………………… When froth appears on the milk, the mixer is switched off. After pouring it in a tall glass it is served cold.

Answer:

(a) is taken

(b) are added

(c) is switched on

Question 2.

Given below are the instructions on How to Make Orange Squash. Refer, to the notes and complete the paragraph given below: (3 marks)

Take 1 dozen fully ripe oranges

Remove the rind

Extract the juice

Strain through a thick cloth

Mix 1 /2 kg sugar, 1 /2 tea-spoonful citric acid

Add a pinch of potassium meta-bisulfate, a few drops of colour and essence

Stir till thoroughly dissolved
One dozen fully ripe oranges are taken. Their rinds (a).....................and the juice (b)..................... Then the juice (c).....................through a thick cloth into a stainless steel vessel. 1/2 kg of sugar, 1/2 teaspoonful of citric acid, a pinch of potassium meta – bisulphate, a few drops of colour and essence are added to the juice. The mixture is stirred till it is thoroughly dissolved.
Answer:
(a) are removed
(b) is extracted
(c) is strained
Question 3.
Given below are a set of instructions for using a clinical thermometer. Complete the paragraph describing the process of using a clinical thermometer: (3 marks) (Board Term-1 2012, Set EC2,052)

Wash the thermometer with fresh water thoroughly.

Stake it well to bring down the reading below 37°C.

Place the die bulb of the thermometer under the patient's tongue.

Ask the patient to keep the mouth closed.

Keep the thermometer under the patient's tongue for at least 2 minutes.

Take out the thermometer and read the temperature.
How to Use a Clinical Thermometer
The clinical thermometer (a).....................with freshwater and the reading (b).....................by shaking it well. Then the bulb of the thermometer (c).....................under the patient's tongue and he is asked to keep the mouth closed. The thermometer should be kept there for at least two minutes. It is then taken out and the temperature is read.
Answer:
(a) is washed
(b)) is brought down
(c) is placed
Question 4.
Given below are instructions on how to make lemonade. Refer to the notes and complete the paragraph: (3 marks) (Board Term-1 2012, Set EC2,048)

Take a glass of water.

Add four spoonfuls of sugar.

Squeeze the juice of a lemon and add.

Add salt, roasted cumin seed powder, and ice.

Serve chilled.

To prepare lemonade, a glass of water is taken and four spoonfuls of sugar (a)....................to it. A lemon (b)....................and juice is added to it. Salt, roasted cumin seed powder and ice (c)..................... It is served chilled.

Answer:

(a) are added

(b) is squeezed

(c) are added and stirred

Question 5.

Given below are instructions on how to make instant coffee. Refer to the given notes and complete the paragraph: (3 marks) (Board Term-1 2012, Set EC2,083)

Put coffee powder and sugar into a cup – pour some hot milk – stir it well for 5 minutes – add hot milk to it – Add a pinch of cinnamon powder for flavour – serve hot.

To prepare instant coffee, coffee powder, and sugar (a)....................in a cup. Some hot water (b)....................into the cup and the mixture is (c)....................for about 5 minutes. Hot milk is then added to it. It is then served hot with cinnamon powder for taste.

Answer:

(a) is put

(b) is poured

(c) stirred

Question 6.

Given below are instructions to make tomato soup. Read the given notes and complete the paragraph that follows: (3 marks) (Board Term-12012, Set EC2,018)

Place tomatoes in a pan-fill the pan with water–add onions and green chilies –cook for 10 min.-remove from the pan–peel tomatoes–grind tomatoes, onion, green chilies–add salt to taste–boil and serve hot.

To prepare tomato soup tomatoes (a)....................in a pan and the pan is filled with water. Onions and green chilies (b)....................and cooked for 10 minutes. Tomatoes are then (c)....................and peeled. Tomatoes, onions, and chilies are ground. After adding salt the mixture is boiled and served hot.

Answer:

(a) are placed

(b) are added

(c) removed from the pan

Question 7.

Given below are the instructions on dyeing a piece of cloth. Refer to the given notes and complete the , sentences given below: (3 marks) (Board Term-1 2012, Set EC2,039)

Take a strong, white-coloured cotton cloth.

Boil water and add the desired colour.

Dip the cloth in coloured hot water and soak it for half an hour.

Take the cloth out

Spread the cloth and let it dry.
A strong, white-coloured
cotton cloth is taken. Water
(a)......................and the
desired colour
(b)...................... The cloth
(c).....................in the
coloured water for half an
hour. The cloth is taken out.
Finally, it is spread and
allowed to dry.
Answer:
(a) is boiled
(b) is added to it
(c) is soaked
Question 8.
Given below are the
instructions on how to use a
thesaurus. Refer to the given
notes and complete the
paragraph: (3 marks) (Board
Term-1 2012, Set EC2,061)

Locate the word for which you
need synonyms in the
Thesaurus.

Note the number given after
that word.

Look up the alternatives listed
against that number.

Choose the one that best suits
the purpose.
First, the word for which
(a).....................in the
Thesaurus. Next, the number
given is noted. After these
alternatives listed
(b)..................... Finally,
the one best
(c).....................

Answer:
(a) synonyms are needed is
located
(b) are looked up against the
number
(c) that suits the purpose is
chosen
Question 9.
Read the instructions given
below and complete the
following: (3 marks) (Board
Term-12012, Set EC2,053)

Don't leave valuables inside
your vehicle.

Don't display large sums of
cash in public.

Don't touch any unidentified
object.

Don't get distracted by
unknown persons trying to
approach you with any offer of
help.
Make your city safe and sound
by following certain
instructions. No valuables
(a).....................inside a
vehicle as they may attract
anti-social elements. While
carrying cash it
(b)..................... If we find
some unidentified object lying
in the market it
(c)..................... We
should not get distracted by
unknown persons trying to
approach us with an offer to
help.
Answer:
(a) should be left
(b) should not be displayed in

public
(c) should not be touched
Question 10.
Given below are the instructions on how to make coconut burfi. Refer to the given notes and complete the paragraph: (3 marks) (Board Term-I 2012, Set EC2,059)
Stir together grated coconut mid condensed milk — cook on high in the microwave for 7 mins — switching off, opening and stirring every 30 seconds — add the almonds and cardamom in the hot and bubbling coconut mixture-pour the mixture into the prepared pan.
To prepare 'coconut burfi' grated coconut and condensed milk are stirred together in a large microwave-safe bowl. Then, it (a)....................on high in the microwave for 7 minutes. It (b)...................., opened, and stirred every 30 seconds. When the coconut mixture is hot and bubbling, almonds, and cardamom (c)..................... The mixture is poured into a prepared pan and after cooling, cut into small squares with a greased knife.
Arts.
(a) is cooked
(b) is switched off
(c) are added
Question 11.
Some steps for an experiment to prove that unlike charges attract each other. Complete the paragraph given below, using suitable words. (3 marks) (Board Term-I 2011, Set 42)

Take a hard rubber rod and a piece of flannel.

Electrify the rod by rubbing it with flannel.

Suspend the rod with a silk thread.

Electrify a glass rod by rubbing it with a silk cloth.

Bring the glass rod near the suspended rubber rod.

The glass rod would attract the rubber rod.
First of all, a hard rubber rod and a piece of flannel are taken. The rod is, then (a)............. A glass rod is, then, (b)................... by rubbing it with a silk cloth. The glass rod (c)................... near the suspended rubber rod. The rubber rod will be attracted by the glass rod.
Answer:
(a) electrified
(b) again electrified
(c) is then brought
Question 12.
Using the information given below, complete the paragraph that follows. The fust one has been done as an example. Don't write the printed words. (3 marks) (Board Term-I 2011, Set 29)
Cut a fresh onion into small pieces.
(ii) Boil these pieces in 10 ml of distilled water for 3-4 min.
(iii) Coal the solution.

(iv) Filter the content to be used as food extract.
(v) Perform Benedict's test.
(vi) The solution turns green, then orange, and finally red.
(vii) This confirms the presence of glucose in onion.
In order to test the presence of glucose in onions, the following experiment must be performed. First, the onion is cut into small pieces. Then these onion pieces (a)................... for 3-4 minutes. The solution is allowed to cool. It is then (b)................... Now (c)................... on the content. You will observe that initially, the solution turns green, then orange, and finally red. Thus, the presence of glucose in onion is confirmed.
Answer:
(a) are boiled in 10 ml of distilled water.
(b) filtered to be used as food extract.
(c) Benedict's test is performed.
Question 13.
Given below are instructions for making soup. Refer to the given notes and complete the paragraph that follows: (3 marks)

Mix the soup powder with 750 ml, of water without allowing it to form lumps.

Pour the mixture into a heavy-bottomed vessel.

Bring it to boil, stirring continuously.

Let the soup simmer for five minutes.

Pour the soup into soup bowls and serve garnished with fried croutons.
The packet containing soup powder is opened and the contents are mixed with 750 ml of water without allowing it to form lumps. The mixture (a)....................into a heavy-bottomed vessel. It is stirred (b)....................boil. The soup (c)....................on a slow flame for five minutes. Finally, after the soup is ready, it is served garnished with fried croutons.
Answer:
(a) is poured
(b) and brought to boil
(c) is allowed to simmer
3. News Headlines (3 marks each)
Question 1.
Read the newspaper headlines given below. Complete the sentences that follow: (3 marks) (Board Term-1 2014, Set EC2,049)

70% INFANT DEATHS IN-FIRST 29 DAYS
Nearly 70% of infant deaths in the country in the year 2010...................
..during the first 29 days of the infant's life.
(b) PARKING ROW: MAN BATTERED TO DEATH
A 45-year-old

autorickshaw driver……………… …..to death over a parking issue in Geeta Colony on Sunday.
(c) MINOR POLIO VICTIM HURT IN HOSPITAL
17-year-old polio afflicted girl …………………..inside a government hospital.
Answer:
(a) took place
(b) was beaten
(c) was hurt
Question 2.
Read the news items given below. Use the information in the headlines to complete the sentences that follow. (3 marks) (Board Term-1 2012, Set EC2,058)
Govt, raises DA; announcement made
The government…………………..for its employees with effect from 1st July 2012
(b) Kalka Shatabdi cancelled due to heavy rains
The heavy rains caused flooding of the railway tracks because of which Kalka Shatabdi
(c) Petrol, diesel prices likely to be raised
The government…………………..the prices of petrol and diesel to ensure that the public sector oil companies do not face losses
Answer:
(a) has announced a raise in DA

(b) has been cancelled
(c) is considering raising
Question 3.
Read the newspaper headlines given below and complete the news items: (3 marks) (Board Term-1 2012, Set EC2,038)
NEGLECT CAUSED MALL TRAGEDY, SAYS PROBE
The tragedy at The Great Adventure Mall…………………..due to neglect on the part of authorities.
(b) FOUR HURT AS CYLINDER BLAST TRIGGERS COLLAPSE
Four members of a family including two children…………………..when portions of their first-floor house collapsed following a gas cylinder explosion in Delhi's Nand Nagri on Sunday morning.
(c) TWO AUTO – LIFTERS NABBED, POLICE CRACK 30 CASES
The South District Police claims to have …………………..the arrest of two persons on Sunday.
Answer:
(a) was caused
(b) were injured
(c) cracked 30 cases of auto-lifting with
Question 4.
Read the given headlines and complete the reports that follow: (3 marks) (Board Term-1 2012, Set EC2,034)
CHIEF SEEKS MORE TIME FROM CBI
NEW DELHI: Army chief General VK

Singh…………………..the CBI for more time to provide details on his allegation that he was offered ?Rs.14 crore bribe.

(b) Rs.1 CR TO THE WIFE OF ACCIDENT VICTIM

The Delhi High Court………………..a compensation of ? 1 crore to the widow of a businessman who died in a road accident five years ago.

(c) DEATH PENALTY TO THREE FOR KILLING GIRL OVER PROPERTY

NEW DELHI: A man, along with his daughter and son………………..death penalty by a Delhi court for burning alive his daughter-in-law to comer her property.

Answer:

(a) has asked

(b) has awarded

(c) have been given

Question 5.

Read the heading given below and complete the news stories : (3 marks)

Pawar, Daughter Deny Involvement In IPL

Sharad Pawar and his daughter Supriya Sule on Friday………..cricket team.

(b) IM Declared Terror Outfit

The Indian Mujahideen (IM), suspected to be a shadow outfit of the banned Students' Islamic Movement of India……………a terror outfit.

(c) 5 Passengers Killed as Train Rams into Mini-Bus

………….at an unmanned level crossing on Friday when a train rammed into a mini-bus.

Answer:

(a) denied having any involvement in any Indian Premier League

(b) has been declared

(c) Five persons were killed

Question 6.

Read the news items given below. Use the information in the headlines to complete the sentences. Write the answer in your answer sheet against the correct blank numbers. Do not copy the whole sentences: (3 marks) (Board Term-1 2011, Set 16)

Stone chamber of 3rd-century tomb unveiled

A third-century stone chamber………………..by Japanese archaeologists today. It was excavated from an ancient tomb in Nara.

(b) Abducted Bengal cop released by Maoists.

Two days after being taken hostage, police officer A. Dutt………………..unharmed by the Maoists in Lalgarh.

(c) Singaporean trade team to visit India.

According to the Singapore Chamber of Commerce, a high-level trade team…………….. India soon to finalize the setting up of the trade development council in New Delhi.

Answer:

(a) has been unveiled

(b) has been released

(c) will be visiting/is going to visit

Use of Conditionals

Meaning: Condition:

We can distribute it in two parts in which the 1st part is a condition and the 2nd part is the result of that particular condition.

Condition: It can never be in future. (this is the basic rule of these type of sentences) So whenever you find a condition in future in your exam then the error will definitely in that part.

Result: It can be in past, present, and future also.

Here are four words that is used in a conditional and with the help of these words we can understand whether a sentence is a conditional sentence or not.

1. If/when   2. Suppose   3. In case   4. Provided

First of all we'll give you some examples of conditionals sentences and these sentences will help you to understand the conditionals sentences.

Example:

If our government takes some strong steps to protect women, they can go anywhere freely.

Explanation: In this sentence the first part of our sentence is a condition and the second part is the result of our conditional part.

We can see that the whole sentence is in present we haven't use any past or future form in this sentence.

Your health will remain good if you do yoga daily.

Explanation: In this sentence our first part is a result and the second part is a condition because we have a word if in our second part.

We can see in this sentence that our result is in future but our condition is still in present as I told you that our condition can never be in future.

Note:

In 1st sentence if is in the beginning and in 2nd sentence if is in the center now the point is it when we use if in the beginning of a sentence we have to use a comma (,) in our sentence but when we use if in the center we don't need to use comma in our sentence.

Rule:

If we have our conditional part in present, we don't need to follow any rule for 2nd part means in result. It can be in present, past and future.

If our conditional part is in past (it can be in simple past and perfect past), we have to follow this rule:

If:

2nd form of verb/had + V3rd form

Result:

Would + V1st form / would have + V3rd form

Could + V1st form / could have + V3rd form

Might + V1st form / might have + V3rd form

Examples:

Example 1.

In case you will fail in your exam, what will you do?

In case you fail in your exam, what will you do?

Explanation:

We have to remove will from the 1st part of our sentence because we can't use a condition in future.

Example 2.

If you came last night, you can also enjoy the party.

If you came last night, you could also enjoy the party.

Explanation:

In this sentence our conditional part is in simple past so we have to follow this rule: Could + V1st form

Example 3.

I went there for you if it was possible for me.

I would go there for you if it was possible for me.

Explanation:

In this sentence we have result in our 1st part and 2nd

part is conditional part and when we have a condition in simple past we have to follow this rule: Would + V1st form

Now the question is why we are using would in this sentence while we can use could and the reason behind it because in this sentence we are talking about the past plan, we always use would to describe our past plans and could is used for the ability.

Example 4. If you had seen yesterday's cricket, 1 am sure you would enjoy seeing our team bating.

If you had seen yesterday's cricket, I am sure you would have enjoyed seeing our team bating.

Explanation: In this sentence we can see that our conditional sentence is in past perfect so we have to follow this rule: would have + V3rd form

Example 5. If I have the courage, I would have answered him back.

If I had the courage, I would have answered him back.

Explanation: In this sentence there can be a confusion because as we told you if our conditional is in present, in our result we can use any rule but we can see that in our result we have would + have + V3rd form so we have to change our conditional in past perfect.

Example 6. I will be very happy if you will select in the hockey team.

I will be very happy if you select in the hockey team.

Explanation: In this sentence we are using will in our conditional part which is wrong so we have to remove will and use simple present tense.

Rule of Verbs

Transitive Verb

A transitive verb is a verb that requires an object to receive the action.

Eg:

The speaker discussed different marketing strategies in the video. →Correct

The speaker discussed in the video. →Incorrect

The verb discuss requires an object (different marketing strategies). It is necessary to state what the speaker discussed.

Some other examples of transitive verbs are address, borrow, bring, discuss, raise, offer, pay, write, promise, and have.

Eg:

The instructor addressed the student's question.

Rani borrowed the methodology book from her classmate because she forgot her copy.

Can you bring your copy of the textbook to our study group meeting?

Shiva gave the gift to his sister.

The committee members will raise money for the new project.

Direct and Indirect Objects

A transitive verb can take more than one object. Consider the example given below:

Shiva gave his sister a laptop.

In this sentence, there is an indirect object, his sister, and a direct object, a laptop. However, there is another way to say this same idea using a prepositional phrase.

Shiva gave a laptop to his sister.

An indirect object may come between a transitive verb and the direct object, like the first example sentence about Shiva, or the indirect object could be in the form of a prepositional phrase, like the second example sentence about Shiva.

An indirect object is only needed if the action is being done to or for somebody; when using a transitive verb, you need to include a direct object, but you may not need to include an indirect object.

Finding the Object

The direct object can be figured out by using this question format: "The subject did what?" or "The subject [verb] what?"

The instructor addressed what? → the student's question

Rani borrowed what? → the methodology book

Can you bring what? → your copy of the text book

The speaker discussed what? → different marketing strategies

The committee members will raise what? → money

The indirect object can be figured out by asking the question "To whom?" or "For whom?"

Shiva gave a laptop to whom? → his sister

Commonly used transitive verbs that must be followed by a direct object:

Bring, send, owe, contain, buy, show, take, tell, verify, check, get, wash, finalize, annoy, lay, lend, offer, edit, make, phone

Intransitive Verbs

An intransitive verb does not take an object. Using an object immediately after an intransitive verb will create an incorrect sentence. However, there may be other information after the verb, such as one or more prepositional phrases or an adverb. Eg:

The students arrived at the residency in Houston. →Correct

The students arrived Houston. →Incorrect

The second sentence is incorrect because the verb cannot take an object.

Some other examples of intransitive verbs are deteriorate, vote, sit, increase, laugh, originate, fluctuate, and trend.

The patient's health deteriorated quickly.

Ahmad voted in the local election.

May I sit here?

Attendance increased at the weekly study sessions as finals drew near.

Susan laughed.

Notes: An intransitive verb can take more than one prepositional phrase or adverb.

The patient's health deteriorated quickly during the night.

Ahmad voted for the incumbent in the local election.

Commonly used intransitive verbs are:

Come, explode, laugh, sit, rise, excel, respond, run, cough, swim, emigrate, smile, act, cry, immigrate, lie, arrive, continue, die, go

Verbs That Are both Transitive and Intransitive

Some verbs can be both transitive and intransitive, depending on the situation. In some instances, such a verb may require an object, while in others it does not require an object.

Continue

We will continue the meeting after the break. (transitive)

The meeting continued after the break. (intransitive)

Play

Three of the students play the guitar. (transitive)

The students will play outside today. (intransitive)

Return

Shiva returned the book to the library. (transitive)

The students returned to school after the winter break. (intransitive)

Grow

I grow roses in my garden. (transitive)

My daughter is growing quickly. (intransitive)

Whether a verb is transitive or intransitive may depend on whether the verb has multiple meanings.

Verbs that can be used as both transitive and intransitive depending on their meanings:

Set, leave, give, study, sit, grow, smell, dance, sing, write, teach, burn, eat, paint, drive, manage, stop, climb, run, check, cost, go, pay, improve.

Rule of Tenses

Present Tense:-
Simple Present Tense
Simple Present Tense sentences include happening of work in present time.

Subject + 1 st form of Verb

1. Subject (Singular form /third person) + 1st Form of Verb + s/es

Noun Subject is also a third person.

2. Subject(Plural) + 1st Form of Verb

3. For I and You , we will not use 's' and 'es' with Verb.

Example :I study on daily basis.

Present continuous tense
Expresses an action continued at present time.

1. Subject (Singular /third person/He,She,It) + is + (1st Form of Verb + ing) + Object

2. Subject (Plural /You,We,They) + are + (1st Form of Verb + ing) + Object

3. I + am + (1st Form of Verb + ing)

Example:I am reading a novel.

Ram is going office.

We are getting late.

Present perfect tense

An action which happened or completed in the present time

1. Subject (Singular /third person/He,She,It) + has + 3rd Form of Verb + Object

2. Subject (Plural /I,You,We,They) + have + 1st Form of Verb + Object

Example:Divya has gone to school.

He has filled a case.

Past Tense :-

Simple Past Tense

1. Subject (Singular/third person/Plural) + 2nd Form of Verb

2. Different number of subject can not change verb.

Example:I worked on the project last night.

Past continuous tense

1. Subject (Singular /third person/He,She,It) + was + (1st Form of Verb + ing) + Object

2. Subject (Plural /You,We,They) + were + (1st Form of Verb + ing) + Object

Example :

I was reading harry potter last night

Past perfect tense

An action which happened or completed in the past time or usually the two actions which happened or completed one by one in the past time.

1. Subject (Singular /third person/Plural) + had + 3rd Form of Verb + Object

Example:Ramya went to school after she had completed her homework.

I had already heard this news.

Future Tense

Simple future tense

1. Subject (Singular/third person/Plural) + will + 1st Form of Verb

2. I or We + shall + 1st Form of Verb

Example:

We shall go to school tomorrow.

You will read a book.

Future continuous tense

1. I,We + Shall be + (1st Form of Verb + ing) + Object

2. Subject(Other than I,We) + will be + (1st Form of Verb + ing) + Object

Example:We shall be coming to your house.

We will be playing football in evening.

Future perfect tense

1. Subject + will have/shall have + 3rd Form of Verb + Object

2. Wherever you'll see the use of the two sentences in this tense, the action which would be completed first would be in 'Future Perfect Tense' and the action completed after would be in 'Present Simple Tense'.

Example:They will have played the match before the sun sets.

I shall have read my book before you come.

Rule 1.

In Present Indefinite sentences the number and the person of the subject play very important role. If the subject is Singular number third person, affix 's' or 'es' to the verb. If the verb ends in any of the following : ss, o , x, z, sh,ch , add, 'es' instead of 's' with the verb.

Eg: Pass-passes, miss-misses, do – does, mix – mixes, fix – fixes etc.

Rule 2.

When the main verb is in Future Tense, use Present Simple in clauses with if, till, as soon as, when, unless, before, until, even if, in case and as.

Eg:

We shall wait till she arrives.

I shall not go there even if it rains.

Rule 3.

Present Simple Tense must be used instead of Present Continuous Tense with verbs of perception (feel, hear, smell etc.), verbs of cognition (believe, know, think etc.), verbs of emotion (hope, love, hate etc.) which cannot be used normally in continuous form.

Eg:

Incorrect – We are seeing with our eyes. Correct – We see with our eyes.

Incorrect – The water is feeling cold. Correct – The water feels cold.

But these words can be used in progressive form in the following cases.

The Session Judge is hearing our case.

We are thinking of going to London next year.

I am seeing my lawyer today.

I am having some difficulties with this puzzle.

Rule 4.

One must not use adverbs of past time like yesterday, last year, last month, ago, short while ago etc. with Present Perfect Tense.

Eg:

Incorrect – He has completed his book yesterday. Correct – He completed his book yesterday.

Incorrect – We have met 3 days ago. Correct – We met 3 days ago.

Rule 5.

If two or more actions took place in sequence, we use Simple Past to denote the actions. (Otherwise Past Perfect is used to denote the earlier action). This is usually used with conjunction Before.

Eg:

He switched on the light before he opened the door.

The train started just before I reached the station.

When Rahul reached home, Tina had had her lunch.

Rule 6.

The use of Simple Past Tense with , 'wish' and 'If only' shows unreal Past and present state of things.

Eg:

I wish I were a millionaire! (I am not a millionaire)

I wish I were a queen! (I am not a queen)

If I only knew her! (I don't know her.)

Rule 7.

In the following structure the use of Simple Past denotes unreal past and present time situation.

Eg:

It is time we went home. (It is time for us to go home.)

It is time you finished. (It is time for you to finish.)

Rule 8.

Use of Past Continuous with 'When' and 'While'

When is usually used when one action was completed and another action was going on.

When gives the meaning 'at the time that'.

Eg:

When he arrived, his wife was washing her clothes.

When she went to Banaras, she bought a sari.

While is used to denote a period.

Eg:

While I was teaching, I put through my best.

While I was in Opera, I could enjoy very much.

Rule 9.

Past Perfect is used when we look back on earlier action from a certain point in the past.

Eg:

She had completed her work, before I reached there.

I had started teaching before Manu came to my class.

Rule 10.

The Past Perfect is also used for an action which began before the time of speaking in the Past and which stopped sometime before the time of speaking.

Eg:

He had served in a bank for twenty years; then he retired and established his business. His children were now well settled.

Rule 11.

Past Perfect Continuous is used when the action began before the time of speaking in the past, and continued up to that time.

Eg:

It is now eight and she was tired because she had been cleaning the house since dawn.

This city has been prosperous since a very long time.

Rule 12.

When two actions are to be taken place on some future time, we use Future Perfect for the action completed first and Present Simple for the action to be completed afterwards.

Eg: The student will have left the class before the teacher comes.

The Principal will have started before I reach there.

Rule 13. Future Perfect is also used for such

incidents/actions about which we presume that another person had the knowledge of that incident or the action is already completed.

Eg:

You will have heard about Mother Teresa.

He will have read the newspaper so far.

Exercise

1.   Adarsh hopes to become(a)/an officer after he complete(b)/his higher education(c)/No error(d)

2. The police have found (a) / who they believe to be (b) / the prime suspect in a murder case (c) / no error (d).

3.   Now-a-days he teaches English (a)/ because the teacher of English. (b)/ has gone for a month's leave. (c)/ No Error (d).

4. I will let you know (a)/ as soon as I will get (b)/ any news in this regard. (c)/ No Error (d)

Answers

1. (B) complete should be replaced with completes ,because 1 verb is in future tense

2. (B) believe should be replaced with believed, as 1st part is in past tense.

3. (A)Replace 'he teaches' by 'he is teaching'.

4. (B) replace i will get with i get.

Rule of Nouns

Rule 1

The nouns such as – Jury, choir, committee, council, crowd, herd, orchestra, team, government, mob, community, union, club, opposition, firm, flock etc. are used as collective nouns to denote a group. They are considered to be singular and a singular verb is used with them.

Example

The committee has submitted its report.

Rule 2

The unit of measurement (such as - hour, pound, kilo, mile…etc.) is always used in the singular form in the structure – 'Half + a/an + unit of measurement'; as, 'Half a kilo', 'Half an hour'.

Note: The   unit   of measurement (such as – hour,

pound, kilo, mile…etc.) is also used in the singular form in the structure – 'A + half + unit of measurement'; as, 'A half kilo', 'A half hour'.

Example

Only Half an hour left to finish this work.

Rule 3

A plural noun is used after 'one and a half'; as 'One and a half kilos'

While 'A/An + singular noun + and + a half' is used in English Language; as,

'A kilo and a half kilos',

'An hour and a half'.

Rule 4

The structure – 'Numeral Adjectives + plural noun + and + a half' or Numeral Adjectives + and + a half + plural noun is used in the English Language. Numeral Adjectives: One, two, three, four…..etc. some, all, many, few…..etc. are called Numeral Adjectives; as,

'Two kilos and a half' 'Five hours and a half' 'Two and a half kilos'.

Rule 5

A plural noun is used after 'Cardinal Adjectives except one'. Cardinal Adjectives: One, two, three, four, five, six….etc. are called Cardinal Adjectives; as 'Five kilometres'

Example

I have fifty rupees.

Rule 6

Generally, the plural of a proper noun is not possible. But the plural of a proper noun can be formed (=made) by adding 's' according to need.

Example

There are two Mohans in my class.

Rule 7

These nouns such as – barracks, corps, crossroads, Innings, headquarters, précis, series, species, Issue, offspring, aircraft, craft, swine are used in the same form both in singular and plural.

Example

All the police barrack of Gorakhpur are old.

Rule 8

The structure – 'Noun + preposition + same noun' is always used in the singular. A singular noun is always used before preposition and after a preposition; as'

Example

Village after village has been swept away.

Rule 9

A plural noun or a plural pronoun is used after these phrases – one of, each of, either of, neither of, any one of, a few of, very few of, half of, a lot of, a large number of etc.

Example

One of the boys was innocent.

Rule 10

If we add 's' or 'es' to some Adjectives, they become plural nouns; as'

Example

We have to taste the sweets and bitters of our lives.

Rule 11

Some nouns always remain in plural form. They take plural verb. These nouns have no singular form. These are -

Assets, alms, amends, annals, archives, ashes ,arrears, athletics, auspices, species, scissors , trousers, pants.

clippers, bellows, gallows, fangs, measles, eyeglasses, goggles, belongings, breeches. Bowels , braces ,binoculars, dregs, earnings, entrails, embers ,fetters, fireworks, longings, lees, odds ,outskirts, particulars, proceeds, proceedings ,riches, remains, shambles, shears, spectacles , surroundings ,tidings ,tactics ,tongs ,vegetables, valuables, wages etc.

Means' — In the sense of income'. Means always takes a plural verb. In the sense way to achieve some end, Means takes a singular verb. When 'a' or 'every' is used before Means', it is singular.

Examples

(a) My means were reduced substantially.

(b) Every means is good if the end is good.

Rule 12

If two adjectives are joined by 'and' and 'The' is used before the first adjectives, A plural noun is used after the second Adjective.

Example

Dr. S.S. Prasad was an examiner of the Patna and Bihar universities.

Incorrect: Dr. S.S. Prasad was an examiner of the Patna and Bihar university.

Rule 13

If two adjectives are joined by 'and' and 'The' used before both Adjectives or each Adjective, A singular noun is used after the second Adjectives.

Example

The first and the second chapter of this book are interesting.

Incorrect: The first and the second chapters of this book are interesting.

Rule 14

Some nouns look plural in form but have singular meaning. Such nouns take singular verb. These are: news, innings, politics, summons, physics, economics, ethics. mechanics, mathematics, measles, mumps, rickets, billiards, draughts, etc.

Rule 15

Some nouns look singular but have plural meaning. Such nouns take plural verbs. These are: cattle, clergy, cavalry, infantry, poultry,peasantry, children, gentry, police etc.

Rule 16

Some nouns are always used in singular . These are uncountable nouns. We should not use article A/An with such nouns. These are -

Scenery, poetry, furniture, advice, information, hair, language. business, mischief, bread, stationery, crockery, luggage, baggage, postage, knowledge, wastage, money, jewellery, breakage etc,

We can not pluralise such nouns by adding `S' or 'es'.

Example It is incorrect to write sceneries, informations, furnitures, hairs.

If hair is used as countable it can be pluralised : e.g., one hair, two hairs.

Example I need three hairs of a black horse.

Rule 17

Some nouns have plural meaning. If a definite numeral adjective is used before them they are not pluralised. e.g., pair, score. Gross , stone

,hundred, dozen, thousand. million. billion. etc.

Otherwise these nouns can well be pluralised:

Dozens of women, Hundreds of people, Millions of dollars, Scores of shops. Many pairs of shoes, thousands millions etc.

Rule 18

If a numeral adjective and a fraction are used with a noun, the noun is used with the numeral and the noun will be in singular.

Examples

(a) He gave me one rupee and a half.

(b) She gave me two rupees and a quarter.

Avoid the following structure

Examples

(a) He gave me one and a half rupees. (Incorrect).

(b) She gave rite two and a quarter rupees. (Incorrect)

If the numeral adjective and the fraction refer the multiplication, the noun be placed in the end (after the fraction) and it must be plural.

Examples

(a) Your deposits has grown two and a half times within two years.

(b) My salary has increased three and a quarter times within three years.

Rule 19

Some nouns are known as common gender nouns. They can be used for either sex; Male or Female. These are called dual gender nouns. Such nouns are : teacher, student, child, clerk, candidate. advocate, worker, writer, author, leader, musician, politician, enemy, client, president, person, neighbour etc. When these are used in singular, use third person singular masculine (his) pronoun with them.

Examples

(a) Every candidate should write his (not her) name.

(b) Every person should perform his (not her) duty.

Each. either, everyone. everybody, no one, nobody, neither, anybody are also common gender pronouns.

Rule 20

Some nouns are used for specifically for feminine gender

only. i.e., blonde, maid, mid wife, coquette, virgin etc.

Now a days nouns 'bachelor' and 'virgin' are being used for masculine and feminine gender as well .

Use of Apostrophe with 's'

(A) You can form the possessive case of a singular noun that does not end in 's' by adding an apostrophe and `s' We should use apostrophe in following situations only

(1) Living things -> Mohan's book

(2) Thing personified; as —> week's holiday

(3) Space time or weight ; as —> a day's leave

(4) Certain dignified objects; as

The court's orders

At duty's call

(5) Familiar phrases; as —

At his wit's end

At a stone's throw

It there are hissing sounds (sounds of sh or s) ending a word, use apostrophe without 's' with such words. e.g., For Jesus' sake, For conscience' sake, The roses' fragrance etc. (It can be noted that if we use apostrophe with s with such words it couldn't be pronounced well)

(B) You can form the possessive case of a plural noun that does not end in 's' by adding an apostrophe and a 's,' as in the following example.

Example The men's cricket team will play as soon as the women's team is finished.

(C) You can form the possessive case of a plural noun that does end in 's' by adding an apostrophe.

Example The concert was interrupted by the 'dogs' barking, the 'ducks' quacking, and the 'babies' squalling.

(D) Do not use apostrophe with possessive pronouns

i.e., his, hers, yours, mine, ours, its, theirs etc.

Yours faithfully, yours truly, ours garden , his pen, hers purse, theirs room.

(E) Use apostrophe with the last word in following titles.

Examples

(a)   Governor-general's instructions.

(b)   Commander-in-chiefs orders. (c)   My   son-in-law's sister.

(d) Ram and Sons's shop.

(F) Do not use 'Double apostrophe'. Avoid double apostrophe in a sentence.

Example

    (a) My wife's secretary's mother has expired. (Incorrect)

    The mother of my wife's secretary has expired. (Correct)

    (G) Apostrophe with 's' is used with; Anybody/ Nobody / Everybody / Somebody / Anyone / Someone / No one / Everyone.

Example Everyone's concern is no one's concern.

If else is used after these words, use apostrophe with else as per following: Example I can rely on your words, not somebody else's.

Common Errors

Mr. Bhatia is my English teacher	Mr . Bhatia is my Teacher of English.
I Frogive him for his faults.	I forgave him his faults.
Chiranjiv Is my cousin Brother.	Chiranjiv is my cousin.
Credit this sum to my name.	Credit this sum to my account.
He is very miser	He is very miserly.
My all friends are very helpful	All my friends are very helpful.
She does not know swimming.	She does not know how to swim.
My uncle lives at Janpath Road.	My uncle lives at Janpath.
He is family man.	He is a man with a family.
This is more batter	This is better.
One must do his duty	One must do one's duty.
He made a blunder mistake.	He made a blunder.
It is a female compartment.	It is a ladies' compartment.
Open your book on page ten.	Open your book at page ten.
He has gone to foreign	He has gone abroad
He married his daughter	He got his daughter married.
Madhu is very proudy.	Madhu is very proud.
He live in the boarding	He lives in the boarding house.
Sachin and myself helped you.	Sachin and I helped you.

Please write with ink.	Please write in ink.
He died from cancer	He died of cancer.
He died of overwork	He died from overwork.
He has no lust of money.	He has no lust for money.
My younger brother goes to the collage daily.	My younger brother goes to college daily.
What a fun!	What fun !
She was crying the glasses in a tray.	She was carrying the glasses on a tray.
He sat in a tree.	He sat on a tree.
He is taller then me.	He is taller than I (am).
He is not as tall as his brother.	He is not so tall as his brother.
I have lost my patience.	I have lost patience.
He likes cutting jokes.	He likes cracking jockes.
You have a chance to win.	You have a chance of winning.
Don't mention.	Mention not.
Are you living in Delhi?	Do you live in Delhi?
It is a true fact.	Is is a fact.
As you like.	As you like it.
Radha resembles to her mother.	Radha resembles her mother.
Please pay for your bill.	Please pay your bill.
The police is looking for the culprit.	The police are looking for the culprit.
He said a lot to lies.	He told a lot of lies.
I believe you are better now.	I hope that you are better now.
He shirks from his studies.	He shirks his studies.
I need a house to live.	I need a house to live in.
I want a pen to write.	I want a pen to write with.
I have no influence on him	I have no influence over him.
I am too happy to see you.	I am very happy to see you.
He invited me on tea.	He invited me to tea.
We go to college by foot.	We go to college on foot.
You have no excuse to be late.	You have no excuse for being late.
Public does not like it.	Public do not like it.
This is somewhat true.	This is partially true.
I do not like the poetries of keats.	I do not like the poetry of Keats.

I prefer lassi than tea.	I prefer lassi to see.
Please give key to your watch.	Please wind up your watch.
There is no harm to do so.	There is no harm in doing so.
He gave a speech.	He made a speech.
I will return just now.	I will return presently.
I will wait here until you do not return.	I will wait here until you come.
He needs not worry.	He need not worry.
He hanged his head in shame.	He hung his head in shame.
The satellite has been sent to space.	The satellite has been launched.
Mohan insisted to go there.	Mohan insisted on going there.
He lives through honest labour.	He lives by honest labour.
Mohan and sohan are fast enemies.	Mohan and Sohan are sworn enemies.
His grandmother is died.	His grandmother is dead.
Send this letter on my address.	Send this letter to my address.
I have seen him today morning	I have been his this morning.
Are you a member in the committee?	Are you a member of the committee?
He is fail in Mathematics.	He failed in Mathematics.
We reached safely.	We reached safe.
Sachin is good in English.	Sachin is good at English.
My elder brother is in the teaching line.	My elder brother is in the teaching profession.
I have read four-fifth of this book.	I have read four-fifth of this book.
Our teacher will take your test tomorrow.	Our teacher will give us a test tomorrow.
All his family members are mad.	All members of his family are mad.
She does not know swimming.	She does not know how to swim.
Our examination starts from Monday next.	Our examination starts on Monday next.
I shall return this book after one week.	I shall return this book in one week.
Thousands were injured in the war.	Thousands were wounded in the war.
He has grown into a beautiful youth.	He has grown into a handsome youth.

There is no other alternative.	There is no alternative.
What is the cost of this pen?	What is the price of this pen?
Translate this passage from English to Hindi.	Translate this passage from English into Hindi.
I have learnt this lesson word by word.	I have learnt this lesson word for word.
I am going to cut my hair.	I am going to have my hair cut.
My watch is two minutes behind .	My watch is two minutes slow.
I asked him that why he was late.	I asked him why he was late.
He pays more attention to Hindi than English.	He pays more attention to Hindi than to English.
Close your door at once.	Shut the door at once
Verbal orders will not be obeyed.	Oral orders will not be obeyed.
Burn the lamp at once.	Light the lamp at once.
Sachin has made ten goals.	Sachin has scored ten goals.
He admitted that he had committed the murder.	He confessed that he had committed the murder.
A dictator generally misuses his political power.	A dictator generally abuses his political powers.
This is the house whose roof leaks.	This is the house, the roof of which leaks.
Being a cloudy day, we did not go out.	If being a cloudy day, we did not go out.
It is possible to score cent per cent marks in Mathematics.	It is possible to score hundred per cent marks in Mathematics.
Mohan has a thirst of knowledge.	Mohan has a thirst for knowledge.
My neighbor is five years elder to me.	My neighbor is five years older than me.
His service has been terminated.	His services have been terminated.
Please see the dictionary to find out the meaning of this word.	Please consult the dictionary to find out the meaning of this word.
Mohan asked his servant to bring water.	Mohan told his servant to bring water.
He got down from his bicycle.	He got off his bicycle.

I lived in that hotel for two days.	I stayed in that hotel for two days.
Please tell us everything in brief.	Please tell us everything in short.
I shall write him tomorrow.	I shall write to him tomorrow.
We have reached the final conclusions.	We have reached the conclusions.
To make dolls is his professions.	Making dolls is his profession.
Finishing his work, he went to see a movie.	Having finished his work, he went to see a movie.
I saw a bad dream last night.	I had a bad dream last night.
If you will abuse me, I will break tour head.	If you abuse me, I shall break you head.
If you will take tae, I shall also take.	If you take tea, I shall also rake.
You need not to tell me all this.	You need not tell me all this.
My elder brother is in the teaching line.	My elder brother is in the teaching profession.
I have read four-fifth of this book.	I have read four-fifth of this book.
Our teacher will take our test tomorrow.	Our teacher will give us a test tomorrow.
All his family members are mad.	All members of his family are mad.
Our examination starts from Monday next.	Our examination starts on Monday next.
I shall return this book after one week.	I shall return this book in one week.
Thousands were injured in the war.	Thousands were wounded in the war.
He has grown into a beautiful youth.	He has grown into a handsome youth.
There is no other alternative.	There is no alternative.
What is the cost of this pen?	What is the price of this pen?
Translate this passage from English to Hindi.	Translate this passage from English into Hindi.
I have learnt this lesson word by word.	I have learnt this lesson word for word.
I am going to cut my hair.	I am going to have my hair cut.
My watch is two minutes	My watch is two minutes

behind.	slow.
I asked him that why he was late.	I asked him why he was late.
He pays more attention to Hindi than English.	He pays more attention to Hindi than to English.
Close the door at once.	Shut the door at once.
Verbal orders will not be obeyed.	Oral orders will not be obeyed.
Burn the lamp at once.	Light the lamp at once.
Sachin has made ten goals.	Sachin has scored ten goals.
He admitted that he had committed the murder.	He confessed that he had committed the murder.
A dictator generally misuses his political powers.	A dictator generally abuses his political powers.
This is the house whose roof leaks.	This is the house, the roof of which leaks.
Being a cloudy day, we did not go out.	It Being a cloudy day, we did not go out.
It is possible to score cent per cent marks in mathematics.	It is possible to score hundred per cent marks in mathematics.
Mohan has a thirst knowledge.	Mohan has a thirst for knowledge.
My neighbour is five years elder to me.	My neighbour is five years older than me.
His service has been terminated.	His services have been terminated.
Please see the dictionary to find out the meaning of this word.	Please consult the dictionary to find out the meaning of this word.
Mohan asked his servant to bring water.	Mohan told his servant to bring water.
He got down from his bicycle.	He got down off his bicycle.
I lived in that hotel for two days.	I stayed in that hotel for two days.
Please tell us everything in brief.	Please tell us everything in short.
I shall write him tomorrow.	I shall write to him tomorrow.
We have reached the final conclusion.	We have reached the conclusion.
To make dolls is his profession.	Making dolls is his profession.

Finishing his work, he went to see a movie.	Having finished his work, he went to see a movie.
I saw a bad dream last night.	I had a bad dream last night.
His father has resigned from his post.	His father has resigned his post.
If you will abuse me, I will break your head.	If you abuse me, I shall break your head.
If you will take tea, I shall also take.	If you take tea, I shall also take.
You need not to tell me all this.	You need not tell me all this.
Let us pass away our time in the canteen.	Let us pass our time in the canteen.
I cannot pull on with this man.	I cannot get on with this man.
First, I told him about his mistakes.	At First, I told him about his mistakes.
Do not interfere in my work.	Do not interfere with my work.
I want a fresh basket of flowers.	I want a basket of fresh flowers.
The students will give their test tomorrow.	The students will take their test tomorrow.
The interview will be held between 10a.m to 12 noon.	The interview will be held between 10a.m and 12 noon.
There was a hell of a rush at the tickets window.	There was a hell of a rush at the ticket- window.
My hairs are black.	My hair is black.
Now, I shall go to my quarter.	Now I shall go to my quarters.
Law and order have to be maintained.	Law and order has to be maintained.
What is the cost of this shirt?	What is the price of this shirt?
Our examination is approaching near.	Our examination is approaching .
Good Night, sir, have a cup of tea.	Good Evening, sir, have a cup of tea.
The chairman is the wholly solely in our establishment.	The chairman is the all in all in our establishment.
We must fight-poverty with tooth and nail.	We must fight-poverty tooth and nail.
The English have left India	The English have left

with bag and baggage.	India bag and baggage.
We go to college by foot.	We go to college on foot.
I have many works to do on Sundays.	I have much works to do on Sundays.
He secured only passing marks in Mathematics.	He secured only pass marks in Mathematics.
Please give me a ten - rupees note.	Please give me a ten - rupee note.
This pen is superior than that.	This pen is superior to that.
I am not on talking terms with Mohan.	I am not on speaking terms with Mohan.
Sachin is our mutual friend.	Sachin is our common friend.
He picks up a quarrel over petty matters.	He picks a quarrel over petty matters.
Summon could not be issued.	Summons could not be issued.
When you say so, I must believe it.	Since you say so, I must believe it.
No less than fifty soldiers were injured in the blast.	No fewer than fifty soldiers were injured in the blast.
What is the fresh news of today?	What is the latest news of today?
I have something to ask from you.	I have something to ask you.
The train left at 3 o' clock.	The train departed at 3 o' clock.
You are requested to substitute the old picture for a new one.	You are requested to replace the old picture by a new one.
Due to illness. I could not go to college.	Owing to illness. I could not go to college.
This news was broadcasted from All India Radio only yesterday.	This news was broadcast from All India Radio only yesterday.
I will teach you reading and writing English.	I will teach you how to read and writing English.
It is the first time I have said so.	This is the first time I have said so.
Failed students cannot be promoted to the next higher class.	Students who have failed in the examination cannot be promoted to the next higher

class.

Please do the needful and oblige.	Please do what is necessary and oblige.
Accompanied with my friends, I went there.	Accompanied by my friends, I went there.
What to speak of English, he cannot speak even Hindi.	Not to speak of English, he cannot speak even Hindi.
The plane circled the airport two times before landing.	The plane circled the airport twice before landing.
He became a rich man by and by.	He became a rich man in course of time.
My dear respected father, you are really great.	My dear father, you are really great.
Send your reply by return post.	Send your reply by return of post.
Please speak to the concerned authority.	Please speak to the authority concerned.
He is a noted dacoit.	He is a notorious dacoit.
It was very wonderful.	It was really wonderful.
I am quite sorry to hear of your failure.	I am very sorry to hear of your failure.

***.

2. Voice Change

Language exhibits Personality.

-   *Chandan Sengupta*

A model combination of verb forms related to voice change is displayed as follows:

ACTIVE VOICE	PASSIVE VOICE
PRESENT TENSE	
SINGULAR	
1. I (a)	1. I am ....
2. Thou (a) .... st.	2. Thou art ....
3. He (a) .... s.	3. He is ....
PLURAL	
1. We (a)	1. We are ....
2. You (a)	2. You are ....
3. They (a)	3. They are ....
PAST TENSE	
SINGULAR	
1. I	1. I was ....
2. Thou .... est.	2. Thou wast (*or* wert) ....
3. He	3. He was ....
PLURAL	
1. We	1. We were ....
2. You	2. You were ....
3. They	3. They were ....
FUTURE TENSE	
SINGULAR	
1. I shall (a)	1. I shall be ....
2. Thou wilt (a)	2. Thou wilt be ....
3. He will (a)	3. He will be ....
PLURAL	

1. We shall (a)	1. We shall be ....
2. You will (a)	2. You will be ....
3. They will (a)	3. They will be ....

PERFECT (OR PRESENT PERFECT) TENSE

SINGULAR

1. I have	1. I have been ....
2. Thou hast	2. Thou hast been ....
3. He has	3. He has been ....

PLURAL

1. We have	1. We have been ....
2. You have	2. You have been ....
3. They have	3. They have been ....

PLUPERFECT (OR PAST PERFECT) TENSE

SINGULAR

1. I had	1. I had been ....
2. Thou hadst	2. Thou hadst been ....
3. He had	3. He had been ....

PLURAL

1. We had	1. We had been ....
2. You had	2. You had been ....
3. They had	3. They had been ....

FUTURE PERFECT TENSE

SINGULAR

1. I shall have	1. I shall have been ....
2. Thou wilt have	2. Thou wilt have been ....
3. He will have	3. He will have been ....

PLURAL

1. We shall have	1. We shall have been ....
2. You will have	2. You will have been ....
3. They will have	3. They will have been ....

ACTIVE VOICE	PRESENT TENSE
SINGULAR	**PLURAL**
1. I am (c)	1. We are (c) ....
2. Thou art (c)	2. You are (c) ....
3. He is (c)	3. They are (c) ....

PROGRESSIVE FORM

Options:

A = strike;   B = struck;   C = striking;

The object of the active sentence becomes the subject of the verb in the passive voice. The preposition 'by' is put before it. The main verb of the active sentence changes into the past participle. The form of the verb to be (am, is, are, was, were, being, been) is placed before the main verb according to the tense. The auxiliary verb is changed according to the new subject in number and person.

Exercise (Solved)

(i) He has missed the train.

Answer: The train has been missed by him.

(ii) Do they speak French?

Answer: Is French spoken by them?

(iii) Was he reading a book?

Answer: Was a book being read by him?

(iv) Compose this letter.

Answer: Let this letter be composed.

(v) Where did you buy this pen from?

Answer: From where was this pen bought by you?

(vi) Who wrote this speech?

Answer: By whom was this speech written?

(vii) One should respect one's elders.

Answer: Elders should be respected.

(viii) I did not praise anybody.

Answer: Nobody was praised by me.

(ix) He hurt his leg in an accident.

Answer: His leg was hurt in an accident.

(x) Someone was knocking at the door.

Answer: The door was being knocked by someone.

(xi) One must do one's duty.

Answer: Duty must be done.

(xii) I know him   Answer: He is known to me.

(xiii) The shop is building by group of artisans.

Answer: The shop is being built by group of artisans.

***.

3. Selected Worksheets

Worksheet 1

Lie is intransitive; lay is transitive. Lie signifies to rest; lay, to place. Insert the correct form in the following:

1. He told me to —— the book on the table. It —— there now.

2. I —— all day waiting for help to arrive. They told me a ……….

3. Where did you —— the purse?

4. I —— it on your desk. You must not tell a ……………..

5. I have —— the letters on your desk. It was ………………… there.

6. They told me to —— down. I —— down for about two hours.

7. As I wished to bleach the clothes, I —— them on the grass.

8. —— the bundle down and listen to me.

9. You will probably find your cap ——ing where it has —— since you dropped it.

10. They let the field —— fallow. We ……….. idle there for an hour.

11. How long has it —— fallow?

12. Yesterday he —— on the grass almost all day.

13. The hunter —— still and watched. His friend ………. under the tree.

14. He —— his gun beside him and waited.

15. It will —— undisturbed till morning.

16. —— down awhile before dinner.

17. I don't know how long he has —— here.

18. He let his tools —— in the rain.

19. You are requested not to tell a ....

20. The draft constitution .... on the table of house.

21. They .... their master plan for further consideration.

22. Civic master was telling a .... regarding his involvement in the incident which took place last night.

23. Somerfield .... Idle on ground before invading the fort.

II. Sit, Set: Sit is intransitive and signifies to rest. Set is transitive and means to place. Insert the correct form:

1. I have —— the ferns in the rain. .... down at your place.

2. —— down for a few minutes. We .... out a plan for the task.

3. She drew up a chair and —— down, while we were ——ting down the probable expenses of the new house.

4. Why don't you —— us a good example?

5. ——ting the table is not strenuous enough for one who has been —— ting all day.

6. The hen is ——ting on her eggs.

7. The man is ——ting out trees.

8. —— still; I'll go. You can .... a new task for the team.

9. Students remain .... on desk and teacher continued to provide a .... of task on the board.

III. Fly, Flow, Flee: Remember that birds fly; rivers flow; hunted creatures flee.

9. Still the river —— on its accustomed course.

10. Every autumn the birds —— south.

11. The birds have not yet —— away.

12. The deer —— before the dogs.

IV. Rise, Raise: Rise is intransitive; raise is transitive.

13. I have been trying all morning to —— this window.

14. I set the bread to ——. You can .... your voice to high pitch.

15. He will surely —— in his profession.

IV. Options: Teach, Learn

16. Will you —— me how to play tennis?

17. I thought you had —— how to play tennis.

18. I —— (past tense) her the new system of filing.

V. Options: May, Can: May signifies permission; can denotes possibility.

19. —— I use your book? I can take it if you .... allow me.
20. —— you write shorthand? You .... help me if you ....
21. —— I go with you? You .... come with me.
22. My mother says that I —— go with you. .... I come with you?
VI. Might, Could: Might is the past tense of may, and could is the past tense of can.

23. He said that I —— go. He frind .... be coming late.
24. He —— do the work if he wished.
25. Did you say I —— use your typewriter?

Worksheet 2

I. Accept, Except: Accept means to receive. Except as a verb means to exclude; as a preposition it means with the exception of. Insert the correct form in the following:

1. Did you —— the position? Yes, no one applied for it —— me.

2. I have no other reason for not ——ing your invitation —— that I shall not be in the city.

3. —— Mary all ——ed the invitation.

4. He would not —— the money —— on one condition.

5. Why do you —— him from the general offer that you are making?

6. I agree with you —— on one point.

7. He ——ed the rebuke in silence.

8. We were forced to —— their conditions.

9. He said he would not —— the money —— that he knew he could return it.

10. You have answered everything —— what I asked you.

II. Affect, Effect: Affect means to influence. It is always a verb. Effect as a verb means to bring to pass; as a noun it means result. Insert the correct form in the following sentences:

1. His opinion does not —— the case. ………….. of sins is fatal.

2. How does war —— trade?

3. His walking has had a good —— upon his health.

4. The ruling did not —— the wholesale dealers, but it had a big —— upon us.

5. What —— did the loss have upon him?

6. The failure of the bank ——ed the small depositors but had no —— upon the big business men.

7. The —— of the law has been startling because of the number of people ——ed by it.

8. They ——ed the consolidation, but thereby produced a bad —— upon the price of their stock.

9. The accident seriously ——ed his nervous system. In fact, the —— of the fall is only gradually disappearing.

10. Did the celebrated physician really —— a cure?

III. Lose, Loose: Lose is a verb, while loose is usually an adjective. The two should be carefully distinguished. Insert the correct form:

1. I have a note book with —— leaves.

2. Aren't you afraid you will —— some of the —— leaves of that book?

3. Be careful that you don't —— that —— bolt.

4. Do you remember that you had warned me that I'd —— the —— button on my coat? I did —— it not five minutes afterward.

5. One of the hinges of the door has become ——.

6. Do not —— the —— change in that pocket.

7. He will —— the parcel as the cord is ——.

8. Did you —— the —— leaf journal?

9. She may —— the money, as the clasp of her purse is ——.

10. I keep my —— journal paper together by a rubber band so that there will be no chance of ——ing it.

IV. Had ought:

Wrong: We had ought to go.   Right: We ought to go.

Wrong: We had ought to have gone.   Right: We ought to have gone.

Correct the following sentences:

1. I had ought to have studied harder.

2. You ought to do it, hadn't you?

3. Hadn't you ought to have gone?

4. Yes, I had ought to have gone yesterday.

5. Do you think I had ought to have accepted?

6. He had ought to come to-morrow.

7. The tickets had ought to have come from the printer's yesterday.

8. We had not ought to stay out so late.

9. You had ought to wear your coat.

10. He had ought to have become naturalized.

11. You had ought to have washed the dishes before you went out.

12. You had ought to take an umbrella.

13. You had ought to have heard what she said.

14. We hadn't ought to disagree.

15. You ought to have invested, hadn't you?

Conjugation of the verb be in the Indicative Mode

Present Tense
Singular   Plural
I am   We are

You are   You are
He is   They are
 Past Tense
I was   We were
You were   You were
He was   They were
 Future Tense
I shall be   We shall be
You will be   You will be
He will be   They will be
 Present Perfect Tense
I have been   We have been
You have been   You have been
He has been   They have been
 Past Perfect Tense
I had been   We had been
You had been   You had been
He had been   They had been

Future Perfect Tense
I shall have been   We shall have been
You will have been   You will have been
He will have been   They will have been

The verb be is used to form the progressive tenses of the active voice and the simple tenses of the passive voice; as,

Passive Voice

Present Tense
   Singular   Plural
I am followed   We are followed
You are followed   You are followed

He is followed   They are followed

Past Tense
I was followed   We were followed
You were followed   You were followed
He was followed   They were followed

Future Tense
I shall be followed   We shall be followed
You will be followed   You will be followed
He will be followed   They will be followed[106]

Present Perfect Tense
I have been followed   We have been followed
You have been followed   You have been followed
He has been followed   They have been followed

Past Perfect Tense
I had been followed   We had been followed
You had been followed   You had been followed
He had been followed   They had been followed

Future Perfect Tense
I shall have been followed   We shall have been followed
You will have been followed   You will have been followed
He will have been followed   They will have been followed

Synopsis of the indicative mood will be as follows if we add the progressive form wherever it may be used:

Passive Voice
Tenses Bracket Primary Bracket Present I am followed (simple)
I am being followed (progressive)
 Past   I was followed (simple)
I was being followed (progressive)

Future I shall be followed
 Perfect Bracket Present Perfect I have been followed
Past Perfect   I had been followed
Future Perfect   I shall have been followed

V. Phrases may be classified:

According to Form	According to Use
Prepositional	Adverbial
Participial (Gerund)	Adjective
Infinitive	Noun

The prepositional and infinitive phrases may have all three uses; the participial phrase has two—adjective and noun (gerund).

Variety of Expression: Phrases are important because, like clauses, they help us to vary the form of our sentences. They help us, above all, to avoid the childish so habit. Thus, instead of They wished to make the ice smooth so they flooded the pond, we may use, for example:

Subordinate clause: Because (as, since) they wished to make the ice smooth, they flooded the pond.

Participial phrase: Wishing to make the ice smooth, they flooded the pond.

Infinitive phrase: To make the ice smooth, they flooded the pond.

Gerund phrase: Flooding the pond made the ice smooth.

Prepositional phrase modifying noun subject: The flooding of the pond made the ice smooth.

Recast each of the following sentences in at least two of the ways shown above:

1. They wished to finish the work so they stayed till six o'clock.

2. John hoped to arrive before the others so he started early.

3. He saw that the cars were not running so he walked so he would be on time.

4. They needed some gasoline so they had to stop at a garage.

5. He wished to make a tool chest so he bought some lumber.

6. They saw that he liked to read so they gave him several books.

7. She wished to make a good appearance at the party so she bought a new dress.

8. He was in a hurry so he walked fast.

9. We were afraid that we'd be late so we ran.

10. The campers thought they'd like a fire so they gathered a quantity of dry leaves and wood.

11. I was very tired when I reached home so I couldn't go to the lecture.

12. The work was difficult so it took three hours to finish it.

13. The clock needed repairing so he took it to a jeweler's.

14. The coat did not fit so she sent it back.

VI. Conjugate the following in the passive voice:

1. Simple present of pay.   2. Progressive past of pay.
3. Present perfect of throw.   4. Future of praise.
5. Past perfect of forget. 6. Progressive present of choose.
7. Past progressive of choose.   8. Future of choose.
9. Future perfect of choose.   10. Past perfect of choose.

VII. Supply the verb forms indicated. Use the active unless the passive is definitely called for.

1. The vegetables (present perfect of lie) in water all the morning.

2. Rumors (past progressive passive of spread) far and wide that Germany would fight England.

3. I thought the gingham (past perfect passive of shrink) before the dress (past passive of made).

4. I am afraid my ear (present progressive of freeze).

5. Is it true that your ring (present perfect passive of steal)?

6. A sudden storm (past of arise) yesterday afternoon, and a little boy (past passive of drown) in the river where he and several of his companions (past perfect progressive of swim) since noon.

7. I (present perfect of speak) of the matter to no one.

8. I suppose that it (present perfect passive of break).

9. I must (present perfect of show) him twenty different styles, but he (past of choose) none of them, for as soon as I (past of show) him one, he (past of shake) his head.

10. She (past progressive of wring) out the clothes when the door bell (past of ring).

11. I am afraid my purse (present passive of lose).
12. The knight (past of say) that he (past perfect of decide) (infinitive of follow) the quest.
13. I thought I (past perfect of bring) you the morning paper.
14. He (past of swim) the river twice yesterday.
15. There he stood (present participle of ring) the dinner bell.
16. His coat (present perfect passive of wet) through more than once.
17. The trip (past of cost) him a hundred dollars.
18. I (past of see) the superintendent yesterday, but he said that there (present of be) no vacancies at present.
19. They (past of lay) the clippings on the desk, and then they (past of sit) down.[108]
20. As he (past of speak), he (past progressive of shake) from head to foot.

21. The clouds (past of lie) low on the horizon.
22. The building in which I work (present perfect passive of burn).
23. Your employer (present perfect deal) fairly with you.
24. I (present perfect of have) the same position for three years.
25. I (future of lend) him no money.
26. The floor (past passive of lay) by an expert workman.

27. The beads (past passive of string) on a waxed thread.

28. He (present perfect of throw) the whole office into confusion.

29. Before he came forward, he (past of set) the child down.

30. After the storm, leaves and twigs (past progressive of lie) thick upon the roads.
31. He (past of drive) to town yesterday. He (future of go) again to-morrow.

32. The dictionary (present progressive of lie) on the table where you (past of lay) it.
33. The dog (past of lay) the bone down, and then he (past of lie) down.
34. He (past of set) the chair by the window and then (past of sit) down.

35. I think we (future of see) him as we pass, for he usually (present of lie) on a couch by the window.

36. The snow (past perfect progressive of fall) for several hours and now (past of lie) deep on every path.

37. Everything (present perfect passive of lay) in readiness.

38. (Present participle of lie) in the hammock, he soon fell asleep.

39. I saw the man (present participle of lie) on the ground.

40. After he (past perfect of lie) there a few minutes, he suddenly (past of sit) up.

41. The biplane, which (past perfect progressive of lie) in the hangar since it (past perfect passive of raise) from the water in which it (past perfect of lie) for two weeks, (past of rise) up over the city.

42. Large crowds (past progressive of sit) on the fields, (present participle of wait) for the aeroplane (infinitive of rise).

43. Many people (past perfect of set) tents on the field during the night and now (past progressive of get) a good view of the flight.[109]

44. All eyes (past progressive of turn) toward the aeroplane, which (past progressive of rise) steadily.

45. The biplane (past of rise) until it (past perfect of rise) about five hundred feet above the tallest building; then it (past passive of raise) about fifty feet more to get it out of an air current that (past progressive of raise) one end of it.

Worksheet 3

I. Insert was or were in each of the following sentence.

1. I wish I —— going with you.

2. As he —— not well, he could not go.

3. If he —— well, he could go.

4. If he —— attentive in class, he would not fail.

5. They treated me as if I —— one of the family.

6. When I —— in the South I visited New Orleans.

7. Suppose she —— your guest, how would you entertain her?

8. He would appear very tall —— it not for the breadth of his shoulders.

9. We decided that if it —— still raining by seven o'clock, we should not go.

10. If our strawberries —— ripe, I'd give you some.

11. If the package —— left yesterday, as you say, it must have been while I —— not at home.

12. If he —— late yesterday, he must start earlier to-day.

13. If every man —— honest, business life would be very pleasant.

14. I saw that he —— not interested.

15. If he —— not interested, he surely looked as if he ——.

16. —— I certain that the bonds —— safe, I should invest in them.

17. As the tablecloth —— stained, we laid it on the grass to bleach it.

Worksheet 4

I. Use suitable alternatives for the following:

[Otions: a, an, the, am, is, are]

Getting .... (a) subject for yourself sometimes seems difficult; you ....(f) likely to think that there .... (e) no topic upon which you can say more than .... (a) few sentences. Isn't it true that when you ....(f) talking to your friends you seldom ....(f) at .... (a) loss for something to say? Of course, what your companion says often suggests .... (b) idea on which you give your opinion. You speak about things that interest you, and .... (a) words come fairly easily. Why not apply .... (a) same principle to more formal composition, whether oral or written? Unless .... (a) subject interests you, do not use it. But be careful that you do not reject it as uninteresting until you have thought about it carefully, considering it from all sides. Often one subject will suggest another akin to it, but more interesting to you because you know more about it. For this reason choose very simple subjects, and become thoroughly familiar with them by thinking or reading about them, before you attempt to explain them.

Sometimes, again, you will find that .... (a) subject you have chosen .... (e) not good because it .... (e) not definite enough. You hardly know where or how to begin to explain it, because it suggests no definite ideas. Perhaps, for instance, you have decided to write on .... (a) automobile and can think of nothing to say until you remember that you once saw .... (b) automobile race about which you can tell several interesting details; or you have seen .... (b) automobile accident and can write on .... (a) topic .... (a) Runaway Electric. If you can speak or write on .... (a) topic taken from your own observation, your composition will probably be good. You know .... (a) facts, you have .... (b) interest in .... (a) subject, and you will very likely say something of interest to others. Subjects taken from school life or neighborhood happenings, especially such things as you yourself have seen, ...(f) excellent. Perhaps on your way to school you noticed that several old houses ....(f) being torn down. You remember that you heard that .... (a) candy factory .... (e) to be erected. At once several suggestions for themes will come to you; as, Why .... (a) Factory .... (e) Being Erected in this Neighborhood, How Neighborhoods Change in .... (a) Large City, ... (a) Work .... (a) Wrecking Company Carries on. Perhaps your father owns property in .... (a) neighborhood, and you could write on How Real Estate Values have Changed in this Neighborhood.

Next to your own experience, ... (a) best source from which to draw subjects .... (e) your reading. This may be divided into (1) books, (2) magazines and newspapers. Recall one of .... (a) books that you read in .... (a) grammar grades, perhaps .... (a) Courtship of Miles Standish. Drawing your material from this source, you can write .... (a) Picture of Early Plymouth Days, or .... (a) sketch of Miles Standish's character, using .... (a) title Practice What You Preach. But to try to tell

.... (a) whole story to any one in two or three minutes would result in failure, for it would be .... (a) subject entirely too big to treat in so short .... (a) time. All .... (a) interesting details would have to be omitted, and, if .... (a) details ....(f) omitted, ... (a) story loses its vitality.

It .... (e) .... (a) newspaper or .... (a) magazine, however, that offers us .... (a) most available source of subjects. Practically all that we know of .... (a) modern world and of .... (a) wonderful progress being made in invention and discovery, as well as of .... (a) accidents and disasters that take place, we have learned first from .... (a) newspaper and have verified later by .... (a) articles in magazines. Every issue of .... (a) newspaper or of .... (a) magazine contains suggestions for many subjects. Such magazines as .... (a) World's Work, System, ... (a) Outlook, ... (a) Technical World, and other magazines that deal with technical subjects in .... (a) popular way ....(f) excellent for this work.

A third important source of subjects .... (e) .... (a) studies that you ....(f) now pursuing. Every new study affords .... (a) new point of view, which should suggest many topics for oral and written themes. Sometimes .... (a) good subject .... (e) .... (a) comparison of two of your studies by which you try to show, perhaps, how .... (a) one depends on .... (a) other.

The subject, of course, ... (e) but .... (a) beginning of .... (a) composition. Developing .... (a) subject .... (e) fully as important as having .... (a) subject to develop. .... (a) ability to develop .... (a) subject clearly .... (e) very important in .... (a) business world. .... (a) business man sells his goods either by talking or by writing; by .... (a) salesman or by .... (a) letter and .... (a) advertisement. Unless .... (a) salesman talks in .... (a) convincing way, he probably will sell few goods. He must know not only what to say, but how to say it.

After you have selected your subject, decide into what divisions it naturally falls. If it .... (e) of .... (a) proper length, it probably will divide itself into two or three divisions. Each of these will constitute one-half or one-third of your composition, and within each division illustrations, reasons, and explanatory details will appear. Arrange .... (a) divisions in .... (a) order in which they naturally come, according to their relative time of happening or according to their relative importance, reserving .... (a) most important for .... (a) last.

Sometimes this sort of division .... (e) difficult to make, because .... (c) subject can frequently be treated from different points of view, ... (a) point of view deciding .... (a) divisions. Sometimes you will find that you have made .... (c) number of small divisions, in each of which you can say only one or two sentences. This will at once suggest that you have not found .... (a) main parts of .... (a) subject, but have made unimportant divisions. Again, it may seem that you cannot divide your subject into satisfactory parts. In that case, you probably do not know enough about it. Think about it again, and, if you find that you really cannot divide it, choose another.

Choose one of .... (a) following subjects. .... (e) .... (a) title definite and clear? If it .... (e) not, change it so that it will be. For example, Photography (5) .... (e) not .... (c) definite title. No one could attempt to explain .... (a) entire subject of photography in .... (c) few minutes. .... (c) better title for .... (c) theme would be one of .... (a) following: How to Develop .... (c) Negative; How to Intensify [or reduce] .... (c) Negative; Our Camera Club; .... (a) Photography Exhibit at .... (a) Art Museum; Kinematography; Flash Light Pictures without Smoke or Odor; .... (a) Conditions Necessary for .... (c) Good Snap Shot Picture; .... (a) Advantages of Using .... (c) Developing Machine; How My Camera Helped Pay for My Vacation. Can you suggest still others?

Most of us get our ideas of what .... (e) taking place in .... (a) world from .... (a) articles that we read in current newspapers and magazines. We cannot always form our opinion from what one newspaper on one day says of .... (c) particular event. We must read what it says on successive days and, if possible, consult other newspapers on .... (a) same subject, for it .... (e) well known that not all newspapers ....(f) non-partisan. If one in .... (a) city .... (e) known to be so, that .... (e) .... (a) paper to read for .... (a) material for this exercise. Then, if we can read what one of .... (a) magazines says on .... (a) same subject, our knowledge will probably be more definite and more nearly true.

Let .... (a) class be divided into different sections, representing different kinds of news; for example, national, local, foreign, and business news. Under national news, you can perhaps find articles on national politics, legislative measures being discussed at Washington, rumors of war, immigration; under local news, anything pertaining to .... (a) city or .... (a) state in which you live; under foreign news, anything of interest to any of .... (a) other countries of .... (a) world; under business news, ... (a) prices of food products, strikes, panics, and their effect on business conditions. These ....(f) but suggestions. Such topics change so rapidly that nothing more definite can here be given.

When you have been assigned to one of these divisions, prepare .... (c) talk on .... (c) topic that you understand thoroughly. Begin your talk with .... (c) clear statement of your subject; amplify it by details or illustrations; and end with .... (c) sentence of conclusion, forecasting .... (a) future of your topic or restating what you have proved.

Answer key 4:

a = the;   b = an;   c = a; d = am;   e = is; f = are;

Worksheet 5

I. Use of apostoph:

The apostrophe (') is used—

1. To show the possessive case of nouns; as,

The boy's writing is excellent.

2. To indicate the omission of one or more letters; as,

I'll attend to the matter.

3. To show the plural of letters, figures, and words that usually have no plural; as,

Your 3's are too much like your 5's, your a's like your u's.

Don't use so many and's.

Write sentences in each of which you use one of the following words correctly:

you're	we're	who's	they're
your	were	whose	there
it's	he's	don't	their
its	his	doesn't	

Explain why the apostrophe is used in the following:

1. I've received no reply.

2. This month's sales exceed last month's by one thousand dollars.

3. Politics doesn't affect the matter very much.

4. The mistake was caused by his making his 7's like his 9's.

5. Have you received the treasurer's report? No, I haven't.

Point out the mistakes in the following:

1. For sale, A ladies fur coat.

2. The boy's have gone skating.

3. We wo'nt worry over the political situation.

4. Lets decide now where were to spend our vacation.

5. Dot your is and not your us.

6. Is this book your's or her's?

7. Students' belongings were kept side before cleaning the classroom.

8. Rikins uncle is a famous doctor.

9. All of her's book will be given to a library.

II. Use of capital letter:

Capitals are used for—
1. The first word of every sentence.
2. The first word of every line of poetry.
3. The first word of a quotation .
4. The first word of a formal statement or resolution; as,
Resolved, That women shall be given the right to vote.
5. The first word of every group of words paragraphed separately in an itemized list, as in an order for merchandise.

6. The pronoun I and the interjection O (not oh).
7. The words Bible and Scripture, the books of the Bible, all names applied to the Deity, and all personal pronouns referring to Him.
8. All proper nouns, proper adjectives, and words that are considered proper nouns; as,
a. Names of the days of the week, holidays, and months of the year, but not names of the seasons.
b. North, South, etc., when they refer to sections of the country, but not when they refer to a direction or a point of the compass.
c. Official titles or titles of honor when they are used in connection with names, but not when they are used without names; as,
Vice-President Roosevelt, ex-President Roosevelt, President Kipling,
Nominations are now in order for vice-president.
d. Names of political parties.
e. Names of religious sects.
f. Names of important events or documents; as,
The Revolution, The Declaration of Independence.
g. The salutation in a letter; as,
Dear Sir, Gentlemen.
h. Words indicating relationship, when they are used in connection with a proper name, or when used alone as a name, but not when used with a possessive pronoun; as,
We expect Aunt Ellen at four o'clock.
I expect my mother at four o'clock.
9. The important words in the title of a book, play, or composition. Prepositions, articles, and conjunctions are not capitalized; as,
The Call of the Wild.

10. Such words as Paragraph, Article, or Section, when accompanied with a number; as,

Frequently, all that shows exactly how the writer wished his thought to be understood is the punctuation. The same words may express different ideas according to the mark of punctuation that follows them. Read the following to show the meaning that the writer wished to convey by each. Explain the circumstances under which each might have been spoken.

1. The price is too high.   2. The price is too high!

3. The price is too high?

4. The crop will not be good. There'll be no corn.

5. Corn! There'll be no corn!   6. You didn't tell him that.

7. You didn't tell him that!   8. You didn't tell him that?

9. You are enjoying yourself.   10. You are enjoying yourself?

11. You are enjoying yourself!

III. Quotation marks:

1. When a speaker's words are quoted exactly, they should be enclosed in quotation marks. This is called a direct quotation.

He said, "The business is growing."

Notice that the word said is followed by a comma, and that the quotation begins with a capital letter.

2. If the quotation itself is a question, although it forms part of a declarative sentence, it requires an interrogation mark before the quotation mark; as, Have you been waiting long?

She opened the door and said, "Have you been waiting long?"

3. The same applies to a quotation that requires an exclamation mark; as,

Look!   He cried, "Look!"

4. When the words of explanation follow the quoted words, the punctuation is as follows:

(a) When the quotation is a declarative sentence, put a comma after the quotation and begin the words of explanation with a small letter; as,

"The business is growing," he said.

(b) When the quotation is a question, conclude it with an interrogation mark, and begin the words of explanation with a small letter; as,

"Have you been waiting long?" she asked.

(c) When the quotation is an exclamation, conclude it with an exclamation mark, and begin the words of explanation with a small letter; as,

"Look!" he cried.

5. When the author's words of explanation interrupt the speaker's words, the punctuation is as follows:

(a) When the interrupted parts are not naturally separated by any punctuation mark, the comma is used as follows:

I do not believe that the report is true.

"I do not believe," he said, "that the report is true."

Notice in what way the quotation marks show that the words he said do not belong to the quoted words.

(b) Whatever mark of punctuation would naturally appear between the interrupted parts must be used; as,

(1) I shall buy the Boston ferns; they seem to require but little care.

"I shall buy the Boston ferns," she said; "they seem to require but little care."

(2) Oh! The flames are higher!

"Oh!" she cried. "The flames are higher!"

4. Division into sentences is made within a quotation just as elsewhere. When the thought ends, the sentence must end. The different sentences, however, must not be divided by quotation marks; as,

"The train came in," said he, "half an hour ago. I do not see them in the waiting room. I think they did not come."

5. When a quotation is very long, consisting of several paragraphs, quotation marks should be placed at the beginning of the quotation, at the beginning of each succeeding paragraph, and at the end of the quotation—not at the end of each paragraph.

6. When a quotation occurs within a quotation, the one within is distinguished by single marks; as,

John explained, "After I had told Mr. Brown how I thought the work could be done more easily, he said, 'Thank you for your suggestion.'"

7. Any words quoted from a book or article, or any words quoted with a special significance, such as slang, should be enclosed in quotation marks; as,

The day of the salesman who is satisfied with the "good old way" is fast passing.

8. A formal question, statement, or resolution for a debate is not enclosed in quotation marks; as,

The question we are to discuss is, Shall women vote?

Punctuate the following, dividing into sentences wherever the sense demands division:

1. Thank you for your suggestion said Mr. Brown

2. Mr. Brown said thank you for your suggestion

3. Thank you said Mr. Brown for your suggestion

4. If you will ask the shipping clerk I volunteered I think you can get definite information

5. How can we enforce the law asked the man

6. The law cried the man how can we enforce the law

7. Tell me said the man how we can enforce the law

8. Tell me this said the man how can we enforce the law

9. The question before us is how can we enforce the law

10. John whispered did you hear his mother say yes you may go

11. As I was walking along the river he continued I heard a voice cry help

12. Halt shouted the captain the bridge is down

13. The captain shouted halt the bridge is down

14. We cannot cross said the captain the bridge is down

15. The bridge is down said the captain and I fear there is no other way to cross

16. Is the bridge down asked the captain does no one know another way to cross

Worksheet 6

Direct and Indirect speech: When the substance of the thought is given in slightly different form, we have an indirect quotation, or indirect discourse, in which no quotation marks are used. An indirect quotation is usually a subordinate clause depending on a word of thinking, saying, telling, or the like. Indirect statements are usually introduced by that, and indirect questions by when, where, why, whether, if, who, which, what, and the like. When a sentence is changed from direct to indirect discourse, the person and usually the tense of the direct quotation are changed; as,

Direct: He said, "I do not believe the report."

Indirect: He said that he did not believe the report.

Direct: He said, "Germany is over-populated."

Indirect: He said that Germany is over-populated.

Direct: She said, "I did my work before I went to school."

Indirect: She said that she had done her work before she went to school.

Indirect: She inquired when she might go.

In the following change the specific parts to direct quotations.

1: The Seal's Lesson   2: The baby seal said that he could not swim.

3: His mother answered that he could try.

4: The little fellow persisted that he could never learn.

5: His mother looked at him sternly, and said that every seal must learn to swim.

6: He replied that the water was cold and that he liked the sand better, but because his mother insisted, he slid into the water whimpering.

7: After he had gone a short distance, he turned around and called out that the water was much pleasanter than the sand.

8: His mother said that she knew that it would be so. She said that young people must do as they are told because they have not had enough experience to judge for themselves.

Worksheet 7

I. Select suitable alternatives from the options provided:

A certain old time king said that .... (a). He said he knew that such a man is difficult to secure, and in the hope of getting the right one, he would hire two.

When he had engaged them, he took them to a well and, showing them a large basket, told them to fill it with water. He said that (b) ....

The men were very much in earnest when they began the work, but, after pouring five or six bucketfuls of water into the basket, (c)

……………............, as soon as he poured the water in, it ran out again, and his time was lost.

His companion replied that (d) …………………..; that they were paid to do the work; and, whether it seemed useful to them or not, they ought to do it.

The first speaker said that (e) ………………………….., he did not expect to waste his time on such foolish work. Throwing his bucket down, he walked off.

The one that was left continued at the work until about sunset, when he had nearly emptied the well. Looking into the basket, (f) ……………….., he found in the basket (g)……………………… He said that now he knew why the king had wanted the water poured into the basket.

Shortly afterward, (h) …………………., he knew that the man had obeyed him, and he said that (i) …………….., and as a reward for obedience (j) …..

Provide suitable alternatives

Options:

1. when the king came up with some of his officers and saw the ring in the basket;
2. a ring of great value which his bucket had scooped up from the mud at the bottom of the well;
3. he knew he could trust him;
4. he would make him master over other servants;
5. one of them stopped and said that he did not see any use in doing that because;
6. he saw something glittering. Stooping to look more closely;
7. the kind of work that their master gave them was no concern of theirs;
8. the other man could do as he pleased, but, as for him ;
9. he would return at night to see what they had done.
10. he needed a servant who could be depended upon;

II. Select correct options:

Literature, the ministry, medicine, the law, (a) .... To test this statement thoroughly you need only hunt up a first-class editor, reporter, (b) .... You will find that he is already hired. He is (c) .... He cannot get a day's holiday (d) .... But if you need idlers, shirkers, (e) .... lawyers, doctors, and (f) ....

Options:

1. sober, industrious, capable, reliable, and always in demand.
2. half-instructed, unambitious, and comfort-seeking editors, reporters,
3. mechanics apply anywhere.—Mark Twain
4. and other occupations are hindered for want of men to do the work ;
5. except by courtesy of his employer, or of his city, or of the great general public.
6. business manager, foreman of a shop, mechanic, or artist in any branch of industry and try to hire him;

III. Look at the notes below. Then use the information to complete the paragraph by choosing a suitable word or phrase in each space.
Bishnois – always – nature worshippers – 1730 A.D. – Maharja Abhay Singh's men – fell – khejri trees – Amrita Devi – hug a tree – protested – insisted – to cut her head first – men obliged – Amrita – a legend.
Bishnois have (a) _____________. In 1730 A.D. Maharaja Abhay Singh's (b) _____________ fell Khajri trees. Amrita Devi, a true Bishnoi, (c) _____________ and expressed (d) _____________. She insisted that if they wanted to cut the tree (e) _____________. The unrelenting men of the Maharaja obliged her and the (f) _____________.
(a) (i) always been regarded as nature worshippers
(ii) always been called as nature worshippers
(iii) always knew nature worshippers
(iv) always done nature worshippers

(b) (i) men coming to   (ii) men started
(iii) men began to   (iv) men came to
(c) (i) hug a tree   (ii) hugging a tree
(iii) hugged a tree   (iv) hugs a tree

(d) (i) his protest   (ii) her protest
(iii) their protest   (iv) protesting

(e) (i) they may cut her head first
(ii) they would have to cut her head first
(iii) they can cut her head first
(iv) they should cut her head first

(f) (i) woman became a legend
(ii) woman becomes a legend
(iii) women became a legend
(iv) woman read a legend

IV. Rearrange the following words and phrases to form meaningful sentences. The first one is done for you as an example. Write the answers in your answer sheet.

Q: are / the / dreams scenarios/picture perfect houses/not a speck of dust/and no cobwebs ever/with a wrinkle-free bedcover/on the shelves

Ans: Picture perfect houses with a wrinkle-free bedcover, not a speck of dust on the shelves and no cobwebs ever are the dream scenarios.

(a) of its residents/becomes a/it reflects/a house/the personality/home when (a) ____

(b) has to look/no rules/how our/there are/as to/home
(b) ____

(c) thing is/ inhabiting them/should enjoy/the important/that we
(c) ____

(d) about/houses are/our lives/personal statements
(d) ____

(e) the confidence/in ourselves/they reflect/we have
(e) ____

(f) we have/will be/the more/ individualistic/confidence/the more/our homes (f) ____

V. Complete the following passage on Dance by choosing the correct word from the given options. The first one has been done for you.
The fact that dance (a) is an art form is a well known fact. (b) _________ dance as a therapy is not known (c) _________ many. Dance therapy involves a synthesis of the grace and vigour (d) _________ Indian classical and folk dance movements into (e) _________ innovative and holistic therapy. It brings (f) _________ the inner feelings (g) _________ the participants and can help them (h) _________ develop a healthy personality.

(a) (i) is   (ii) been   (iii) as
(iv) being
(b) (i) For   (ii) Although
(iii) But   (iv) While
(c) (i) by   (ii) to
(iii) in   (iv) about
(d) (i) on   (ii) in   (iii) of   (iv) into

(e) (i) the   (ii) a   (iii) an   (iv) as

(f) (i) in   (ii) of   (iii) over   (iv) out

(g) (i) about   (ii) for   (iii) in   (iv) of

(h) (i) with   (ii) in   (iii) to   (iv) into

VI. Use the information in the headlines to complete the sentences. Choose the correct option from those given.
(a) Women Rescue Child
Two brave women of Rampur village _____________ kidnapped by his father's distant relative.

1. have rescued a child who has been
2. have rescued a child who was being
3. rescued a child who had been
4. rescued a child who was

(b) Two killed in Collision
Two passengers travelling in a car died _____________ . The driver of the truck is absconding.
1. after their collision of a truck
2. in a collision with a truck

3. after their car collided in a truck
4. when their car collided with a truck

(c) Ban on Smoking

Smoking _____________ in all public places.

1. has been banned   2: is being banned

3: banned   4: was banned

(d) Old Building Demolished

Keeping in mind the dilapidated condition of _____________ yesterday.

1. the building, it was demolish
2. the building, it was demolished
3. the building, it has been demolished
4. the building, it will be

Answer key I:

a	b	c	d	e	f	g	h	i	j
10	9	5	7	8	6	2	1	3	4

Answer key II:

a	b	c	d	e	f
4	6	1	5	2	3

Answers III:

(a) (i) always been regarded as nature worshippers

(b) (iii) men began to   (c) (iii) hugged a tree

(d) (ii) her protest   (e) (iv) they should cut her head first

(f) (i) woman became a legend

Answers IV:

(a) A house becomes a home when it reflects the personality of its residents.

(b) There are no rules as to how our home has to look.

(c) The important thing is that we should enjoy inhabiting them.

(d) Houses are personal statements about our lives.

(e) They reflect the confidence we have in ourselves.

(f) The more confidence we have the more individualistic our homes will be.

Answers V:

(b) (iii) But   (c) (ii) to   (d) (iii) of   (e) (iii)

(f) (iv) out   (g) (iv) of   (h) (iii) to

Answers VI:

(a) (iii) rescued a child who had been

(b) (iv) when their car collided with a truck

(c) (i) has been banned   (d) (ii) the building, it was demolished

Worksheet 8

I. Some of the fragments of the paragraph are replaced and indexed in the options as given. Use all such options to rewrite this paragraph.

To begin, then: the influence of our name makes itself felt from the very cradle. As a schoolboy I remember the pride (a) ....; and the feeling of sore disappointment that fell on my heart when (b) .... Look at the delight with which two children find they have the same name. They are friends from that moment forth; (c) .... This feeling, I own, wears off in later life. Our names lose their freshness and interest, become trite and indifferent. But this, dear reader, is merely one of the sad effects of those "shades of the prison house" (d) ....; it affords no weapon against the philosophy of names.

In after life, although we fail to trace its working, that name (e) .... and influencing with irresistible power the whole course of your earthly fortunes. But the last name is no whit less important as a condition of success. Family names, we must recollect, are but inherited nicknames; and if the sobriquet were applicable to the ancestor, it is most likely applicable to the descendant also. You would not expect to find Mr. M'Phun acting as a mute or (f) .... Therefore, in what follows, we shall consider names, independent of whether they are first or last. And to begin with, look what a pull Cromwell had over Pym—(g) .... Who would expect eloquence from Pym—who would read poems by Pym—who would bow to the opinions of Pym? He might have been a dentist, but he should never have aspired to be a statesman. I can only wonder that he succeeded as he did. Pym and

Habakkuk stand (h) ...., over the most unfavorable appellations. But even these have suffered; and, had they been more fitly named, the one might have been Lord Protector and the other have shared the laurels with Isaiah. In this matter (i) .... Chaucer, Spenser, Shakespeare, Milton, Pope, Wordsworth, Shelley—what a constellation of lordly words! Not a single commonplace name among them—not a Brown, not a Jones, not a Robinson; (j) .... Now, imagine if Pepys had tried to clamber somehow into the enclosure of poetry, what a blot would that name have made upon the list! The thing is impossible. In the first place, a certain natural consciousness that men have would have held him down to the level of his name, would have prevented him from rising above the Pepsine standard, and so haply withheld him altogether from attempting verse. Next, (k) .... on the mere evidence of the fatal appellation. And now, before I close this section, I must say one word as to punnable names, names that stand alone, that have a significance and life apart from him that bears them. These are the bitterest of all. One friend of mine goes bowed and humbled through life under the weight of this misfortune; (l) ....and when even the intimation of his death bids fair to carry laughter into many a home.

So much for people who are badly named. Now for people who are too well named, (m)...................... A man, for instance, called William Shakespeare could never dare to write plays. He is thrown into too humbling an apposition with the author of Hamlet. His own name coming after is such an anti-climax. "The plays of William Shakespeare?" says the reader—"O no! The plays of William Shakespeare Cockerill," and he throws the book aside. In wise pursuance of such views, Mr. John Milton Hengler, (n) ....but has chosen a new path and has excelled upon the tight-rope. A marked example of triumph over this is the case of Mr. Dante Gabriel Rosetti. On the face of the matter, I should have advised him to imitate the pleasing modesty of the last-named gentleman, and confine his ambition to the sawdust. But Mr. Rosetti has triumphed. He has even dared to translate from his mighty name-father; and the voice of fame supports him in his boldness.

Options:

1. with which I hailed Robin Hood, Robert Bruce, and Robert le Diable as my name-fellows
2. first upon the roll of men who have triumphed, by sheer force of genius
3. which careless godfathers lightly applied to your unconscious infancy will have been moulding your character
4. Mr. M'Lumpha excelling as a professor of dancing
5. they are all names that one would stop and look at on a door-plate
6. we must not forget that all our great poets have borne great names
7. they have a bond of union stronger than exchange of nuts and sweetmeats
8. for it is an awful thing when a man's name is a joke, when he cannot be mentioned without exciting merriment,
9. which come gradually betwixt us and nature with advancing years
10. the booksellers would refuse to publish, and the world to read them,
11. the one name full of a resonant imperialism, the other mean, pettifogging, and unheroic to a degree
12. who go topheavy from the font, who are baptized into a false position, and who find themselves beginning life eclipsed under the fame of some of the great ones of the past
13. I found a freebooter or a general who did not share with me a single one of my numerous praenomina
14. who not long since delighted us in this favored town, has never attempted to write an epic,

Answer key:

a	b	c	d	e	f	g	h	i	j	k	l	m	n
1	13	7	9	3	4	11	2	6	5	10	8	12	14

***

4. Popular Phrases

Language displays Personality.

- *Chandan Sengupta*

Smell a Rat
(feel that something is wrong)
How come the front door is
open? Didn't you close it before
we went shopping?
I'm sure I did. I can't understand
it.
Frankly, I smell a rat.
Me, too. I'm convinced that
something is definitely wrong
here.
We'd better call the police.
Goto the Dogs
(become run-down)
Have you seen their house
lately? It's really gone to the
dogs. It's true that it has become
run-down and in serious
need of repair, but I'm sure that
it can be fixed up to look like
new.

I guess with a little carpentry
work and some paint it could
look pretty decent.

Fishy
(strange and suspicious)
When the security guard saw a
light in the store after closing
hours, it seemed to him that
there
was something fishy going on.
He called the central office and
explained to his superior that he
thought something strange and
suspicious was occurring.

Take the Bull by the Horns
(take decisive action in a
difficult situation)
Julie had always felt that she
was missing out on a lot of fun
because of her clumsiness on
the
dance floor. She had been
putting off taking lessons, but
she finally took the bull by the
horns
and went to a professional dance
studio for help. She was tired of
feeling left out and acted
decisively to correct the
situation.

Horse of a Different Color
(guite a different matter)
Eric likes to play jokes on his
friends, but he makes sure that
nobody is hurt by any of his
pranks. A prank that hurts
someone is a horse of a different
color! Being playful is one
thing,
but hurting someone by one's
prank is quite a different matter.

Let the Cat Out of the Bag
(inform beforehand)
Bob was going to retire from
teaching in June, and the foreign
language department was
planning on presenting him with
some luggage at his retirement
dinner. He wasn't supposed to
know about it, but someone let
the cat out of the bag. At the
dinner Bob acted surprised,
even
though someone had told him
what he was getting lief ore the
official presentation.

For the Birds
(unlnteresting and meaningless)
They went to a poetry reading,
but they got bored and restless.
As far as they were concerned,
it was for the birds! They left
during an intermission because
they found the reading totally
uninteresting and meaningless.

Straight From, the Horse's
Mouth,
(from a reliable source)
How did you find out that Jill
was engaged? I got the
information from a very reliable
source. You mean Jill
told you so herself? That's right.
I got it straight from the horse's
mouth 1

Horse Around
(play around)
Did you hear about Dave's back
injury?
No. How did he get hurt?
Well, after the coach left the
gym he decided to stay and
horse around on the parallel
bars. He somehow lost
his grip and fell on his back.
That's too bad, but he shouldn't
have been aimlessly
playing around on the
equipment without proper
supervision.

Cat Got Your Tongue?
(can't talk?)
Come on, Connie! Tell us what
you think about our little
ride down the rapids yesterday.
Well,uh... Wasn't it exciting?
I,uh...

What's the matter? Cat got your tongue? If you must know, I'm keeping quiet because I was scared out of my wits!

Get in Someone's Hair
(bother someone)
Children! Would you please stop making so much noise! And for heaven's sake, pick up your clothes and toys!
It's hard enough trying to keep this house clean
without your throwing your things all over the
place! Clara, I know that the children get in your hair, but you should try not to let it upset you so much. Listen, Jim. I can't help it. The children bother me and make me very angry when they're so noisy and messy.

Shoot Off One's Mouth,
(express one's opinions loudly)
Jim doesn't play tennis very much, but he's always shooting off his month about how good he
is. Yet he's fooling nobody. Jim is somewhat of a braggart and everyone knows that he gives opinions without knowing all the facts and talks as if he knew everything about the game.

Jump Down Someone's Throat

(become angry with someone)
That's it, Greg! You'd better not come in after midnight again tonight! I know, dad. You don't have to jump down my throat! I told you that I'd make it home around 11:30.1 don't intend to be late! Well, you've said that before and in you come at 2:30 in the morning. You can't blame me for getting angry and scolding you. I've got good reason.

Pay Through, the Nose (pay too high, a price)
At last Mr. Smith came upon the rare stamp he had been seeking at an auction. Since many other stamp collectors would also be bidding for it, he realized that he would have to pay
through, the nose in order to have it. After considering the increasing value of the stamp, he
decided that he would not mind paying such a high price for something so rare.

Tongue-In-Cheek (not serious)
Why were you teasing Sonia about her new hairdo? She really took offense at what you said. I didn't mean to offend her. I was simply making a

tongue-in-cheek remark when I
said that it was
too elaborate for a girl of her
young, tender age. Well, she
thought you were serious. She
had
no idea that
you were just saying that as a
joke. I'm really sorry. I suppose
I owe her an apology.

Pull Someone's Leg
(fool someone)
Hey, Al. I was invited to be a
judge for the Miss America
Beauty Pageant!
Oh, really? Come on, you're
pulling my leg! No, honestly.
Do you really think that I'm
trying to
fool you with a ridiculous story?
Well, you've told me foolish
stories before. I can assure you
that this one is for real.

Play It by Ear
(improvise as one goes along)
Let's go to the movies, agreed?
Sure. And what'll we do after
that?
Oh, I don't know. Let's play it
by ear.
Well, I would like to have a
more definite plan of action.
Don't be like that. It's always
more fun not knowing

what to expect and deciding
what to do as we go along.

Stick Out One's Neck
(take a risk)
How come they're asking me to
act as their guide through the
jungle?
Evidently they think you're the
only one who can lead them to
the lost temple.
That jungle has danger lurking
around every corner. Why
should I stick my neck out for
them?
They didn't pay me for my
services.
They know that you would be
taking a great risk and could
possibly get hurt, but you're the
only one with enough
knowledge to take them to their
destination. I'm sure you'll be
amply
rewarded.

Shake a Leg (hurry!)
Mary, you always take such a
long time to put on your
makeup. Come on, shake a leg!
I'll be finished in a minute. Be
patient. You've got to hurry or
else we won't arrive on time to
see the last show.

All Thumbs (clumsy)

Hey, Bea. Can you help me out? I don't seem to be able to button up the back of my dress.
Sure. Let's see if I can do it for you.
I guess I'm all thumbs because I'm so nervous. I'm already late for my date.
Well, I suppose that being so nervous would make you clumsy and awkward. But don't worry.
I'm sure your date will wait.

physics exam. I won't be able to make
it tonight. You've been studying for a long time. Why don't you take a break? Come on! Let's go!
Forget studying for a while! Look! Get off my back! I can't go anywhere! OK. I'll stop bothering you only if you promise to
let me know the minute you're finished.

Not Have a Leg to Stand On
(to have no good defense for one's opinions
or actions)
Tom maintains that the firm owes him some back wages for having worked overtime. However,
he won't have a leg to stand on unless he can prove that he put in all those extra hours. He doesn't stand a chance of getting his money without a strong foundation of facts to support his position.

Drive Someone Up a Wall
(annoy someone greatly)
Wow! What a great set of drums!
Yeah, they're great, but I can't play on them when my folks are at home. They say I drive them up a wall with all the loud banging. I get the same thing at home. My folks tell me that I annoy
them and get them really angry whenever I turn up the volume on my stereo.

Get Off Someone's Back
(stop bothering someone)
Hey, John. I'm bored. Come on, let's go out and do
something. Sorry, I'm right in the middle of studying for a

String Someone Along
(lead someone on dishonestly)
Liz had high hopes of marrying Dean. When he ran off with another woman, she realized that he

was just stringing her along. She
had felt very strongly about him
and was really hurt to see
that he was deceiving her and
had no intentions of ever
marrying her.

Sell Someone Down the River
(betray someone)
I heard that poor Jud landed up
in jail.
Yeah. His so-called girlfriend
sold him down the river and
claimed the reward on him.
I can't understand that. I thought
she was devoted to him.
She couldn't have been very
devoted to him if she betrayed
him and informed the police
about his hiding place.
That just goes to show you what
people will do for money.

Leave Someone High, and Dry
(abandon someone)
Say, Jill. I thought that John was
going to help you do the dishes
tonight.
So did I. But he left me high and
dry. Where did he go? Well, he
got a call from some of his
pals at work to go bowling, and
he left me alone to do all this
work without any help at all!

Sell Someone Short
(underestimate someone)

Just because he does not say
very much is no reason to sell
him abort. Actually, he's a
profound thinker and a most
talented writer. People tend to
underestimate him and not give
him the credit he deserves
because they think he's shy.

Snow Job
(insincere talk)
The salesman tried to convince
a group of investors that the
properties he was selling would
soon be worth much more
money than he was asking.
However, no one bought
anything from
him because they felt he was
giving them a snow Job. Wo
one was deceived by his
insincerity
and exaggerated claims about
the worth of the properties.

Spill the Beans
(reveal a secret)
Did you know that Harry was
going to take Kathy on a
Caribbean cruise? Yes, I did. He
was planning on surprising her
with the
tickets for their anniversary, but
someone spilled
the beans. What a shame! That
was supposed to have been a

surprise. Yes, it's too bad that someone told her about the trip beforehand and ruined Harry's surprise. That's OK. Her enthusiasm was not dampened in the
least!

Feed Someone a Line
(deceive someone)
Mr. Jones had been telling Louise how efficient she was and how much he admired her work at
the office. He had promised her a promotion in the near future, but she soon discovered that he was feeding her a line when he passed her by and gave the promotion to someone less capable. Louise was acutely disappointed to find out that Mr. Jones was not telling her the truth, and that he was deceiving her.

On Ice (set aside for future use)
We've been working on this sales report for some time now. Don't you think we should take a
break for some dinner? Now that you mention it, I am kind of hungry. Let's put the report on ice

awhile and grab a bite to eat. That's fine. I'd be happy to stop working on it and set it aside until we get some food. Great! Let's lock up and go.

Shoot the Breeze
(chat informally)
What are you going to be doing this afternoon?
Oh, I don't have anything in particular in mind.
Why don't you come over to my place? We can listen to some records and shoot the breeze.
That sounds OK to me. I'd like to relax listening to music and visit and chat informally until my
folks get back from shopping.

Bite the Dust (go down in defeat)
Andy did exceptionally well in all of the track events, but he bit the dust in the high jump competition. Much to the disappointment of his fans, he went down in defeat, losing to a competitor from the visiting team.

Bend Over Backwards (try very hard)
When Joan first started teaching she was afraid that she would have a lot of trouble getting

used to the kids and to the
faculty. Her fears turned out to
be unfounded, since everybody
bent
over backwards to help her.
Everyone tried very hard to help
her feel comfortable and adjust
to the school.

Hit the Hay (go to bed)
Listen, Kim. We're going to be
really busy with moving
tomorrow, and we've got to get
an early
start.
I guess you're right. We'll need
all the rest we can get.
What do you say we hit the hay
now?
Agreed. Let's go to bed and get
a good night's sleep. It's going to
be a long day.

Cough Up (give unwillingly)
Say, Greg. Did you finally get
that computer that you
wanted so much? Not yet. I
needed to raise a couple of
hundred dollars more.
Is it going to take you a while to
raise the money? It would have
taken me forever, but dad said
he'd cough
up the money I need since I'm
going to he using the

computer for my school work.
Maybe it was difficult for your
dad to give you the
money—but then, he knows that
it's for a good cause.

Jump the Gun (to be hasty)
Denise was planning on telling
her grandparents that the doctor
said she was going to have
twins, but when her dad found
out he jumped the gun and told
them before Denise could say a
word. He was so excited that he
became hasty and revealed the
news before Denise had a
chance to tell them.

Scratch Someone's Back
(return a favor)
Hey, Bea. I need some help
stacking these boxes. Would
you please give me a hand? OK.
And
I need some help tidying up the
house. How about your helping
me out after that? OK. If you
scratch my back, I'll scratch
yours. I know you don't like
doing housework, but I'll help
you
with the boxes if you promise to
return the favor. No problem. I'll
even do the windows.

Hit the Ceiling
(become very angry)

Don's father hit the celling when
he was informed that his son
had been detained by the police
for disorderly conduct. He
became violently angry, since
he had often warned his son not
to
keep company with that group
of boys.

Fork Over (hand over, give)
Hey, Dan. How come you're
looking so sad?
It's nothing, really. I
unexpectedly bumped into
Ralph and he asked me to fork
over the ten
bucks I owed him.
Did he expect you to pay him
back right then and there? Yes,
he did. It was all the money I
had,
and I had to hand it over to him.
Don't complain. After all, he did
you a favor by lending it to you
in the first place.

Turn Someone Off
(disgust someone)
How was your date with Marty
last night?
Well, it started off OK, but he
really turned me off when we
went for a snack after the
movies.
Did he say or do something to
annoy you? Frankly, he

disgusted me when he tried to
talk with
his mouth full. I don't blame
you. That would have really
bothered me too.

Go Fly a Kite (go away!)
For the past three hours Jerry
had been trying to convince
Linda to go to the art exhibition
with
him. She had been refusing all
along and finally in desperation
she told him, "Go fly a kite!"
Jerry didn't like to be told to go
away in such, a forceful manner.
Nevertheless, he finally
stopped trying to get Linda to
attend the exhibition.

Kick the Bucket (die)
It's been said that the old man
knew of a buried treasure, but
lie kicked the bucket before
telling anyone where it was. If
the treasure exists, the old man
unfortunately took the secret of
its location with him when he
died.

Raise a Stink
(protest strongly)
Listen! Don't try to use any of
your sister's clothes without
asking her first. She's liable to
raise a

stink if she finds something
missing.
I'm sure that there will be no
problem. She's borrowed some
of my things before, and I've
never
said anything. I really doubt that
she will protest very strongly.

Wet Blanket
(dull or boring person who
spoils the
happiness of others)
James was not invited to go on
the outing with the rest of the
group because he's such a wet
blanket. On many previous
occasions he has kept others
from enjoying themselves by his
pessimism and lack of
enthusiasm. It's understandable
that no one wants him around.

Keep Under One's Hat
(keep something a secret)
Although, the contestants were
most anxious to know who won
the prizes in the piano
competition, the judges kept the
results under their hats. They
kept the results a secret so
that the formal announcements
could be made in public at the
awards ceremony.

Up One's Sleeve
(concealed)

All right, Sara. We know that
you're planning something big
for Jean-Paul's birthday. Mind
telling
us just what you have up your
sleeve?
I wanted to make his birthday a
very special event. Jean-Paul
has a sister living in France, and
I
sent her an airplane ticket so
that she could be here for his
birthday.
Boy! That is something special!
We kind of guessed that you had
some concealed plan and
were waiting for the right time
to reveal it.
Well, I didn't want to say
anything until I was sure she
could come.

Dressed to Kill
(wear one's finest clothing)
The reception for the new
Swedish ambassador at the
Jennison's was quite lavish.
Naturally,
everybody was dressed to kill.
Since it was a formal occasion,
everyone was dressed in their
finest, most elegant clothes.

Give Someone the Slip
(make a getaway)
The police were chasing the
thief through the streets of the

city, but he managed to give them
the slip. No wonder. There were
so many people around that the
thief managed to escape by
getting lost in the crowds.

Knock Someone's Socks Off
(enthuse and excite)
Hi, John. What's new?
Oh, nothing too much with me,
but you ought to see Al-fredo's
new car. It'll knock your socks
off!
So, he finally got that Italian
sports car he's been dreaming
about.
He sure did! When you see all
the custom features that it has,
you'll get so enthused and
excited you won't know what to
do!
Boy, I can hardly wait to go for
a ride in it!

Talk Through One's Hat
(make foolish statements)
We were discussing ethnic
traditions and customs with Fred
the other day, and he showed
just
how little he knew about other
cultures.
What do you mean?
Well, he said that as far as he
could tell, there wasn't much
difference in behavior and

temperament between the
English and the Hispanics.
It's plain to see that he was
talking through, his hat!
True, but Fred thinks he's an
authority on everything. It was
difficult to convince him that he
was
talking ignorantly. He's got a
reputation for making foolish,
inaccurate statements.

Lose One's Shirt
(lose a great deal of money)
I happened to bump into Doug
at lunch yesterday afternoon.
What's new with Doug these
days?
He wasn't doing so well. For
one thing, he told me he lost his
shirt at the races.
Doug has always liked to bet on
the horses. I'm not surprised that
he lost a great deal of
money.
Yeah. At this rate he'll never
have a penny to his name!

In Stitches
(laughing very hard)
Danny was hilarious at the party
the other night. He had us all in
stitches! I didn't realize that
he was such a comedian.
He's always been funny, but last
night he outdid himself. He had
us laughing so hard that it

hurt our sides.

Dressed to the Teeth
(dressed elegantly)
Did you see Hilda at the party
last night?
Yes, I did. She was really
dressed to the teeth!
Well, she had on her finest,
most elegant clothing because
she was out to make a good
impression, on
Bill.

Lemon
(something defective)
Have you seen Joanne's new car
yet?
Yeah. It looks good, but she's
had nothing but problems with
it.
That's too bad. It sounds like she
got a real lemon. She sure did!
No sooner did she drive it
home from the dealer's than it
proved defective and started
breaking down.

Out of the Woods
(out of danger)
Although Eric was well on his
way to recovering from his bout
with pneumonia, he was still not
out of the woods. The doctors
told him that he would have to
take it easy and avoid exposure

to cold, since he was not out of
danger and difficulty yet.
Get Up on the Wrong Side of
the Bed
(wake up in a toad mood)
What's the matter with Bernard
today? He started shouting from
the moment he stepped into
the office. I don't know. He
usually doesn't act that way at
all.
I guess he got up on the wrong
side of the bed. Just because he
woke up in a bad mood is
no reason for him to toe so cross
and to go around shouting at
everybody.
Hopefully he'll relax as the day
goes on. Amen!

Out on a Limb
(in a risky position)
The members of the committee
realized that their position
against expanding the student
aid
program was an unpopular one,
and that they were going out on
a limb by voting against the
program. Nevertheless, their
position was justified to a
certain extent. Although they
knew that
they were placing themselves in
a risky position, they felt that
other budgetary considerations
were of greater urgency.

Eating Someone
(bothering or worrying
someone)
Hey, Alice. What's been eating
you lately? Don't you realize
how rude and irritable you've
become?
I know. I'm really sorry for the
way I've been acting.
Well, why don't you tell me
what has been bothering and
upsetting you and maybe we can
work your problem out together.
I'll admit that it would help to
talk to someone about it.

Get the Ax (toe dismissed, fired)
I feel sorry for Richard. He was
feeling quite depressed when I
ran into him. Did he tell you
what
was bothering him? Among
other things, he informed me
that he got the ax at work. That's
strange. He's always teen a
conscientious worker.
I wonder why they dismissed
him from his job? Evidently he
had a disagreement on company
policies with one of the top
executives.

In the Hole (in debt)
Unfortunately, Peter had to sell
his neighborhood hardware

store. Because of competition
from
the bigger stores in the shopping
center, he was going in the hole
every month. His store was
small and did not generate
enough income to meet
expenses. As a consequence, he
was rapidly losing money and
going into debt.

Section Seven
When Things
Go Well

For a Song
(for very little money)
Sara, I picked up the perfect
chair for the living room the
other day.
That's wonderful. I know you've
been looking for some time.
Where did you finally come
across
what you wanted?
I was really quite lucky. I got it
for a song at a little furniture
store. I was able to buy it for
very
little money because the owners
of the store were right in the
middle of their spring
liquidation
sale.

Make a Splash.

(be successful and attract attention)
Do you remember Andre and Jack?
Yes, I do. Weren't they working together on some kind of a novel?
That's right. It was finally published and I understand that it made quite a splash both domestically and abroad.
That's great news! They're both talented and hardworking. It's good to hear that the book was so successful and attracted such a great deal of attention.

Have the World by the Tail
(be successful and happy)
Marc finished school at the top of his class and he was offered an excellent position with an accounting firm Now he feels that he has the world by the tail. Everything has been working out for him lately, and it's no wonder that he's feeling so successful and happy.

Sitting Pretty
(in a fortunate position)
I heard that Michael and Jennifer got a good price when they sold their house. Yes, they did. Now they're really sitting pretty. As a

matter of fact, they're thinking of going on a long vacation.
I wish I were in such a fortunate position. I haven't had a vacation in years.

Feel Like a Million Dollars
(feel wonderful)
I bumped into Nick at the barbershop yesterday. He looked great, but I noticed that he had a
slight limp when he walked.
I guess you didn't know that he had an operation on his knee.
No, I didn't. How's he feeling?
He says he's feeling like a million dollars now. Apparently the pain in his knee is all gone.
It's good that he's feeling so wonderful. It must be a refreshing change not having to put up
with all that discomfort.

Kick Up One's Heels
(celebrate)
The prerequisites for admission to the Theater Arts School are quite demanding, and those students who were finally accepted had reason to kick up their heels. It was only natural that
those who made it through the exams and interviews would

want to celebrate the occasion
by
going out and having a good
time.

Bury the Hatchet
(make peace)
Somebody told me that you and
Doug had been quarreling over
the construction site of the new
building.
That's true, but we worked out
the problem and decided to bury
the hatchet.
Glad to hear that. You guys
have always worked well
together.
Well, once we came to the
conclusion that we both had the
same goal in mind, we put an
end
to our bitter feelings and made
peace with each other.

Paint the Town Red
(carouse and have a good time)
How did you enjoy your
vacation to Europe last summer?
It was marvelous. I'll never
forget the time we had when we
were in Rome. There was no
end to
things to see and do.
And how was the night life?
Great! We painted the town red
the first three nights we were
there.

Didn't that get to be pretty
expensive?
I guess so, but we were so
excited by all that the city had to
offer that we went out carousing
without thinking about the cost.

Get Away Clean
(escape punishment)
After robbing a neighborhood
bank, the robbers sped off in a
waiting car and got away clean.
In spite of all
police efforts to apprehend
them, the criminals were never
caught and punished for their
crime.

Come Alive
(brighten up and become active)
Up to now the guests at the
party had been eating and
making small talk, hut when the
rock
band arrived, everyone came
alive. When the band started
playing all the latest rock hits,
everybody brightened up and
became very active.
Section Eight
Do Your Best

Toot One's Own Horn
(boast)
Michael's last novel was a best
seller. He has no need to toot his
own horn about his literary

accomplishments. His readers
and critics alike will now
become aware of his talent. He
won't
have to boast about his skill and
success as a writer.

Stick to One's Guns
(maintain one's position)
In spite of the fact that it was
inadvisable to have a
controversial figure address the
club, the
chairman stuck to his guns and
insisted that it would make good
sense to hear the other side
of the question before taking a
vote on the issue. He maintained
his opinion and position on
the matter, even though a
number of members tried to
make him change his mind.

Get the Ball Rolling
(initiate action)
Look! You've been talking
about repairing the roof for
weeks now. Don't you think it's
about time
to get the ball rolling?
I know, but I've been busy with
other things. I promise I'll get to
it this weekend. The time to
start doing it is right now!
According to the weather report
it's supposed to rain tomorrow.

Mind One's P's and Q's
(take care in speech and action)
Listen, Larry. If you want an
invitation to Clarissa's
party you'd better mind your P's
and Q's. But I haven't been
doing anything to offend her. I'll
tell you one thing. You're going
to have to be careful
of what yon say and how yon
act around Susan. Come on!
Susan and I are just friends. I
know that, but Clarissa is the
jealous type. She's liable
to think that something is going
on between the two
of you.

Hang On
(persevere)
During the depression years the
Smiths had a great deal of
trouble with their business, but
somehow or other they were
able to hang on. Although they
almost lost their store, they
managed to persevere until
things got better.

Give It One's Best Shot
(try hard)
Can you do anything about
repairing this TV set? I'm not
much of an electrician, but I'll
give it
my best shot.

Many thanks. I'd be most
appreciative. OK. I'll try my
hardest to fix it, but I'm not
promising that
I'll succeed. At this point, I'll
take all the help I can get.

Make Ends Meet
(pay one's bills)
It's almost impossible trying to
keep up with the high cost of
living.
It's true. Things are so
expensive nowadays that it's
very difficult to make ends
meet.
You know, even with Lucie's
salary, our combined income is
hardly enough to pay all the
bills.

Get the Jump on Someone
(get the advantage over
someone)
Did you have a nice time at the
school dance last night?
To tell you the truth, I would
have enjoyed myself more if I
had been able to go with Teresa
instead of Elena.
Why didn't you ask Teresa in
the first place?
I was about to, but Benito got
the jump on me.
How did he manage to do that?

He got the advantage over me
by telling Teresa that if she went
with him, he'd take her out to
dinner and then to the dance in
his brand new convertible.
Well, now, she can hardly be
blamed for accepting an offer
like that!

Pull Strings
(exert influence)
Steven had been unsuccessful in
getting tickets for the opening
game of the season. However,
he pulled some strings with the
manager of the team and got
excellent seats. There's no
doubt that he got the tickets only
by exerting his influence with a
person important enough
to help him get what he wanted.

Spread Oneself Too Thin
(become involved in too many
activities)
Although Teresa has always
been an excellent student, her
marks have been going down
lately
because she is spreading herself
too thin. Besides spending a
great deal of time in afterschool
sports, she got a part-time job as
a clerk in a department store. It's
only natural that her

grades would suffer. She is becoming involved in so many activities that she cannot devote the time that it takes to excel in any one of them.

Go to Bat for Someone
(help out and support someone)
Is it true that Don got into some trouble at work last week? Yes, he did. He was reproached for not turning in his sales reports, but his secretary went to bat for him.
What was she able to do? She helped him out a great deal by admitting that she had misplaced the reports that he gave her to be typed.
So, it was her fault, not his.
Bight.

Duck Soup
(easy, effortless)
Can you help me hook up my new stereo equipment? I'm having quite a bit of trouble with all these connections.
Sure. That's duck soup for me.
Well, with all your experience in electronics, I have no doubt that it will be very easy for you to do.
No problem. Glad to help out.

Section Nine
You Don't Say

Money Talks
(money can influence people)
We've been waiting for three months to get delivery on our car, and people who put in their order after us have already gotten theirs.
Well, money talks. Why don't you try giving the dealer a little something extra to move things along?
I know full well that money has the power to influence people, but I refuse to pay extra for a service that is owed to me as a client.
If you want to have your car maybe you'd better reconsider.
Let Sleeping Dogs Lie
(do not agitate a potential source of trouble)
You'd better not say anything to the owner of the building about painting your apartment. If I were you I'd let sleeping dogs lie. The last time you asked him to do some repairs, he raised your rent.
You're telling me not to make trouble if I don't have to, but I'm going to risk making him angry, since I can no longer stand to look at the paint peeling off the walls.

Shape Up or Ship Out
(behave properly or leave!)
Al had been constantly
reprimanded for being negligent
on the job. Finally, in
desperation his
supervisor exclaimed, "Shape
up or ship out!" Al admitted that
he had not been taking his
work seriously and realized that
he should be more conscientious
about his job or he would
be discharged.
If the Shoe Fits, Wear It
(admit the truth)
Joe feels rather badly because
he's always being criticized for
his sloppy personal appearance.
With reason. "If the shoe fits,
wear it," I always say.
Still, I can't help feeling sorry
for the guy. I know that what
people say about him is true,
and
that he should admit it. He
doesn't seem to want to improve
his appearance. Evidently, he
himself can't see anything
wrong with the way he looks.
Different Strokes For
Different Folks
(everyone has different interests
and tastes)
It's hard to understand how
Millie and Ron ever got
together. She has always gone in
for sailing

and he can't stand to be on
water. He enjoys the opera and
she likes jazz.
You know what they say:
"Different strokes for different
folks!"
You don't have to tell me that
everyone has different interests
and tastes. I still can't figure
out what attracted them to each
other in the first place.
Haven't you heard that opposites
attract?
Bark Worse Than One's Bite
(not as bad-tempered as one
appears)
On occasion Mr. Hopkins
speaks harshly to his students,
especially when they fail to
complete
their homework assignment.
Nevertheless, they all know that
his bark is worse than his bite.
He threatens to keep them after
school and to inform their
parents, but he's not really as
badtempered
as he appears.
Eyes Are Bigger Than One's
Stomach
(take more food than one can
eat)
Chris, why don't you finish
eating that third helping of
dessert?

I guess my eyes were bigger than my stomach when I said I wanted more.

I'm not surprised. The same thing happens to me.

Sometimes, when I'm really hungry, I'll take

more food than I can possibly eat.

Put One's Money Where One's Mouth Is

(follow through with a stated intention)

You've been promising to take us to Disneyland for the past two years. Since the kids are free,

how about putting your money where your mouth is?

You don't have to remind me. I have every intention of doing exactly what I said I'd do. But you yourself know that in the past we have been unable to go because of other financial obligations. Things have eased up and it looks like we'll be able to go this year.

The Early Bird Catches the Worm

(arriving early gives one an advantage)

Marc, the lines for the rock festival are going to be miles long! If you expect to get tickets for you

and Marika, remember that old saying, "The early bird eatches the worm."

I guess you're right. Marika is looking forward to the concert, and I'd hate to disappoint her. I'll

get up real early to get a place at the head of the line. That way I'll get the tickets I want, for sure!

People Who Live in Glass Houses Shouldn't Throw Stones

(one should not criticize when one is equally at fault)

Janet has often criticized her friend Lois for driving too fast, yet she herself has had her license

suspended for exceeding the speed limit. Lois once tried to tell her that people who live in glass houses shouldn't throw stones, but it didn't do much good. Janet simply didn't accept the fact that she should not pass judgment on other people when she is just as bad as they are.

All's Well That Ends Well

(a successful outcome is worth the effort)

Hi, Benito. How are things going?

Well, everything's OK now. Remember that teaching job

for which I applied? Yes, I sure do. Well, I was finally hired, but I had a bit of a rough time before I got it. Between all that paperwork and all those interviews, I'm all worn out. Thank goodness it's all over. Great! All's well that ends well. After all that you went through, I'm happy to hear that things finally turned out satisfactorily for you. Yes. I'm happy, too. It was really worth the effort.

Index to Idioms

A

all's well that ends well (a successful outcome is worth the effort) _______

all thumbs (clumsy) _____

at the end of one's rope (at the limit of one's ability to cope) _____

B

bark worse than one's bite (not as badtempered as one appears) _____

bend over backwards (try very hard) _____

bite the bullet (endure in a difficult situation)

_____

bite the dust (go down in defeat)

_____

blow it (fail at something) _____

bury the hatchet (make peace)

_____

C

cat got your tongue? (can't talk?) _____

come alive (brighten up and become active)

_____

cough up (give unwillingly)

_____

D

different strokes for different folks (everyone has different interests and tastes)

_____

dressed to kill (wear one's finest clothing)

_____

dressed to the teeth (dressed elegantly) _____

drive someone up a wall (annoy someone greatly) _____

duck soup (easy, effortless)

_____

E

early bird catches the worm (arriving early gives one an advantage) _____

eating someone (bothering OF worrying someone) _____

eyes are bigger than one's stomach (take more food than one can eat)

_____

F

face the music (accept the consequences)____

feed someone a line (deceive someone) ____

feel like a million dollars (feel wonderful)

____

fishy (strange and suspicious)

__

for a song (for very little money) ____

for the birds (uninteresting and meaningless)

__

fork over (hand over, give) _____

G

get away clean (escape punishment) ____

get In someone's hair (bother someone) ____

get off someone's back (stop bothering someone) ____

get the ax (be dismissed, fired)____

get the ball rolling (initiate action) ____

get the jump on someone (get the advantage over someone) ____

get up on the wrong side of the bed (wake up in a bad mood) ____

give it one's best shot (try hard)

____

give someone the slip (make a getaway)

____

go fly a kite (go away!) ____

go to bat for someone (help out and support someone) ____

go to the dogs (become rundown) __

H

hang on (persevere) ____

have the world lay the tall (be successful and happy) ____

hit the celling (become very angry) ____

hit the hay (go to bed) ____

horse around, (play around) __

horse of a different color (quite a different matter) __

hot under the collar (extremely angry) ____

I

If the shoe fits, wear It (admit the truth) ____

in stitches (laughing very hard)____

in the hole (in debt) ____

J

Jump down someone's throat (become angry with someone)

____

jump the gun (to be hasty) ____

K

keep under one's hat (keep something a secret)

____

kick the bucket (die) _____
kick up one's heels (celebrate)
_____
knock someone's socks off
(enthuse and
excite) _____
L
leave someone high and dry
(abandon
someone) _____
lemon (something defective)
_____
let sleeping dogs lie (do not
agitate a potential
source of trouble) _____
let the cat out of the bag (inform
beforehand)
__
lose one's shirt (lose a great deal
of money)
_____
M
make a splasb (be successful
and attract
attention) _____
make ends meet (pay one's bills)
_____
mind one's P's and Q's (take care
in speech
and action) _____
money talks (money can
influence people)
_____
N
not have a leg to stand on (to
have no good

defense for one's opinion or
actions) _____
O
on ice (set aside for future use)
_____
on one's last legs (sick and
failing) _____
on the line (in danger of being
lost) _____
out of the woods (out of
danger)_____
out on a limb (in a risky
position) _____
P
paint the town red. (carouse and
have a good time) _____
pay through the nose (pay too
high, a price) _____
people who live in glass houses
shouldn't
throw stones (one should not
criticize when one is
equally at fault) _______
play it by ear (improvise as one
goes along)
_____
pull someone's leg (fool
someone) _____
pull strings (exert influence)
____
put one's money where one's
mouth is (follow
through with a stated intention)
_____
R
raise a stink (protest strongly)
_____

S
scratch someone's back (return a
favor) _____
sell someone down the river
(betray someone) _____
sell someone snort
(underestimate someone) _____
shake a leg (hurry) _____
shape up or ship out (behave
properly or leave!) _____
shoot off one's mouth (express
one's opinions loudly) _____
shoot the breeze (chat
informally) _____
sitting pretty (in a fortunate
position) _____
smell a rat (feel that something
is wrong) __
snow job (insincere talk) _____
spill the beans (reveal a secret)

_____
spread, oneself too thin (become
involved in
too many activities) _____
stick out one's neck (take a risk)

_____
stick to one's guns (maintain
one's position)

_____
straight from the horse's mouth
(from a
reliable source) __
string someone along (lead
someone on
dishonestly) _____
T

take the trail toy the horns (take
decisive action
in a difficult situation) __
talk through one's hat (make
foolish
statements) _____
tongue-in-cheek (not serious)

_____
toot one's own horn (boast)

_____
turn someone off (disgust
someone) _____
U
up one's sleeve (concealed)

_____
W
wet blanket (dull or boring
person, who spoils
the happiness of others) _____

5. Idims

A good many
Meaning: A lot of.
Dialogue example:
Speaker A: Did anyone enter the building while you were talking?
Speaker B: A good many people I should think.

All hands on deck
Meaning: The phrase is said when there is some kind of emergency, and it requires everyone to work hard; something that takes a lot of effort.
Example: It's been a bit of an all hands on deck effort organizing this meeting.

All hell broke loose
Meaning: A situation that suddenly gets out of control and people start fighting or arguing.
Example: When a fan at a rock concert jumped onto the stage, all hell broke loose.

All walks of life
Meaning: People of all social and economic classes.
Example: In the 19th century, this game was played by all walks of life.

A mile a minute
Meaning: Extremely fast; very rapidly.
Example: My friend talks a mile a minute about his cars.

An awful lot
Meaning: A large amount; very much.
Dialogue example:
Speaker A: Our friend is completely devastated by the death of his parents.
What can we do about it?
Speaker B: Not an awful lot, unfortunately.

Any port in a storm
Meaning: To emphasize that in a bad situation you will accept any help or take advantage of any opportunity.
Example: Thanks, Dan! It's not an ideal solution, but hey, any port in a storm.

Article of faith
Meaning: Something you deeply believe in.
Example: This book is an article of faith for her.

As broad as it's long
Meaning: With no significant difference; without any advantage; the same.

Example: Hotel A is a little cheaper, but Hotel B has free breakfast, so it's as broad as it's long.

As drunk as a lord
Meaning: Extremely drunk.
Example: He was as drunk as a lord.

As good a place as any
Meaning: Not perfect, but not worse than any other.
Example: This hotel is as good a place as any to spend the night; It was just as good a place as any to spend the weekend.

As keen as mustard
Meaning: Extremely excited, interested, or enthusiastic.
Example: John got a job at a big company because he was as keen as mustard.

As long as one's arm
Meaning: Extremely long.
Example: My wife owes money to a list of people as long as my arm.

At a low ebb
Meaning: In a state of weakness.
Example: Our economy is at a low ebb; Her health is at a low ebb; My business is now at a low ebb.

At long last
Meaning: Finally; after a long wait.

Example: At long last pizza has arrived; At long last the project was finished.

A torrid time
Meaning: A difficult period filled with problems and challenges.
Example: Our team will definitely face a torrid time in tomorrow's game; I had a torrid time during the championship.

At your earliest convenience
Meaning: As soon as possible.
Example: Please reply to my letter at your earliest convenience.

Avoid something like the plague
Meaning: To avoid something as much as possible.
Example: Rita's been avoiding me like the plague ever since I confessed my love for her.

Back the wrong horse
Meaning: To support something unsuccessful; make the wrong choice or decision.
Example: You really backed the wrong horse when you bought this abandoned house; Despite their vast experience, investors sometimes end up backing the wrong horse.

Barking up the wrong tree

Meaning: Follow the wrong course of action; doing something that will not produce the result you want.

Example: If you expect me to solve all your financial problems, then you, my dear friends, are barking up the wrong tree.

Batten down the hatches

Meaning: To prepare for a difficult or unpleasant situation.

Example: Many companies are battening down the hatches before the crisis.

Be a barrel of fun

Meaning: Be very cheerful, sociable, and enjoyable.

Example: My friend Joe is a real barrel of fun; Festivals are always a barrel of fun.

Be at a loose end

Meaning: Not knowing what to do; have nothing to do.

Example: You can come and help me clean up if you're at a loose end; Get out and take a walk if you're at a loose end.

Beat someone hollow

Meaning: To defeat someone easily and thoroughly.

Example: We scored an incredible 130 points per game and beat that team hollow.

Be beside yourself

Meaning: Being overwhelmed by strong feelings or emotions; unable to think clearly or control oneself.

Example: Tanya was beside herself with grief when her husband died; John was beside himself with excitement.

Be chasing your own tail

Meaning: To do something extremely inefficient or unproductive.

Example: I need to start taking only effective steps towards my goal and stop chasing my own tail.

Bee's knees

Meaning: Excellent; of a very high standard; ideal.

Example: Ron thinks he's the bee's knees; This TV show is the bee's knees; Christmas dinner was just the bee's knees.

Be for the high jump

Meaning: Prepare to be punished; to warn someone that you will punish them if they do something wrong/illegal.

Example: If I catch you stealing, you'll be for the high jump.

Before your very eyes

Meaning: Right in front you; while you are watching.

Example: Thank you for coming to see our magic show! Before

your very eyes, I will make this ball disappear.

Beggar belief (or "beggar description")

Meaning: Impossible or not worth believing; impossible to describe or explain.

Example: It almost beggars belief that you completed the project on your own, without any help; Her beauty beggars description!

Be in a tight corner

Meaning: To be in a difficult or tough situation.

Example: With funding being cut, my science project is in a tight corner.

Be in deep water

Meaning: To get into serious trouble.

Example: Having lost all his savings in the casino, he is now in deep water; Sarah has been in deep water since she lost her job.

Be in over your head

Meaning: To be involved in a difficult, dangerous, or unpleasant situation that you cannot handle due to lack of strength, knowledge, or experience.

Dialogue example:

Speaker A: I can beat them all, I have enough resources.

Speaker B: No, you can't! You are in over your head and you know it.

Be in the soup

Meaning: To be in serious trouble.

Example: If Tony and his wife find out what you've done, you'll be in the soup.

Belt and braces

Meaning: Do some extra actions to make sure something is safe; providing double security.

Example: I have a very important meeting tomorrow, so I set an alarm on my phone, tablet, and watch - belt and braces, I admit.

Be on the best of terms with someone (or "be on good terms")

Meaning: To have a good/excellent relationship with someone.

Dialogue example:

Speaker A: Do you think Dan will agree to hire me?

Speaker B: I'm not on the best of terms with Dan at the moment, so you'll have to ask him yourself.

Be on tenterhooks

Meaning: Very nervous, excited, and thrilled because you are wondering what is going to happen in a specific situation.

Example: We were on tenterhooks all evening waiting for the big news; I've been on tenterhooks all month, waiting for the DNA test results.

Be on the cusp of

Meaning: To be at the time when a situation/condition is going to change.

Example: We're on the very cusp of the new world.

Be on the skids

Meaning: To be in a difficult or bad situation.

Example: Their family business seems to be on the skids.

Between the devil and the deep blue sea

Meaning: In a bad situation with two equally unpleasant options.

Example: With all my debts, I'm really between the devil and the deep blue sea, because I need to sell either my house or business.

Blot on something

Meaning: A fault or mistake that ruins someone's reputation; something that spoils something.

Example: A serious blot on my career; This incident is a blot on our family name.

Blow something or someone out of the water

Meaning: Completely destroy, ruin, or defeat someone/something.

Example: These terrible reviews from the critics will blow my restaurant out of the water.

Bone of contention

Meaning: Something that people argue about; subject of a disagreement.

Example: The main bone of contention between us is money.

Bring something to the table

Meaning: To contribute; to provide something useful to others in your group; bring up for discussion.

Example: Our new worker will bring many important skills to the table; So, John, what are you going to bring to the table besides your vast experience?

Burn the midnight oil

Meaning: To work/read/study late into the night.

Example: I have to burn the midnight oil to finish my homework.

Bursting at the seams

Meaning: Extremely full or crowded.

Example: When the whole family comes home for Christmas, our house is bursting at the seams.

Burst someone's bubble

Meaning: To end someone's illusions, dreams, beliefs, or hopes by telling
them the truth.
Example: I don't want to burst your bubble, but she's gone and won't come back to you.

By jove
Meaning: To emphasize that you are very surprised or excited.
Dialogue example:
Speaker A: Thank you for your testimony, sir. But before we let you go,
there's one more thing I need to do.
Speaker B: What exactly?
Speaker A: I will take your fingerprints and a hair sample.
Speaker B: Will you, by jove? Well, get on with it then!

By leaps and bounds
Meaning: Extremely fast.
Example: His English is improving by leaps and bounds; Her admiration for him was growing by leaps and bounds.

By the look of things/it
Meaning: Based on the information you have at the moment.
Example: By the look of things, he did not commit a crime; Prices are going to go up, by the look of it.

Call a spade a spade
Meaning: Speak directly and clearly about something, even if it is
unpleasant.
Example: Let's call a spade a spade - you cheated on me with my best
friend!

Cannot do something for toffee
Meaning: Be very incompetent and extremely bad at something.
Example: I can't drive a truck for toffee; I can't sing for toffee.

Can't make head nor tail of something
Meaning: Can't understand something at all.
Example: I couldn't make head nor tail of that old book.

Carved in stone
Meaning: Cannot be changed; permanent.
Example: You can pitch us your ideas about our product, we haven't carved anything in stone yet.

Cast a shadow over/on
Meaning: To make a situation less encouraging, enjoyable, or hopeful and more unpleasant.
Example: The sad news about his health condition cast a shadow over our meeting.

Catch someone red-handed
Meaning: To discover (or catch) someone in the act of

committing a crime or doing something bad or illegal.
Example: Finn was caught red-handed in a robbery; The police caught her red-handed with stolen diamonds in her purse.

Cat got your tongue?
Meaning: To emphasize that someone is unusually quiet.
Dialogue example:
Speaker A: You have lipstick marks on your neck. Who is she?
Speaker B: Ohhh.
Speaker A: What's the matter? Cat got your tongue?

Champagne tastes, beer wages (or "champagne taste on a beer budget")
Meaning: Someone with expensive preferences and low income.
Example: Tina spent her entire salary on a designer jacket, she definitely
has champagne taste on a beer budget.

Clip someone's wings
Meaning: To limit someone's power, freedom, or comfort.
Example: Her parents clipped her wings by refusing to pay for her
luxurious life.

Close the door/stable door after the horse has bolted
Meaning: To emphasize that it is too late to take action to prevent
something
undesirable/unwanted from happening, because it has already
happened.
Dialogue example:
Speaker A: Hello sir! We would like to offer you a free alarm system for
your store.
Speaker B: Thanks for the offer, but I've already been robbed, so it's a bit
late to close the door after the horse has bolted.

Come a cropper
Meaning: To fail badly; to fall down.
Example: Investors have come a cropper on this project; Dan came a
cropper on the ski slopes and broke his arm.

Come from behind
Meaning: To win unexpectedly while in a losing position.
Example: The red team came from behind to beat the green team 6-5.

Cook someone's goose
Meaning: To ruin someone's plans; prevent success.

Example: This front-page scandal news will surely cook his goose.

Cook the books
Meaning: To falsify a company's financial records.
Example: He made thousands from cooking the books before the fraud department caught him.

Couldn't fight their way out of a paper bag
Meaning: Weak or ineffective; without much energy or ability.
Example: He's absolutely useless as an ally - he couldn't fight his way out of a paper bag!

Counsel of despair
Meaning: An admission of defeat or failure.
Example: It is sad to hear such a counsel of despair from our government about the situation with our economy.

Crawl out of the woodwork
Meaning: To suddenly or unexpectedly appear after a long time (usually for selfish purposes).
Example: After his song became a number one hit, his ex-girlfriend came crawling out of the woodwork.

Cry for the moon
Meaning: To wish for something unattainable.

Dialogue example:
Speaker A: I do not have time for anything. I wish there were at least 40 hours in a day.
Speaker B: Well, you're crying for the moon!

Cute as a button
Meaning: Adorable; graceful; very cute.
Example: Your little sister is cute as a button.

Cut short
Meaning: To end something earlier than expected or planned.
Example: He was a promising surgeon, but his career was cut short by a terrible accident with his left hand.

Cut something to the bone
Meaning: To cut down severely; reduce to the bare minimum.
Example: We need to cut our expenses to the bone.

Die in vain
Meaning: To die for nothing; to sacrifice yourself for a cause that ends up being useless.
Example: Commander, you need to retreat! Don't let your warriors die in vain.

Dig one's heels in
Meaning: To emphasize that you do not want to change your plans; to

refuse to do something.

Example: I tried to persuade her to choose another restaurant, but she dug her heels in.

Discretion is the better part of valour

Meaning: To emphasize that it is better to avoid unnecessary risks or

unpleasant situations.

Example: Danny, my boy, discretion is the better part of valour, so don't be a hero and go home!

Dock someone's wages

Meaning: To reduce the amount of money you pay someone as a penalty/punishment.

Dialogue example:

Speaker A: Boss, John delivered the package, but it's damaged. Should I

accept it and pay him?

Speaker B: Fine, but dock his wages.

Don't give up the day job

Meaning: Make it clear to someone that you do not believe in the success of their new idea, plan, project, or hobby (in a playful and non-offensive manner).

Dialogue example:

Speaker A: What do you think of my new book idea?

Speaker B: Hmm, interesting idea, but don't give up the day job.

Do someone a world of good

Meaning: To make someone feel better or much healthier; to be very helpful for someone.

Example: The mountain air will do you a world of good.

Down in the dumps

Meaning: Extremely sad; unhappy; very depressed.

Example: Vince has been down in the dumps ever since his wife died.

Dress in layers

Meaning: Dress warmly; wear several types of clothing at once to keep

warm.

Example: You're going to Norway, so dress in layers.

Drop a clanger

Meaning: To say or do something foolish or embarrassing.

Example: I dropped a clanger when I asked him about the wedding on our first date.

Easy on the eye/ear

Meaning: Pleasant to look at or listen to.

Example: I painted my bedroom in pastel colours to make it easy on the

eye; I like classical music because it's easy on the ear.

Eat someone out of house and home
Meaning: To eat a lot of someone's food, especially when you're a guest in their house (often said in a humorous manner).
Example: Aunt Lucy, Uncle John, I didn't invite you here to eat me out of house and home.

Educated guess
Meaning: An assumption based on knowledge of the situation and therefore most likely correct.
Example: As a mechanic, I can't say exactly how much it will cost to repair your car, but I can make an educated guess.

Every dog has its day
Meaning: Everyone has at least one happy or successful moment in life.
Example: Your startup has failed, but don't lose hope and remember that every dog has its day.

Fall by the wayside
Meaning: To fail to finish an activity; no longer be effective.
Example: Many clubs and resorts fall by the wayside during a recession.

Fall into the wrong hands
Meaning: To be discovered by your enemy; to be discovered by unfriendly/dangerous people.
Example: If this document falls into the wrong hands, then it could be catastrophic.

Fat chance
Meaning: Not likely to happen; extremely unlikely.
Example: Let's face it, you have a fat chance of getting the job; Fat chance we can get there on time.

Faux pas
Meaning: A social mistake; embarrassing error; something socially awkward.
Example: Arriving at the party early or on time is a faux pas.

Fit to drop
Meaning: Very tired.
Example: After the marathon we were fit to drop.

Flatter to deceive
Meaning: Looks promising at first glance, but ends up being very disappointing.
Example: As with most new investment companies, their early success flattered to deceive.

Flog/beat a dead horse
Meaning: To keep wasting energy or time on something when there is no chance of success.
Dialogue example:

Speaker A: Stop asking me these questions, I won't tell you anyway.

Speaker B: But I need answers. Tell me everything you know!

Speaker A: You do like flogging a dead horse, don't you?

Fly off the handle

Meaning: To become very angry; to lose control; react too angrily to something insignificant.

Example: I'm sorry I unintentionally pushed your girlfriend, but there's no need to fly off the handle.

For donkey's years

Meaning: For a very long time.

Example: I've had this ring for donkey's years; The new railway won't be ready for donkey's years.

For want of a better word/term

Meaning: Lacking a more precise word/term; to emphasize that you cannot think of a more accurate way of explaining what you mean.

Example: He is, for want of a better word, a grumbler; She should behave more respectfully or, for want of a better word, decently.

Friends in high places

Meaning: Influential and powerful people who will help you in case of emergency.

Example: I have plenty of friends in high places, so finding a new job is not a problem.

Get a grip on yourself

Meaning: To make an effort to control your behaviour, manners, or emotions.

Example: Get a grip on yourself and stop crying!

Get your hands on someone

Meaning: To catch or find someone.

Example: When I get my hands on him, he will have to pay off his debts.

Give someone the runaround

Meaning: To delay someone by providing useless information or directions.

Dialogue example:

Speaker A: When do you plan to launch the project?

Speaker B: On Monday or Wednesday. Maybe Saturday. Or maybe a week from now.

Speaker A: Sounds like you're giving me the runaround. I need to know exactly when this project will be launched!

Go at it hammer and tongs

Meaning: With great energy, power, passion, or enthusiasm; very intensively; to have a very noisy argument.

Example: Our neighbors were going at it hammer and tongs all night.

Go down like a lead balloon

Meaning: To be extremely unsuccessful, unloved, or unpopular.

Example: His political joke went down like a lead balloon; These stupid questions go down like a lead balloon.

Go down like ninepins

Meaning: To be damaged in large numbers; when a lot of people suddenly become ill.

Example: Trees and road signs were going down like ninepins in a storm.

Go easy on someone

Meaning: To treat someone more gently, less harshly.

Example: Go easy on your son, he's just a kid.

Go off-book

Meaning: To not follow the script; disturb the order of things.

Dialogue example:

Speaker A: I have an idea! Let's take half of Mike's share for ourselves.

Speaker B: I have a better idea! Let's split the money between the three of us and leave Mike aside.

Speaker C: Stop arguing! Let's stick to the plan. I don't like it when you two go off-book like this.

Go off the rails

Meaning: Start behaving in an uncontrollable or intolerable way.

Example: My daughter started going off the rails shortly after graduation.

Go the extra mile

Meaning: To make an extra effort; do more than is expected of you.

Example: We need to go the extra mile to release the game on time.

Go through the floor

Meaning: To fall to an ultra-low level.

Example: Due to the crisis, resort prices have gone through the floor.

Guard your tongue

Meaning: Being very careful about what you say.

Example: Guard your tongue, woman, you're talking about my mother!

Hang in the balance

Meaning: Not yet decided; unsure of the future; not certain what will happen to it.

Example: After that scandal, the future of my company still hangs in the balance.

Have a bone to pick with someone

Meaning: To talk to the person about the things that annoy you; to have an issue to discuss or argue about.

Example: Darling, I've got a bone to pick with you. Why did you decide to have dinner with your ex-boyfriend again?

Have a bee in your bonnet

Meaning: To talk a lot about something or be extremely passionate about it (mostly in a very annoying way).

Example: He's got a bee in his bonnet about video games.

Have another string to one's bow

Meaning: To emphasize that you have another plan/idea/skill to use if it's needed.

Example: You're right, my plan didn't work, but I have another string to my bow.

Have a short fuse

Meaning: To get angry/mad very easily.

Example: Her boss is known to have a short fuse.

Have bigger fish to fry

Meaning: Have more important things to do.

Dialogue example:

Speaker A: Could you help me with my project?

Speaker B: Sorry, I've got bigger fish to fry!

Have feet of clay

Meaning: To have hidden flaws or weaknesses.

Example: Most of the greatest minds in history had feet of clay; Fans don't want to see their idols with feet of clay.

Have it in you

Meaning: To have a certain quality/skill.

Example: You don't have it in you to make the difficult choices.

Have one's blood up

Meaning: To be angry or inflamed; to be in an aggressive or violent mood.

Example: Her offensive jokes really got my blood up.

Have the stomach for something

Meaning: To have enough determination to do something difficult, risky, or unpleasant.

Example: I don't have the stomach for a real fight; I have no stomach for horror movies.

Have your back to the wall
Meaning: Find yourself in an extremely difficult situation with limited
options for action.
Example: He really has his back to the wall because of all his debts and
loans.

Have your fair share of something
Meaning: A lot or more than enough of something.
Example: Listen to me Jonny, I've done my fair share of travelling and I'm telling you the most delicious desserts can be found in Norway; He's had his fair share of failures in his life.

Hold sway
Meaning: To have a great influence on someone's opinion or behaviour; to control someone/something.
Example: His warriors hold sway over much of the continent; Traditional values still hold sway in our home.

Hot on the trail of
Meaning: Close to catching someone; close to finding something.
Example: A detective is hot on the trail of a murder; Recruiters are hot on the trail of young soccer stars.

Hot under the collar
Meaning: Extremely angry or embarrassed.
Example: I got really hot under the collar when my ex-girlfriend showed up at the party.

If all else fails
Meaning: If all other attempts have failed; if what was planned cannot
happen.
Dialogue example:
Speaker A: You look gorgeous! You've always been so stylish and unique in your outfits.
Speaker B: Thanks! If all else fails, I can get into the fashion business.

In a bind
Meaning: To be in a difficult, tough, or threatening situation.
Example: I'm in a bind to pay my bills; This new schedule has put me in a bind.

In a stew
Meaning: Worried; confused; upset.
Example: Jennifer is all in a stew over her lost mobile phone.

In cold blood
Meaning: In an unemotional way; in a cruel and calm way.
Example: She shot him in cold blood.

In fits and starts

Meaning: Not stable; not smooth; often stops and then starts again.

Example: The music player works in fits and starts.

In full swing

Meaning: At the peak of activity.

Example: When my girlfriend and I arrived, the party was in full swing.

In one piece

Meaning: Unscathed; without being damaged.

Dialogue example:

Speaker A: Ouch, an icicle just fell on me.

Speaker B: You in one piece?

Speaker A: And still breathing, thanks.

In someone's bad books

Meaning: In someone's disfavour.

Example: I'm in her bad books at the moment because I forgot to buy her a birthday present.

In store for someone

Meaning: Forthcoming; about to happen to someone; planned for someone.

Example: I have a big surprise in store for you.

In the fullness of time

Meaning: Eventually; after a long time.

Example: I'm sure she'll forgive me everything in the fullness of time; All her secrets will be revealed in the fullness of time.

In words of one syllable

Meaning: In clear and simple language without complicated words and expressions.

Example: Please explain this theorem to me in words of one syllable; Could you repeat your speech in words of one syllable?

Itching to do something

Meaning: Being extremely impatient because you want to do/get something as soon as possible.

Example: She's itching to go to college; He's itching to get back to work.

It's high time

Meaning: To emphasize that it's time to do what should have been done a long time ago.

Example: It's high time you realize that you're a father; It's high time you got a job.

It's no skin off my nose

Meaning: To emphasize that you don't care if someone does something, because it's not your responsibility.

Dialogue example:

Speaker A: They will stop working with us if we do not fulfil all the terms of the contract.

Speaker B: It's no skin off my nose, I'm just a trainee in this company.

Jog someone's memory

Meaning: To refresh someone's memory; to help someone remember something.

Example: His old diary jogged his memory; That family photo jogged my memory.

Jumping-off point

Meaning: A starting point for an activity, journey, or project.

Example: Amsterdam is the best jumping-off point for a trip to the Netherlands.

Jumping on shadows

Meaning: Being intensely frightened by things that shouldn't normally frighten you.

Example: Ever since she returned from the expedition, she's been acting strangely - jumping on shadows, constantly checking if the front door is closed.

Keep a low profile (or "keep the spotlight off")

Meaning: To avoid attracting attention.

Example: I hope you will try to keep a low profile tonight. Don't forget that the police are looking for you.

Keep one's chin up

Meaning: To stay cheerful during difficult or challenging times.

Dialogue example:

Speaker A: Don't worry so much about bad test results, you'll retake them in a month and get the highest possible score. I believe in you!

Speaker B: I'll try my best to keep my chin up, thanks dad.

Keep one's nose to the grindstone

Meaning: To do intensive, heavy, or continuous work.

Example: Dina's got to keep her nose to the grindstone to feed her family.

Keep one's powder dry

Meaning: To remain calm and be fully prepared for a particular situation/event.

Example: Conflict may not arise, but there is no harm in keeping your powder dry.

Keep one's eyes peeled

Meaning: To watch very carefully.

Example: Just drive slowly and keep your eyes peeled.

Keep one's hair on

Meaning: To urge someone not to panic and stay calm.

Example: Keep your hair on, we're almost there!

Keep tabs on

Meaning: To watch someone/something carefully; always know where someone/something is.

Dialogue example:

Speaker A: Where is Jimmy?

Speaker B: How should I know? I don't keep tabs on him.

Kill or cure

Meaning: Either success or total failure.

Example: This project will be kill or cure for our company; This discovery will kill or cure our research.

Know something by heart

Meaning: To memorize something completely.

Example: I'm pretty sure I know this song by heart.

Labour the point

Meaning: Keep talking or pitching your idea/plan in a boring or annoying manner.

Example: I don't want to labour the point, but you should know that my project is much better.

Lead someone a merry dance

Meaning: To treat someone unfairly or badly over period of time; to cause a lot of problems.

Example: She led me a merry dance before I finally got her to sign the divorce papers.

Lead someone down the garden path

Meaning: To mislead; cheat; deceive.

Example: Vince may have led me down the garden path with that investment opportunity.

Leap in the dark

Meaning: An action performed without the certainty of what will happen as a result.

Example: It would be a leap in the dark to start a company without testing your product; My move to Europe was a leap in the dark.

Leave in the lurch

Meaning: To leave/abandon someone at a time when they really need your assistance or support.

Example: My colleagues left me in the lurch and I had to finish the report myself.

Leave no stone unturned

Meaning: To do everything you can to find something.

Example: Ginny left no stone unturned in her search for her real parents.

Lend an ear

Meaning: To listen to someone in a friendly and sympathetic manner.

Example: Could you please lend me your ear for a minute? I have a

confession to make; My friends are always ready to lend an ear to me.

Lie low

Meaning: To remain hidden; to try not to be seen or noticed.

Example: After the last fraud, the scammers decided to lie low for a while.

Load the dice against someone

Meaning: To put someone at a disadvantage.

Example: Lack of experience loaded the dice against Sarrah as a candidate for the position.

Long shot

Meaning: With very little chance of success.

Example: It's a long shot, but I still want to try to get the job.

Loosen someone's tongue

Meaning: To make someone speak more openly or freely.

Example: The beer had loosened John's tongue.

Lose one's bottle

Meaning: To lose one's nerve or courage in a stressful situation.

Example: I wanted to fight him back, but I lost my bottle at the last minute.

Magic touch

Meaning: The ability to do something extremely well.

Example: He has a magic touch in the kitchen; Dan seems to have a magic touch with cars.

Make a meal of something (or "make a big deal of something")

Meaning: To treat something in a way that makes it seem more significant, valuable, or important than it actually is.

Example: Students always make such a meal of the simplest test; He made such a meal of that task - it only took him half an hour!

Make a rod for your own back

Meaning: To do something that will cause you trouble/problems in the future.

Example: Our management made a rod for their own back when they fired all the highly skilled workers.

Move heaven and earth

Meaning: To try as hard as you can to achieve something; to stop at nothing.

Example: I had to move heaven and earth to get my dream job.

Nip something in the bud
Meaning: To stop something at an early stage before it becomes a big
problem.
Example: It is extremely important to nip this problem in the bud.

Nod is as good as a wink
Meaning: To emphasize that there is no need to explain something further,
because the person already understands or knows enough about it.
Dialogue example:
Speaker A: Do you know why Tanya is so upset?
Speaker B: All I know is that she met her ex-boyfriend at the supermarket.
Speaker A: Come on, a nod is as good as a wink. It's all because of him.

No holds barred
Meaning: Without any restrictions or limits.
Example: In my house you can do whatever you want, no holds barred.

No picnic
Meaning: Quite difficult or unpleasant.
Example: College life is no picnic; Being a single parent is no picnic.

No prizes for guessing
Meaning: To emphasize that it is very easy to guess something; something that is very obvious.
Example: No prizes for guessing where John is; No prizes for guessing the answer to that simple question.

Not a bed of roses
Meaning: Having some unpleasant aspects.
Example: My job is not a bed of roses.

Not a hair out of place
Meaning: To have a very neat/tidy appearance.
Example: He was so gorgeous in his new suit, not a hair out of place; She was splendidly dressed, not a hair out of place.

Not budge an inch
Meaning: To refuse to change your mind/position.
Example: I tried to negotiate a better offer but they wouldn't budge an inch.

Not have a care in the world
Meaning: Without worrying about anything.
Example: I miss the old school days, when I didn't have a care in the world.

Not have a leg to stand on

Meaning: To have no proof of your rightness/correctness.
Dialogue example:
Speaker A: What is your evidence?
Speaker B: I don't have a leg to stand on. It's only my word against hers.

Not in one's right mind
Meaning: Mentally ill; cannot think clearly.
Example: Leave her alone, she's not in her right mind; I know he's scared to death, but I need him in his right mind!

Not best pleased
Meaning: Annoyed; irritated; angry; unhappy.
Example: I wasn't best pleased when my mother married again; and so soon after my father's death!

No two ways about it
Meaning: Definitely; for sure; without a doubt.
Example: If you leave me here alone and go drink beer with your friends,
I'll break up with you! No two ways about it!

Off one's hands
Meaning: Removed from one's responsibility; no longer needing to be looked after.

Example: If you are unable to complete these tasks, I'll be glad to take them off your hands.

Off the mark
Meaning: Not correct; inaccurate; wrong ("on the mark" - correct/right).
Example: Your remark is off the mark; The facts she provided are way off the mark.

Of the essence
Meaning: Absolutely necessary in a particular situation.
Example: Speed is of the essence in dealing with an emergency; We must hurry, time is of the essence!

On a hiding to nothing
Meaning: Without the slightest chance of success; sure to fail.
Example: He's on a hiding to nothing in this competition.

One for the books
Meaning: Very surprising or unexpected.
Example: His last-minute goal was one for the books.

On speaking terms
Meaning: Amicable or friendly enough to talk (often used in negative
form).
Example: I'm not on speaking terms with my family; I don't know how after all his intrigues and betrayals she's somehow still on speaking terms with

him; We're on speaking terms with John, but I wouldn't say we're real friends.

On the loose
Meaning: A dangerous animal/criminal who walks free (mostly because they have escaped from prison/cage).
Example: He's still on the loose - but not for long. The police have already blocked all exits from the city.

On the verge of something (or "on the brink of something")
Meaning: Very close to experiencing something; the moment when something is about to happen.
Example: We are on the verge of a big discovery; We stand on a brink of a great change.

On your own head be it
Meaning: To warn someone that they will have to take full responsibility for what they are about to do.
Example: If you choose to disobey my order, then on your own heads be it!

Out of sorts
Meaning: Slightly ill/unwell/unhappy.
Example: He's feeling a bit out of sorts.

Out of the corner of one's eye
Meaning: Looking at something indirectly; when you see something briefly, rather than clearly.
Example: Out of the corner of my eye, I saw my wife talking to some stranger.

Over the hill
Meaning: No longer young and fit; too old to perform as well as before.
Example: Ron is over the hill as a professional basketball player.

Pale into insignificance
Meaning: To appear less important, significant, or impressive when compared with something else.
Example: All my problems pale into insignificance when compared to the problems of the homeless.

Paragon of virtue
Meaning: One who has perfect moral values.
Example: Ron was considered to be a paragon of virtue; I don't expect any billionaire to be a paragon of virtue.

Pass the buck
Meaning: To shift the responsibility to someone else.
Example: It's your fault because you're in charge, so don't try to pass the buck.

Perish the thought
Meaning: To emphasize that the proposed idea/concept/plan is ridiculous
and unlikely to be implemented.
Example: I will never marry her - perish the thought!

Pipe dream
Meaning: Something that is not destined to come true.
Example: His plans to become president of several countries at once are
simply pipe dreams.

Plain sailing
Meaning: Without problems; smooth; easy.
Example: Her surgery was plain sailing; Pregnancy wasn't all plain sailing.

Play into someone's hands
Meaning: To do something that will be to your disadvantage and to your
opponent's advantage; to act in the way your opponent wants you to act.
Example: It would be playing into Rita's hands to react to her humiliating
jokes.

Play your cards right
Meaning: To behave in a way that is beneficial in a given situation; to do
something in a well-planned way.

Example: If you play your cards right, you can win this competition.

Pull out all the stops
Meaning: To make every possible effort; do the best you can.
Example: The police pulled out all the stops to find the robber; Dan pulled
out all the stops to finish the project on time.

Pull someone's leg
Meaning: To tell someone a lie, as a joke.
Example: Calm down Ian, it's not true, I was only pulling your leg.

Pull the plug
Meaning: To prevent further activity; to prevent something from continuing.
Example: I have enough power to pull the plug on your career; She decided to pull the plug on her research.

Put it down to experience
Meaning: To regard a bad, difficult, or unpleasant situation as a learning
experience rather than a punishment.
Example: Everyone makes mistakes, don't worry so much and put it down to experience.

Put someone wise to something

Meaning: To clarify something for someone; to tell someone about something.

Example: I showed up at the appointed time. Tommy put me wise to the situation and we started negotiations.

Put something to bed

Meaning: To successfully deal with something; to finish work on something.

Example: Before putting the agreement to bed, we must clarify a few clauses; Let's just put the issue to bed and stop arguing!

Put the cart before the horse

Meaning: To do something in the wrong order.

Example: Aren't you putting the cart before the horse by choosing a wedding venue before the actual proposal?

Raining cats and dogs

Meaning: Heavy rain.

Example: Better stay at home, it's raining cats and dogs outside.

Rain on someone's parade

Meaning: To do something that ruins someone's plans; dampen one's excitement.

Example: I hate to rain on your parade, but I think your name on the list of finalists is just a typo. You took 25th place, not third, sorry.

Ride for a fall

Meaning: To do something unwise and reckless that will lead to failure or injury.

Example: Nina's riding for a fall with the dubious investments she's been making lately.

Rob someone blind

Meaning: To cheat someone and take their money; to steal everything someone owns.

Dialogue example:

Speaker A: Hello madam! Would you like to multiply your savings? For just a thousand pounds, I can tell you how to do it.

Speaker B: You are trying to rob me blind. I won't buy it!

Rocky road

Meaning: A difficult/challenging period.

Example: The rocky road to the championship.

Rub shoulders/elbows with

Meaning: To spend time with someone.

Example: She loves rubbing shoulders with the rich and famous.

Rue the day
Meaning: To curse or bitterly regret a moment in your life; to be very sorry for something.
Example: I rue the day I lost my wife; When I find him, he'll rue the day he was born!
Said the pot to the kettle (or "the pot calling the kettle black")
Meaning: A witty remark to someone who says something bad/insulting
about another person, when they themselves are guilty of the same thing.
Dialogue example:
Speaker A: He is so arrogant and selfish!
Speaker B: Said the pot to the kettle.
Sail close to the wind
Meaning: To do something dangerous, risky, illegal, or unacceptable.
Example: Illegal tobacco company was sailing close to the wind.
Salt something away
Meaning: To save something for later.
Example: Don't worry about the wedding expenses, I have fifty thousand
pounds salted away for that.
Say your piece

Meaning: To state your opinion; to say what you want to say.
Example: Stop glaring at us! Just say your piece about the incident.
See fit
Meaning: To consider proper or desirable.
Example: When you find this fraudster, deal with him however you see fit.
See the light of day
Meaning: To come into existence; first time to appear.
Example: This video game first saw the light of day in 2005.
Serve someone right
Meaning: To emphasize that someone deserves all the bad things that
happen to them.
Dialogue example:
Speaker A: He is in trouble with the law again.
Speaker B: It serves him right!
Set someone's mind at ease
Meaning: Help someone to calm down/stop worrying.
Example: He could set her mind at ease by telling her the truth.
Set something in motion
Meaning: To start a process/series of events.
Example: By not taking their money, you set the bankruptcy in motion.
Settle a score

Meaning: To punish or harm someone for something bad that they did to
you in the past; take revenge; pay the debt off.
Dialogue example:
Speaker A: Will you join us to fight the hooligans from 15th Street?
Speaker B: Yes, I have some scores to settle with them.

Shadow of one's former self
Meaning: Not as good, powerful, or capable as before.
Example: Three years after her injury, she returned to the basketball court,
but was only a shadow of her former self.

Shed some light
Meaning: To provide additional/missing information about something.
Example: Hopefully these documents will shed some light on her past.

Sitting duck
Meaning: Easy target; someone who is very easy for the enemy to attack.
Example: Without body armor and a helmet, I'm a sitting duck for the
enemy; children are often sitting ducks for scammers.

Sitting pretty

Meaning: To be in a good, comfortable, privileged, or favored position.
Example: Cariba really is sitting pretty with her new job as CEO; With
profits up 200 percent, my company is sitting pretty.

Slip of the tongue
Meaning: Something that was said by accident/mistakenly.
Example: Did I call you Rachel? It must have been a slip of the tongue.

Small wonder
Meaning: Not surprising.
Example: It's small wonder he wanted me back, I'm the best girlfriend on a planet; It's small wonder the kids are bored.

Smarten up your act
Meaning: To improve your behavior; make more of an effort.
Example: Tell your king that he'll have to smarten up his act if he needs me as an ally.

Someone's lot in life
Meaning: General state of life; general situation in life.
Example: John seems happy enough with his lot in life; He tried to accept the bankruptcy of his company as his lot in life, but he could not.

Splinter off from something

Meaning: To separate from the greater part of something; to separate from a larger group.

Example: Small group splintered off from main camp.

Squeeze something out of someone

Meaning: To force someone to do or give something (mostly information).

Example: It's just a shame we couldn't squeeze anything out of Dan and his accomplices. They probably could have told us some interesting things about the robbery!

Stand your ground (or "hold your ground")

Meaning: To refuse to change your opinion; continue to support a particular position or point of view in an argument; to stay where you are when someone threatens or intimidates you.

Example: Our meeting was unsuccessful because Harry stood his ground and refused to accept any of our offers; The hooligans threatened him, but John stood his ground.

Stem the tide

Meaning: To stop the growth or continuation of something.

Example: These strict measures are designed to stem the tide of illegal immigration.

Straight from the horse's mouth

Meaning: To hear information from someone who knows for sure that it's true (mainly because that person has personally seen or heard something that confirms the accuracy of the information).

Example: Oh, you're here! John already told me what's been happening, but I'd like to hear it straight from the horse's mouth.

Strain every nerve

Meaning: To make every possible effort; do the best you can.

Example: I will strain every nerve to finish the book.

Sure as eggs is eggs

Meaning: Without any doubt; for certain.

Dialogue example:

Speaker A: Are you sure you are pregnant?

Speaker B: Sure as eggs is eggs!

Sweep something under the carpet

Meaning: To deliberately ignore a problem/issue in the hope that it will be overlooked or forgotten.

Example: You can't just sweep your financial problems under the carpet.

Sweep the board
Meaning: To win everything possible.
Example: My team swept the board in the boxing competition.

Take a hint
Meaning: To understand something that is suggested or offered to you indirectly.
Dialogue example:
Speaker A: Nancy, would you like to have dinner with me tonight?
Speaker B: I'd love to, but I have a lot of work to do. And besides, my knee hurts. So, uh...
Speaker A: Okay, I can take a hint.

Take it from me
Meaning: To emphasize that you are absolutely sure of what you are saying.
Dialogue example:
Speaker A: What is your opinion of John?
Speaker B: You can take it from me, he's a wonderful man.

Take matters into your own hands
Meaning: To do something yourself because others have refused or failed.
Example: We failed his order to eliminate the target. So he took matters into

his own hands and killed the target.

Take something as read
Meaning: To agree/accept that something is true without any evidence.
Example: We took it as read that he was a spy; Let's take it as a read that he was the first to invent this method.

Take the bull by the horns
Meaning: To confidently deal with a dangerous or difficult situation.
Example: I know that you are a very empathetic person, but it's time to take the bull by the horns and fire inefficient employees.

Tall order
Meaning: A request or task that is extremely difficult to complete.
Example: Completing this task on time was a tall order, but we did it;
Spending more time with kids is a tall order for busy parents.

Thank your lucky stars
Meaning: To be extremely grateful.
Example: You should thank your lucky stars that you managed to survive the accident.

That's one way of putting it

Meaning: To emphasize that someone said something completely different from the intended meaning of their words (mostly in a sarcastic or flirty manner).

Dialogue example:

Speaker A: You look really hot!

Speaker B: Well, that's one way of putting it.

The jury is still out

Meaning: To emphasize that something has not yet been decided/answered.

Example: The jury is still out on whether red wine can be good for you.

The lion's share

Meaning: Bigger half; largest part.

Example: I spend the lion's share of my salary on rent.

The mists of time/history

Meaning: To emphasize that something happened so long ago that you barely remember it.

Example: The answer is lost in the mists of time; The origins of this phrase are lost in the mists of history/time.

The more the merrier

Meaning: To emphasize that more people will make the event or activity more enjoyable.

Dialogue example:

Speaker A: Can I bring my brother to your birthday party?

Speaker B: Sure, the more the merrier!

There's no telling

Meaning: Impossible to know for sure.

Example: If he fails in negotiations, there's no telling how many people will lose their jobs.

There's no time like the present

Meaning: To emphasize that now is the best time to do something.

Dialogue example:

Speaker A: When would you like to meet?

Speaker B: There's no time like the present. See you in an hour at our favourite cafe.

There's safety in numbers

Meaning: To emphasize that when you are in a large group with other people, you are less likely to be harmed.

Dialogue example:

Speaker A: We are lost in the woods at night. What should we do?

Speaker B: We must stick together. There's safety in numbers.

The worse for wear
Meaning: Exhausted; tired; in poor condition; beaten up from use.
Example: He was slightly the worse for wear after a grueling workout; Your jacket seems to be the worse for wear - I'll buy you a new one.

Throw a spanner in the works
Meaning: To prevent things from going as planned (mainly by causing
problems or difficulties).
Example: I was ready to publish my novel when my little sister threw a
spanner in the works by deleting the book from my computer.

Throw cold water on something
Meaning: To destroy someone's enthusiasm for something; be extremely
pessimistic about someone's plans or ideas.
Example: You're always throwing cold water on my ideas!

Tie up loose ends
Meaning: To deal with little issues/problems left unresolved from
something; to complete minor matters that are the result of a previous
action.

Example: It was almost a perfect heist. With all the witnesses under control,
all that remained was to tie up loose ends.

Till the cows come home
Meaning: For a long period of time.
Example: You can convince me till the cows come home, but I won't
change my mind.

To someone's liking
Meaning: Fitting someone's preferences; enjoyable to someone.
Dialogue example:
Speaker A: Everything to your liking, thus far?
Speaker B: Couldn't be better, thank you.

To the untrained eye/ear
Meaning: Without special knowledge of the subject.
Example: To the untrained eye, it looks like a stack of old papers. But,
believe it or not, this is the original manuscript of my first book.

Tough act to follow
Meaning: Someone or something so successful, exemplary, or effective that it overshadows anything that follows.

Example: John was a tough act to follow - a Nobel laureate with 40 years of experience in the field; Finding a replacement for my colleague Dan will be a tough act to follow.

To your heart's content
Meaning: As long as you wish; as much as you want.
Example: You can circle Paris to your heart's content; His wife let him eat and drink to his heart's content.

Treat/handle with kid gloves
Meaning: To treat someone/something very gently and carefully; be extremely polite and kind.
Example: She needs to be handled with kid gloves; We must treat the situation with kid gloves.

Trouble is brewing (or "something is brewing")
Meaning: A dangerous or difficult situation is developing.
Example: The informant made it clear that something was brewing and that you and your family were in great danger.

True to form
Meaning: Behaving in expected or predictable manner; as usual.
Example: True to form, Rita and Sam are late again; True to form, John

asked to borrow some more money; True to form, she missed the flight.

Try your hand at something
Meaning: To do something for the first time.
Example: I've always wanted to try my hand at scuba diving.

Until all hours
Meaning: Very late; until a very late hour.
Example: We were up talking until all hours.

Until the dust settles
Meaning: Until the situation becomes calmer.
Example: You've caused a lot of trouble, and we'll have to leave town until the dust settles.

Walk with a spring in your step
Meaning: Walk energetically and happily.
Example: As Rita walked into the school that morning, there was a spring in her step.

Water under the bridge
Meaning: Something that happened a long time ago and doesn't bother you anymore.
Example: I forgive you, my dear friend! And that quarrel is just water under the bridge!

When push comes to shove
Meaning: When a situation becomes critical and you need to act; when a

decision needs to be made; when something can no longer be ignored.
Example: Only Bella was there to help me when push came to shove.

With flying colours
Meaning: Successfully.
Example: He passed his college entrance exam with flying colours.

With one accord
Meaning: All together; in full agreement; at the same time.
Example: With one accord they left the room; We made the decision with one accord.

Without a hitch (or "with no hitches")
Meaning: Smoothly, easily, without any difficulties or problems.
Example: The parade went off without a hitch; The knee surgery went
without a hitch.

Worth your while
Meaning: Something that is worth your attention/time and you can gain
some benefit or advantage from it.
Dialogue example:
Speaker A: Is it really worth your while to keep looking for your
grandmother's necklace?

Speaker B: Yes, that necklace is a family heirloom.

6. Modals

Modals
Modals are auxiliary verbs used to form the tenses, moods, voices, etc. of other verbs. They are helping verbs that cannot be used on their own but to be used along with other main verbs mainly to express attitudes.
1. When something happens, they form a tense of the main verb.
Examples:
- I shall go.
- He was going
2. They express permission, necessity, or possibility to do something.
Examples:
- They may go.
- You must go.
- I can't go.
- I might go.
- She would go if she could.

Observe the highlighted words in these sentences.
- We can make our nation a superpower by the year 2020.
- Kalam says that we need to do things ourselves. We must not import equipment from other nations.
- In twenty years, each one of us ought to have our destiny worked out.

All the highlighted words are Modal Auxiliaries that are used with another verb, and express the mood of the speaker.
- The main MODALS are: can, could; may, might; shall, should; will, would; must; ought to; need to; have to.
- The negative modals are: couldn't, wouldn't, shouldn't, mustn't, needn't, oughtn't.

1.Must and have to:
- Must is used for all persons in the present and the future tenses.
- The negative is must not (mustn't).
- The interrogative form is, must I?
- Must has no infinitive and no past tense. It is followed by the infinitive without "to'.

(i) Must is used to express obligation:
- You must obey your parents.
- You must go to school in time.

(ii) It is used to express compulsion, e. ordering someone to do something because it is necessary or important to do so:
- You must answer all questions.
- You must return by the evening.

(iii) It is used for saying that something is probably true because nothing else seems possible:

- You must be tired after your long journey (inference).
- There must be some mistakes.

(iv) The negative form of must (must not) is used for prohibition:

- You must not come here.
- You must not use the office phone for private calls.

(v) It is used to give emphatic advice:

- She must consult a doctor at once.
- You must work hard if you want to get good marks.

You can master in English Grammar of various classes by our articles like Tenses, Clauses, Prepositions, Story writing, Unseen Passage, Notice Writing, etc.

Must and have to:

Have to, like must, expresses obligation in the present while had to does so in the past. Must expresses an obligation imposed by the speaker. Have to/Had to expresses external obligations—an obligation by some authority or circumstances.

- I must reach there in time (the speaker himself feels so).
- You must reach in time (ordered to do so by some external authority).

Had to is used when describing something belonging to the past.

- He had to go early to catch the train.

For example:
Have you to obey his orders?
or
Do you have to obey his orders?   Had you to work on Sundays?
or
Did you have to work on Sundays?
Do you have to mind your watch every day?
Did you have to pay customs duty on your watch?
You can master in English Grammar of various classes by our articles like Tenses, Clauses, Prepositions, Story writing, Unseen Passage, Notice Writing etc.

2. Have to/Had to:

(i) Have to express obligation and necessity in the present. Had to does so in the past:

- She has to look after her mother.
- He had to finish his work before 5 p.m.

(ii) Have to and had to are used for giving advice:

- First you have to mix the water and the sugar.
- She had to take those pills to get better.

(iii) Have to and had to are used to draw a logical conclusion:

- There has to be some reason for his mischief.

- This has to be a part of the whole plan.

(iv) Have to is used for supposition or to describe something based on possible ideas or situations:

- You will have to work very hard to stand first.
- If she has to choose, she won't marry him.

(v) Have to is used to indicate that something is very important or necessary:

- We have to be more careful in the future.
- They will have to clear all their debts before December.

3. Should:

(i) Should is the past tense of shall. In the indirect form of speech 'shall' changes into should:

- I said, "I shall go to school tomorrow."
- I said that I should go to school the next day.

(ii) Should is used to express obligation, duty, etc.

- You should look after your old parents.
- You should pay all your taxes.

(iii) Should is used to give advice or suggestion:

- You should consult a doctor.
- She should do yoga exercises daily.
- He should learn English if he wants to get a good job.

(iv) Should is used to express purpose:

- Mohan walked fast so that he should catch the train.
- Satish worked hard so that he should stand first in the class.

(v) Should is used to state imaginary results:

- He should get angry if he had come to know about it.

(vi) Should is used to express polite requests:

- I should be thankful if you give me some money.

4. Need:

As a modal verb, need is usually followed by an infinitive without 'to':

The modal verb need is mainly used in questions and negatives, which are formed without 'do':

Need I go now? You need not go.

The negative need not is often shortened to needn't in the conversation and informal writing.

Need does not change its form, so the third person singular of the present tense does not end in' —s' :

He need not go there.

The modal verb need has no past tense. But it can be used in the pattern followed by a past participle:

Need not have/needn't have

You needn't have waited for me.

The negative and interrogative forms of the past tense are:

Did not (didn't) need and did I need?

In the present and future tenses, the negative and interrogative can be formed in either of the two ways:

	Negative	Interrogative
Present Tense	Need not or don't/ doesn't need	Need I? or do I need?
Future Tense	Need not or shan't/won't need	Or need I? / shall I need?

(i) The nigtive need expresses absence of obligation:

- They need not send the letter now.
- You need not go. (i.e., It is not necessary for you to go).
- He need not come now.

(ii) Need is used to express obligation or necessity:

- Need I attend the class today?
- Need he solve all the sums?

(iii) Need not + perfect infinitive is used to express an unnecessary action which was performed:

- You needn't have gone to see the doctor. He was on leave today.
- You needn't have carried an umbrella as it was not raining.

5. Ought

Ought is usually followed by 'to' and an infinitive:

- You ought to tell the truth.

It does not change its form so that the third person singular form does not end in '-s':

- She ought to work a little harder.

It can be used as a present, past, or future tense.

The negative is ought not (oughtn't) and the interrogative is ought I?, Ought you?, Ought he?, etc:

- Ought I do it at once?
- He ought not disobey his teachers.

(i) Ought to is used for expressing what is the right or sensible thing to do, or the right way to behave:

- You ought to get up earlier.
- We ought to exercise daily.
- Teachers ought not smoke before students.

(ii) Ought to is used when we believe strongly or expect that something will happen:

- The Indian team ought to win.
- Satish ought to pass.
- The meeting ought to have finished by 2 o'clock.

(iii) Ought to see/hear/meet, is used for emphasising how good, impressive or unusual something or someone is:

- You ought to see their new house.
- You ought to meet his elder brother.

(iv) Ought to have is used when we realise that we did not do the right thing in the past:

- You ought to have listened to my advice.
- She ought to have taken the money.

Ought, must, have to, and should

Note: Ought is used to express the subject's obligation or duty. But it indicates neither the speaker's authority as with must nor an outside authority as with have to. The speaker is only reminding the subject of his duty. Besides this, he is giving advice or indicating a correct or sensible action.

Ought can be used in exactly the same way as should:

- You ought to/should obey your parents.
- Have to and must:
- You have to be regular. (These are the rules.)
- You must obey your teachers. (The speaker insists on it.)
- You have to take this medicine. (The doctor insists on it.)
- You must take this medicine. (The speaker insists on it or It is the speaker's emphatic advice.)
- You mustn't drink this, it is poison, (prohibition)
- You oughtn't to smoke so much. (It is not right or sensible.)

Exercise (Solved)

Fill in the blanks with appropriate modals:

1. We........................ obey our teachers, (have to, must)
2. She........................ .... pass this time, (ought to, has to)
3. He..................... not buy a car. (has to, need)
4. He works hard lest he...................... fail, (should, must)
5. Do you........................ cook your own meal? (should, have to)
6. The villagers..................... use kerosene lamps a few years ago. (must, had to)
7. The old lady.............. take a bath every day before taking meals, (ought to, should)
8. She.................. finish this work before I go. (has to, must)
9. Ramesh said that they................. report for duty on Monday, (should, ought to)
10. We........................... .. prepare our lessons well before the examination. (ought to, must)

Answer:

1. must
2. ought to
3. need
4. should

143

5. have to
6. had to
7. should
8. must
9. should
10. ought to

Exercise (Unsolved)

Fill in the blanks with appropriate modals:

1. We...................... pay attention to our studies, (ought to, should)
2. You......................... ... not litter the classroom, (should, could)
3. I talk to you immediately, (need to, ought to)
4. They will.................... clear all the doubts before the starting of meeting, (have to, had to)
5. He...................... take those medicines to get better, (has to, had to)
6. You.................. consult a physician, (should, ought to)
7. You..................... exercise daily, (ought to, need)
8. They.................. not send the letter now. (need, would)
9. Sahil ran fast so that he.................... catch the train, (should, needs)
10. You......................... ... not use the office phone for private calls, (must, have to)

We have already studied some of the uses of '*be*' (i*s, am, are, was, were, being* and *been*), '*do*' (*does* and *did*) and '*have*' (*has, have, had*). Be, do and *have* are *Primary Auxiliaries*. They help to form *tenses*, *questions* and *negatives*. They are also used in changing voice.

The forms of '*be*', '*do*' and '*have*' can be used as Principal Verbs also; as—

Smriti *is* in her class.

I *have* a lot of work to do.

Do as I tell you.

Be careful in this matter.

She *has* no friend in this locality.

Modals express the mode of action. The most common modals are: may, might, can, could, shall, should, will, would, must, dare, need, have and used to.

GENERAL CHARACTERISTICS OF MODALS

1. Modals are never used alone. A Principal verb is either present or implied; as—

    I *can* sing. He *will* help you.

2. Modals do not change according to the number or person of the subject; as—

    I *can*. We *can*. You *can*. We *can*. They *can*. etc.

    I *may*. We *may*. You *may*. He *may*. They *may*. etc.

3. Modals have no *Infinitive, Present Participle* or *Past Participle* forms.

4. Modals cannot be used in all the tenses. When a modal does not fall in this pattern, it works as a Principal Verb; as—
God *willed* so.
He *needs* a pen.
She *dared* to go into the dark forest.
(Here *will, need,* and *dare* a re used as *main verbs*)

Relationship of Modals with Tenses

(i) *May, can, shall,* and *will* are in present forms while *might, could, should,* and *would* are their past forms.

The two forms express different meanings, but usually, no difference of time, e.g. the difference
between *may* and *might* is often that of the *degree of probability,* as—

She *may* come today. (*possibility / likely to happen*)

She *might* come today. (*remote possibility/less likely*)

(ii) However, if the verb in the main clause is in the past tense, the forms *might, could, should* and *would* serve as regular past tenses; as—

1. He said, "I *can help* you."
He said that he *could help* her.

2. You said, "She *will come* back soon."
You said that she *would come* back soon.

3. Sheetal said, "May I *use* this pen, madam?"
Sheetal asked her teacher if she *might* use that pen.

(iii) When we want to express the past time in verb phrases involving modals, we use the Present Perfect Tense of the Principal Verb; as
She *must have reached* home by now.
You *ought to have told* me all the facts.

General Functions of Modals

1. Modals express *probability, logical necessity, possibility, future confirmation* etc. These are not conceptions of the mind. *Modals are not used to state facts.*

2. Modals are used in the main clause of conditional sentences. Since the condition is contrary to facts, the main statement cannot be actual. Hence a modal is used; as—
If I *were* you, I *should help* the old beggar.
If it *were* fine, we *might play* a cricket match.
If you had told me, I *could have helped* you.

Apart from these general functions, modals are used in various ways. Let us consider them separately.

USE OF MODALS

CAN/COULD

Can is used for all persons in the *present tense.*

Could is used for all persons in the *past tense.*

CAN is used

1. to express permission:
   You *can* go now. (= I give you permission to go)
   You *cannot* touch the flowers. (= I don't permit you to touch the flowers)

2. to express ability:
   I *can* swim. (= I know how to swim)
   He can speak Sanskrit. (= He is able to speak Sanskrit)

3. to express possibility:
   Anyone *can* make mistakes.
   Accidents *can* happen to anyone.

4. 'Can't help' is an idiom. It means 'Can't avoid'; e.g.
   He has a bad cold. He *can't help* sneezing.
   The boys *can't help* laughing on seeing the clown.
   COULD must be used to express *ability, permission* and *possibility* when the main verb is in the past tense; as—
   I *could* swim well when I was younger. (*ability*)
   Could you lend me some money, please?
   Could you tell me the time, please?
   Could you wait for a few minutes?

MAY/MIGHT

'May' is used for all persons of the present and future tense.

'May' is used

1. to express or to seek permission: [*in a formal way*]
   You *may* go (= I permit you to go.)
   May I come in, Sir? (= seeking permission)
   Students *may not* bring any book or paper in the examination hall. (*permission refused*)

2. to express possibility:
   It *may* rain. He *may* come today.

3. to express a wish:
   May he live long! *May* she enjoy good health!

4. to express purpose:
   He works hard so that he *may* pass.

MIGHT

Might is used for all persons of the past tense.

(i) to seek permission:

'Might I' can be used instead of '*May* I' when asking for permission and '*Migh*t I' is a more polite form. The use of '*might*' shows that the speaker is rather hesitant or doubtful about making the request; as—

(i) *May* I use your phone?

(ii) *Might* I use your phone?

Both express the same idea, but the second sentence is more polite.

(ii) to express possibility:

'*Might*' expresses greater doubt than 'may'.

'*Might*' suggests remote/distant possibility; as—

It *might* rain. He *might* come today.

(iii) to put forward a suggestion:

'*Might*' is often used to put forward a suggestion or offer advice which you are a little hesitant about; as—

You *might* try again. (= But I am not certain if you should)

You *might* wait.

(iv) in conditional sentences:

'May / Might ' can be used instead of 'shall / will' and 'should / would' in the conditional sentences respectively to express a possible result; as—

If you work hard, you *may* pass, (possibility)

If she had left early, she *might* have reached by now.

Might must be used when the main verb of the sentence is in the past tense.

(i) to express permission:

He said that I *might* borrow his car.

The teacher said that the boy *might* go.

(ii) to express possibility:

He thought that I *might* like it.

Sudha said that she might go abroad next year.

(iii) to express speculation (guess) about past actions. '*Might have*' is used for past time.

He told me that she *might have* finished her work.

This medicine *might have* cured your cough.

Both '*May*' and '*might*' are used to suggest '*there is a good reason*'-, as—

You *may* as well say so.

She *might* as well come by the next train.

You might just as well go as not.

(*There is just as much to be said in favour of going as against it*)

EXERCISE 1

(Solved)

Fill in the blanks with 'can' or 'could':

1. .... you prepare a cup of tea for me, please?

2. She .... not help to laugh at the joker.

3. We .... execute your plan at once.

4. He said that he .... walk twenty kms at a stretch.

5. A lame person .... not walk.

6. .... you lift this box for me?

7. She .... read without glasses till last year.

8. You .... not see the principal now.

9. He worked hard but .... not pass the examination.
10. She .... play the piano when she was only eleven.

Answers:

1.*could* 2. *can* 3. *can* 4. *could* 5. *can* 6. *could* 7. *could* 8. *can* 9. *could* 10. *could.*

EXERCISE 2

(Solved)

Fill in the blanks with May' or ''Might':

1. The news .... not be true.
2. With a little more effort we .... win this time.
3. The examinations .... be postponed.
4. We .... have gone if they had invited us to dinner.
5. With a little push, he .... have got the job.
6. .... your future be bright!
7. You .... not attend the meeting this evening.
8. He said that it .... not rain.
9. She asked if she .... see the director.

10. The sky is overcast. It ....rain at any time.

Answers:

1. *may* 2. *might* 3. *may,* 4. *might* 5. *might* 6. *may* 7. *may* 8. *might* 9. *might* 10. *may*

EXERCISE 3

(Solved)

Fill in the blanks with 'can', 'could', 'may' or 'might' appropriate to the sense given in brackets:

1. He .... do this if he tried.   (*possibility*)
2. She .... not run as fast as you.   (*ability*)
3. He .... enter college next year.   (*possibility*)
4. I knew that I .... borrow his car.   (*ability*)
5. You .... tell me what he said.   (*claim*)
6. You .... tell me what he said.   (*ability*)
7. I .... help him if he asked me to.   (*wish*)
8. He works hard so that that he .... get good marks.   (*purpose*)
9. When I was young, I .... write Hindi verse.   (*capacity*)

10. Had you worked hard, you .... have won a scholarship   (*possibility*)

Answers:

1. *might* 2. *can* 3. *may* 4. *could* 5. *might* 6. *could* 7. *may* 8. *may* 9. *could* 10. *might*.

WILL/SHALL

(a)   With the second and third persons, will is used

1. to express simple future:
    She *will leave* for Ambala tomorrow.
    Lata *will sing* a song.
    You *will study* in the evening.

2. to express an invitation or request Here 'will you'? is not a question in the ordinary sense; as—
    Will you care for a cup of tea?   *(Invitation)*
    Will you please lend me your pen?   *(Request)*

3. to express command in an informal or impersonal manner expecting that it will be surely obeyed; as—
    All new boys *will* report for a medical check-up.
    ''You *will* not leave the class before completing your homework,'' said the teacher.
    Officers *will* appear properly dressed in public places.

4. to express something that happens again and again

and is likely to recur; as—
The old woman *will* sit in the park and sing songs.
Vinod *will* go to the coffee house and discuss politics.
Some persons *will* walk in the middle of the road.

5. to express quantity or capacity; as—
    This jug *will* hold two litres of water.
    Two hundred persons *will* be seated in this tent.

6. to express prediction; as—
    It is too close, it *will* rain.
    You *will* fall ill, if you eat all that.

7. as a Principal Verb:
    God *willed* otherwise. We waited under different clocks and could not meet each other.

(b)   'Will' with the First Person is used

1. to express willingness or offer; as—
    I will help you as far as possible.
    I will carry that parcel for you.

2. to express intention or promise; as—
    I *will* go home to see my mother.
    We *will* come in time.

3. to express threat; as—
    I *will* beat you.
    I *will* teach him a lesson.

4. to express determination; as—

I will lay down my life for my country.

I will not take eggs; I am a strict vegetarian.

SHALL

(a) With the first person, 'shall' is used

1. to express simple future; as—

We *shall* leave for Delhi tomorrow.

I *shall* go for a long drive this evening.

2. to express the plan or intention of the speaker; as—

We *shall* shift to our new house next week.

I *shall* go to Chandigarh via Rohtak.

3. to express an offer or suggestion; as—

Shall I shut the window?

Shall we sit in the lawn?

(b) With the second and third persons, 'shall' is used

1. to express a command; as—

You *shall* do it.

You *shall* remain here till he comes.

He *shall* report for duty at 8.30 a.m. tomorrow.

2. to express a threat; as—

You *shall* die for it. You shall not study further if you fail.

She *shall* be punished for her misdeeds.

He *shall* be sacked for his negligence.

3. to express a promise; as—

You *shall* get leave today.

You *shall* have a scooter if you pass.

He *shall* get a reward for his faithfulness.

4. to express command or wish of the person addressed if used with the third person; as—

Shall he carry your luggage?

Shall he wait outside for you?

EXERCISE 4

(Solved)

Use shall or will in the blanks in the following sentences:

1. He .... leave this office at once. It is final.

2. I .... file a case of defamation against the paper.

3. We .... not allow this type of misrule to continue.

4. All traitors .... die.

5. How long .... you stay at Manali?

6. ....you attend her farewell party?

7. ....we be invited to her mango party?

8. She .... just sit and brood over her past life.

9. We .... not visit the Trade Fair tomorrow.

10. .... we refresh ourselves with some coffee now?

Answers:

1. *shall* 2. *will* 3. *will* 4. *shall* 5. *will* 6. *will* 7. *shall* 8. *will* 9. *shall* 10. *shall.*

EXERCISE 5

(Solved)

Fill in the blanks with 'shall' or 'will' whichever is appropriate:

1. You .... not steal. *(command)*

2. We ....be very glad to see you. *(simple future)*

3. My son ....be twelve next month. *(natural occurrence)*

4. .... you do it or shall I? *(enquiry)*

5. All right! You .... have what you want. *(promise)*

6. I .... meet you again if you so desire. *(determination)*

7. I .... meet you again next week, I expect. *(simple future)*

8. You .... stay till you have finished your work. *(threat)*

9. You .... not prevent me from saying what I want, *(simple future)*

10. If you carry the chairs I .... carry the table. *(willingness)*

Answers:

1. *shall* 2. *shall* 3. *will* 4. *will* 5. *shall* 6. *will* 7. *shall* 8. *shall* 9. *will* 10. *will.*

WOULD/SHOULD

Would is the past tense of '*will*'. '*Would,*' is used

1. to denote the past tense of will/shall in indirect speech; as—

   He said that he *would* go.
   The officer said that he would look into the matter.

2. to express a habitual or customary activity in the past; as—

   He *would* go for a swim in the sea every morning.
   She *would* sit in the sun and talk all day.

3. to make a polite request (with the second person); as—

   Would you spare some time for me?
   Would you mind telling me the way to the post office?

4. To denote courtesy; as—
   Would you stay for dinner?

Would you take a cup of tea?
(Note. Here '*would you* ' is more polite than '*will you*')

5. to express a wish; as—
   Would that I were a film star!
   Would that I were rich!

6. to express a preference; as—
   I *would* like to ask you something.
   I *would* rather die than beg.

7. To express improbable or unreal conditions; as—
   If I won a lottery prize, I *would* build a hospital.
   If I were an astronaut, I *would* take you to Mars.
   Had you helped her, she *would* have succeeded.

SHOULD

Should is the past tense of shall. It is used

1. to denote the past tense of shall in indirect speech; as—
   I said that I *should* go.
   He said that they *should* report for duty on Monday.

2. to express obligation or advice:
   We *should* respect our elders.
   You *should* do your job well.

3. to express purpose:
   She works hard lest she *should fail.*

He worked hard so that he *should* pass the examination.
Hire a taxi, so that you *shouldn't* miss your train.

4. to express probability or likelihood; as—
   Should they play well, they will win.
   If they should play well, they will win.

Here the use of '*should*' is preferred to the present tense to express a very unlikely condition.
If Urvi *should* come, I'll inform you.

EXERCISE 6
(Solved)
Fill in the blanks with 'would' or 'should':

1. You .... work hard to win a scholarship.

2. He .... rather starve than beg.

3. .... you post this letter?

4. They .... arrive here at any moment.

5. If I were a judge, I .... do fair justice.

6. I .... like you to help him with his studies.

7. We .... help the poor and the needy.

8. .... she walks fast, she will catch the train.

9. .... you like to listen to music?

10. I wish he .... not fail this time.

Answers:

1. *should* 2. *would* 3. *Would* 4. *should* 5. *would* 6. *would* 7. *should* 8. *should* 9. *would* 10. *would.*

EXERCISE 7

(Solved)

Fill in the blanks with the right word out of those given in brackets against each sentence:

1. .... she works hard, she will pass. (*would, should)*

2. I ....pre fer to keep quiet. *(would, should)*

3. Work hard lest you .... fail. *(would, should)*

4. I am sure we ....cro ss the forest easily. *(will, shall)*

5. ....yo u please stop talking so loudly. (*will, shall)*

6. If I were you, I .... not do it. *(would, should)*

7. ....yo u please lend me your scooter? (*would, should)*

8. I .... carry out your orders at all costs. *(w ould, should)*

9. I ....lik e to inform you of my inability to attend the meeting. *(would, should)*

10. Walk carefully lest you ....fall down. *(would, should)*

11. He .... ra ther resign than submit to injustice. *(would, should)*

12. You .... not ask me to do anything against my will. *(should, will)*

13. You .... catch a cold, if you go out in the rain. *(shall, will)*

14. I .... n

ot budge an inch from the righteous
path.   *(shall, will)*
15. You

..............................not
go in for that old
car.
(would, should)

Answers:
1. *should* 2. *would* 3. *should* 4. *shal l* 5. *will* 6. *would* 7. *would* 8. *would* 9. *would* 10. *should* 11. *would* 12. *should* 13. *will* 14. *will* 15. *shou ld.*

MUST

'Must' refers to the Present or the Future Tense.

Must is *used*

1. to express compulsion or necessity; as—
   A servant *must* obey his master.
   Every member *must* participate in the discussion,

2. to express duty or a very strong obligation; as—
   We *must* work for the country.   *(dut y)*
   You *must* practise virtue.
   (duty)
   We *must* respect our parents.   *(obligat ion)*
   We *must* obey the laws of our country.   *(obligation)*

3. to express emphatic advice; as—

You *must* reach home before sunset.
You *must* use seat-belt while driving a car.

4. to express determination; as—
   I *must* see you again before the meeting.
   You *must* become a doctor.
   She *must* qualify the test.

5. to express certainty or strong belief; as—
   All *must* die sooner or later.
   Everyone *must* grow old and perish.

6. to express possibility or inference; as—
   She *must* be at least fifty years old.
   Nina *must* have reached the station by now.

7. to express logical necessity or expectation; as—
   There *must* be some error in computation.
   You *must* feel sorry for your misbehaviour.

8. to express strong negation by 'must not'; as—
   He *must* not waste time in street plays.
   You *must* not be rude to your elders.

MUSTN'T

Must not (Mustn't) is used

1. to express prohibition or negative command; as—
   You *mustn't* jump the traffic lights.

One *mustn't* smoke in the presence of ladies.

2. to express the prohibition of "very strong obligation'; as—
A peon *mustn't* disobey his officer.
You *mustn't* leave home without mother's permission.

3. to express the prohibition of necessity; as—
You *mustn't* bring cameras or sticks inside the hall.
Candidates *mustn't* write anything except their roll numbers.

OUGHT

'Ought' refers to Present, Past, or Future Tense.

'Ought' is used

1. to express the sense of duty or moral obligation; as—
Students *ought to* prepare well for their examinations.   (*duty*)
You *ought to* maintain communal harmony.   (*social obligation*)
We *ought to* love our neighbours.   (*moral obligation*)
She *ought to* consult some doctor.   (*a dvice*)
We *ought not to* use unfair means in the examination.   (*advice*)
Note. The sense of moral obligation springs from within. There is no outside force or compulsion. '*Must*' suggests the speaker's authority and emphatic advice 'should'

implies what is the proper or right action.

'*Ought to*' is less forceful and has the same meaning as '*should*'.

2. to express strong probability.
She ought to pass this time.
The past tense of ought is expressed with ought to have + Third form of the verb; as—
You *ought to* have *attended* the meeting.
The driver *ought to have applied* the brakes.
She *ought to have helped* the old woman.
You *ought not to have criticised* me in public.

HAVE TO

1. Have to is *used to express compulsion or necessity* from without; as
I *have* to cook my own meals these days.
She *has to* help her mother in domestic affairs.
People *had* to walk miles to fetch drinking water.

2. Questions and negatives have formed both ways i.e. with or without 'Do'; as—
Negatives: We *don't have to* clean our own shoes.
We haven't to clear our own shoes.
Questions: Do you *have* to cook your own meals?
Have you to cook your own meals?

EXERCISE 8
(Solved)

Fill up the blanks with should, must, mustn't, have to, or ought to:

1. You .... respect your elders.
2. He .... be more careful in the future.
3. You .... to take regular exercise.
4. She is headstrong. She .... have her way in everything.
5. You .... not tell lies. It is not good for you.
6. She .... to develop good manners.
7. She .... contact the doctor at once.
8. They .... to have been more generous.
9. Teachers .... have affection for their students.
10. Mohit, you .... waste a minute now. Your examination is at hand.
11. Varun, you .... squander your parents' hard-earned money.
12. The students .... be in school at nine a.m.
13. You .... disobey the laws of the land.
14. You .... mend your ways before you criticise others.
15. You .... disobey your parents.

Answers:

1. *must* 2. *should* 3. *ought* 4. *must* 5. *should* 6. *ought* 7. *must* 8. *ought* 9. *should* 10. *mustn't* 11. *mustn't* 12. *have to* 13. *mustn't* 14. *have to* 15. *mustn't.*

NEED

1. As a regular verb, 'need' expresses requirement; as—
   She *needs* money for a camera.
   He *needed* your help.
   I *do* not *need* any apples.
2. As modal auxiliary, need is used to express necessity or obligation.
   It is used only in the Present Tense; as—
   Need I to go there?
   Need she to stay here more?
   Need he bring more milk tomorrow?
3. Needn't implies absence of necessity or obligation; as—
   You *needn't go there again:*
   She *needn't wait for me.*

Needn't he go to the office today?

DARE

1. As a regular verb, 'Dare' means 'Challenge\ It is used in all tenses. Its forms are dare (dares), dared and dared.

   He *dares* to go into the forest.

   She *dares* to go into the forest.

   She *dared* to go alone.

   I *dare say* that you are a liar.

   He *did not dare* to come out with the truth.

   She *does not dare* to offend me.

2. As a modal auxiliary, it means '*to take courage*' or '*venture*'. Its other forms are *dare, durst (dared), durst*. It is used only in the *Negative* or *Interrogative sentences*.

   He *dare not* enter my room.   *(Present)*

   She *dare not* oppose me.

   He durst not open my letters.   *(Past)*

   How *dare* you open my letter?   *(Present)*

EXERCISE 9

(Solved)

Fill in the blanks with the right word out of *'Must'*, *'Ought'* , *'used to'*, *'need'*, *'needn't'*, *'dare'*:

1. How .... you say so?
2. She .... have been ill.
3. You .... worry about the child. He will recover soon.
4. .... you disobey your father.
5. Do I .... to come here again?
6. You .... to have obeyed your teacher.
7. He .... not come tomorrow. We are going out on a picnic.
8. I .... to have been there this time.
9. Gandhiji .... spin every day.
10. You .... engag e a tutor for your son.

Answers:

1. *dare* 2. *must* 3. *needn't* 4. *Dare* 5. *need* 6. *ought* 7. *need* 8. *ought* 9. *used to* 10. *must*.

EXERCISE 10

(Solved)

1. Fill in the blanks with suitable modals:

may, ought to, would, must, need.

(i)   You .... go home now.

(ii) The doctor told me that I .... not smoke anymore.

(iii) You .... not see him. Just write a letter to him.

(iv) We .... show respect to

our elders.

(v) ………….. you possibly lend a thousand rupees?

2. Fill in the blanks with appropriate modals:

may, could, must, ought, shall.

(i) You ………….. not enter my class. I forbid it.

(ii) He has been absent for a fortnight, he ………….. be ill.

(iii) ………….. I come in? I'm sorry to be late.

(iv) You ………….. to respect your elders.

(v) ………….. I speak to the Principal for a minute?

3. Fill in the blanks with appropriate modals:

will, shall, should, can, could, must, ought to, need.

(i) I ………….. go there even if it rains.

(ii) You have burnt the midnight oil. You ………….. win a scholarship.

(iii) If you have a ticket, you ………….. go inside.

(iv) I ………….. not come yesterday since I was too busy.

(v) We ………….. go to the station by taxi; it is getting late.

(vi) You ………….. not bring your umbrella. I'll lend you mine.

(vii) Work hard lest you ………….. fail.

(viii) ………….. he brings the dinner now?

Answers:

1. (i) *may* (ii) *must* (iii) *need* (iv) *ought to* (v) *Could/Would*

2. (i) *shall* (ii) *must* (iii) *May* (iv) *ought* (v) *Could*

3. (i) *will* (ii) *ought to* (iii) *can* (iv) *could* (v) *must* (vi) *need* (vii) *should* (viii) *will.*

EXERCISE 11

(Solved)

1. Fill in the blanks with appropriate modals:

May, must, can, could, should, would, ought, need.

1. She ………….. run ten kms an hour.

2. You ………….. go home now; it is getting dark.

3. He ………….. to like this film?

4. Walk carefully lest you ………….. stumble.

5. You ………….. clean your teeth every morning.

6. You ………….. not hurry; there's plenty of time.

7. She ………….. cross such obstacles very easily when she was young.

8. The old man ………….. lie in the sun and dream of his past.

Answers:

1. *can* 2. *must* 3. *ought* 4. *should* 5. *should* 6. *need* 7. *could* 8. *would*

2. Fill in the blanks with suitable modals to convey the sense indicated in the brackets:

1. I

………………………… speak

English fluently. (Present ability)

2. You .... have the money tomorrow. (Promise)

3. When I was young, I .... run faster. (Past ability)

4. .... he disobeys his father? (Courage)

5. He .... apologise or face the consequences. (Command)

6. You .... leave these papers on my desk and go.(Permission)

7. .... we go to a movie? (Suggestion)

8. I .... wait till you return. (Willingness)

9. We .... not give up fighting. (Determination)

10. You .... not touch those exhibits. (Prohibition)

11. You .... not worry about your son now. (Absence of necessity)

12. I fear the weather .... not improve soon. (Possibility)

13. You .... go (permission), if you .... (Compulsion)

14. They .... sit together in the lawn and talk for hours. (Habitual action in the past)

15. We .... to serve our nation. (Moral obligation)

Answers:

1. *can* 2. *shall* 3. *could* 4. *Dare* 5. *must* 6. *may lean* 7. *shall* 8. *will /must* 9. *will* 10. *must* 11. *need* 12. *may* 13. *can; must* 14. *would* 15. *ought.*

EXERCISE 12

(Solved)

Complete the following dialogue using suitable modals:

Father : (a) .... you go to the post-office just now and send these letters by registered post.

Son:

There (b) .... be a rush at this hour. Moreover,

I (c) .... not
go to the post office on foot.
Father: But,
why (d) .... yo
u go on foot? What happened to
your scooter?
Son: It has no .petrol.
I (e) .... not
get it filled because there was a
strike at the petrol station.
Father: O.K.,
You (f) .... use
my scooter, but
you (g) ....
post the letters today. They are very
urgent.
We (h) ....
suffer a loss if they were delayed.
Answers:
(a) *Could* (b) *might* (c) *can* (d) *shou
ld* (e) *could* (f) *can* (g) *must* (h) *cou
ld/might.*
EXERCISE 13
(Solved)
Complete the following paragraph
by filling in the blanks with
suitable modals:
If we sit in an incorrect posture,
it (a) ....
strain our back. As far as possible
this (b) ....
. be avoided. If the posture
becomes a part of the habit, a low
back pain invariably develops.
It (c) ....
cured if we become conscious of
our posture.
We (d) ....
. also take time out to perform a
few exercises. If the exercises are

done regularly the
backache (e) ....
.... certainly be cured.
It (f) ....
also improve blood circulation
within the spine.
Answers:
(a) *will* (b) *should* (c) *can* (d) *shoul
d* (e) *can /will* (f) *can / will.*
EXERCISE 14
(Solved)
1. Fill in the blanks with
appropriate modals:
(a) I *(i)* .... smell
something burning in the
kitchen, *(ii)*.................... you?
It *(iii)* .... be the
pudding in the oven. (b) Your essay
is full of mistakes.
You *(iv)* .... to be
more careful.
You *(v)* .... do
much better if you tried
harder. *(c)* She *(vi)* ....
... to play tennis before her
marriage.
Answers:
*(a) (i) can (ii) can't (iii) may /must
(b) (iv) ought (v) could I would
(c) (vi) used.*
2. Complete the following dialogue
using suitable modals.
Mother:
You (a) .... take an
umbrella. It isn't going to rain.
Son: Well, I don't know.
It (b) ....
Mother: O.K., then take care.
You (c) .... lose it.
Answers:

(a) *needn't* (b) *might/may* (c) *mustn 't/shouldn't.*

INTEGRATED TASKS

I. ERROR CORRECTION

EXERCISE 14

(Solved)

Make corrections wherever necessary:

1. All the traitors may die.
        (threat)
2. Will I open the window?
        (offer)
3. I wish she will come one time.
        (wish)
4. Shall you post this letter, please?
        (request)
5. I shall come if you need my help.   *(willin gness)*
6. He shall rather die than beg.   *(preference)*
7. Shall you live long!
        (wish)
8. Work hard lest you may fail.
        (fear)
9. Can you give me five hundred rupees?   *(polite request)*
10. Shall you care for a cup of coffee, please?   *(polite request)*
11. None will leave the class.
        (prohibition)
12. Will you lift this heavy bag?
        (ability)
13. You need not walk in the middle of the road.   *(prohibition)*
14. When we were students we play games regularly *(past habit)*
15. If she worked harder, she will pass.   *(condit ion)*

Answers:

1. All the traitors *shall* die.
2. *Shall* I open the window?
3. I wish she *would come* one time.
4. *Will* you post this letter, please?
5. I *will* come if you need my help.
6. He *would* rather die than beg.
7. *May you* live long!
8. Work hard *lest* you *should* fail.
9. *Could* you *give* me five hundred rupees?
10. *Would* you *care* for a cup of coffee, please?
11. None *shall leave* the class.
12. *Can* you *lift* this heavy bag?
13. You *must not walk* in the middle of the road.

14. When we were students
    we *used to play* games
    regularly.
15. If she worked harder,
    she *would* pass.

**.

7. Mistakes to be Avoided

Mistakes to be avoided

1. accept / except

INCORRECT: Please except this gift.

CORRECT: Please accept this gift.

Except, as a verb, means to exclude or leave out. As a preposition it means "with the exception of." Accept means "to receive willingly." For example: We visited every landmark except the Eiffel Tower. The school is accepting only those students who have had their shots; all others are excepted.

2. advice / advise

INCORRECT: He refused to take my advise.

CORRECT: He refused to take my advice.

Advise is a verb. The s has the sound of "z." Advice is a noun. The c has the sound of "s."

3.all right / alright

INCORRECT: He's alright after his fall.

CORRECT: He's all right after his fall.

Although arguments are advanced for the acceptance of the spelling, alright is still widely regarded as nonstandard. Careful writers avoid it.

4. awhile / a while

INCORRECT: I'll be staying in Paris for awhile.

CORRECT: I'll be staying in Paris for a while.

Awhile is an adverb that means "for a while." While is a noun that means "a period of time." A while is a phrase that means "for a period of time." Because awhile means "for a while," to say for awhile is like saying "for for a while."

5. alot / a lot

INCORRECT: I like you alot.

CORRECT: I like you a lot.

Despite being used widely, "alot" is not a word. A lot is the correct spelling.

6. allude / elude / illude

INCORRECT: The writer eluded to the Odyssey.

CORRECT: The writer alluded to the Odyssey.

Elude means "to escape," usually by means of swift or clever action. Allude means "to refer to indirectly." Illude is an obsolete spelling for delude and elude.

Spelling Mistakes

7. cannot / can not

INCORRECT: I can not go with you today.

CORRECT: I cannot go with you today.

In speech and informal writing, cannot is frequently contracted as can't. In writing the uncontracted form, cannot is preferred.

8. complement / compliment

INCORRECT: I want to complement you on your writing style.

CORRECT: I want to compliment you on your writing style.

Complement, most frequently used as a verb, means "to complete." Compliment, used as a verb, means "to make a courteous remark." As a noun, it means "a courteous remark." For example: The illustrations complement the text. She complimented his singing. Sallie has difficulty accepting compliments.

9. effect / affect

INCORRECT: His death really effected me.

CORRECT: His death really affected me.

The most common use of effect is as a noun meaning "something produced by a cause." The most common use of affect is as a transitive verb meaning "to act upon." For example: The disease had a lasting effect on the child. The family's lack of money affected his plans.

Spelling Mistakes

10. every day / everyday

INCORRECT: Dan walks the dog everyday at six p.m.

CORRECT: Dan walks the dog every day at six p.m.

Everyday is an adjective that means "daily." Every day is a phrase that combines the adjective every with the noun day. For example: Walking the dog is an everyday occurrence. I practice the flute every day.

11. forty / fourty

INCORRECT: She made the check out for fourty dollars.

CORRECT: She made the check out for forty dollars.

The number 4 is spelled four. The number 40 is spelled forty.

12. its / it's

INCORRECT: Put the saw back in it's place.

CORRECT: Put the saw back in its place.

It's is a contraction that represents two words: it is. Its is a one-word third-person singular possessive adjective, like his. For example: The man lost his hat. The dog wagged its tail.

Spelling Mistakes

13. irregardless / regardless

INCORRECT: I want you here at six a.m., irregardless of how late you go to bed tonight.

CORRECT: I want you here at six a.m., regardless of how late you go to bed tonight.

Although listed in dictionaries and widely used colloquially, the word "irregardless" is to be avoided as nonstandard usage.

14. *inquire / enquire

These are two spellings of the same word. Enquire tends to be more common in British usage, while inquire is more common in American usage. The British newspaper The Guardian prefers inquire, and the Oxford

English Dictionary considers enquire to be "an alternate form of inquire." The forms inquire and inquiry are the safe choices when no official writing guidelines are being followed.

15. *license / licence

license: verb, "to grant permission

licence: noun, "permission, liberty"

In British usage, licence is the spelling of the noun; license is the spelling of the verb. In American usage, both

the noun and the verb are spelled license.

Spelling Mistakes

16. lightning / lightening

INCORRECT: The hen house was struck by lightening last night.

CORRECT: The hen house was struck by lightning last night.

Lightning means the flashing caused by an electrical discharge in the atmosphere. Lightening means "state of becoming brighter," or "lessening the weight of something." Mixing in some white is one way of lightening the dark blue paint. The camel driver is lightening the load by removing the trunk.

17. loose / lose

INCORRECT: I'm afraid you'll loose your way in the dark.

CORRECT: I'm afraid you'll lose your way in the dark.

As an adjective, loose means "not tight." Lose is a verb with such meanings as "go astray from," "fail to keep up with," "suffer deprivation." For example: Athletes prefer loose clothing for exercise. He frequently loses his car keys. Note: The s in loose has a soft sound. The s in lose has the sound of z.

18. passed / past

INCORRECT: The car past the train.

CORRECT: The car passed the train.

Spelling Mistakes

Past is used as an adverb of place, or as a preposition. Passed is the past tense of the verb to pass. For

example: The past few days have been hectic. The deadline has passed. He passed her the biscuits. The boys

ran past the gate. As we stood in the doorway, the cat ran past.

19. pore / pour

INCORRECT: The students were up until midnight, pouring over their books.

CORRECT: The students were up until midnight, poring over their books.

Pore is a verb meaning "to look at attentively." Pour is a verb meaning "to cause to flow."

20. prescibe / proscribe

INCORRECT: What did the doctor proscribe for your headache?

CORRECT: What did the doctor prescribe for your headache?

Prescribe in this context means "to give directions for." Proscribe means "to condemn or forbid as harmful."

The use of any kind of drug is proscribed in the workplace.

21. principle / principal

INCORRECT: The principle kept us after school.

CORRECT: The principal kept us after school.

10

Spelling Mistakes

As a noun, principle means "a general truth." As a noun referring to a person, principal means "the person in

authority." The cloying but useful mnemonic for this one is "The principal is your pal."

22. pronunciation / pronounciation

INCORRECT: I have trouble understanding his pronounciation.

CORRECT: I have trouble understanding his pronunciation.

Although the verb is pronounce, the noun is pronunciation.

23. quiet / quite

INCORRECT: We spent a quite evening reading.

CORRECT: We spent a quiet evening reading.

Quiet is an adjective meaning "marked by little or no activity." Quite is an adverb meaning "to a considerable

extent." Example: The children are quite amiable today. Quiet can also be used as a noun. For example: We enjoyed the quiet by the lake. (The suffix "ness" should never be added to the abstract nouns quiet and calm.)

24. then / than

INCORRECT: I have more eggs then you.

CORRECT: I have more eggs than you.

Spelling Mistakes

Then is an adverb that indicates time. It can go anywhere in a sentence. For example: The man paused by the

door and then entered. Then the noise started. As conjunction or preposition, than will always be followed by a noun or a pronoun. I like Melville better than Hawthorne.

25. thought / tough / through / though

The ough spelling in each of these words represents a different vowel sound: thought, ough= [aw]; tough,

ough= [uh]; through: ough= [oo], and though: ough= [ō].

thought: "the action or process of thinking": He was lost in thought. As a verb, it is the past tense of think: I thought you had already gone.

tough: adjective, "not easily broken or taken apart": The hide of the rhinoceros is extremely tough. Figuratively one can

speak of "a tough person" or "a tough job."

through: preposition expressing the relation of movement within something, from one end to the opposite end or side. The train passed through the tunnel. The needle went through the cloth.

though: conjunction, "although" or "in spite of the fact that." Though he had a broken leg, he managed to reach the fort. As an adverb, though can mean "nevertheless" She said she would not attend the wedding. She did, though.

26. there / they're / their

INCORRECT: They parked there car on the lawn.

CORRECT: They parked their car on the lawn.

Spelling Mistakes

There is an adverb of place. It can stand anywhere in a sentence. They're is a contraction of "they are." There is a possessive adjective. It must be followed by a noun. For example: I don't know why they're always late. Tell them to put their coats on the bed. I don't want to go there.

27. to / two / too

INCORRECT: I'm to tired to go out again.

CORRECT: I'm too tired to go out again.

To is a preposition that indicates direction. It is also a particle used with a verb infinitive. Too is an adverb

used to indicate excess. Two is the spelling of the numeral 2. For example: Let's all go to the lobby. Remember

to brush your teeth. They ate too much pizza. You may have two pieces.

28. weather / whether / wether

INCORRECT: He never knows weather to phone or just drop by.

CORRECT: He never knows whether to phone or just drop by.

Weather is a noun that refers to the state of the atmosphere. (It can also be used, literally or figuratively, as a verb with the meaning "to stand up to and survive.")

Whether is a function word with various uses. A wether is a castrated sheep or goat. Examples: When will you know whether or not you can come? The weather should be mild this weekend. The passengers weathered the storm without too much sickness. The bell-wether led the flock.

Spelling Mistakes

29. wreck / wreak

INCORRECT: The wizard plans to wreck vengeance on the outlanders.

CORRECT: The wizard plans to wreak vengeance on the outlanders.

Wreck, as a verb, means "to reduce to a ruinous state by violence." It is pronounced with a short e, rhyming with neck. Wreak means "to inflict" or "bring about." It is pronounced with a long e, rhyming with sneak.

30. who's / whose

INCORRECT: I don't know who's dog you're talking about.

CORRECT: I don't know whose dog you're talking about.

Who's is the contracted form of "who is." Whose is the possessive adjective form of who. For example: Who's

your daddy? Whose car are we going in?

31. your / you're

INCORRECT: Give me you're advice.

CORRECT: Give me your advice.

You're is a contraction that represents the words "you are." Your is the second person plural possessive

adjective. For example: You're my best friend. Is that your key on the ground?

Spelling Mistakes
UUsSAaGgE eMIS TMAKIESS TAKES
32. averse / adverse
INCORRECT: I'm not adverse to a glass of wine at dinner
CORRECT: I'm not averse to a glass of wine at dinner.
Averse is an adjective meaning "having an active feeling of repugnance or dislike." Adverse is an adjective
meaning "being in opposition to one's interests." For example: Is he averse to eating meat? Do you think the judge will deliver an adverse opinion?

33. abstract nouns ending with -ness
INCORRECT: Anwar Sadat was admired for his courageousness.
CORRECT: Anwar Sadat was admired for his courage.
The suffix -ness is correctly added to many adjectives to form an abstract noun. For example, good/goodness, red/redness. However, many English adjectives have abstract noun forms that are not formed with a suffix.
With a few exceptions, it is a weakness of style to create a "ness" form when a distinctive form already exists.

Examples: silent/silence, curious/curiosity, brave/bravery, courageous/courage, valiant/valor, cowardly/cowardice, greedy/greed, mature/maturity.
Usage Mistakes
34. a / an
INCORRECT: Meet me here in a hour.
CORRECT: Meet me here in an hour.
The rule is to use the article a before words beginning with a consonant sound, and an before words beginning with a vowel sound: a dog, an eel, an hour.
Only a few English words begin with an unvoiced h: an heir to the throne, an honest man, an honorable man.
The same principles of pronunciation apply to abbreviations, acronyms and the like: a URL, an @ symbol, an SUV.

35. anyway / anyways / any way
INCORRECT: Who reads my paper anyways?
CORRECT: Who reads my paper anyway?
Anyway is an adverb, and it means "regardless" or "in any event": Penelope never completes her homework assignments, but she expects to go to college anyway. Any way

is a phrase meaning "any particular course, direction, or manner": Our dog tries to get out of his pen any way he can.

"Anyways" is a nonstandard form to be avoided by careful speakers and writers.

Usage Mistakes

36. bring / take

Both bring and take indicate the conveyance of something from one place to another. Which to use depends upon context. A mother organizing her family for a trip to the zoo, for example, might say "Everybody bring a jacket." She's going too. If, however, she's staying home, she would say "Everybody take a jacket." Something going away from the speaker is taken. Something going to or with the speaker is brought.

37. between you and me / I

INCORRECT: Keep this information just between you and I.

CORRECT: Keep this information just between you and me.

Between is a preposition. Me is the object form of the pronoun I. When a pronoun follows a preposition, the object form is required.

38. before / ago

INCORRECT: He left his money to a woman he had met many years ago.

CORRECT: He left his money to a woman he had met many years before.

Ago means "at a certain time before now." It refers to a time before the present. Before means "at any time before now."

When the event referred to occurred at a specific time in the past, the simple past form of the verb is used: Alexander the Great lived many years ago.

Five years ago, my brother worked in Detroit.

Usage Mistakes

If the event referred to occurred before another past event, then the choice of adverb should be before,

earlier, or previously: We learned that our favorite tree had been cut down many years before.

39. beg the question / raise the question

INCORRECT: His position on tax reform begs the question, does wealth redistribution really help the poor?

CORRECT: His position on tax reform raises the question, does wealth redistribution really help the poor?

To beg the question is a rhetorical term to describe the logical fallacy of assuming the truth of an unsupported

assertion. For example, Dr. Locke grades unfairly because he never gives me any grade higher than a C on my papers. The unproved assumption is that the papers are of a quality to merit a higher grade. The student is "begging the question." If you find yourself following "beg the question" with a question, you are using the expression incorrectly. The expression you are looking for is "raise the question."

40. *could care less / couldn't care less

Much breath and ink are expended in arguing about this expression, yet both forms of it have been in the language for more than half a century, and both are used with exactly the same meaning.

Pedants argue that "I could care less" is illogical because if one could care less, one therefore cares a little.

When it comes to idiom, logic is frequently irrelevant. Whether the "not" appears or not, speakers who use the expression are not chopping logic. What they mean is that they don't

care. Linguist Mark Liberman estimates that in American English anyway, the use of "could care less" exceeds that of "couldn't care less" by a ratio of Usage Mistakes

about 5 to 1. Nevertheless, the proponents of "couldn't care less" can be quite excitable. If you're going to be graded, better go with the negative form.

41. can / may

INCORRECT: He wants to know if he can borrow the car tonight.

CORRECT: He wants to know if he may borrow the car tonight.

The difference between can and may is one of ability versus permission. Not everyone observes the

distinction, but it is a graceful usage.

42. double negative

INCORRECT: I don't get no respect.

CORRECT: I don't get any respect.

Although common in regional dialects and in earlier forms of English, the use of a double negative is

considered to be incorrect in modern standard English. Double negative: a construction that contains two negative elements such as no and not.

43. disinterested / uninterested

INCORRECT: Charlie is totally disinterested in algebra.

CORRECT: Charlie is totally uninterested in algebra.

Usage Mistakes

Disinterested implies impartiality. Uninterested implies lack of interest. For example: The financial dispute was settled by a disinterested third party. Many students are uninterested in their assignments.

44. *different from / different to / different than

Preferred by H. W. Fowler in his landmark Modern English Usage, different from is considered by many

speakers, both British and American, to be the only correct form of the comparative phrase. According to Ask Oxford, "There is little difference in sense between different from, different to, and different than. Different from is generally regarded as the correct use in British English, while different than is largely

restricted to North America." Different to is also common in British speech.

45. either is / either are

INCORRECT: Either Jack or Joan are correct.

CORRECT: Either Jack or Joan is correct.

Either, which may be either a pronoun or an adjective, is singular. Its modern meaning is "one or the other of two."

When either introduces a choice between two things, the verb must be singular: Either the Honda or the Ford belongs to Harry. Either one of the books is a good choice.

Confusion arises when either introduces an either...or construction in which one of the choices is singular and one is plural. In such a case, the verb will agree with the nearer noun: Either hot dogs or pizza is on the menu for tonight. Either pizza or hot dogs are on the menu for tonight.

Usage Mistakes

Neither, like either, is a singular word that usually takes a singular verb. In a neither...nor construction that contains a singular noun and a plural noun, the verb agrees with a plural noun that comes before it: Neither bad morals nor hypocrisy is wanted in a public official. Neither hypocrisy nor bad morals are wanted in a public official.

46. *each / their

Each writer should have their own computer.

All writers should have their own computers.

Because each is singular, words relating back to each should be singular. Their is plural and therefore does not agree in number with each. The same goes for everyone, everybody, and all singular nouns. However, many speakers and writers have been breaking this rule in certain contexts since at least the 16th century.

In the past, no objection was made to the use of singular his in a construction like this one: Each writer should have his own computer. Concerns about gender equality have made this use of "his" unacceptable when the antecedent is perceived to include women as well as men. Bottom line: each/their is no longer perceived as a gross grammatical fault. Writers who still shudder at the yoking of each and their can rewrite such sentences in the plural.

47. economic / economical

INCORRECT: Eating at home is more economic than dining out.

CORRECT: Eating at home is more economical than dining out.

Usage Mistakes

Economic refers to economics and the economy. Economical refers to getting the most value for one's money.

The government must address serious economic problems. Families living on reduced means must make economical food choices.

48. e.g. / i.e.

INCORRECT: Boswell asked Dr. Johnson about every trivial detail, e.g., he made himself a daily nuisance.

CORRECT: Boswell asked Dr. Johnson about every trivial detail, i.e., he made himself a daily nuisance.

The abbreviation e.g. stands for the Latin expression exempli gratia and means "for example. The abbreviation i.e. stands for the Latin expression id est ("it is") and is used in English to mean "in other words." The farmer grows several kinds of soft fruit, e.g., strawberries, blueberries, and grapes.

49. free rein / free reign

INCORRECT: Unfortunately, their parents give them free reign on the weekends.

CORRECT: Unfortunately, their parents give them free rein on the weekends.

Free rein is a term that originated with riding. It refers to holding the horse's reins loosely, so as to permit the horse to move more freely. The figurative sense relates to any kind of unimpeded freedom. Reign refers to the authority of a monarch. Although commonly seen, "free reign" is incorrect.

Usage Mistakes

50. flammable / inflammable

INCORRECT: These pajamas can't burn because they're inflammable.

CORRECT: These pajamas CAN burn because they're inflammable.

Both words, flammable and inflammable, mean "capable of bursting into flames." In modern usage the term inflammable is being dropped because the prefix -in, which means "into" in inflammable, is often confused with the prefix -in which means "not." The better practice is to use nonflammable as the opposite of flammable.

51. *farther/further

Farther is the comparative of the adjective far. It is used as an adverb to mean "to or at a more advanced point." For example:

He rode farther down the road. Some speakers argue a difference between the adverbial uses of farther and further. In general usage, however, the choice between farther and further is a matter of preference. He rode further down the road.

As a verb, further means "to help forward, to assist." He would stop at nothing to further his ambition.

52. good / better / best

INCORRECT: Who's the best runner, Jack or Jill?

CORRECT: Who's the better runner, Jack or Jill?

Usage Mistakes

Good has the irregular comparative forms better and best. The word better is used to compare two people or things: This rope is better than that one. The word best used to compare three or more people or things: Charlie is the best player on the football team.

53. good / well

INCORRECT: I hope I did good on the exam.

CORRECT: I hope did well on the exam.

Good is an adjective. Well is an adverb. When describing an action, the word to use is well. A great many

English speakers cringe when they hear "I'm doing good" as the response to the polite question "How are you doing?" Writers aiming at standard usage acceptable to a wide audience will do well to avoid using good as an adverb.

54. historic / historical

INCORRECT: The signing of the bill today will be a historical event.

CORRECT: The signing of the bill today will be a historic event.

Historical is an adjective that refers to anything that has happened in the past. Historic is an adjective to

describe an event or invention that had or will have a major impact on future events. For example: The novel is

based on historical events in the settling of the American West. The driving of the Golden Spike was a historic

event. Note: Some speakers use an before the words historical and historic.

Usage Mistakes

55. incident / incidence

INCORRECT: The witness described the incidence to the police.

CORRECT: The witness described the incident to the police.

Incidence is a noun meaning "the extent of something's influence." Incident is a noun meaning "an occurrence or an event." For example: The incident involved a trailer truck and a Miata. What is the incidence of poverty among women?

56. imply / infer

INCORRECT: His use of that word infers that he doesn't trust you.

CORRECT: His use of that word implies that he doesn't trust you.

The verb imply means to suggest a meaning. The person who implies something hints at it without saying it directly. The verb infer means to take meaning from. The person who infers draws a conclusion by

interpreting words or actions. For example: Because you are always late, I infer that you don't want to work here.

57. in / on

INCORRECT: The ship is sailing in the water.

CORRECT: The ship is sailing on the water.

Usage Mistakes

The use of prepositions in English is frequently idiomatic. General guidelines exist, but they cannot cover all the expressions involving prepositions. In denotes "state of being somewhere within." On indicates "proximity and position, above or outside."

58. less / fewer

INCORRECT: This box contains less fire crackers.

CORRECT: This box contains fewer fire crackers.

Less is used with uncounted nouns: less soup, less intelligence, less forage.

Fewer is used with countable nouns: fewer voters, fewer apples, fewer commercials.

59. lend / loan / borrow

INCORRECT: Will you loan me a pencil?

CORRECT: Will you lend me a pencil.

The verbs lend and loan both mean "to grant the temporary possession of a thing." The verb borrow means "to take a thing with the intention of returning it." In a business transaction, lend, loan, and borrow all imply an exchange of money and securities.

In a non-business context, lend and borrow do not imply the existence of a financial transaction. May I borrow the car for the evening? Will you lend me a pencil? However, for many speakers, the connotation of lending for hire clings to the word loan. For that reason lend is preferable to loan in an informal situation.

Usage Mistakes

60. Miss / Mrs / Ms

INCORRECT: Address the letter to Miss Jones.

CORRECT: Address the letter to Ms. Jones.

Miss, denoting an unmarried woman, is an honorific no longer considered acceptable in common use because it identifies a woman according to marital status.

Mrs., denoting a married woman, is considered unacceptable for the same reason.

Ms. is an honorific that pertains to any woman, without indicating marital status.

NOTE: In American usage, both Ms. and Mrs. are written with periods. In British usage the periods are omitted.

61. *mankind / humankind

The word mankind has been used for many generations with the meaning of "all humankind." In recent years, however, many English speakers have come to feel that mankind excludes women. Modern usage prefers the use of the word humankind.

62. people / persons

INCORRECT: I don't know any of the persons in this room.

CORRECT: I don't know any of the people in this room.

Usage Mistakes

Although the word person has the plural persons, in most non-legal contexts people is the preferred plural of person.

63. Scotch / Scots / Scottish

INCORRECT: The Scotch people value education.

CORRECT: The Scottish people value education.

Scotch is an adjective still used in certain established expressions such as Scotch whisky or Scotch broth. In other contexts, however, it is considered unacceptable. For example: "Scotchmen" or "the Scotch government."

Use Scots or Scottish in a general context to convey the idea of belonging to or being from Scotland: a Scotswoman, The Scotsman (newspaper), the Scottish weather, the Scottish parliament. The word for the nationality is Scots. Example: Robert the Bruce is a hero to the Scots.

64. sooner than / when

INCORRECT: No sooner had the dogcatcher turned his back when the boy released the stray.

CORRECT: No sooner had the dogcatcher turned his back than the boy released the stray.

Modern usage prefers than to when as the conjunction to be used in this expression.

Usage Mistakes

65. there is / are

INCORRECT: There's some children at the door.

CORRECT: There are some children at the door.

There's is a contraction of "there is." When the word there used to begin a sentence, the verb that follows it

should agree with the true subject of the sentence. For example, There is a cat on the fence. ("cat" is the true subject) There are some children at the door. ("children" is the true subject.)

A tendency in spoken English is to begin "there" sentences with the contraction "there's," regardless of

whether the subject word is singular or plural. In writing, however, there's no reason not to make the verb "to be" agree in number with the true subject of the sentence. Note: Sentences that begin with there can usually be improved by putting the true subject first and replacing is or are with a more vivid verb.

66. these / those

INCORRECT: Do you see these books over there?

CORRECT: Do you see those books over there?

These is the plural of this. Used as either a demonstrative adjective or a demonstrative pronoun, these

indicates objects or persons nearby.

Those is the plural of that. Used as either a demonstrative adjective or a demonstrative pronoun, those

indicates objects or persons at a distance.

Usage Mistakes

Used together, the words these and those indicate contrast or opposition: Do you want these or those? Note: The same is true of the singular forms this and that: Eat this, not that.

67. waiting on / waiting for

INCORRECT: We waited on the bus, but it never came.

CORRECT: We waited for the bus, but it never came.

The expression wait on means "to serve," as in a business establishment: The woman waited on the customer.

Wait for implies expectation or anticipation. The child is waiting for Santa Claus.

Usage Mistakes

GRAMMAR MISTAKES

68. dangling participle

INCORRECT: Reported missing a month ago, police have recovered the body of a young girl.

CORRECT: The body of a young girl reported missing a month ago has been recovered by police.

Verb forms ending in -ing or -ed are called participles. They can be used as adjectives, either alone, or as the first word in a descriptive phrase. A common error is to follow a participial phrase with the wrong noun, as in the example above. The noun being described by "reported" is "girl," not "police."

69. if I was / if I were

INCORRECT: If I was a rich man, I'd buy houses for all my children.

CORRECT: If I were a rich man, I'd buy houses for all my children.

Although more and more English speakers fail to observe the use of were in an if clause that makes a

statement contrary to fact, it's a usage that careful writers will probably continue to observe for a while yet. If the statement is contrary to fact, use were. In some contexts the if clause may contain a factual statement for which "was" is the suitable choice: If I was listening at the door, I had my reasons. (The speaker had in fact

been listening at the door.)

Grammar Mistakes

Grammar MISTAKES

70. if I would / if I had / if I did

INCORRECT: If I would have known about the party, I would have gone to it.

CORRECT: If I had known about the party, I would have gone to it.

When speaking of an event that might have happened in the past but didn't, we use an if clause containing the helping verb "had" followed by a main clause containing "would": If I had known you were coming, I would have baked a cake. This use is sometimes called the "third conditional."

Another error made with the third conditional is to use the auxiliary "did" in the if clause:

INCORRECT: If Captain Jones didn't pull me from that burning car, I would be dead.

CORRECT: if Captain Jones hadn't pulled me from that burning car, I would be dead.

71. lay / lie (to recline)

INCORRECT: I think I'll lay down for a few minutes.

CORRECT: I think I'll lie down for a few minutes.

Lay is the past tense of the verb to lie, "to recline." For example: Today I lie in the hammock. Yesterday I lay in the hammock. I have lain in the hammock for hours. I am lying there because I like it.

Grammar Mistakes

72. lay / lie ("to place")

INCORRECT: Lie the book on the table.

CORRECT: Lay the book on the table.

Lay is the present tense of the verb to lay, "to place." For example: Today I lay the book on the table.

Yesterday I laid the book on the table. I have already laid the book on the table. I am laying the book on the table. Note: When lay means "to place," it will always have an object.

73. *Microsoft is/are

American usage: Microsoft is settling with another software distributor.

British usage: Microsoft are settling with another software distributor.

In British English, collective nouns and the names of organizations can take either a singular or plural verb, depending upon whether the entity is being thought of as a single thing or as a collection of individual things

or persons. In American usage, such words almost always take a singular verb.

74. me / I

INCORRECT: Me and Jamie are going to Mexico.

CORRECT: Jamie and I are going to Mexico.

Me is the object form of the pronoun I. It should never be used as the subject of a verb. The same applies to the other object pronoun forms him, her, us, and them.

Grammar Mistakes

This error occurs most frequently in compound subjects:

INCORRECT:

Him, Sallie, and Fred moved to Arizona.

Her and her children live behind the stadium.

Laurie and them said "hello."

CORRECT:

Sallie, Fred,and he moved to Arizona.

She and her children live behind the stadium.

Laurie and they said "hello."

75. myself / I

INCORRECT: Sophie and myself volunteer three days a month at the homeless shelter.

CORRECT: Sophie and I volunteer three days a month at the homeless shelter.

Myself is a pronoun whose function is to restate the subject I: I cut myself shaving. Sometimes I talk to myself as I work. I wouldn't have believed it myself. It is never correct to use myself as the subject of a verb, or anywhere in a sentence in which I is not the subject.

76. none is / none are

INCORRECT: None of the boys are qualified to play.

CORRECT: None of the boys is qualified to play.

Grammar Mistakes

None is a singular word. It means "not one." It takes a singular verb.

77. *preposition at the end of a sentence

Many writers go to great lengths in the effort to avoid ending a sentence with a preposition in the mistaken belief that to do so is to break a rule of "good

English." This superstition arose from the practice of 17thcentury writers like John Dryden (1631-1700) whose familiarity with and admiration for Latin led them to apply

rules of Latin grammar to the writing of English. The result was often at odds with English idiom. Whether or not to end a sentence with a preposition is a stylistic choice, not an unforgivable sin.

78. ran/run

INCORRECT: The dog has ran away.

CORRECT: The dog has run away.

Run is an irregular verb whose past participle form (run) is the same as the present form. The simple past is ran. Examples: Today I run. Yesterday I ran. I have run every day this week.

A common error is to use the simple past (ran) when the past participle (run) is called for. The form ran

should never be used with the helping verbs has, have, or had. Other irregular verbs susceptible to the same kind of error with the past participle are go, come, write, give, and eat. The correct use of these verbs: have gone, have come, have written, have given, have eaten.

79. should have / should of

INCORRECT: I should of listened to my instincts.

CORRECT: I should have listened to my instincts.

Grammar Mistakes

The contraction should've combines the words should and have.

80. superlatives

INCORRECT: This movie is the most awesomest I've ever seen.

CORRECT: This movie is the most awesome I've ever seen.

Adjectives have three forms:

Positive: the adjective's "plain" form. Example: awesome.

Comparative: the form used to compare two things. Example: more awesome.

Superlative: the form used to compare more than two things. Example: most awesome.

Adjectives of one or two syllables usually form their comparisons by adding the endings -er and -est: This is a fine story. This is a finer story than that one. This is the finest story of all. This is a simple solution. This is a simpler solution. This is the simplest solution of all.

Adjectives of three or more syllables form their comparisons by preceding the adjective with more and most:

This is a beautiful flower. This is a more beautiful flower than that one. This is the most beautiful flower of all.

The most common error in the use of the comparative forms is to use more and most in combination with –er and -est forms. Constructions like "the most awesomest" are often seen on the web. They may be meant to be humorous, but they come across as babyish.

Grammar Mistakes

81. suppose to / supposed to

INCORRECT: I'm suppose to wash the windows on Saturday.

CORRECT: I'm supposed to wash the windows on Saturday.

Suppose is a verb. Used with a helping verb it takes the past participle ending: -ed. The participle form in –ed can also be used as an adjective, as in the expression "an old-fashioned girl."

82. *toward / towards

Towards may be more common among British speakers, but, used prepositionally, both are acceptable: The child ran towards the road. The child ran toward the road.

83. went / gone

INCORRECT: Fame had went to his head.

CORRECT: Fame had gone to his head.

The verb go has irregular past and past participle forms. The simple past is went. The past participle form is (had) gone. Never use went with had.

84. who / whom

INCORRECT: Whom shall I say is calling?

CORRECT: Who shall I say is calling?

Grammar Mistakes

Whom is the object form of who. Like me, him, her, us, and them, its correct grammatical use is to serve as the

object of a verb or a preposition: Whom do you mean? (direct object of the verb "do mean")

To whom shall I give this puppy? (object of the preposition "to")

That is the man whom I saw running away. (object of the verb "saw.")

Because so many speakers and writers of standard English have come to use who as both subject and object, it's not necessary to use whom at all. However, some speakers and writers mistakenly try to use whom as a subject. This is a nonstandard use to avoid.

The example given above is incorrect because the sentence is

made up of two clauses: I shall say and Who is
calling. As the subject of "is calling," who requires the subject form.
85. which / who
INCORRECT: That's the boy which started the fire.
CORRECT: That's the boy who started the fire.
The relative pronoun which stands for inanimate things only.
86. who / that
INCORRECT: The woman that sold you the car didn't own it.
CORRECT: The woman who sold you the car didn't own it.
Grammar Mistakes
Although many speakers and writers consider the words who and that be interchangeable, others prefer to reserve who for speaking of humans or humanized creatures, and that for referring to inanimate entities.
Sometimes there are stylistic reasons to use that to stand for a person, but in general, use who when referring to people.
Grammar Mistakes
PUNCTUATION MISTAKES
87. apostrophe to form plural
INCORRECT: King Alfred the Great lived in the 800's.
CORRECT: King Alfred the Great lived in the 800s.

The use of an apostrophe to form the plural of letters or numerals is to be avoided. The only time that it can
be justified is with lower-case letters.
88. comma splice
INCORRECT: The fire truck tore around the corner, flames spurted from the burning car.
CORRECT: The fire truck tore around the corner. Flames spurted from the burning car.
A comma splice occurs when two independent clauses are joined by a comma.
89. comma missing after introductory clause
INCORRECT: If I were you I'd do what you have done.
CORRECT: If I were you, I'd do what you have done.
An adverbial clause that begins a sentence is set off by a comma: When the rains came, everyone stayed
inside.
Punctuation Mistakes
Punctuation MISTAKES
90. comma missing after introductory words/phrases
INCORRECT: To be perfectly honest I don't like her one bit.
CORRECT: To be perfectly honest, I don't like her one bit.
Single words and phrases that begin a sentence are set off by a

comma: Yes, you may go. In my opinion, James Fenimore Cooper is unjustly ignored.

91. *comma with lists

Disagreement exists as to whether or not a comma should be placed before the conjunctions and, or, or nor in a list.

I like cats, dogs, birds, and moles.

I like cats, dogs, birds and moles.

The first example illustrates the serial comma. Also called the Oxford comma and the Harvard comma, the serial comma is a comma placed before the conjunction.

Some usage guides, like the Associated Press Stylebook, recommend leaving out the last comma except in cases where confusion might arise because of another conjunction in the sentence: I had orange juice, toast, and ham and eggs for breakfast.

Using the serial comma consistently eliminates the necessity of making decisions on a case by case basis.

Punctuation Mistakes

92. comma after main clause

INCORRECT: The King of Siam held absolute power over his subjects, when Anna Leonowens lived at his court.

CORRECT: The King of Siam held absolute power over his subjects when Anna Leonowens lived at his court.

When the adverbial clause follows the main clause, a comma is not usually needed.

93. comma instead of semi-colon

INCORRECT: We missed the bus, we did not know what to do.

CORRECT: We missed the bus; we did not know what to do.

Using a semi-colon to join closely-related main clauses is another means of avoiding a comma splice. If the clauses are very short, commas may be used: He came, he saw, he conquered.

94. dash instead of comma

INCORRECT: My best friend – Colin Blakely – is acting at the Old Vic.

CORRECT: My best friend, Colin Blakely, is acting at the Old Vic.

The em dash is frequently used unnecessarily to replace more appropriate punctuation marks. In the example above, the name is in apposition to the word "friend." Nouns in apposition are set off by commas.

Punctuation Mistakes

95. multiple end marks

INCORRECT: We're going to Paris in April!!!! Do you want to go with us???

CORRECT: We're going to Paris in April! Do you want to go with us?

Multiple exclamation marks or question marks at the end of sentences are unnecessary and amateurish.

96. possessive apostrophe

INCORRECT: Mr. Thomas' opinion was that the dog should be returned.

CORRECT: Mr. Thomas's opinion was that the dog should be returned.

Nouns whose singular form does not end in s form the possessive by adding the apostrophe plus an s ('s):

Mary's veil. The house's roof. The trunk's latch. Nouns that form their plurals by adding the letter s form the

possessive by adding an apostrophe: The birds' beaks. The teachers' salaries. The street lamps' bulbs. A few

nouns do not form the plural by adding s. Their possessive is formed by adding apostrophe s ('s): The

children's teacher. The deer's meadow. The salesmen's catalogs.

Singular nouns that end in s also form the possessive by adding apostrophe s ('s): St. James's Park. Arkansas's

scenic beauty.

Not all authorities agree that the addition of 's to a singular noun ending in s should be a hard and fast rule.

For example, with ancient names ending in s, a conventional practice is to add only the apostrophe: Jesus'

name. Achilles' heel.

Punctuation Mistakes

Writers who prefer a one-rule-fits-all approach may simply follow the practice of forming the plural of any

singular noun by adding 's.

97. *punctuation outside or inside the quotation mark

American usage places the period inside the quotation marks whether the quoted material includes a period or

not.

Examples of American usage: Franklin Roosevelt said that the only thing Americans had to fear was "fear itself."

Winston Churchill said "Never in the field of human conflict was so much owed by so many to so few."

British usage places periods that are not part of the quotation outside the closing quotation mark.

Examples of British Usage:

Franklin Roosevelt said that the only thing Americans had to fear was "fear itself".

Winston Churchill said "Never in the field of human conflict was so much owed by so many to so few."

98. quotation marks for emphasis

INCORRECT: All "anoraks" are now on sale.

CORRECT: All anoraks are now on sale.

Punctuation Mistakes

The chief use of quotation marks is to set off the exact words used by a speaker or by another writer: "You

can't be serious," Percy said. According to Dickens, the year 1775 was "the best of times" and "the worst of

times."

An additional use of quotations marks is to indicate that the writer is using a word in an ironical sense:

Screaming at the top of her lungs, my "meek and mild" nanny sent the burglar running for his life.

Using quotation marks to emphasize a word or phrase is unnecessary and confusing.

99. run-on sentence

INCORRECT: The fishing boat ran aground on a reef all the men were rescued.

CORRECT: The fishing boat ran aground on a reef. All the men were rescued.

A run-on sentence occurs when an independent clause follows another independent clause without

punctuation or a joining word.

100. semi-colon instead of colon

INCORRECT: The winners are the following films; The Lion King, Silas Marner, and Kim.

CORRECT: The winners are the following films: The Lion King, Silas Marner, and Kim.

The most common use of a colon is to introduce a list following an independent clause.

The next most common use is to separate an example, explanation, or reason from a preceding independent clause:

It's over between us: you won't stop drinking to excess.

I learned a useful mnemonic for remembering the colors of the rainbow: Roy G. Biv.

**.

Question Bank

Set 1

1. Food prices have been … steadily for at least ten years.
a) rising
b) lifting
c) raising
2. I'll have to study hard, … I can pass the exam.
a) so that
b) such
c) in order
3. You … to eat if you are not hungry.
a) needn't
b) haven't
c) don't have
4. We'll dance and … we'll have lunch.
a) straight away
b) so
c) then
5. She has to go to Germany for the next … of the training.
a) step
b) stage
c) point
6. When the meeting had finished, we went … the plan once again.
a) up
b) down
c) over
7. I locked the animals in the cage to … them from getting away.
a) avoid
b) hinder
c) prevent
8. You're … your time trying to persuade her.
a) wasting
b) losing
c) missing

9. Our last cook was better than our … one.
a) latter
b) instant
c) current
10. I am grateful to Mary for being so patient … us.
a) for
b) with
c) at
11. Have you exchanged that lovely car … this?
a) with
b) by
c) for
12. The weather was … the poor harvest.
a) condemned for
b) found fault with for
c) blamed for
13. Olivia is teaching three classes and she is examining at a literature exam

tomorrow. …, she is chairing a meeting at the Bright Owl Club.
a) On top of it
b) At top
c) On the top of it

14. I don't see any … in arriving early at the show.
a) cause
b) point
c) reason

15. Your application for a vise was turned … by the consulate.
a) aside
b) over
c) down

16. Shopping malls account for 70 percent of the retail business in this
country because they are controlled environments which … concerns about
the weather.
a) justify
b) foster
c) eliminate

17. It is … impossible to tell the twins apart.
a) virtually
b) closely
c) extremely

18. The man claimed that he was the … heir to the throne.
a) due
b) correct
c) rightful

19. The rather humid climate in no way … from the beauty of these places.
a) protracts
b) detracts
c) attracts

20. … no need to buy traveller's cheques.
a) It's
b) It has
c) There's

21. Is there … bread for all the sandwiches?
a) enough
b) plenty
c) equal

22. Teaching is not a/an … which pays very well.
a) work
b) post
c) occupation

23. This letter didn't come through the post. It was delivered personally, … hand.
a) from
b) by
c) with

24. I … do that if I were you.
a) shan't
b) won't
c) wouldn't

25. There was nothing to … her with the burglary until the police found two
gold ring in her car.

a) link

b) place

c) join

26. The manufacturers are advertising a new … of perfume.

a) mark

b) pack

c) brand

27. … my stay in hospital, I lost three kilos.

a) During

b) On

c) In

28. I'm sorry to hear that they have … . They were good friends.

a) dropped out

b) fallen out

c) dropped against

29. Shall I use this … to fry the eggs?

a) dish

b) tin

c) pan

30. She … being given a receipt for the bill she had paid.

a) insisted on

b) demanded

c) asked to

31. These cars historically had two doors but the latest … has four.

a) brand

b) mark

c) model

32. That girl is far ahead … everyone else in the class.

a) of

b) with

c) from

33. She is also interested … art.

a) with

b) in

c) about

34. It's impossible to prevent the boys from quarreling … each other.

a) for

b) with

c) by

35. I'm thinking … looking for a new job in another city.

a) on

b) at

c) of

36. Steve prefers football … tennis.

a) to

b) over

c) than

37. The experience in a psychiatric ward … for the rest of his life.

a) had an influence on him

b) had influence on him

c) had an influence at him

38. If I had known the way to her house, I … her last Monday afternoon.

a) have been visiting

b) had been visiting

c) would have visited

39. He ... that he had been involved in the decision.

a) refused

b) declined

c) denied

40. As brown as ... . This phrase means having a tanned skin after sunbathing.

a) dust

b) a berry

c) chocolate

41. It's an awful ... your friend couldn't come.

a) shame

b) sorrow

c) shock

42. There is a problem at our TV station. Please do not ... your set.

a) repair

b) change

c) adjust

43. Be careful! The cat may ... you.

a) kick

b) scratch

c) tear

44. They agreed to ... the question of payment.

a) discuss

b) control

c) increase

45. Owing to the bad weather, the garden party was ... .

a) shouted off

b) spoken against

c) called off

46. I am sorry I opened your bag but I ... it for mine.

a) confused

b) imagined

c) mistook

47. The ... of these volunteers for hard work is remarkable.

a) ability

b) efficiency

c) capacity

48. I like this country, but I wish it ... rain quite so much.

a) won't

b) didn't

c) hasn't

49. She was so tired that she ... asleep in the chair.

a) fell

b) went

c) became

50. Mike has just taken an examination ... chemistry.

a) on

b) in

c) for

51. They shouldn't have ... the incident. It wasn't my fault.

a) accused me of

b) blamed me for

c) blamed me

52. They won't lend you the money without some ... that you will pay it

back.
a) profit
b) charge
c) guarantee
53. When you come tomorrow why not … your brother with you?
a) carry
b) bring
c) fetch
54. After she had broken her leg, Marry could only go up and down stairs
… .
a) with difficulty
b) in difficulties
c) hardly
55. Who does this laptop belong … ?
a) for
b) with
c) to
56. All her handbags … of leather.
a) being made
b) are made
c) had been made
57. John is the perfect person to take on this difficult job. He's a really hard-
… person and won't stand for any nonsense.
a) ship
b) nosed
c) bargain
58. What does a sabbatical year mean?

a) a miserable year
b) a year in which previously made plans are bound to
c) a year in which one is released from one's normal duties

59. It always … me as odd that she should go to work so late in the day.
a) hit
b) smacked
c) struck
60. I walked away as calmly as I could … they thought I was the thief.
a) in case
b) or else
c) to avoid
61. If it's raining tomorrow, we shall have to … the match till Sunday.
a) cancel
b) put off
c) put away
62. Call in and see our … of spring fashions today.
a) reputation
b) election
c) selection
63. We have no … in our files of your recent letters to the company.
a) record
b) account
c) list

64. When her aunt dies, she ... a lot of money.
a) earned
b) inherited
c) paid

65. Give him a telephone number to ring ... he gets lost.
a) whether
b) unless
c) in case

66. Her parents never allowed her ... .
a) smoking
b) a smoking
c) to smoke

67. Bill is only interested ... making money.
a) in

b) about
c) on

68. The boy was very upset by the ... of his English examination.
a) failure
b) result
c) effect

69. Their actions caused the rate of inflation to ... sharply.
a) lift
b) raise
c) rise

70. They were good friends. I was surprised when they ... .
a) fell out
b) fell off
c) fell down

71. I had to leave early ... I didn't feel very well.
a) too
b) because
c) also

72. After closing the envelope, the assistant manager ... the stamps on firmly.
a) licked
b) stuck
c) struck

73. Don't be so sure ... yourself! You might be wrong.
a) on
b) from
c) of

74. This book will prove useful ... you.
a) for
b) to
c) on

75. You should not be so sensitive ... criticism.
a) to
b) at
c) on

76. I am not familiar ... his novels.
a) with
b) about
c) for

77. You should study the college ... for full particulars of enrolment.
a) prospect

b) syllabus

c) prospectus

78. A novel is a form of …
which may include many facts.

a) short story

b) legend

c) fiction

79. The relationship that matters
most in the life of a … is the
one between
him and his constituency party,
they say.

a) judge

b) politician

c) captain

80. The case of the missing
millionaire has become the …
of considerable
interest in the press.

a) focus

b) middle

c) target

81. These people are thought …
less friendly than people from
our country.

a) been

b) being

c) to be

82. Would you give this report
to Mr. Smith? Sorry, I can't. He
doesn't … .

a) any more work here

b) work any more here

c) work here any longer

83. After hitting her arm, she
had a large black … .

a) bruise

b) cut

c) swelling

84. This is not the right … to
ask for my help; I am away on
business.

a) situation

b) moment

c) opportunity

85. I hadn't seen him for years,
but when I saw him in the street,
I … him at
once.

a) reminded

b) realized

c) remembered

86. The dog was so frightened
that it ran … the bed to hide.

a) along

b) beside

c) under

87. John was unable to … my
party as he was ill.

a) visit

b) attend

c) be present

88. Jane bought red shoes to …
her red dress.

a) match

b) pair

c) mate

89. We'll have to … the
meeting until next month.

a) put down

b) put off

c) put round

90. I am not sure … the black coat is.
a) whom
b) who
c) whose
91. I don't think he'll beat the opponent. He's out of … .
a) fitness
b) practice
c) play
92. She is a very … person, but she has no sense of humour.
a) pleasant

b) amusing
c) enjoyable
93. The university arranges a … to Madrid every year.
a) travel
b) rout
c) trip
94. Beware … these people.
a) from
b) of
c) at
95. If you fail … this attempt, don't count on me for help.
a) on
b) at
c) in
96. I separated them … each other because they were fighting.
a) of
b) from
c) against

97. I have to leave before six and so … .
a) do you
b) leave you
c) you do
98. There were no lifeboats on the little ship because it was … to be unsinkable.
a) claimed
b) told
c) believed
99. This church was … by a famous architect.
a) outlined
b) designed
c) produced
100. Mary is plain, but her sister is very … .
a) attractive
b) complex
c) sympathetic

101. Her boyfriend treated her badly. I'm surprised she … it for so long.
a) put off
b) put through
c) put up with
102. The manager … me to open a deposit account.
a) warned
b) approved
c) advised
103. This organization tries to send food to countries where people are

suffering … malnutrition.
a) from
b) for
c) by
104. If they are to understand the notice, the instructions must be … clearer.
a) wrote
b) made
c) done
105. … you like what I want to do or not, you won't make me change my mind regarding this situation.
a) If
b) When
c) Whether
106. Doctors usually have to study for at least eight years before becoming fully … .
a) tested
b) proved
c) qualified
107. The weather was pleasant with … a gentle wind to cool us down.
a) just
b) almost
c) nearly
108. I wish you wouldn't … your clothes all over the room.
a) sprawl
b) scatter
c) straggle

109. … she had no money for a bus, Olive had to walk all the way home.
a) As
b) For
c) Thus
110. I didn't want to make up my mind until I had heard her … of the story.
a) angle
b) edge
c) side
111. It's strange that Jane is as … as her mother is beautiful.
a) dull
b) plain
c) raw
112. Since the accident he has been walking with a … .
a) slope
b) lame
c) limp
113. I flew to the island, then … a car for five days and visited most places.
a) charged
b) bought
c) hired
114. In Russia, surgeons have given a man a/an … heart.
a) artificial
b) unreal
c) false
115. The examiners had to … most of the candidates.
a) fire
b) fail

c) fall

116. Our company made a record ... last year.

a) benefit

b) wage

c) profit

117. They must economize ... fuel.

a) on

b) in

c) with

118. When I understood what she was saying, everything ... .

a) fell into the place

b) fell into place

c) fell off the place

119. I had to give a full ... of my car when I reported it stolen.

a) detail

b) account

c) description

120. His version of the facts doesn't ... with the version I heard from Jane.

a) accord

b) argue

c) amount

121. They have ... to accommodate us and the children too.

a) such a small house

b) too small a house

c) a too small house

122. After they had ... the carpet, the employees went back to the office.

a) laid

b) lain

c) lied

123. It will ... be Christmas again.

a) fast

b) next

c) soon

124. Be careful not to ... your coffee on this rug.

a) drip

b) spill

c) filter

125. Mary had to leave her family ... when she went abroad to work.

a) at all costs

b) out

c) behind

126. Metal ... at high temperatures.

a) grows

b) expands

c) enlarges

127. Because of the poor harvest, cereals prices have ... in the last three months.

a) gone up

b) jumped up

c) sprung up

128. I'm ... worried about Mary; she always seems to be exhausted.

a) as

b) such

c) so

129. I have difficulty … without glasses.

a) read

b) of reading

c) in reading

130. He arrived rather late. The party was already … .

a) in full swing

b) at full tilt

c) in full bloom

131. My neighbour plays his records … in his flat at night and nobody can get enough sleep.

a) at full tilt

b) at full blast

c) in full cry

132. It's unwise to … in a quarrel between husbands.

a) involve

b) poke

c) interfere

133. I will … the project with other members and see what they think about it.

a) discuss

b) talk

c) explain

134. The poor farmer was very angry … the dogs chasing his sheep.

a) about

b) because

c) with

135. I think she's quite honest … her intentions.

a) about

b) with

c) in

136. I will be waiting … them at the entrance door.

a) on

b) for

c) at

137. It's no use complaining … the cold during winter.

a) of

b) from

c) on

138. Manufacturers are now … of the latest credit restrictions.

a) smelling the rat

b) feeling the pinch

c) cooking the books

139. This music type is an American art form which is now … in Europe through the efforts of expatriates.

a) foundering

b) waning

c) flourishing

140. She was … disappointed when she learned that she hadn't got the job she dreamt of.

a) fully

b) highly

c) bitterly

141. They have … the castle and it is now a luxury hotel.

a) undone
b) remade
c) transformed

142. I … so much last night: I feel terrible.
a) shouldn't have eaten
b) mustn't have eaten
c) didn't have to eat
143. The man stole one of the officers' uniforms and managed to escape by
passing himself … as a guard.
a) out
b) off
c) through
144. … we set off in the next minutes, we'll be there on time.
a) In case
b) So long
c) Provided
145. If he drinks any more beer, I don't think he'll be … to football this
afternoon.
a) skilled
b) capable
c) fit
146. My manager's … of my work doesn't matter to me at all.
a) opinion
b) belief
c) meaning
147. The recent … domestic violence is worrying the police.
a) increase in
b) increase of

c) increase about
148. There's … to hurry.
a) no purpose
b) no need
c) impossible
149. The officers … the kidnapper from escaping by blocking all exits.
a) allowed
b) avoided
c) prevented

150. This meat isn't suitable … .
a) the grill
b) for grilling
c) being grilled
151. A bridge is already … over the river.
a) being built
b) erecting
c) been erected
152. The painting is …; the thief will be disappointed.
a) invalid
b) priceless
c) worthless
153. Even though he is thirty-three, he lives … his mother's salary.
a) from
b) at
c) on
154. It should be obvious … you that this problem will be solved.
a) for
b) to

c) at

155. Mike often forgets to do what he has been told and is scolded for being

… .

a) rebellious

b) malicious

c) disobedient

156. The house is quite warm. The oil heater gives … .

a) out a good heat

b) off a good heat

c) out good heat

157. In the middle of my trip I stopped … a rest on the river bank.

a) have

b) to have

c) having

158. After ruling that the article had unjustly … the reputation of the

businessman, the judge ordered the magazine to … its libelous statements

in print.

a) praised…publicize

b) injured…retract

c) sullied…communicate

159. When she heard the news she went completely … .

a) fuse

b) thunder

c) spare

160. I won't … those children making a noise in my apartment!

a) have

b) allow

c) let

161. It's great that your father managed to … that man. Somehow he had deceived many people.

a) see to

b) see through

c) see out

162. My car is much older … than yours.

a) form

b) manufacture

c) model

163. I … in bed all night thinking about it.

a) laid

b) led

c) lay

164. According to the medical doctor, there's absolutely nothing the … with you.

a) wrong

b) matter

c) problem

165. I looked everywhere but I couldn't find … at all.

a) anyone

b) no one

c) someone

166. It was … a simple question that everyone answered it.
a) much
b) such
c) too
167. I like my eggs soft …, not hard.
a) cooked
b) steamed
c) boiled
168. I was utterly amazed when the train arrived exactly … time.
a) on
b) by
c) in
169. I'd like to take this … of wishing you all the best.
a) chance
b) opportunity
c) occasion
170. Learners of English may fail to .. between unfamiliar sounds.
a) separate
b) differ
c) distinguish
171. … her opinion, English cheese is better than French cheese.
a) To
b) By
c) In
172. Their parents would not ... them to go there for the weekend.
a) agree
b) permit
c) consent
173. Every Sunday the old man's dog goes to the shop to … him a newspaper.
a) carry
b) fetch
c) take
174. It's late! It's time we … .
a) are gone
b) are going
c) were gone
175. I drove around the area for half an hour but I couldn't find a car … .
a) park
b) plan
c) garage
176. The smell was so bad that it … me off my food.
a) took
b) put
c) got
177. Although she hasn't said anything she … to be upset about it.
a) seems
b) acts
c) behaves
178. It's strange: his sister is blonde, … he is very dark.
a) therefore
b) however
c) whereas

179. I very much … that you will come to dinner next Monday.
a) hope
b) want
c) wish

180. Crops are sometimes completely destroyed by … of locusts.
a) bands
b) swarms
c) flocks

181. There's something wrong with my watch: it has … five minutes in the last hour.
a) gained
b) won
c) advanced

182. Keep in mind that if you are … to customers, they'll walk out of the shop.
a) brush

b) rough
c) rude

183. The air in the house felt cold and … after some days of bad weather.
a) wet
b) damp
c) moist

184. Do you want to wait for a table at this restaurant or shall we go …
else?

a) anywhere
b) everywhere
c) somewhere

185. Children who use escalators should always be accompanied … an adult.
a) with
b) by
c) beside

186. I took someone else's coat by … .
a) fortune
b) error
c) mistake

187. How long does it … to get home in the morning?
a) take you
b) need you
c) demand

188. It's becoming more and more … that the Government has lost its confidence.
a) apparent
b) expected
c) anticipated

189. You need a special … to go into this building.
a) agreement
b) allowance
c) permit

190. I don't like her, so I have no intention … speaking to her.
a) about

b) of

c) with

191. I had to drive carefully because the road was icy in several … .
a) places
b) blocks
c) pieces

192. Don't invite him; I can't stand his bad … .
a) mood
b) mind
c) temper

193. Not only … the movie, but she had also read the book.
a) she did see
b) she saw
c) had she seen

194. I had a meeting at work which went … much longer than I expected.
a) in
b) on
c) by

195. Tom … me to take a lawyer to court with me.
a) suggested
b) insisted
c) advised

196. Poor woman! She has so much to cope … .
a) with
b) in
c) by

197. Tim has always gone … strange hobbies like inventing secret codes.
a) by

b) into
c) in for

198. As he is an expert, his opinions would be worth … .
a) to have
b) having
c) of having

199. Nowhere … this room.
a) is as cold as in
b) is it as cold as
c) it is as cold as in

200. There's just something about him that really puts my … up.
a) handle
b) teeth
c) back

201. The explorer walked all the way along the river, from its mouth to its
… .
a) cause
b) source
c) well

202. She soon received promotion, for her superiors realised that she was a woman of considerable … .
a) ability
b) future
c) possibility

203. It is … knowledge that they quarrel violently several times a month.
a) complete
b) normal

c) common

204. After his mother died, he was … up by his grandparents.
a) taken
b) brought
c) grown

205. You should do something worthwhile with your time instead of … it!
a) spending
b) using
c) wasting

206. The police have issued … to local citizens to be on the lookout for thieves.
a) warnings
b) advice
c) information

207. If you require any more … about the event, please telephone us.
a) news
b) fact
c) information

208. Wait … you get at the office before you unpack this.
a) when
b) until
c) after

209. The students … names appear on the list all failed the exam.
a) whose
b) which
c) their

210. When the police appealed for witnesses, many people came … .
a) across
b) on
c) forward

211. Can you give me a rough … of how much it will cost?
a) esteem
b) value
c) estimate

212. I do play billiards, but I … tennis.
a) prefer
b) like
c) would rather

213. The consultant gave me … useful information.
a) one
b) some
c) the

214. One of the … has fallen off the clock.
a) hands
b) pointers
c) arms

215. How old do you have to be … you can drive a car in your country?
a) when
b) since
c) before

216. I'll let you have the book back next Friday without … .
a) miss
b) fail

c) doubt

217. ... I ask him for money he owes me, he says he will bring it in a few
weeks.
a) However
b) Whatever
c) Whenever

218. I ... to inform you that we cannot exchange articles.
a) resent
b) regret
c) sense

219. I am responsible ... what has happened.
a) with
b) for
c) by

220. They have to arrange for the ... of their furniture accessories.
a) sole
b) sale
c) seal

221. The boy wouldn't go into the sea ... his parents went too.
a) unless
b) except
c) but

222. The ... part of the week is always busy for Steven.
a) start
b) near
c) early

223. I ... to take my neighbour to court if he didn't stop making so much noise.
a) offered
b) suggested
c) threatened

224. It wasn't his ... that he was late.
a) blame
b) fault
c) error

225. She sat there with her arms ... doing nothing.
a) turned
b) folded
c) twisted

226. Our neighbours ... their hedge cut once a year.
a) have
b) do
c) make

227. I could tell she was pleased ... the expression on his face.
a) at
b) by
c) for

228. Steve calls himself Steve Milton, but his ... surname is Smith.
a) natural
b) current
c) real

229. If you keep trying you might ... to do it.
a) succeed
b) manage
c) understand

230. Their child was born in the ambulance … to the hospital.
a) on the way
b) by the way
c) a long way

231. The meeting is now … .
a) on end
b) at the end
c) at an end

232. She promised to write … I never heard from her again.
a) except
b) but
c) because

233. I … to Tim for my bad behaviour.
a) coped
b) excused
c) apologised

234. Ever … she was in school she has wanted to become a medical doctor.
a) since
b) always
c) after

235. The bottle was on the top shelf, out of … .
a) achievement
b) arrival
c) reach

236. Laptops are supposed to … time, but I'm not so sure they do!
a) spare
b) save
c) waste

237. I didn't mean to do it; it was … accident.
a) in
b) on
c) by

238. His speech was …, eliciting thunderous applause.
a) tedious
b) cowardly
c) well-received

239. What does "a wild goose chase" mean?
a) a wild night on the town
b) a search for something that cannot be found
c) a dangerous race in the streets between cars

240. You should have avoided risking …, General!
a) the lives of your soldiers
b) your soldiers' life
c) the life of your soldiers'

241. … goes the train; now we will have to walk!
a) On time
b) There
c) At once

242. Jane is important to him. He wouldn't get … without her.
a) by
b) over
c) round

243. They live in the house … the blue door.
a) which
b) where
c) with

244. I phoned the bank to …
how much money I had to pay.
a) control
b) check
c) test

245. His parents give him
anything he wants and as a
result he's very … .
a) ruined
b) spoilt
c) damaged

246. … I am studying at the best
university and I hope to get a
job soon.
a) In a moment
b) At present
c) At this instant

247. He is a fast typist but his
letters are full of spelling … .
a) mistakes
b) wrongs
c) faults

248. The officers have asked
that … who saw the accident
should inform
them.
a) one
b) someone
c) anyone

249. If the greengrocer has some
tomatoes … buy some?
a) you will
b) would you
c) shall you

Set 2

250. I will offer a small … to
anyone who finds my missing
cat.
a) reward
b) receipt
c) repayment

251. The party has … to win the
elections.
a) achieved
b) managed
c) attained

252. You … do the washing-up:
we can do it later.
a) wouldn't
b) daren't
c) needn't

253. They demand higher wages
because prices are … .
a) growing
b) exceeding
c) rising

254. You should be careful
when you wash this … blouse.
a) weak
b) feeble
c) sensitive

255. My parents always fall …
in front of the TV.
a) asleep
b) sleepy
c) sleeping

256. You can never rely … her
to be punctual.

a) of
b) with
c) on
257. Are you interested … rock music?
a) on

b) in
c) of
258. You should reply … his letter.
a) on
b) for
c) to
259. I will certainly act … your advice.
a) with
b) at
c) on
260. as sound as … . This phrase means healthy, in good condition.
a) steel
b) a monkey
c) a bell
261. Buy the … of soap which is now on sale.
a) model
b) brand
c) mark
262. My uncle took … jogging when he retired.
a) up
b) on
c) over

263. There has been a rather worrying … five per cent in our profits last
year.
a) drop in
b) fall in
c) drop of
264. … you hurry, you won't catch the train.
a) Unless
b) Except
c) As
265. The customer … his money back.
a) asked
b) demanded
c) requested

266. I … him to go to the Lost Property office.
a) noticed
b) announced
c) advised
267. I couldn't resist having another slice of pizza even … I was supposed
to be on diet.
a) though
b) however
c) although
268. These old buildings are going to be … soon.
a) laid out
b) run down
c) pulled down
269. … as I like ice-cream, I can't eat any more now.

a) Much
b) Even
c) So
270. You may borrow ten books, provided you show them to … is at the desk.
a) who
b) whoever
c) whom
271. Is he playing computer games? He's … to be washing the car.
a) hoped
b) supposed
c) expected
272. Mary was angry with me for breaking the windows, but it happened … accident.
a) by
b) in
c) on
273. The room was crowded with over fifty people … into it.
a) pushed
b) packed
c) stuck

274. Beware of the friends who appear to be enthusiastic … your success.
a) of
b) with
c) about
275. They want to watch the latest movie … TV.

a) in
b) at
c) on
276. … to leave early is rarely granted.
a) Permission
b) Leave
c) Allowance
277. …, my colleagues didn't laugh at me.
a) For my surprise
b) To my surprise
c) As to surprise me
278. If you had gone there, you … my sister.
a) would have met
b) would meet
c) had met
279. She never goes in lifts because she is terrified of … spaces.
a) constricted
b) compressed
c) contained
280. It never … to me that she would be there.
a) recurred
b) occurred
c) contemplated
281. The assistant was … helpful, but Mike felt she could have given him more information.
a) exactly
b) totally
c) quite

282. The meal was excellent;
the steak was particularly … .
a) flavoured

b) tasteful
c) delicious
283. Are there any seats left for
this evening's …?
a) opera
b) act
c) performance
284. Having … the table, she
called the family for supper.
a) laid
b) spread
c) ordered
285. As I have been ill, I have
had no … to discuss the
business plan.
a) suitability
b) possibility
c) opportunity
286. Tom … to turn up for the
football match.
a) omitted
b) failed
c) stopped
287. The manager's presence
was helpful, but he could … us
more money.
a) give
b) gave
c) have given
288. There are five lawyers in
my town and I have consulted
… of them in
turn.

a) every
b) each
c) any
289. The final course was so
difficult that I didn't … any
progress at all.
a) do
b) create
c) make
290. I'm tired of looking at
ancient … .
a) ruins
b) foundations
c) remnants

291. My bike is gone: it must …
.
a) have been stolen
b) have stolen
c) be stolen
292. There's a … to her
patience.
a) top
b) limit
c) bottom
293. I … hands with the guests.
a) gave
b) nodded
c) shook
294. We had a great … of
trouble getting through customs.
a) level
b) lot
c) deal
295. Rose trees need to be …
regularly.
a) cut

b) clipped
c) pruned
296. What made you think …
such a thing?
a) of
b) on
c) at
297. I would go to the pool if
the weather … good.
a) is
b) were
c) has been
298. I rang you up while he …
his report.
a) was finishing
b) has been finishing
c) had finished
299. The bus … is 50 cents.
a) cost

b) fare
c) charge
300. Before the invention of
refrigeration, the … of meat was
a problem.
a) preservation
b) keeping
c) maintenance
301. Could I have another one?
Oh, there doesn't seem to be …
.
a) any left
b) some left
c) left any
302. I will go on working on the
farm … I can.
a) through

b) during
c) as long as
303. I'll ask Ms. Thompson to
… to you as soon as she returns.
a) ring
b) contact
c) speak
304. This new model works by
letting light through a small …
at the front.
a) leak
b) hole
c) break
305. You will have to … your
holiday if you are too ill.
a) cut down
b) call off
c) put aside
306. If you go to the market you
might find a … .
a) chance
b) bargain
c) trade
307. The train was ... by three
hours because of bad weather.
a) postponed
b) put off
c) delayed

308. My guests didn't leave
until 3 a.m.; they … have
enjoyed themselves.
a) can't
b) must
c) might
309. She was sitting just ...
Steve and John.

a) beside

b) off

c) besides

310. Mary remembered the correct address only … she had posted the letter.

a) since

b) following

c) after

311. I have never … any experience of living in a small village.

a) wished

b) made

c) had

312. I'm very … of cash at the moment.

a) down

b) empty

c) short

313. The … were told to fasten their seat belts.

a) passengers

b) flyers

c) customers

314. There are … trains running today.

a) scarcer

b) fewer

c) little

315. Mary isn't … well with the new manager.

a) going on

b) taking on

c) getting on

316. Has this idea ever occurred … you?

a) at

b) to

c) on

317. I'm … with your stupid ideas.

a) get rid

b) fed over

c) fed up

318. If they had been able … it for you, they would have helped you.

a) to do

b) doing

c) is doing

319. The officers carried out a … search for the missing diplomat.

a) through

b) thoughtful

c) thorough

320. Fitting together the fragments was a … task.

a) minute

b) minuscule

c) painstaking

321. It will … rain later so we should go now.

a) probably

b) likely

c) usually

322. I would have cleaned this mess if I … you were coming.

a) would have known

b) had known

c) have known

323. We have … to meet at the station at 8 o'clock.
a) confirmed
b) combined
c) arranged

324. There is always … traffic in the city centre.
a) full
b) strong
c) heavy

325. He's … to drink too much at parties.
a) adequate
b) apt
c) common

326. We must get there … or other.
a) somehow
b) anyhow
c) anywhere

327. She was left to make all the … for the meeting.
a) procedures
b) provisions
c) arrangements

328. The new girl … type at 45 words per minute.
a) need
b) can
c) dare

329. I'll wait over there until … ready.
a) you are
b) you will be
c) you were

330. You must move your car; … I have to give you a ticket.
a) whether
b) therefore
c) otherwise

331. A manager of a large company is given a big … .
a) money
b) pay
c) salary

332. Heavy goods delivery vehicles may not carry … of more than fifteen tons.
a) masses
b) sizes
c) loads

333. After they went on strike there was a … of water.
a) shortage
b) drain
c) loss

334. She's entitled to a pension, but she won't dream … retiring yet.
a) on
b) of
c) to

335. Mix the contents … a little water.
a) of
b) with
c) at

336. You can try … if you really need to improve your language skills.

a) listening to BBC
b) listening at BBC
c) to listening to BBC

337. His … of Alexander the Great was acclaimed as one of the best.
a) entertainment
b) portrayal
c) spectacle

338. The army … defeat at the hands of such powerful enemies.
a) bore
b) supported
c) suffered

339. Their accounts were phony. They had been cooking the … for years.
a) books
b) spinner
c) trade

340. Practical … is desirable for candidates.
a) exploit
b) initiative
c) experience

341. The director opened the letter without … to read the address on the envelope.
a) worrying
b) bothering
c) caring

342. Hurry! She's already here. I didn't think she … till tomorrow.
a) was coming
b) is coming
c) is to come

343. If you have any … concerning this report please phone us.
a) requests
b) wishes
c) queries

344. Could you … exactly what you saw?
a) inform
b) describe
c) point

345. He has brought you a … of flowers.
a) branch
b) bunch
c) bush

346. The child seems to be incapable … keeping his room tidy.
a) at
b) with
c) of

347. In the summer I often sleep in the … air on the terrace.
a) clean
b) clear
c) open

348. This dress … you perfectly.
a) likes
b) suits
c) matches

349. I bought the phone because the colours … the colours of the car.
a) match
b) fit
c) suit
350. To promote her so quickly you must have a high … of her ability.
a) view

b) idea
c) opinion
351. We … as well go without him.
a) can
b) may
c) just
352. She … out of the window for a moment and then went on writing.
a) glanced
b) glimpsed
c) regarded
353. You should keep receipts from shops as proof …
purchase.
a) to
b) for
c) of
354. Don't mention it … my girlfriend, but I paid $80 for this perfume.
a) to
b) at
c) with

355. The child knocked … the door.
a) on
b) for
c) at
356. You must have … the examination before Friday.
a) passing
b) entered for
c) sit for
357. They … for you for more than one hour now.
a) have waited
b) have been waiting
c) wait
358. I would have come home earlier if you … me.
a) had told
b) have told
c) told

359. Petrol is so expensive … they use public transport.
a) then
b) thus
c) that
360. There has been some … in their bilateral relations.
a) destitution
b) deterioration
c) depreciation
361. They take too much … of his kindness.
a) profit
b) use
c) advantage

362. I can easily … you up for
the night.
a) put
b) take
c) keep
363. My car is very old, but I
can't … to buy a new one.
a) achieve
b) reach
c) afford
364. Two passengers were
killed and the other was …
injured.
a) hardly
b) severely
c) unusually
365. After ten years the
bedroom wallpaper had
considerably … .
a) faded
b) mixed
c) lighted
366. My attempt to pass the
final exam was … .
a) unmerciful
b) unhelpful
c) unsuccessful
367. She … at the Latin College
for French.
a) enlisted

b) inscribed
c) enrolled
368. I admit I suffer from a …
of patience with old people.
a) lack
b) limit

c) shortage
369. The building is in good …
though it needs to be painted.
a) state
b) condition
c) position
370. I can't be sure I'll be there
in time. I … be late.
a) should
b) must
c) may
371. His suit didn't … him
properly.
a) meet
b) fit
c) frame
372. She may be quick …
understanding, but she's not
capable of doing it.
a) at
b) in
c) for
373. We have some important
business to attend … .
a) with
b) at
c) to
374. Steve, you should not boast
… your success.
a) of
b) with
c) from
375. I'm sorry, I haven't got …
change.
a) all
b) any
c) lots

376. An oppressive ..., and not
the festive mood characterized
the mood of
the gathering.
a) senility
b) inanity
c) solemnity
377. I think it's ... your luck to
drive without a license.
a) risking
b) tempting
c) pushing
378. If you looked back far
enough, you would see that you
are ... related
to Karl Marx.
a) distantly
b) slightly
c) previously
379. I can't understand it; your
handwriting is … .
a) illegible
b) illicit
c) illusive
380. Hello! You ... be the new
employee.
a) could
b) should
c) must
381. Last year the cereals
harvest was disappointing, but
this year it looks
as if we shall have a better … .
a) crop
b) amount
c) product

382. She was in ... of a large
number of men.
a) direction
b) leadership
c) charge
383. Tom was born during the
last war, which would ... him
about 50 now.
a) give
b) make
c) calculate

384. The actor never married,
choosing to remain ... all his
life.
a) separate
b) single
c) individual
385. The consultant showed me
... the washing machine.
a) the working of
b) to work
c) how to use
386. The driver failed to signal
his ... to turn left.
a) idea
b) purpose
c) intention
387. I wish you wouldn't call
her ... that name.
a) by
b) with
c) under
388. I had ... reached the park
when I saw everyone leaving.
a) quite
b) almost

c) rather

389. She tried to … to see him
at least once a week.
a) call up
b) come on
c) drop in

390. No, Kate isn't stupid. …,
she's rather clever.
a) Now
b) Currently
c) Actually

391. The Minister resigned as
a/an … of the incident.
a) effect
b) result
c) cause

392. The names of the winners
will be … in the next magazine
issue.
a) told

b) informed
c) announced

393. When the clock … twelve,
I left.
a) struck
b) beat
c) shot

394. The store is only open …
weekday mornings now.
a) for
b) in
c) on

395. They think he is very good
… drawing.
a) at
b) for

c) in

396. Every day thousands of …
fly the Atlantic for negotiations.
a) dealers
b) merchants
c) businessmen

397. Prices continued to rise …
the ruling party became
unpopular.
a) on condition that
b) with the result that
c) on the chance that

398. I would help the old lady in
her shopping if she … me.
a) will ask
b) ask
c) asked

399. … for a trip last Friday?
a) Did you go
b) Will you go
c) Have you gone

400. The child was taught that it
was … to interrupt.
a) coarse
b) rude
c) crude

401. She was … better than her
brother at chess.
a) miles
b) feet
c) inches

402. I often speak to her on my
… to work.
a) travel
b) way
c) road

403. The noise prevented me from … to sleep.
a) starting
b) going
c) beginning

404. This horse is famous for … the National race two times.
a) gaining
b) conquering
c) winning

405. Before starting a new chapter, I'd like to … what we discussed yesterday.
a) run up
b) run along
c) run through

406. I think it's time we … on our way.
a) are
b) were
c) will be

407. Would you … taking care of the cat for two hours?
a) mind
b) matter
c) agree

408. The world record for this event is almost impossible to … .
a) beat
b) meet
c) compare

409. We've been … with this business partner for many years.
a) competing
b) shopping
c) dealing

410. She applied for training as a pilot, but they turned her … .
a) down
b) over
c) back

411. The child wasn't accustomed … by coach.
a) travel
b) to travel
c) to travelling

412. She has left her phone at home. She's always so … .
a) forgetful
b) forgotten
c) forgetting

413. Newly-… coins always look clean.
a) moulded
b) minted
c) printed

414. I had to go to the library to … some books.
a) give
b) return
c) buy

415. It was such a hot day … the surface of the material was damaged.
a) as
b) so
c) that

416. She always … out in a crowd because of her style.
a) stood
b) found

c) looked

417. Please apply … the secretary for this type of information.

a) for

b) at

c) to

418. Though the concert had been enjoyable, it was overly … .

a) sublime

b) protracted

c) extensive

419. A skillful …, John adopted a posture of patience and … toward the protestors.

a) academician/understanding

b) pundit/tolerance

c) negotiator/compromise

420. Could you give me a rough … of the costs?

a) estimate

b) value

c) correlation

421. There is a … of $2,000 for information leading to the thief.

a) gift

b) reward

c) prize

422. The manager didn't pay for the meal himself – he put it on his company's … account.

a) expense

b) price

c) value

423. I knew her … we were young.

a) until

b) as

c) when

424. I … them run away from the bank.

a) allowed

b) saw

c) felt

425. I only have … days left in Spain.

a) little

b) a few

c) a little

426. She pretended that she agreed with me to avoid … my feelings.

a) hurting

b) to hurt

c) hurt

427. Many fires could be … if new safety standards were introduced.

a) protected

b) excluded

c) prevented

428. My watch stopped so I had no way of knowing the right … .

a) moment

b) time

c) hour

429. He came … an unknown poem while he was searching for something

else.
a) round
b) across
c) off

430. I couldn't beat him at chess; I'm just not in his … .
a) class
b) type
c) set

431. Too much exercise can be harmful but walking is good … you.
a) by
b) with
c) for

432. I find it difficult to talk to her because we have so … in common.
a) few
b) less
c) little

433. His attitude … his parents is very disrespectful.
a) as far as
b) towards
c) as for

434. Surely Anna is not going to drive, … she?
a) does
b) will
c) is

435. You … pay for this. It's free.
a) shouldn't
b) mustn't
c) don't have to

436. A child learns a language best … .
a) when being brought up to it
b) by being brought up to it
c) while being brought into it

437. Urgent discussions will continue … .
a) behind the scenes
b) behind the curtain
c) behind the bars

438. Our house is nothing out of the … .
a) normal
b) usual
c) ordinary

439. "A ladies' man" means:
a) a man most women fall for
b) a man who dresses up like a woman
c) a man who enjoys the company of women

440. The manager warned Kate that the laziness and … could result in her dismissal.
a) procrastination
b) ambition
c) fortitude

441. The butcher cut some steak and … it up.
a) closed
b) wrapped
c) wound

442. The man … to take a breath test after the incident.
a) denied
b) objected

c) refused

443. I do my best to practise every day … it is difficult sometimes.
a) although
b) also
c) even

444. His arm was so … injured that he couldn't play anymore.
a) deeply
b) badly
c) hardly

445. His home is a … between a palace and a hotel.
a) union
b) link
c) cross

446. The woman … case was described in the article never fully recovered.
a) what
b) whom
c) whose

447. I … put my money there if I didn't consider it was safe.
a) didn't
b) wouldn't
c) hadn't

448. Driving in this city is supposed to be confusing but I didn't find it at … difficult.
a) all
b) once
c) least

449. I enjoy … but don't like jogging.
a) to swim
b) in swim
c) swimming

450. Would you … the kettle on for some coffee?
a) set
b) put
c) have

451. I suggest … the "meal of the day" rather than fish.
a) to have
b) we have
c) for us having

452. Her father won't … to my marrying Olivia.
a) agree
b) allow
c) approve

453. It was way to hot. I couldn't … it any longer.
a) carry
b) hold
c) stand

454. They had always liked the sea … they moved to the Coast.
a) so
b) since
c) such

455. Just keep .. on him, will you?
a) a look
b) an eye
c) a care

456. By the time you receive
this message, I … for China.
a) will leave
b) have left
c) will have left
457. You can depend … me.
a) in
b) of
c) on
458. I invested a lot of money
… residential buildings.
a) in
b) for
c) at
459. She is trying to lose weight
by … sweets.
a) cutting down at
b) stopping down at
c) cutting down on

460. The terrorist tried to
persuade the hostage that he was
neither … nor …
. He was just interested in
calling attention to his cause.
a) impeccable/sincere
b) antagonistic/vindictive
c) recalcitrant/clandestine
461. The professor was
surprised that her English was
so … .
a) liquid
b) definite
c) fluent
462. I went to … some pictures
by a renowned painter.
a) watch

b) look at
c) see to
463. If it … fine, she shall go
out.
a) was
b) were
c) is
464. The idea of a balanced diet
is difficult to … in this group.
a) put across
b) take in
c) make over
465. There was a small room
into … we all gathered.
a) where
b) that
c) which
466. You … go to dentist's.
a) rather
b) ought to
c) better
467. His speech was interesting
at first, but it was … long.
a) so much
b) far too
c) too much
468. The soldier has been on …
for twenty-four hours without a
break.
a) work

b) job
c) duty
469. When she braked on the
icy road, the car … .
a) slid
b) slipped

c) skidded
470. This is the … building in
the city.
a) oldest
b) elder
c) elderly
471. You must put your name
on this side and then sign on the
… side.
a) other
b) under
c) back
472. I will always … our
wonderful holidays.
a) reflect
b) remind
c) remember
473. The Prime Minister … his
intention to retire.
a) told
b) announced
c) informed
474. As the child walked
through the fields, he heard
sheep … .
a) braying
b) bleating
c) crying
475. I'm afraid I can't comment
… your project yet.
a) about
b) with
c) on
476. Steve was employed … a
factory in 2010.
a) in
b) to

c) by

477. It was such a good weather
that I decided to go … .
a) fish
b) fishing
c) to fishing
478. I think she … you my
regards when you met two days
ago.
a) gave
b) has given
c) give
479. Not … did she refuse to
speak to me, but she also
blamed me for
failing.
a) even
b) at all
c) only
480. "To come through flying
colours" means:
a) to succeed in one's study
b) to accomplish something with
great success
c) to be understood loud and
clear
481. I hope she is … to buy
some milk.
a) proposed
b) suggested
c) remembered
482. If I were you, I … that
gaming PC.
a) would buy
b) will buy
c) am buying

483. The vet decided that he had to operate … the dog.
a) with
b) on
c) at

484. I … like to apologize.
a) could
b) must
c) would

485. Many accidents in the home could be … by taking simple safety measures.

a) protected
b) avoided
c) preserved

486. Try to remember … bring your debit card.
a) me to
b) yourself to
c) to

487. The bride looked … in her dress.
a) beauty
b) lovely
c) handsome

488. We didn't leave for the station until the very … moment.
a) late
b) least
c) last

489. When are you going to give back that book you … me?
a) owe
b) debt

c) lend

490. The poor man was … by a gang last month.
a) murdered
b) destroyed
c) slaughter

491. Each … of the family had to do the washing up.
a) person
b) member
c) individual

492. The woman performs beautifully … the piano.
a) in
b) from
c) on

493. The boy comes … drawing lessons four times a week.
a) to
b) for
c) at

494. She … a coloured thread round her finger so as not to forget about the meeting.
a) rang
b) wound
c) curved

495. You have a new baby?! …!
a) What wonderful news
b) What a wonderful news
c) How wonderful news

496. If my diploma … last week, I would have been able to come sooner.
a) are found

b) were found

c) had been found

497. Old people do not take kindly to having their daily … upset.

a) routine

b) habit

c) custom

498. You were warned never … with those members.

a) to assign

b) to assume

c) to associate

499. If your company wants to attract workers it must … the wages.

a) spread

b) raise

c) rise

500. This computer package is totally … for our need.

a) unsuitable

b) undeniable

c) unspeakable

501. Some people think it is … to use little-known words.

a) clever

b) skilled

c) sensitive

502. He decided to … from the committee.

a) cancel

b) resign

c) prevent

503. Be here at nine o'clock without … .

a) fault

b) late

c) fail

504. The children were … by the cartoons.

a) fascinated

b) fascinating

c) fascination

505. The murderer … escape from the prison.

a) could

b) managed to

c) succeeded in

506. A witness … now been found.

a) was

b) had

c) has

507. She couldn't tell the truth. She had to … a story.

a) invent

b) manage

c) combine

508. She woke up crying because she had … a nightmare.

a) seen

b) dreamt

c) had

509. I hope to get an answer to my final letter by … of post.

a) round

b) return

c) back

510. Didn't it ever … to you that you would be caught?

a) occur

b) enter

c) strike

511. I started early … to avoid the worst of the traffic.
a) so that
b) in so far
c) in order

512. The children threw snowballs at … on their way.
a) themselves
b) each other
c) their own

513. Don't be so sure … yourself.
a) of
b) with
c) on

514. My grandmother buys eggs … the dozen.
a) to
b) for
c) by

515. She's entitled … a pension, but she doesn't want to retire.
a) to
b) on
c) in

516. Before you run … other people, you should consider your own faults.
a) over
b) up
c) down

517. The child won't go to sleep … we leave a light on.
a) except
b) unless

c) but

518. The effectiveness of his work relies … the use of advanced technologies.
a) on
b) by
c) of

519. The minority are suing the government for the return of their … lands.
a) antique
b) ancestral
c) inherited

520. Some species are on the … of becoming extinct.
a) edge
b) side
c) verge

521. One … of my job is that it is near where I live.
a) advantage
b) pleasure
c) preference

522. The little child loved … the old castle.
a) hunting
b) detecting
c) exploring

523. This is a photo of the university I … when I lived in Hamburg.
a) used
b) attended
c) joined

524. It's the first time … here.

a) I have been

b) I was

c) I am coming

525. Many accidents in this town are caused by … driving.

a) harmful

b) careful

c) careless

526. I was delighted when I … to sell my car so quickly.

a) managed

b) could

c) risked

527. It sounds … the situation isn't about to improve.

a) how

b) as if

c) so that

528. This patient … quickly after his illness.

a) recovered

b) covered

c) discovered

529. Caring for her cousin is a … burden for her.

a) sour

b) bitter

c) heavy

530. The manager made a wonderful … .

a) message

b) talk

c) speech

531. There is a fault at our latest TV station. Please don't … your TV set.

a) repair

b) adjust

c) switch

532. The man … going by plane instead of car.

a) suggested

b) agreed

c) convinced

533. Please concentrate … your tasks!

a) with

b) to

c) on

534. Many men do not approve … blood-sports.

a) for

b) of

c) with

535. You must encourage Mary … her efforts.

a) in

b) at

c) with

536. The ball … two or three times before disappearing.

a) leapt

b) bounced

c) hopped

537. It's … helping that man. He will die anyway.

a) good

b) no good

c) not good

538. Would you agree that a man pays less attention … than a woman does?

a) to dress
b) on dress
c) to the dress
539. Our institution can give you the … number of refugees.
a) unclear
b) suggestive
c) approximate
540. As drunk as … . This phrase refers to someone very drunk.
a) a fish
b) a lord
c) a barrel
541. How … you manage to get there so fast?
a) used
b) had
c) did
542. The touristic guide walked so … that most of the people could not
keep up with him.
a) fast
b) quick
c) rapid
543. Membership of the club, … costs $12,000 a year, is only open to
women.
a) what
b) that
c) which
544. The boy swore that he would take … his family's killer.
a) revenge in
b) revenge on
c) revenge at
545. … she wasn't feeling very well, she went to visit her parents as usual.
a) Still
b) Although
c) However
546. That guy has a dishonest … in his character.
a) stripe
b) strip
c) streak
547. Having looked the place …, the strange man went away.
a) down
b) out
c) over
548. I'm selling the building … of the summer.
a) at the end
b) in the end
c) on the end
549. She was complaining … a headache this morning.
a) at
b) from
c) of

Set 3

550. You need to hurry because the … train leaves in five minutes.

a) latter
b) last
c) latest
551. I am not used … spoken to in such a manner.
a) for being
b) to being
c) to be
552. There was a small house standing … hundreds of palm trees near the
beach.
a) in
b) among
c) between

553. As the team were … at the end of the game, he lost the bet.
a) equal
b) fair
c) correct
554. These little stores are always … of people at Christmas time.
a) stuffed
b) busy
c) crowded
555. Their request … me completely by surprise.
a) left
b) made
c) took
556. I have … why the Browns went to live in that country.
a) puzzled
b) surprised
c) wondered

557. You have to be patient … him.
a) for
b) with
c) about
558. Most women never … with violent crimes.
a) get into contact
b) come into contact
c) get in touch
559. I don't think I … this game before.
a) have played
b) will play
c) would play
560. "A City man" refers to:
a) any man with a higher education
b) a man who works in a city, which is a financial power of an area
c) someone who is constantly showing off
561. Is there a bank where I can … these pounds for euros?
a) turn

b) alter
c) exchange
562. The officer said that he saw no … between the murders.
a) joint
b) connection
c) join
563. Drinking is a bad habit, which many people find difficult to … .

a) beat
b) cough
c) break
564. Would you … passing this magazine to him?
a) mind
b) agree
c) want
565. There's … to be frightened of the cat.
a) a fear
b) no need
c) no fear
566. Her boyfriend won't … her drive his car.
a) allow
b) leave
c) let
567. The competitors in the rally had to follow the … laid down by the sponsors.
a) direct
b) route
c) address
568. If only I …play the piano as well as you!
a) might
b) would
c) could
569. It's a great … that the exhibition was cancelled.
a) sorrow
b) sadness
c) pity

570. On our … to Madrid, the car broke down.
a) way
b) road
c) voyage
571. She has adopted two orphans … her own children.
a) except
b) besides
c) in place of
572. I cannot understand how you put … this residential area.
a) out
b) by
c) up with
573. You will have to take things … .
a) like you find them
b) as you find them
c) so as you find them
574. We … to the concert, but we didn't make it.
a) were to have gone
b) would go
c) were gone
575. No one … she was.
a) could be quicker than
b) can be as quick as
c) could be so quick as
576. This computer is cheap, but that one is … .
a) cheaper yet
b) more cheaper
c) even cheaper
577. If the line is busy, don't wait and … .
a) hang on

b) hang up

c) hang down

578. If they … to that event, they would certainly have decided to attend it.

a) will be invited

b) had been invited

c) were invited

579. If I saw Olive, I … her to my party.

a) invite

b) will invite

c) would invite

580. I was very … not to pass the message further.

a) cajoled

b) tempted

c) elicited

581. After the party the dog was allowed to finish off the … sandwiches.

a) left

b) leaving

c) remaining

582. I would much … a reply by the end of the week.

a) appreciate

b) require

c) value

583. When she heard the joke, she burst into loud … .

a) smiles

b) laughter

c) enjoyment

584. I couldn't get used to … to work so early.

a) go

b) going

c) be going

585. … amount of money can buy a true friend.

a) No

b) Never

c) None

586. They should be spending money on a house … than on a car.

a) other

b) better

c) rather

587. I was very … of myself for forgetting that.

a) disgraced

b) ashamed

c) shocked

588. Mary earns a great … of money.

a) quantity

b) level

c) deal

589. He is an expert … coronaviruses.

a) about

b) on

c) in

590. They look exactly the … .

a) alike

b) identical

c) same

591. There was no need to be uneasy … the results.

a) for

b) about

c) on

592. It's impossible to prevent the boys ... quarrelling with each other.

a) to

b) in

c) from

593. This bike is inferior ... the one I bought last year.

a) to

b) at

c) by

594. Tom plays ... the school team.

a) by

b) in

c) on

595. The teacher despairs ... ever teaching him anything.

a) of

b) in

c) on

596. Our family is fortunate in having sufficient supplies ... the winter.

a) for

b) on

c) to

597. The old man was found guilty ... many crimes.

a) from

b) for

c) of

598. ... Sam, he can't go alone.

a) As if

b) As for

c) As far as

599. I know nothing about that battle. It was ... .

a) behind the times

b) as the same time

c) before my time

600. Many jobs in this area can be directly ... to tourism.

a) attributed

b) attracted

c) dedicated

601. When the director went to China on business his ... took over all his duties.

a) officer

b) deputy

c) caretaker

602. She saw the plane crash when its engines ... .

a) failed

b) struck

c) held

603. You are going to come to the meeting, ...?

a) will you

b) do you

c) aren't you

604. You will not finish that project by tomorrow unless you ... some help.

a) get

b) would get

c) will get

605. It's difficult to pay my bills when prices keep … .
a) rising
b) gaining
c) raising

606. After the death of her father, she was brought … by her uncle.
a) round
b) about
c) up

607. Why did the police suspect you? It doesn't make … to me.
a) right
b) sense
c) truth

608. When they heard that their children had crossed the road without
looking, they told them they … do it again.
a) mustn't
b) needn't
c) didn't need to

609. He went to Germany hoping to find a teaching … .
a) work
b) occupation
c) post

610. I can't … what they are doing; it's way too dark down there.
a) look into
b) make out
c) see through

611. This country has … good transport.
a) the
b) a
c) very

612. I'd like you to meet a very good friend of …, Dave.
a) me
b) my
c) mine

613. We travelled to Australia by the most … route.
a) direct
b) unique
c) easy

614. This film is based … a novel.
a) of
b) on
c) in

615. I should be grateful … any advice you can give regarding this
situation.
a) for
b) about
c) with

616. I was shocked … her indifference!
a) on
b) with
c) at

617. The manager has just gone on her … leave. She gets three weeks'
holiday a year.
a) regular
b) annual

c) regular

618. He have … this minute left for the city centre.

a) ever

b) already

c) just

619. To my …, a pandemic is more dangerous than nuclear arms.

a) mind

b) view

c) disbelief

620. They are always … with each other about investments.

a) shouting

b) arguing

c) annoying

621. I took that faulty laptop back to the shop where I'd bought it and asked the … if they would change it for me.

a) clerk

b) official

c) assistant

622. I … to the cinema last night. I'm so tired now.

a) had not to go

b) shouldn't have gone

c) haven't had to go

623. You will spend at least one year working in this company … you can find out how things operate here.

a) so that

b) so as to

c) because

624. I can … with most things but I cannot stand lies.

a) put aside

b) put up

c) put off

625. I think she is … her time looking for a job here.

a) losing

b) wasting

c) missing

626. It is a very good idea to be … dressed when you have a business meeting.

a) finely

b) smartly

c) boldly

627. I was pleased to see how … he looked after his recent COVID-19 illness.

a) well

b) pleasant

c) nice

628. Let's … across this field instead of going by the road.

a) set

b) come

c) cut

629. Tell me … about your holiday in Spain.

a) every

b) much

c) all

630. It's fairly rude to interrupt when someone is … .
a) talking
b) saying
c) discussing

631. I didn't enjoy the event. No, and … .
a) neither we did
b) we didn't either
c) so didn't we

632. … of the week, I hope I shall have lost another kilo.
a) By the end
b) At the end
c) To the end

633. I reasoned … her, but she would not listen to me.
a) to
b) for
c) with

634. She is responding … treatment and will be cured.
a) on
b) for
c) to

635. Nothing will prevent me … succeeding.
a) on
b) from
c) in

636. Jennifer criticised everything and even ran … his friends.
a) up

b) down
c) into

637. Why did you have … his last tutorial?
a) such difficulties to follow
b) such a difficulty to follow
c) such difficulty in following

638. I was sitting in a famous café … afternoon when I saw her.
a) one
b) in
c) the

639. The … question in this case is whether she was there or not.
a) crucial
b) valuable
c) supreme

640. He's the best employee I've ever had. I couldn't … for a better one.
a) abide
b) average
c) ask

641. You are not allowed … in this room.
a) smoke
b) smoking
c) to smoke

642. I think you'd better … before the manager returns.
a) be gone
b) be going
c) being gone

643. "I … you all", she said, as she left.
a) am hating
b) can hate

c) hate

644. I'm sorry. It's all my …!
a) guilt
b) fault
c) wrong

645. I chose these because they
are my … shade of blue.
a) popular
b) favourite
c) fancy

646. I wonder … like to travel
by boat.
a) what it is
b) how it is
c) what is it

647. Two other … in their
report are worth mentioning.
a) effects
b) points
c) notices

648. Many soldiers were …
wounded in the war. They
needed a lot of help.
a) hardly
b) seriously
c) utterly

649. She's a luck person. She
always seems to fall on her … .
a) ankles
b) legs
c) feet

650. … experience of working
in a factory is required.
a) Previous
b) First
c) Initial

651. For a short time after the
car crash, I suffered from
constant … in my
back.
a) hurt
b) pain
c) ache

652. An enormous … of rubbish
had built up here.
a) pile
b) hill
c) tower

653. Children can be instructed
… swimming at a very early
age.
a) with
b) for
c) in

654. Marry will come … home
late. Don't wait for her.
a) to
b) into
c) back

655. I was instructed … driving
once upon a time.
a) in
b) about
c) at

656. How can you agree … such
an idea?
a) with
b) at
c) by

657. It was … to meet you.
That's what she said to me.
a) pleasure

b) a pleasure

c) some pleasure

658. Only by shouting loudly …
a taxi.

a) she got

b) she's got

c) did she get

659. The lights … out and I was
left in the darkness.

a) turned

b) went

c) gave

660. For this meal to be a real
success, you … cook the meat
for at least
three hours.

a) need

b) ought

c) must

661. It is logical that when
factories are … workers tend to
lose their jobs.

a) automatic

b) automation

c) automated

662. They are not used …
supper so late.

a) to having

b) of having

c) to have

663. Be careful; she has her
eyes … you.

a) for

b) at

c) on

664. In spite of the anesthetic, I
was fully … during the
operation.

a) awake

b) sensitive

c) conscious

665. Today a man was … down
the street by my dog.

a) chased

b) hunted

c) sped

666. I don't … to see her again
until next month.

a) think

b) expect

c) wait

667. Some drivers, after …,
annoy their fellows.

a) passing by

b) taking over

c) overtaking

668. I had … news of what she
was doing in London.

a) several

b) little

c) few

669. Now that he is retired, he
enjoys … more time watching
documentaries.

a) spending

b) to take

c) taking

670. His debt now amounts …
$10,000.

a) in

b) with

c) to

671. You demand too much of them; they are not really equal … the project.
a) for
b) to
c) with

672. The student is still dependent … his parents.
a) on
b) from
c) with

673. Will you have … to tell your manager about it?
a) some nerves
b) some nerve
c) the nerve

674. Boys and girls … enjoyed the show.
a) both
b) either
c) alike

675. The reconstruction of the city is now … .
a) well under way
b) well in the way
c) through the way

676. The production goes well now, although there were some … .
a) last straws
b) teething troubles
c) starting problems

677. If I could understand this alphabet, I … the article.
a) read

b) will read
c) would read

678. Please … and see me some time – you are welcome.
a) come to
b) come away
c) come around

679. I could … panic in her voice.
a) desist
b) detect
c) detest

680. Thousands of tourists use the … of footpaths across these hills.
a) network
b) grid
c) circuit

681. The professors … with coronavirus infection one after the other.
a) went down
b) went off
c) went under

682. He agreed to give me $100, … the $300 he had already lent me.
a) extra to
b) surplus to
c) in addition to

683. What do you usually … for delivering things?
a) demand
b) charge
c) cost

684. We chose some attractive
… paper for the present.
a) covering
b) wrapping
c) packing

685. It was a beautiful cloth …
from velvet.
a) worn
b) threaded
c) woven

686. We have … of time to
catch the flight.
a) enough
b) plenty
c) great deal

687. She put the letters into the
wrong envelopes … mistake.
a) on

b) with
c) by

688. Mike seems confident but
you … never judge by
appearances.
a) might
b) should
c) could

689. I couldn't go fishing
because it began to … with rain.
a) flow
b) drench
c) pour

690. They … for the same job.
a) chose
b) referred
c) applied

691. The plane was … for over
two hours because of fog.
a) delayed
b) landed
c) cancelled

692. She has to be careful which
soap she uses, because her skin
is … .
a) sensible
b) senseless
c) sensitive

693. The local authorities want
people to set … their own
businesses.
a) off
b) up
c) in

694. She is quite intelligent but
she … common sense.
a) wants
b) fails
c) lacks

695. I wonder who drank all the
wine. It … have been Mike
because he was
out all day.
a) can't
b) could
c) must

696. They are opposed …
giving people large pay rises.
a) for
b) to
c) against

697. I will show you the
document if I … it.

a) could find
b) will find
c) find
698. Being exhausted, he sent a request asking that his colleagues … their meeting for one hour.
a) defray
b) defer
c) commence
699. The reporter gave a dramatic … of his adventures.
a) tale
b) saga
c) account
700. Some people are camping for the … of rare species hunting.
a) extinction
b) abolition
c) annihilation
701. I am … in information about this laptop.
a) interested
b) bored
c) concerned
702. They say we're likely to have a … winter.
a) calm
b) smooth
c) mild
703. Do you think Sarah and Tom marry …?
a) lastly
b) at last
c) in the end

704. You should … a lawyer before you sign that contract.
a) check
b) consult
c) counsel
705. "You can take a horse to water, but you can't … it drink!"
a) make
b) compel
c) save
706. The old man is a little bit … in his right ear.
a) disabled
b) deaf
c) dead
707. Some explorers did not survive the terrible … across the mountains.
a) journey
b) step
c) travel
708. Heavy snowfalls have … all flights.
a) omitted
b) delayed
c) postponed
709. The rainstorms … more than three days.
a) went
b) took
c) lasted
710. There will be a … interval for snacks.
a) small
b) short

c) light

711. The play was very long, but there were three … .
a) rests
b) intervals
c) gaps

712. The jewels were … a lot of money.
a) cost
b) valued
c) worth

713. They had a plan to trick me, but I didn't fall … it.
a) for
b) to
c) at

714. It is unreasonable to demand this … Mary.
a) in
b) at
c) of

715. It took me a long time to get rid … the infection.
a) of
b) against
c) from

716. They differ … each other so much.
a) of
b) with
c) from

717. There is little … in this company.
a) hanging around
b) to hang around
c) hung around

718. I would let her go, if I … all about this mission.
a) know
b) have known
c) knew

719. They were … for smuggling perfumes into the country.
a) judged
b) warned
c) arrested

720. They didn't believe his theory because it didn't seem at all … .
a) feasible
b) plausible
c) creditable

721. … you leave for the airport, you'll miss the flight.
a) Unless
b) However
c) When

722. I haven't met her, but I did once … across her boyfriend.
a) look
b) go
c) come

723. She … her next appointment at the dentist's.
a) erased
b) cancelled
c) wiped

724. Because of the earthquake, the windows … in their frames.
a) rattled
b) slapped

c) shocked

725. I would … go by air than spend two days travelling by car.
a) prefer
b) better
c) rather

726. It's all over between them: she's walked … on him.
a) off
b) away
c) out

727. Our best player got infected and won't be … to play tomorrow.
a) adequate
b) fit
c) proper

728. Sarah spoke so fast I couldn't understand … she was talking about.
a) what
b) which
c) how

729. Mr. Smith is free … you now.
a) see
b) will see
c) to see

730. Everyone felt … for Mr. Brown when he lost his management position.
a) discontent
b) sorry
c) unhappy

731. What … will this decision have on the future of this company?
a) effect
b) result
c) answer

732. This year the trees were … two weeks earlier than usual.
a) in full cry
b) in full bloom
c) at full blast

733. During the last meeting everyone shared … his happiness.
a) in
b) against
c) at

734. The professional climber failed … his attempt.
a) with
b) at
c) in

735. I tried to reason … her, but she was rude to me.
a) on
b) with
c) for

736. Are you aware … the difficulties that lie ahead?
a) by
b) on
c) of

737. It's just an illusion. He's not different … anyone else.
a) for
b) from
c) on

738. Dave usually goes there …
him.
a) with

b) to
c) at
739. Alexia worships the sun
and … she spends her holidays
in Greece.
a) yet
b) however
c) accordingly
740. I can't come. I'm tied … at
the office.
a) in
b) up
c) down
741. Guests wore … they liked
to the party.
a) everything
b) anything
c) nothing
742. The pilot drives so quickly
that I am afraid that one day he
will …
someone.
a) crash down
b) turn over
c) knock down
743. Don't worry. This dog is
perfectly … .
a) harmless
b) harmful
c) tame
744. One of the main
advantages … the new operating
platform is that it is

very simple to use.
a) for
b) of
c) on
745. You'd better set off twenty
minutes early … there is traffic.
a) in case
b) so that
c) as if
746. When I saw Olivia's
reaction, I regretted … told her.
a) to have

b) to having
c) having
747. The shirt I was wearing
that day was dirty, but I don't
think anyone …
.
a) watched
b) noticed
c) remarked
748. This is the oldest house …
the village.
a) in
b) by
c) to
749. Jane was singing an old
rock song, a favourite of … .
a) her
b) herself
c) hers
750. So … people came to the
meeting that they had to cancel
it.
a) a few
b) few

c) little

751. Scientists are still looking for a cure … COVID-19.

a) for

b) against

c) to

752. Put the salt in the water and let it … before adding anything else.

a) melt

b) dissolve

c) soften

753. It's too hot for you … this parcel.

a) digging

b) for digging

c) to dig

754. He told Steve … for borrowing his laptop without permission.

a) on

b) out

c) off

755. In this company, if you interfere … other people's affairs, you will regret it.

a) with

b) to

c) about

756. Are you at least partially aware of the difficulties that lie ahead … you?

a) for

b) of

c) to

757. I left my office after I … the report.

a) had written

b) have written

c) should have written

758. Her medical doctor made her … in bed for two weeks.

a) to stay

b) staying

c) stay

759. As quick as … . This phrase means very quick.

a) cats

b) fire

c) lightning

760. The officers haven't had time to complete the investigation, but they have concluded … that he committed suicide.

a) tentatively

b) tenuously

c) temporally

761. I'm going to buy a new car; I'm tired … this one.

a) of

b) in

c) with

762. … a personal computer can help you work much faster.

a) To have

b) In having

c) Having

763. I … be delighted to show you the way.

a) might

b) ought to

c) would

764. ... the weather, the match went ahead.

a) Owing to

b) In spite of

c) However

765. Melania rang to make an early ... at the hairdresser's.

a) order

b) appointment

c) date

766. Adrian was the ... in his family.

a) lowest

b) littlest

c) shortest

767. Could you buy a cake please ... they come this afternoon?

a) if only

b) in case

c) on account of

768. One ... of old public transport is its unreliability.

a) disorder

b) dislike

c) disadvantage

769. Did you know that she is ... a baby?

a) expecting

b) hoping

c) waiting

770. The main ... to progress is not technical but political.

a) clash

b) obstacle

c) prevention

771. The best rooms in this hotel ... the bay.

a) regard

b) overlook

c) view

772. All dogs ... be kept on a lead in public.

a) must

b) ought

c) need

773. You should separate the eggs and then beat with a ... .

a) whip

b) wick

c) whisk

774. The man was ... to steal the laptop when he saw it on the table.

a) dragged

b) tempted

c) brought

775. My parents ... me to learn English when I was a child.

a) let

b) heard

c) persuaded

776. I am accustomed ... bad weather.

a) to

b) of

c) from

777. She was afraid ... mentioning it to her husband.

a) in

b) at

c) of

778. I warned them … the danger.

a) at

b) of

c) in

779. Gold is feared … in price this week.

a) to go up

b) going up

c) to be going up

780. I will ask Jane to come if I … her.

a) saw

b) will see

c) see

781. In the jar there was a … which looked like jam.

a) material

b) solid

c) substance

782. Because his presentation was so confusing, … people understood it.

a) clever

b) few

c) less

783. I am … her to arrive at any moment.

a) expecting

b) waiting

c) hoping

784. You … worry about the bill – I've already paid it.

a) daren't

b) might not

c) needn't

785. I've made an appointment for 11 o'clock. Is that … for you?

a) fit

b) convenient

c) right

786. You look … you've seen a ghost!

a) so that

b) that

c) as if

787. You … blame yourself. It wasn't your fault.

a) daren't

b) won't

c) mustn't

788. I'm … that I didn't pass the examination.

a) deceived

b) despaired

c) disappointed

789. This magazine has … interesting article on space travel.

a) quite an

b) a partly

c) nearly an

790. Your sister is much taller … you.

a) how

b) than

c) from

791. They always quarrel about coffee; she likes it strong, but he wants it …

.

a) small

b) feeble

c) weak

792. Getting divorced was a ... decision for us.

a) firm

b) hard

c) large

793. Mr. Smith was … in a road accident.

a) damaged

b) wronged

c) injured

794. I expected her at eight but she finally … at midnight.

a) came to

b) turned up

c) came off

795. Buses into town run … ten minutes or so.

a) each

b) all

c) every

796. Can you make … what she has written there?

a) for

b) out

c) up for

797. I can't say what his name is though it is … .

a) on the tip of my tongue

b) on top of my tongue

c) on my tongue's tip

798. Whether or not to abolish corporal punishment is still … in political circles.

a) proposal of contention

b) a bone of contention

c) bone of agreement

799. I … a nice watch two days ago.

a) was given

b) have been given

c) would give

800. As bold as … . This phrase means cheeky, impudent.

a) bones

b) a bear

c) brass

801. He was an … writer because he persuaded many people.

a) ordinary

b) influential

c) accurate

802. I … seeing Mary tomorrow so I will give her your message.

a) may be

b) shall be

c) could be

803. The temperature yesterday was about … for this season.

a) average

b) middle

c) moderate

804. Steven swims well and … does his sister.

a) also

b) even

c) so

805. The old man was very …
for my help.

a) grateful

b) pleased

c) delighted

806. … it was raining she went
out without a raincoat.

a) In spite

b) However

c) Although

807. Your progress will be … in
three months' time.

a) valued

b) evaluated

c) counted

808. I don't know why she
complains. She doesn't earn as
… as I do.

a) less

b) few

c) little

809. The organization will not
be … any new members.

a) taking up

b) taking off

c) taking on

810. She can make a delicious
… out of almost anything.

a) food

b) meal

c) plate

811. From now on, everything
will be … sailing, I hope.

a) plain

b) simple

c) pretty

812. She could hardly … such a
generous offer.

a) turn for

b) turn off

c) turn down

813. Tom has made his money
by developing a travel … .

a) shop

b) business

c) affair

814. Do you believe … all that
nonsense? I honestly don't.

a) in

b) to

c) at

815. I'm not sure … the exact
date.

a) with

b) of

c) for

816. She's not capable …
bringing up this child.

a) of

b) on

c) for

817. Steven was born … .

a) without wedlock

b) out of a wedlock

c) out of wedlock

818. Although he has travelled
extensively, he has never been
… .

a) to the Antipodes

b) at Antipodes

c) to Antipodes

819. At that hour, the street was … as people were fast asleep in bed.
a) denuded
b) deserted
c) devastated

820. Artists struggle with the conflict between … their own talent and
knowledge that very few succeed.
a) faith in
b) neglect of
c) dissolution to

821. My house isn't difficult to find. It's … the high school.
a) against
b) beside
c) between

822. A lot of my friends have … smoking in the last year.
a) put off

b) given up
c) held back

823. Please tell me … there is anything special that you would like to eat.
a) which
b) so
c) if

824. I'm making you responsible for this report. Please see … it that it is finished on time.
a) for

b) into
c) to

825. Olivia suggested … to the cinema together.
a) that we should go
b) us to go
c) we are going

826. It will be mostly cloudy, with … of rain in the west.
a) bursts
b) outbreaks
c) times

827. I … of people who smoke.
a) dislike
b) distrust
c) disapprove

828. Jane bought a new … for the party.
a) dress
b) clothes
c) vest

829. When the organization got a new computer, we had to … a programming course.
a) do
b) make
c) study

830. This history lesson seemed to go … .
a) over and over

b) on and on
c) off and on

831. I know her by …, but I don't what her name is.
a) sight
b) heart

c) chance
832. The bus burst into … but the driver managed to escape.
a) heat
b) fire
c) flames
833. I know Jane is slow … understanding, but please be patient.
a) to
b) at
c) on
834. I'll be absent … class this week.
a) from
b) at
c) to
835. It gives me … to introduce her.
a) great pleasure
b) a great pleasure
c) much pleasures
836. They … in Germany for more than two years now.
a) were staying
b) are staying
c) have been staying
837. Look, I'm not drunk. I am as … as a judge.
a) calm
b) sober
c) clear
838. The working atmosphere has gone downhill. You have a lot to … for.
a) agree
b) abide

c) answer

839. That incident happened because of the … of the employees.
a) infallible
b) negligence
c) diligence
840. "A sore point" means:
a) a very dangerous crossroads
b) a matter that irritates or hurts when it is brought up
c) a blister on a foot
841. She likes to sit there and … what goes on below.
a) look
b) gaze
c) watch
842. Keep … the good work!
a) with
b) on
c) up
843. … he joined the army, Steve had never been abroad.
a) Until
b) Since
c) While
844. If you want to join our club, you must first … this application form.
a) do up
b) fill in
c) make up
845. I haven't got … furniture like theirs.
a) some
b) any

c) the

Set 4

846. The librarian went to search for the book in a place … rare ones were kept.
a) where
b) there
c) that

847. A teacher must … children to be kind to each other.
a) let

b) force
c) encourage

848. You'll … a lot of time if you take the car.
a) spend
b) make
c) save

849. They took out a/an … to that newspaper.
a) inscription
b) subscription
c) conscription

850. The local authorities … increase taxes soon.
a) may
b) need
c) dare

851. The child hit the vase with his elbow and it … to the floor.
a) crashed
b) smashed

c) broke

852. I completely … with what has been said.
a) accept
b) agree
c) approve

853. She lost her homework and she … do it again.
a) ought
b) needs
c) has to

854. You are not … to smoke inside.
a) let
b) allowed
c) accepted

855. I believe … this town needs is a new shopping mall.
a) as
b) how
c) what

856. It's still not … that I am going to Madrid tomorrow.
a) certain
b) right
c) exact

857. Even though the old man was often cruel to his dog, it remained faithful … him.
a) for
b) in
c) to

858. You should encourage your daughter … her efforts.
a) to

b) for

c) in

859. The artists … our town by … .

a) have taken/by surprise

b) have taken/by storm

c) have brought/by storm

860. There is an increasing … to make films portraying love.

a) trend

b) surge

c) tradition

861. I felt sorry … him when he lost his job.

a) with

b) to

c) for

862. It was difficult for me to … what the recommendations I should make.

a) decide

b) realize

c) settle

863. The gorgeous lady walked to the … of the pool and jumped in.

a) extent

b) border

c) side

864. I thought she would like me to buy her a … brown bag.

a) black

b) French

c) new

865. The officer … me the way.

a) said

b) told

c) directed

866. Her boyfriend was sent to prison for … a bank.

a) stealing

b) robbing

c) lending

867. I'm going to stay here … she phones me.

a) for

b) when

c) until

868. You can trust what Daniel says. He's a very … person.

a) trustful

b) profitable

c) reliable

869. Don't worry. I still have one or two … up my sleeve.

a) tricks

b) defenses

c) jokes

870. The Prime Minister got up to … a short speech.

a) tell

b) make

c) hold

871. Mike was an … writer who persuaded many people.

a) influential

b) accurate

c) ordinary

872. If I hadn't done that, I think you … .

a) could die

b) might have died

c) may have died

873. People who live in big
cities … to suffer from stress.
a) develop
b) tend
c) lean

874. She has provided … every
emergency.
a) to
b) with
c) for

875. There was a note attached
… the package.
a) to
b) with
c) on

876. They say Italian is a
splendid language … .
a) for singing in
b) to sing in
c) for sing in

877. I saw him … the street.
a) crosses
b) to cross
c) cross

878. Although we have a large
number of employees, each one
receives …
attention when needed.
a) only
b) individual
c) single

879. We negotiated for hours
but we weren't able to … at an
agreement.
a) agree
b) abide

c) arrive

880. The missing climber
appeared at the mountain hut …
and kicking.
a) alive
b) hale
c) safe

881. Sarah had had a special …
with her aunt ever since her
mother died.
a) sense

b) feeling
c) relationship

882. The little boy was so noisy
that his mother told him not to
be such a …
.
a) trouble
b) nuisance
c) worry

883. I took … football again at
the beginning of this month.
a) up
b) with
c) by

884. Would you … the stamps
on to the documents?
a) spit
b) suck
c) stick

885. The robber … everyone in
the bank lie on the floor.
a) obliged
b) made
c) forced

886. There are … employees
who always cause trouble.
a) these
b) that
c) some
887. I am late because my alarm
clock … this morning. I'm
sorry.
a) came on
b) went off
c) turned on
888. In spite of his protests,
Steve … the athlete train two
hours a day.
a) made
b) let
c) cause
889. The man was standing …
of the diving board, showing off
his muscles.
a) by the end
b) on the end
c) in the end

890. I mustn't stop … on this
project for another two hours.
a) to work
b) working
c) to have work
891. Would you mind if I … the
windows? It's hot in here.
a) did open
b) opened
c) were opening
892. The next time you see Jane,
you … apologize.
a) ought to

b) need
c) dare to
893. If she's not back …
midnight, I'm going to phone
the police.
a) on
b) till
c) by
894. The man … his wife and
children and left them to take
care of
themselves.
a) let
b) spoilt
c) abandoned
895. The customer … on
complaining to the manager in
person.
a) insisted
b) argued
c) demanded
896. They have a great … for
that island because they spent
their
honeymoon there.
a) feeling
b) affection
c) connection
897. Like her, I hope …
something better.
a) to
b) in
c) for

898. I would go to Rome if I …
time to do it.
a) have

b) had

c) would have

899. I will play the piano but I'm a little … .

a) out of practice

b) out of use

c) out of turn

900. In this area coal is mined day … night.

a) into

b) after

c) and

901. I had to leave my family … when I went abroad to work.

a) at a loss

b) behind

c) out

902. The author had qualified as a medical doctor but later gave up the … of medicine.

a) practice

b) procedure

c) prescription

903. It was … . I had to talk quickly to keep warm.

a) fresh

b) mild

c) cold

904. Her novel was more exciting … any she has written.

a) than

b) as

c) to

905. I'm having a party on Sunday. …?

a) Will you come

b) Don't you come

c) Need you come

906. The boy … his head, wondering how he could solve the equation.

a) shaved

b) screwed

c) scratched

907. She swatted some flies on the windows and … the glass.

a) crashed

b) smashed

c) cut

908. She received a e-mail this morning … her a place at university.

a) inviting

b) offering

c) proposing

909. The Browns spent so much money that they're … debt.

a) out of

b) with

c) in

910. … you open the windows, please?

a) Need

b) Will

c) May

911. Will you … what you said? It was rude!

a) take off

b) take up

c) take back

912. Stick this … on the parcel that says "fragile".

a) label
b) sign
c) advice
913. The manager … that the people he works with are very committed.
a) talks
b) says
c) tells
914. The girl learnt to ski on a slope that was not too … .
a) high
b) tall
c) steep

915. The trade … of the company if a bee.
a) mark
b) class
c) brand
916. You will not succeed … working harder on this project.
a) although
b) if
c) without
917. The old lady will never part … her precious possessions.
a) from
b) to
c) with
918. I am grateful … you.
a) to
b) for
c) by

919. They have to work hard for money while the fat … in the city make money doing very little.
a) pack
b) fish
c) cats
920. Youngsters need all the help and … when applying for jobs.
a) incentive
b) stimulation
c) encouragement
921. I'm sorry but I haven't got … change.
a) some
b) lots
c) any
922. Volkswagen is one of the most popular … of car in Germany.
a) makes
b) brands
c) marks
923. I must … shopping tomorrow.
a) to go
b) going
c) go
924. I can't see any … to this complicated problem.
a) result
b) solution
c) reason
925. Yesterday I came … a beautiful old car.

a) across

b) over

c) down

926. I can't find my book anywhere; it has simply … .

a) missed

b) lost

c) vanished

927. Scientists have discovered a close … between smoking and cancer.

a) action

b) connection

c) union

928. He came in quietly … not to wake the children.

a) so as

b) if so

c) as if

929. I decided to … a party to celebrate my promotion.

a) offer

b) give

c) make

930. I have no doubt … the innocence of the accused.

a) over

b) on

c) about

931. Everybody … me for the incident.

a) blamed

b) arrested

c) charged

932. Tomorrow the children are going to see the works … Van Gogh.

a) from

b) of

c) with

933. I consulted my lawyer … the matter and I shall continue.

a) for

b) to

c) on

934. She didn't enjoy … at her aunt's.

a) to stay

b) staying

c) stayed

935. There are … when I have to drive for long distances.

a) times

b) a long time

c) at times

936. … by the rejections of his articles, Daniel … to submit his works to other publishers.

a) Undaunted/continued

b) Elated/planned

c) Inspired/complied

937. When Mary heard the latest bad news, she hit the … .

a) head

b) bend

c) roof

938. It has been suggested that environment is the … factor in the incidence of drug addiction.

a) logical
b) conclusive
c) predominant

939. If the door bell ... she would rush to answer it.
a) rings
b) rang
c) has rung

940. The five friends all ... for the same job.
a) applied
b) referred
c) requested

941. My laptop is out of order, which is a ... .
a) hurt
b) harm
c) nuisance

942. We decided to go ahead with the match ... the bad weather.
a) unless
b) in spite
c) despite

943. She kept the job ... the manager had threatened to sack her.
a) although
b) even
c) unless

944. It takes most people seven to ten days to ... from COVID-19.
a) cure
b) recover
c) prevent

945. The building has been left empty for five years; it will be expensive to ... the damage that has been done.
a) fix
b) repair
c) mend

946. The children were ... by the noise in the forest.
a) afraid
b) feared
c) frightened

947. No, thanks. I'm trying to ... weight.
a) lose
b) rid
c) throw

948. Is there ... at all I can do to help you?
a) someone
b) anything
c) no one

949. I'll have to wait until the mechanic ... .
a) will come
b) is coming
c) comes

950. ... you improve this project, you won't pass the exam.
a) When
b) Unless
c) If

951. We got up early this
morning … pack the car for the
journey.
a) in order to
b) so that
c) in case

952. I … that a shame!
a) calling
b) might call
c) call

953. When there are people
about a deer … for the shelter of
the forest.
a) takes
b) makes
c) seeks

954. I am anxious about the …
of the negotiations.
a) output
b) outlook
c) outcome

955. We have been
corresponding … each other for
some years.
a) with
b) to
c) by

956. When questioned about the
missing report, he firmly … that
he had
ever seen it.
a) defied
b) refused
c) denied

957. Have you ever been
introduced to …?

a) royalty
b) the royalty
c) royalties

958. Mary's rung … . I must
have said something wrong.
a) off
b) round
c) back

959. The officers set a … to
catch them.
a) trap
b) plan
c) device

960. The rise in the flat prices
… him to sell his for a large
profit.
a) achieved
b) enabled
c) managed

961. She enjoyed the dessert so
much that she accepted a second
… .
a) load
b) pile
c) helping

962. The little boy put a …
against the tree and climbed up.
a) scale
b) grade
c) ladder

963. This is one of the London's
most … hotels.
a) well-off
b) luxurious
c) rich

964. Some truck drivers expect everyone else to get … their way.
a) away from
b) off
c) out of

965. It's … long time since I last saw you.
a) such a
b) so
c) too

966. The dentist told me to open my mouth … .
a) broad
b) greatly
c) wide

967. Tom left home more than two hours ago. He … be at the office by now.
a) can
b) must
c) would

968. I … you wear the blue coat.
a) say
b) suggest
c) encourage

969. When I was in London I went on a few short day … to tourist sights.
a) travels
b) voyages
c) trips

970. The purple curtains began to … after some time in the sun.
a) fade
b) dissolve
c) melt

971. Our new colleague seems calm enough, but he has a very violent … .
a) mood
b) temper
c) stage

972. It's three years … I went to Cambridge.
a) for
b) last
c) since

973. They can only cure Mary … her illness if they operate on her.
a) of
b) on
c) in

974. I believe … taking my time to finish this project.
a) on
b) in
c) with

975. That man is often extremely rude … people.
a) for
b) with
c) to

976. You demand too much … him.
a) of
b) for
c) in

977. The branch gave … and the cat found itself suddenly on the ground.
a) in
b) way
c) back

978. Mira saw her little sister … after the dog.
a) run
b) ran
c) runs

979. If you … Harry, tell him to come and see me.
a) have met
b) meet
c) met

980. Our study … in March if we receive all feedback.
a) is published
b) published
c) will be published

981. I kept the door open by putting a … under it.
a) triangle
b) block
c) wedge

982. … from Sarah, all the employees said they would go.
a) Apart

b) Except
c) Only

983. This cloth … quite thin.
a) touches
b) feels
c) holds

984. The boy says he has got … in his stomach.
a) hurt
b) pains
c) suffering

985. The drivers are complaining that their fares are too … .
a) small
b) little
c) low

986. The terrorist … the pilot to change direction.
a) forced
b) demanded
c) made

987. As soon as the alarm rang everyone walked quickly downstairs, …
gathered in the car park.
a) while
b) then
c) before

988. She has a strong … to see her town again.
a) liking
b) feeling
c) desire

989. Don't … your drink on the table. Be careful!
a) spill
b) flood
c) flow

990. This wet weather has lasted for two weeks; … rained every single day.
a) there has

b) it has

c) there was

991. It is a long ... from Berlin to Moscow.

a) tour

b) track

c) flight

992. Do you mind not ...?

a) to smoke

b) smoke

c) smoking

993. We will have to ... sales during the coming year.

a) expand

b) increase

c) extend

994. The meeting, ... I was the guest of honour, was enjoyable.

a) by which

b) for which

c) at which

995. That's the woman ... daughter I nearly kissed when I was young.

a) whose

b) whom

c) that

996. I am thankful ... any advice you could give me.

a) about

b) on

c) for

997. We haven't accused him ... anything.

a) by

b) of

c) to

998. The spy surrendered himself ... the enemy.

a) in

b) with

c) to

999. This shows continues to ... various audiences.

a) enthrall

b) bored

c) catching

1000. The ... of supplies and equipment has hampered the progress of medical research for a cure.

a) scarcity

b) rationing

c) discontinuance

1001. In this country home ownership has ... rapidly since 1990.

a) raised

b) grown

c) enlarged

1002. Unfortunately, nobody ... that airplane crash.

a) lived

b) released

c) survived

1003. We were so late reaching the station that we ... missed the train.

a) almost

b) already

c) soon

1004. The director didn't offer her the job because of her untidy … .
a) sight
b) presence
c) appearance
1005. You … have seen them yesterday. They're on holiday.
a) mustn't
b) can't
c) needn't
1006. The mansion has been built on the … of a lake.
a) border
b) edge
c) front
1007. Her performance was …; everyone was delighted.
a) faultless
b) unmarked
c) worthless

1008. Please … your bill before you leave the shop.
a) control
b) figure
c) check
1009. I can't even make … where the road is.
a) out
b) up
c) over
1010. I found the articles rather dull; I couldn't read it … .
a) by the end
b) to the end
c) on the end

1011. She has to work hard to keep the house … and tidy.
a) smooth
b) neat
c) plain
1012. How much have you borrowed … me already? Don't you think that's enough?
a) of
b) from
c) on
1013. This coat will protect you … the cold.
a) from
b) about
c) of
1014. Spies may have a number of … names and documents.
a) false
b) artificial
c) synthetic
1015. They were … after working all day.
a) tired out
b) worn out
c) tired down
1016. If I had known about the problem, I … him to go away.
a) told

b) would tell
c) would have told
1017. You … better be careful not to miss the class.
a) would
b) had

c) should

1018. I hope you don't mind me
... so late at night. It's urgent.
a) telephone
b) telephoning
c) to telephone

1019. As cunning as a ... . This
phrase means very clever, very
smart.
a) a fox
b) a leopard
c) an owl

1020. Molecular biology is one
of the most interesting scientific
... .
a) divisions
b) disciplines
c) matters

1021. Take the bus and get ... at
Black Lake Road.
a) off
b) down
c) outside

1022. Tom's sister had a baby
daughter yesterday and she is
his first ... .
a) cousin
b) relation
c) niece

1023. Will the company be able
to ... all their difficulties?
a) overcome
b) dismiss
c) defeat

1024. There was nothing ... to
eat in the refrigerator.
a) at last

b) at all
c) at least

1025. The professor was angry
with them because they kept ...
talking.
a) up
b) up with
c) on

1026. After going to several
interviews, she ... to get a job.
a) managed
b) could
c) achieved

1027. If only he ... told the
police the truth in the first place.
a) has
b) would have
c) had

1028. A small ... of students
was waiting outside the class.
a) team
b) group
c) gang

1029. Many countries rely on
rice as the ... food.
a) capital
b) staple
c) winning

1030. Please take your place in
the ... .
a) queue
b) tail
c) file

1031. I like to sit ... the river
and fish.
a) beside

b) next

c) along

1032. The poor man fell … in front of a train.

a) in full

b) in full cry

c) full length

1033. Her professor brought her some books … art.

a) on

b) for

c) with

1034. I am thinking of looking … a new job.

a) to

b) for

c) after

1035. I've never been good … math.

a) with

b) at

c) in

1036. It's pointless … .

a) asking her for help

b) to ask help from her

c) to ask her of helping

1037. There is no need for you to shout … .

a) at your top voice

b) on top of your voice

c) at the top of your voice

1038. I … him about it for more than two weeks.

a) am asking

b) have been asking

c) asked

1039. They … their success to hard work.

a) attribute

b) aim

c) angle

1040. Prescribed treatments can … the pain but cannot … the patient.

a) palliate/cure

b) alleviate/infect

c) abate/affect

1041. When the police found my wallet, it was … .

a) vacant

b) empty

c) deserted

1042. It was a sad day when the company closed and the employees were all … .

a) paid back

b) paid up

c) paid off

1043. You will become ill … you stop working so hard.

a) until

b) unless

c) if

1044. The sooner we leave this place, the …!

a) preferable

b) better

c) ideal

1045. The weather seems to be … .

a) clearing up

b) setting up
c) wearing off
1046. After some time you get used to the people's … of life.
a) habit
b) custom
c) way
1047. I can no longer afford the cost of … two cars.
a) operating
b) running
c) managing
1048. A soldier has to learn to carry … orders as soon as they are given.
a) on
b) off
c) out
1049. Too many players refuse to … the referee's decisions.
a) accept
b) allow
c) agree
1050. It's not fair that I … always have to clean the table.
a) should

b) would
c) must
1051. She won't have any problems. She's a very self-… young lady.
a) reliable
b) confident
c) trusting

1052. This summer was so hot that the … in the woods dried up.
a) bath
b) bowl
c) pond
1053. It's over a year … I visited the medical doctor.
a) past
b) since
c) when
1054. There's an interesting pc game … in today's newspaper.
a) advertised
b) informed
c) issued
1055. The lessons usually start … 8 p.m.
a) with
b) on
c) at
1056. I though you said that you were … to be in Germany this month.
a) supposed
b) intended
c) assumed
1057. Motorway traffic was … after a terrible accident.
a) diverged
b) diverted
c) deflected
1058. She is referred to as a/an … housewife.
a) only
b) sole
c) mere

1059. I wish she … change her mind so often!
a) shouldn't
b) wouldn't
c) couldn't

1060. The famous woman lived a life thought to be … even by her contemporaries.
a) exorbitant
b) extraneous
c) extravagant

1061. When I was a child I wanted to … to play the guitar.
a) know
b) learn
c) discover

1062. I really can't make … what's happening here.
a) away
b) over
c) out

1063. Mary has put on so much weight that her clothes don't … her any more.
a) match
b) fit
c) suit

1064. It's amazing what his mother lets him … away with.
a) get
b) make
c) go

1065. Steve … to the hospital ten minutes before her birth.
a) was
b) got
c) arrived

1066. The man took the stress to write … the complete list for us.
a) out
b) through
c) off

1067. … the papers, the Prime Minister is to give a speech tomorrow.
a) Related to
b) Referring to
c) According to

1068. Clearing the weeds was a much harder … than they had imagined.
a) deed
b) service
c) task

1069. Be careful! It's a minor road and … in places.
a) bending
b) wandering
c) winding

1070. My application was … .
a) turned down
b) let down
c) put down

1071. I am fond of his novels. He is my … author.
a) favourite
b) likely
c) favoured

1072. She studied chemistry at university and … .

a) so did I
b) so I did
c) I did also
1073. Biting one's fingernails is a very bad … .
a) custom
b) habit
c) way
1074. You … be serious about that. I won't do it.
a) mustn't
b) might not
c) can't
1075. He is so keen … learning. He should be encouraged.
a) in

b) on
c) for
1076. Don't blame me … that! It's not my fault.
a) to
b) with
c) for
1077. I don't think she had … me about her problems.
a) tells
b) to tell
c) telling
1078. The judge shouted to counsel on both sides that he would … no argument.
a) hear
b) brook
c) accept

1079. The professor was … out of his job after the scandal.
a) wiped
b) eased
c) wiped
1080. He was unsure that the speech was word … .
a) perfect
b) precise
c) accurate
1081. Mike often … about his expensive car.
a) praises
b) boasts
c) prides
1082. Have you heard? Steven has got married … Susan.
a) to
b) with
c) by
1083. The boy went to bed … very ill.
a) feels
b) having felt
c) feeling

1084. Could you … me fifty dollars? I'll pay you back next Friday.
a) lend
b) take
c) borrow
1085. We hope that one day a cure for cancer will … .
a) find
b) be found
c) been found

1086. We have much pleasure in … the invitation.

a) taking

b) accepting

c) thanking

1087. Tom is a … player. He practises for three hours every morning.

a) keen

b) excited

c) impatient

1088. I had a … that something terrible was going to happen.

a) sense

b) view

c) feeling

1089. If you're trying to lose weight, you should … off fats.

a) eat

b) keep

c) go

1090. Tom decided to … a priest instead of joining the army.

a) train for

b) study for

c) become

1091. Jennifer … drive to the station every day.

a) using to

b) used to

c) had used to

1092. … hard he tries, she never wins at tennis.

a) Wherever

b) Whatever

c) However

1093. When the little boy was hit on the head, he … consciousness.

a) lost

b) fell

c) dropped

1094. The kid got a bad mark because he had … a lot of mistakes in his homework.

a) done

b) committed

c) made

1095. The student who … in his exams was expelled.

a) cheated

b) tricked

c) deceived

1096. The racing car came round the corner … full speed.

a) for

b) at

c) to

1097. I dreamt … you last night.

a) on

b) in

c) of

1098. He … .

a) set off to a stroll

b) set off on a stroll

c) set down to a stroll

1099. If I can't be back on time, she … her dinner alone.

a) has

b) will have

c) would have

1100. As black as … . This phrase means very dirty.
a) the Ace of Spades
b) ink
c) night

1101. I'm very … in this information.
a) concerned
b) interested
c) surprised

1102. Since his wife died, he has gone to … .
a) fragments
b) bits
c) pieces

1103. I hope that you have read the report and understand … it means.
a) what
b) how
c) that

1104. The crowd's … was amazing.
a) inactive
b) reaction
c) interacted

1105. Sarah met her husband … a computer dating agency.
a) out of
b) from
c) through

1106. As far as I'm …, it's all right to leave now.
a) regarded
b) consulted
c) concerned

1107. There was a serious … of cholera last year.
a) outbreak
b) fallout
c) overflow

1108. The … of the employees led to a series of troubles.
a) sending
b) dismissal
c) parting

1109. She struggled for a time before she … to free herself.
a) managed
b) achieved
c) enabled

1110. She tried to find a good excuse to … the awkward situation.
a) get over for
b) get away
c) get out of

1111. This meat isn't that good; you have to … it for a long time.
a) chew
b) bite
c) swallow

1112. I wear a seat-belt … I have an accident.
a) unless
b) if
c) in case

1113. It takes a while to … in a new house.
a) settle up
b) settle down

c) settle on

1114. More people … football than play it.

a) watch

b) look

c) stare

1115. The conductor told her to get off because she couldn't pay the … .

a) fee

b) fare

c) bill

1116. She is qualified … typing.

a) to

b) at

c) in

1117. We have to … museums and encourage legitimate investors.

a) protect

b) undermine

c) perpetuate

1118. Despite some bad reviews, his importance was not … .

a) diminished

b) distilled

c) embellished

1119. "A French window" means … .

a) a windows with no glass

b) a double glass door that opens on to a garden or balcony

c) a windows that turns out to be too small

1120. Our fortune was … at more than $2 million.

a) judged

b) guessed

c) estimated

1121. To my …, her illness proved not to be as serious as I had feared.

a) anxiety

b) eyes

c) relief

1122. You shouldn't let him treat you like that. You must stand … him.

a) up to

b) by

c) for

1123. This public clock is not as … as it should be.

a) true

b) accurate

c) strict

1124. You … stay at home for another day.

a) had better

b) can better

c) would better

1125. The two cars collided with … loud a crash it woke me.

a) so

b) very

c) such

1126. I … the stolen bike when the insurance money arrived.

a) misplaced

b) displaced

c) replaced

1127. I'm looking forward …
you again.

a) to see

b) to seeing

c) seeing

1128. This is a friendly
community and everyone …
each other very well.

a) gets on with

b) gets up to

c) gets down to

1129. Parking …!

a) stopped

b) prohibited

c) denied

1130. It's a good thing to give at
least a two week's … before
you leave.

a) time

b) leave

c) notice

1131. More often … not, it rains
here in autumn.

a) than

b) if

c) as

1132. Now they are the … of
friends.

a) most

b) best

c) nearest

1133. If … I had done it when I
had the chance!

a) just

b) then

c) only

1134. She kept the business …
for as long as possible.

a) to go

b) going

c) go

1135. This employee is very
good .. finding excuses.

a) for

b) in

c) at

1136. … any of these
documentaries before?

a) Did you see

b) Have you seen

c) Will you see

1137. Would you mind … these
plates a wipe?

a) making

b) giving

c) getting

1138. The lung transplant
operation is … complicated.

a) broadly

b) slightly

c) extremely

1139. I … be grateful if you
could let me have the details.

a) should

b) ought to

c) might

1140. Do you know … there?

a) whose

b) who's

c) whom

1141. He looks as if he … be
her brother.

a) can
b) would
c) could
1142. The little girl is as … as a mouse.
a) quiet
b) small
c) slight
1143. After her absence, she found it difficult to … up with the rest.
a) take

b) catch
c) make
1144. I got to the theatre just … to see the actors entering.
a) in time
b) on time
c) at times
1145. This job … many visits to landlords.
a) concerns
b) offers
c) involves
1146. Do you … my turning the laptop on?
a) want
b) mind
c) object
1147. Jack was not pleased about … called an idiot.
a) was
b) being
c) to be
1148. A hot lemon drink is good … a cold.

a) for
b) with
c) to
1149. I heard a … at the door.
a) lean
b) hit
c) knock
1150. The hotel is … walking distance of the sea.
a) close
b) within
c) inside
1151. The main … of this drink are wine and orange juice.
a) parts
b) ingredients
c) components

1152. Our hands smell … honey soap.
a) of
b) with
c) by
1153. I'm sure she … on 16th February.
a) hasn't come
b) don't come
c) didn't come
1154. If I see John, I … to him.
a) talk
b) would talk
c) will talk
1155. If I get tickets, I … you up.
a) will ring
b) ring
c) could ring

1156. Kate did all the work … her own.
a) by
b) on
c) for

1157. The officers arrested the … criminal.
a) famous
b) renowned
c) notorious

1158. The left faction prospers … … the right is losing ground.
a) while
b) until
c) whether

1159. The student took down … quantities of notes.
a) extended
b) detailed
c) copious

1160. Open plains are … of the geography of this country.
a) distinctive

b) specific
c) characteristic

1161. It is a good idea to see your medic for … .
a) a revision
b) a check-up
c) a control

1162. If I had known your address, I … to see you.
a) would come
b) would have come
c) came

1163. Steve has … you some flowers.
a) carried
b) lifted
c) brought

1164. She played an active … in politics.
a) part
b) scene
c) job

1165. Chip-making is a very … work.
a) skilled
b) trained
c) educated

1166. Mary … him of wanting to marry her just for money.
a) cursed
b) accused
c) blamed

1167. It was snowing very … so I took my car.
a) wet
b) badly
c) hard

1168. He was … twenty euros for parking the car illegally.
a) fined
b) punished
c) charged

1169. Do you know what time the train … to Madrid?
a) gets
b) comes
c) reaches

1170. She never turned … at the cinema.
a) out
b) up
c) in

1171. The man … to give the police any more information.
a) objected
b) refused
c) disliked

1172. Can you give me … information about it?
a) any
b) all
c) one

1173. The boy was the only person to … the crash.
a) alive
b) survive
c) cure

1174. I have always been fond … games.
a) with
b) about
c) of

1175. I heard her … to John about holiday plans.
a) talk
b) talked
c) to talk

1176. These sweaters are … by this local firm.
a) well made
b) well-knit
c) well-founded

1177. Many undergraduates think it's east to … a job once they leave university.
a) collect
b) obtain
c) apply

1178. Brian is sucking up to the manager. I guess he's … for promotion.
a) acting
b) adhering
c) angling

1179. Her poetry is rather vague and … .
a) lucid
b) opaque
c) straightforward

1180. As rich as … . This phrase means extremely rich.
a) honey
b) Croesus
c) nails

1181. I ran … the thief, but I didn't catch him.
a) over
b) after
c) near

1182. Could you … me to take back those books?
a) remind
b) remember
c) memorize

1183. The new play is worth … .
a) to see

b) to seeing
c) seeing
1184. I'm not surprised you failed. You … have worked harder.
a) must
b) would
c) should
1185. … no need to buy a car.
a) You're
b) It has
c) There's

1186. She retired early … ill-health.
a) ahead of
b) in front of
c) on account of
1187. … did I have a sore throat, I also felt quite sick.
a) Not only
b) Also
c) In addition
1188. Do you think you could … me $25?
a) let
b) lend
c) borrow
1189. He is … a lot of money in his new job.
a) having
b) earning
c) gaining
1190. She was … of stealing one of the office laptops.
a) judged
b) charged

c) accused
1191. He tried harder than …, but he failed again.
a) ever
b) never
c) better
1192. Traffic is being … because of the parade.
a) altered
b) converted
c) diverted
1193. Don't blame him … this mess.
a) to
b) for
c) at
1194. Mary often suffers … colds.
a) at

b) on
c) from
1195. My competitor ran so fast I couldn't catch up … him.
a) to
b) from
c) with
1196. She has never done any work. She lives … her mother.
a) on
b) from
c) at
1197. His reports … in its remarks on the issue.
a) pulls no punches
b) pulls no needles
c) puts no punches

1198. My car … in the street.
a) has parked
b) is parked
c) had parked
1199. It's probably that the final price will … .
a) relax
b) evolved
c) escalate
1200. When the old lady tried to walk she had a sharp … in her leg.
a) hurt
b) pain
c) cut
1201. She stood on one leg, … against the wall.
a) leaning
b) stopping
c) staying
1202. … of all of us who are here tonight, thank you.
a) In person
b) On account
c) On behalf

1203. It was a mere …; I didn't mean to hurt them!
a) chance
b) accident
c) error
1204. When I was there my money … .
a) were stolen
b) was stealing
c) was stolen

1205. … to an accident, traffic is moving extremely slowly.
a) Because
b) Since
c) Owing
1206. I need to have a short rest as I … a headache.
a) take
b) have
c) feel
1207. Ducks fly in a definite … .
a) formation
b) formula
c) figure
1208. The police are looking … the matter.
a) up to
b) in on
c) into
1209. She must be … for 80.
a) going by
b) going off
c) getting on
1210. The sky is … so we can go fishing.
a) clean
b) clear
c) open
1211. It tasted so … of lemon. I didn't like it.
a) hardly

b) strongly
c) fully
1212. We are not in the least … about his opinion.

a) concerned
b) interested
c) aware
1213. Whenever you go to the sales, you … your money.
a) miss
b) leave
c) waste
1214. Paris lies … the Seine river.
a) on
b) over
c) at
1215. At the end of the day I watch a little TV … going to bed.
a) then
b) upon
c) before
1216. She decided to … early.
a) retire
b) resign
c) retreat
1217. It's obvious to us that the manager is not responsible … this mistake.
a) for
b) of
c) about
1218. The officer's orders were perfectly … .
a) exercised
b) executed
c) applied
1219. I'm going to get a top job soon. I'm a real high … .
a) cats

b) flier
c) market
1220. The girl takes … her mother.
a) over
b) for
c) after
1221. The … thing about travelling by train is that you can sleep.
a) enjoyed
b) enjoyable
c) enjoyment
1222. I let it ring several times before I … the receiver.
a) raised up
b) picked up
c) took out
1223. I have arranged special insurance to cover medical … .
a) expenses
b) prices
c) money
1224. You will be given an intelligence … during today's interview.
a) fitting
b) proof
c) test
1225. If you hear the baby … please call me.
a) say
b) cry
c) shout
1226. In the last months, a record number of cars … .

a) have been sold
b) have sold
c) had been sold
1227. Tim thought … getting a new job for a long time.
a) at
b) on
c) about
1228. I'm a millionaire … I expect everyone in this club to be a millionaire too.
a) then

b) but
c) and
1229. I'm disgusted … your behaviour!
a) to
b) for
c) at
1230. You forgot to thank her … the present.
a) for
b) on
c) at
1231. She's not fond … dancing.
a) at
b) of
c) on
1232. I was afraid of mentioning it … him.
a) on
b) for
c) to

1233. They have a … future ahead with little comfort and food.
a) grim
b) cruel
c) fierce
1234. Sarah … me all about her new job next Friday.
a) will tell
b) told
c) tells
1235. Mike … for Germany last weekend.
a) has left
b) had left
c) left
1236. I would have bought that PC, if I … money.
a) had have
b) had had
c) have had

1237. As soon as you … to the place, call me.
a) will get
b) has got
c) get
1238. If I had more time, I … some of those studies.
a) will read
b) would read
c) had read
1239. I'd be … to go to China one day.
a) interested
b) fond
c) helpful

1240. The product is a success. We're doing a roaring … in it.
a) ship
b) deal
c) trade

1241. I shouldn't imagine there is … in this organization who can answer
that question.
a) anyone
b) no one
c) somebody

1242. Here they learn how to get … with other people.
a) away
b) along
c) across

1243. Hello. Please put me … to the marketing manager.
a) up
b) over
c) through

1244. … pleasant it is to sit here in the garden!
a) So
b) How
c) What

1245. I'm going to … my suit cleaned.
a) make

b) send
c) have

1246. I'm afraid his writing is becoming more and more … .
a) illegible
b) illiterate
c) eligible

1247. I had to … some trees so that I could extend my herbs plantation.
a) cut
b) cut down
c) cut off

1248. I … rather not go there.
a) would
b) will
c) should

1249. Thank goodness you have come …!
a) finally
b) at the end
c) at last

Set 5

1250. It was an unique car which must have belonged to a … person.
a) plentiful
b) expensive
c) wealthy

1251. I'll give him your message the … I see him.
a) minute
b) soon
c) time

1252. I had a … problem with my laptop.
a) like
b) same
c) similar

1253. She is quite stubborn, so it will be difficult to … her to go.
a) suggest
b) persuade
c) make

1254. In the city park the officer came face … face with the thief.
a) to
b) for
c) by

1255. I can't afford a laptop so we'll just have to do … one.
a) down
b) up with
c) without

1256. I am intent … passing the exam.
a) with
b) to
c) on

1257. … the evening we will meet again.
a) In
b) About
c) On

1258. When I was washing the car, the telephone … .
a) would wing
b) rings
c) rang

1259. The bank is obliged to refuse your application for an extended … .
a) estimate
b) overdraft
c) balance

1260. The delay was brought … by bad weather.
a) up
b) down
c) about

1261. Jane … the office when I arrived.
a) was leaving
b) has left
c) leaves

1262. I will do the work and then send you the … for it.
a) sum
b) note
c) bill

1263. She seems to be … of leaving the house on time. She is always late.
a) unable
b) incapable
c) unaware

1264. She would not … her boyfriend's advice.
a) follow
b) agree
c) want

1265. She has never been too friendly to her colleagues and keeps them at a … .
a) space
b) reserve
c) distance

1266. I … rather go to Spain than Russia for my holiday.
a) would

b) had

c) did

1267. Our organization is a small one with only a few … .

a) employees

b) employs

c) employers

1268. Catching this flight will give us the … to do some shopping.

a) luck

b) occasion

c) opportunity

1269. I've … had time to read the report. I can't give an opinion on it.

a) nearly

b) hardly

c) hard

1270. You … have rushed to the airport. The plane was delayed.

a) needn't

b) mustn't

c) couldn't

1271. They have helped the tourist business … .

a) no end

b) on end

c) at an end

1272. She looked embarrassed … than pleased.

a) apart

b) instead

c) rather

1273. I have been waiting for this day for years, and at … it has come.

a) the end

b) last

c) the finish

1274. This year the company made a … but next year I hope to make a small profit.

a) loss

b) lose

c) loose

1275. The old man was cruel … his dog.

a) for

b) with

c) to

1276. I expect a great deal … you, Daniel.

a) on

b) from

c) at

1277. Mary is very efficient … her work.

a) on

b) with

c) at

1278. If he … me to do it, I would do so.

a) asks

b) asked

c) has asked

1279. I don't believe that this preposterous plan is … of our consideration.

a) worthy

b) worth

c) worthless

1280. They say Mary is an excellent manager. She runs a tight … .

a) deal

b) ship

c) bargain

1281. The gun fell into the river and was … along by the fast current.

a) caught

b) swept

c) thrown

1282. There is a lot of … when fruit and vegetables are not sold because

they are scraped.

a) rot

b) ruin

c) waste

1283. Why don't you look it … the dictionary?

a) up

b) at

c) in

1284. Do I have to make that course? No, you … .

a) haven't

b) mustn't

c) needn't

1285. I had no way of making a fire so I had to eat the meat … .

a) crude

b) rude

c) raw

1286. My plane takes … at 4 p.m.

a) out

b) off

c) up

1287. The child was told to … for being rude.

a) apologize

b) excuse

c) forgive

1288. I'll have to … to you. I don't want him to hear.

a) whisper

b) shout

c) say

1289. I'll call … you at 7 o'clock.

a) up

b) for

c) in

1290. Try to write the report the way Jane … .

a) puts

b) makes

c) does

1291. The concert was so … that I almost fell asleep.

a) boring

b) bored

c) tired

1292. When he entered the room, Mike looked rather pale and in … of a shave.

a) lack

b) need

c) necessity
1293. The traffic lights … to
green.
a) removed
b) shone
c) turned
1294. There were people who
escaped … prison camps.
a) from
b) off
c) in
1295. How long have you been
working … this project?
a) to
b) in
c) at
1296. I hope she won't … his
offer.
a) have Steve up on

b) take Steve up on
c) get Steve up on
1297. After I had discussed my
plans with him, I … to work on
my project.
a) have started
b) started
c) would start
1298. Absenteeism per
employee in our company …
out at 7 days per year.
a) averages
b) acts
c) arrives
1299. The storm played … with
these houses.
a) down

b) havoc
c) along
1300. If you have a … of cards,
I can show you a trick.
a) packet
b) set
c) pack
1301. This is the … of the
laptop which was stolen.
a) detail
b) example
c) description
1302. It is … unlikely that the
new manager will agree to that.
a) highly
b) mainly
c) greatly
1303. I've grown … to the noise
of the trains.
a) familiar
b) accustomed
c) aware
1304. He … me of the first time
we met.
a) reminded
b) recalled
c) remained

1305. The noise got … as the
bike disappeared into the fog.
a) smaller
b) slighter
c) fainter
1306. … of all colleagues, I
would like to wish you a happy
retirement.
a) In place

b) On account

c) On behalf

1307. While studying, she depended … her family for money.

a) on

b) of

c) from

1308. Never before … seen such an enormous cake.

a) I had

b) had I

c) I have

1309. I wish she … her phone number before she left.

a) gave

b) would give

c) had given

1310. She always refuses … advice of any kind.

a) accepting

b) to reject

c) to accept

1311. I apologize … keeping you waiting so long.

a) for

b) from

c) with

1312. I appealed … her for help.

a) for

b) by

c) to

1313. The man is responding to treatment and will soon be cured … his illness.

a) from

b) of

c) with

1314. In the sky a … of birds was flying southward.

a) pack

b) swarm

c) flock

1315. A general manager … over all employees.

a) has ultimate authority

b) is an ultimate authority

c) is having ultimate authority

1316. It was … a hot tea that I burnt my mouth.

a) such

b) so

c) so and so

1317. I … to read this book before I found an interesting review about it.

a) had told

b) was told

c) had been told

1318. As I was … through the newspaper this morning I saw a picture of her.

a) staring

b) gazing

c) glancing

1319. Many of his remarks were derogatory and … lawsuits against him.

a) came upon

b) resulted in

c) assuaged

1320. There is no … that the new policy has been in any way disastrous.
a) indiscretion
b) indication
c) inducement

1321. When she retired from the job, the manager … Jane with a symbolic
gift.
a) offered

b) presented
c) pleased

1322. The boat was … without trace during the storm.
a) crashed
b) vanished
c) lost

1323. … she comes, don't forget to call me.
a) If
b) In case
c) That

1324. He's the …-looking man I have ever met, said Mary about me.
a) most
b) best
c) well

1325. You can always count … me.
a) in
b) by
c) on

1326. My favourite … is roast chicken.
a) eat
b) dish
c) menu

1327. At seven o'clock, the old man still had some … to do in the garden.
a) job
b) task
c) work

1328. I … dark chocolate to white chocolate.
a) prefer
b) want
c) like

1329. You can't have this toy back … you promise to be a good boy.
a) when
b) until
c) while

1330. There was so … noise that I could hardly understand anything.
a) many
b) much
c) plentiful

1331. If you want to have a cat you must be ready to look … it for some
time.
a) after
b) at
c) for

1332. She wishes she could … smoking.
a) give away

b) give from

c) give up

1333. The United States … from voting.

a) abstained

b) refused

c) rejected

1334. Don't worry. She always comes … time.

a) in

b) on

c) at

1335. My best friend confessed to me that he had been converted …another religion.

a) on

b) for

c) to

1336. You must have avoided risking …!

a) the life of your soldiers

b) the lives of your soldiers

c) your soldiers' life

1337. Before I decided to buy a plane ticket I … to wife.

a) had talked

b) talked

c) has talked

1338. I'm fed up to the back … with this pandemic.

a) ceiling

b) teeth

c) handle

1339. Given her … the manager's decision, she has no choice but to resign.

a) antipathy towards

b) pretense of

c) support for

1340. I like you because you aren't afraid to tackle … subjects.

a) concurrent

b) consecutive

c) controversial

1341. A crazy driver cut … so suddenly that I had to brake hard.

a) in

b) out

c) by

1342. If she … a little harder, her results would be better now.

a) works

b) worked

c) has worked

1343. The lights … out and we were left in darkness.

a) turned

b) put

c) went

1344. I had no … that the divorce rate was so high.

a) doubt

b) knowledge

c) idea

1345. I don't think he will … the shock of his sister's death.

a) get over

b) get through

c) get by

1346. … he is over seventy, Mr. Smith still goes jogging every day.

a) Despite

b) Unless

c) Although

1347. In today's newspaper it … that a coronavirus cure has been discovered.

a) notices

b) says

c) writes

1348. There is a large park … to the station. You will find an empty space.

a) across

b) close

c) right

1349. Seeing the room, I was … and complained to the manager about it.

a) disgusted

b) ashamed

c) disgusting

1350. … from anything else, he is always late.

a) As well

b) Except

c) Apart

1351. You should keep your dog on a … in this park.

a) lead

b) line

c) link

1352. Margaret has said that she will … the ceremony.

a) engage

b) impart

c) attend

1353. I'm not sure that this is … a good idea after all.

a) as

b) such

c) so

1354. They were unprepared … the news.

a) to

b) at

c) for

1355. The employees have embarked … a new scheme.

a) on

b) with

c) at

1356. What does this drink consist …?

a) with

b) from

c) of

1357. … I had to stand.

a) There's being no seats left

b) There being no seats left

c) There are no seats left

1358. I refused to give up work, … I'd won a big prize.

a) despite

b) however

c) even though

1359. We believe that the latest project will … expectations.

a) undermine
b) succeed
c) surpass
1360. It's distressing to see a kid … in the street.
a) begging
b) pleading
c) imploring
1361. The manager explained that he hoped to … new procedures to save time and money.
a) manufacture
b) control
c) establish
1362. Medicines should be kept out of the … of children.
a) hold
b) reach
c) grasp
1363. The manager … the employees to return to work.
a) ordered

b) insisted
c) suggested
1364. On holiday, I … always on the beach.
a) be
b) were
c) am
1365. Travelling to Moscow … air is quicker than driving.
a) by
b) on
c) over

1366. I'm not going to help you with your project and neither … Steve.
a) isn't
b) is
c) is going to
1367. … is a very good exercise, said the doctor.
a) To swim
b) A swim
c) Swimming
1368. The detective … to open a window at the back of the house.
a) managed
b) forced
c) succeeded
1369. I … going to the concert. It was marvelous.
a) hated
b) wanted
c) enjoyed
1370. She noticed the old lady … to get out of bed.
a) has tried
b) trying
c) tried
1371. Although the town had changed, much of it was still … to me.
a) common
b) relative
c) familiar

1372. If you want to change the item, make sure that you keep the … .

a) ticket
b) bill
c) notice
1373. When are they going to
sell that car? Didn't you know?
They decided
… .
a) not to
b) not to be
c) not
1374. After the officers had
questioned him for days, he
broke … and
confessed.
a) up
b) down
c) out
1375. While studying she was
financially dependent … her
husband.
a) to
b) of
c) on
1376. Luckily, I remembered …
up with diesel.
a) to fill
b) filling
c) filled
1377. I've looked … the phone
everywhere, but I can't find it.
a) at
b) on
c) for
1378. This country is well-
known for its impressive
mountainous … .
a) views

b) scenery
c) scene
1379. If they … to that event,
they would attend it.
a) were invited
b) are invited
c) will be invited

1380. I will lend you this book
collection next month if I … it.
a) am reading
b) were read
c) finish reading
1381. Our house is … at the
corner of a busy street.
a) stood
b) situated
c) stood
1382. If I were you I … go to
the doctor.
a) could
b) will
c) would
1383. The new chimney was …
than all the trees around it.
a) longer
b) taller
c) deeper
1384. The police officer … me
$10 for parking there.
a) fined
b) asked
c) demanded
1385. His mother was very …
because he was out so late that
night.
a) sorry

b) worried

c) overcome

1386. Take a toothbrush just in … .

a) time

b) order

c) case

1387. The answer … higher employment is a greater production.

a) for

b) with

c) to

1388. We meet for dinner … every Friday.

a) hourly

b) up to date

c) at the same time

1389. On the … to the woods there is a beautiful restaurant.

a) way

b) direction

c) street

1390. We don't have any … sizes in stock.

a) higher

b) larger

c) greater

1391. The patient … to listen to doctor's advice.

a) lacked

b) hindered

c) refused

1392. Children with … diseases should not be allowed to go to school.

a) infectious

b) contact

c) influential

1393. … twenty minutes of the game one player had been sent off.

a) Before

b) Inside

c) Within

1394. It happened … I was asleep.

a) while

b) during

c) for

1395. It's obvious … everyone that she's not responsible for this situation.

a) at

b) from

c) to

1396. His … for the services was a seat in the Cabinet.

a) reward

b) repayment

c) recompense

1397. The documents need … .

a) sorting out

b) sorting off

c) sorting out of

1398. I hope the project … by next month.

a) has been finished

b) had been finished

c) will have been finished

1399. I don't know the answer but I will … around.

a) attend

b) ask

c) accord

1400. I thought the way my cousin behaved was … outrageous.

a) very

b) extremely

c) quite

1401. The only way to clean this is to … it in soap and warm water.

a) polish

b) wash

c) wipe

1402. It's … to rain again today.

a) likely

b) possibly

c) probably

1403. The little girl hasn't … her shyness yet.

a) got under

b) get through

c) get over

1404. The store gave me a 10 per cent … for paying cash.

a) sale

b) discount

c) bargain

1405. My leg was very … after the wasp stung me.

a) swollen

b) wide

c) thick

1406. … I have a beer, please?

a) Must

b) Shall

c) Could

1407. They met yesterday to discuss the … at the factory.

a) closing

b) block

c) strike

1408. I was unable to warn you because my telephone was … .

a) off duty

b) out of order

c) out of work

1409. Don't … her to arrive early.

a) expect

b) judge

c) think

1410. Sometimes I can't … the professor.

a) keep at

b) keep up to

c) keep up with

1411. The car broke … on my way there so I wasn't able to be on time.

a) up

b) down

c) in

1412. He signed the agreement … the General Manager.

a) on behalf of

b) because of

c) on account of

1413. Who is going to pay … this mess?

a) on

b) in

c) for

1414. He is jealous … his older brother.
a) to
b) at
c) of

1415. She might be good … her job, but I can't rely on her.
a) at
b) in
c) on

1416. I felt considerably … after a meal and a rest.
a) renewed
b) refreshed
c) remade

1417. My eldest sister intends to take … skiing next winter.
a) up
b) to
c) away

1418. The bank … planned to escape using a plane.
a) thieves
b) robbers
c) bandits

1419. Which soldier is … this morning?
a) on call
b) on the call
c) at call

1420. Your laziness and … could result in your dismissal.
a) ambition
b) zeal
c) procrastination

1421. Tom is stubborn, so it will be difficult to ... him to go.
a) make
b) suggest
c) persuade

1422. When the time came to … the bill she left.
a) pay
b) pay out
c) pay up

1423. The film … several scenes that might upset some people.
a) admits
b) contains
c) involves

1424. My house is going to be knocked … when the new highway is built.
a) out
b) down
c) away

1425. I returned the laptop to he shop because it was … .
a) mistaken
b) wrong
c) faulty

1426. Can you come here? I … speak to you about something.
a) must
b) can
c) should

1427. I've never had to … such things before.
a) get out of
b) put up with

c) go off with

1428. I don't think I have …
eaten something like this before.
a) always
b) rarely
c) ever

1429. We all felt sorry … her.
a) with
b) for
c) about

1430. Which … choose between
these two?
a) do your rather
b) would you rather
c) did you rather

1431. Everything was …, just
like any other day.
a) normal
b) average
c) common

1432. The mechanic … me $10
for mending my bicycle.
a) asked
b) demanded
c) charged

1433. … I tell you yesterday not
to go there?
a) Hasn't
b) Didn't
c) Haven't

1434. Inflation and its upward
… is worrying.
a) bend
b) stream
c) trend

1435. I apologized for causing
so much … .
a) problem
b) trouble
c) damage

1436. I am … to come to the
meeting.
a) capable
b) excused
c) unable

1437. I suppose I can count …
you for help?
a) on
b) in
c) from

1438. We began by
experimenting … rats.
a) of
b) in
c) on

1439. I bought the land with a
… to building a new office.
a) purpose
b) goal
c) view

1440. In all … there will never
be a third World War.
a) odds
b) probability
c) certainty

1441. The defendant's wife was
present at the … .
a) court
b) hearing
c) law

1442. I don't … with your
decision. It's fine.
a) disagree
b) displease
c) dislike
1443. … I lock the door?
a) Will
b) Need
c) Shall
1444. My car was badly … in
the accident.
a) hurt
b) damaged
c) broken
1445. Come … instead of
standing on the doorstep.
a) in
b) to
c) by
1446. Everyone in the city …
about the plans for the new
road.
a) was concerned
b) took care
c) had concerned
1447. I … my friends to go
camping with me.
a) attracted
b) suggested
c) persuaded

1448. What needs …?
a) to do
b) to be done
c) to be doing
1449. I ... my family very much
when I'm away from home.

a) miss
b) lack
c) long
1450. The … age of the
population is rising.
a) medium
b) general
c) average
1451. You can't get these pills
unless you go to the doctor and
get a … .
a) receipt
b) prescription
c) recipe
1452. Driving a bike with faulty
brakes is … quite a risk.
a) taking
b) putting
c) setting
1453. The assistant apologized
and said that she didn't have any
of them …
yet.
a) in stock
b) in store
c) out of stock
1454. You … have passed that
exam. I believe you didn't work
hard
enough.
a) must
b) should
c) can
1455. Jennifer hadn't seen her
brother for twenty years and …
she
recognized him.

a) so
b) despite
c) yet

1456. You … be exhausted after that mission.
a) must
b) can
c) need

1457. These pills are round, so they're easier to … .
a) eat
b) chew
c) swallow

1458. I … myself and left the party. It was late.
a) refused
b) excused
c) thanked

1459. Do you … to go to the meeting?
a) pretend
b) attempt
c) intend

1460. I … the plumber to install an extra radiator.
a) arranged
b) got
c) intend

1461. I'm free this evening. … we go out to dinner?
a) Will
b) Shall
c) Won't

1462. The officer threw the drowning woman a lifebelt in the … of time.
a) nick
b) end
c) quick

1463. Children have to stay … school until 1 p.m.
a) with
b) on
c) at

1464. The management received a lot of … about the service.
a) information
b) advice
c) complaints

1465. It has been raining for five days … now.
a) at an end
b) on end
c) in the end

1466. The opening … of the play took place in camp.
a) stage
b) sight
c) scene

1467. I don't know what to do this Saturday. Perhaps I … at home and so some work.
a) stay
b) will stay
c) am staying

1468. When you … the Smiths, give them my best wishes.
a) will visit
b) would visit
c) visit

1469. The sign asks people …
smoke.
a) not to
b) to not
c) don't
1470. He never became the …
of the local chess club, despite
his
intelligence.
a) member
b) champion
c) winner
1471. … for Adam, we enjoyed
the play very much.
a) Except
b) Apart
c) Aside
1472. Mary is unemployed.
She'd feel much happier if she
were in … .
a) touch

b) job
c) work
1473. Five meters of this
material … at $35.
a) add up
b) fetch down
c) work out
1474. It was difficult to … a
date which was convenient for
us.
a) elect
b) arrange
c) organize
1475. There was nothing I could
do … leave the car there.

a) unless
b) but
c) instead of
1476. Did anything emerge …
your meeting?
a) from
b) on
c) of
1477. You can't rely … Steve.
He's away on holiday all the
time.
a) at
b) on
c) with
1478. The concert began … a
new instrumental song.
a) on
b) in
c) with
1479. When I realized it was
three o'clock, I stopped … a
rest.
a) having
b) have
c) had
1480. Are you … to leave?
a) thinking
b) planned
c) about

1481. The soldier … a
dangerous mission.
a) undertook
b) agreed
c) entered
1482. What a lovely suit … on!
a) have you

b) you've got

c) have you got

1483. They have just released a new graphic card, … you must buy.

a) that

b) what

c) which

1484. Because nobody admitted breaking the windows, the … class was punished.

a) all

b) whole

c) each

1485. It was a good attempt, but it didn't really come … .

a) off

b) on

c) away

1486. Your test result is poor, … you have failed.

a) because

b) therefore

c) however

1487. Would you … talking a little bit more quietly?

a) care

b) rather

c) mind

1488. The bank seems to have credited my account with $500 in … .

a) error

b) fortune

c) accident

1489. I'm sorry but I don't … you at all.

a) agree to

b) disagree to

c) agree with

1490. This wine is cheap but it is very … .

a) drinking

b) drinkable

c) drank

1491. Do you … bringing your laptop? Mine is broken.

a) mind

b) complain

c) oppose

1492. She has a … temper and often says things, which she later regrets.

a) warm

b) angry

c) quick

1493. The child says he's sorry … what he did.

a) of

b) for

c) from

1494. I'm satisfied … your project.

a) with

b) to

c) at

1495. She cannot be held responsible … other people's mistakes.

a) by

b) to

c) for

1496. I will ask him to return my book when I … him.

a) see

b) saw

c) will see

1497. My speech may have … you.

a) mistaken

b) misled

c) miscalculated

1498. What she told me was a … of lies.

a) load

b) pack

c) flock

1499. The death penalty was … two years ago in this country.

a) absolved

b) aborted

c) abolished

1500. Stop … yourself. Your work is highly valued.

a) belittling

b) interpreting

c) distinguishing

1501. Food prices have been … steadily for the last two years.

a) lifting

b) rising

c) raising

1502. I'll have to study hard, … I can pass the exam.

a) in order

b) such

c) so that

1503. You … to drink if you don't feel like it.

a) don't have

b) haven't

c) mustn't

1504. We'll play football and … we'll have a drink.

a) then

b) so

c) straight away

1505. She has to go to Berlin for the next … of her training.

a) step

b) stage

c) stand

1506. After the meeting had finished, we went … the project once again.

a) over

b) up

c) on

1507. I locked the bird in a cage to … it from getting away.

a) avoid

b) hinder

c) prevent

1508. You're … your time trying to persuade her.

a) losing

b) wasting

c) missing

1509. Out last cook was better than the … one.

a) former

b) current

c) latter

1510. I am grateful to you for being so patient … me.
a) with
b) at
c) for

1511. Do you mean to say you exchanged that performant laptop … this?
a) for
b) on
c) to

1512. The rain floods were … the poor harvest.
a) accused of
b) blamed for
c) condemned for

1513. I have so many things to get done today. …, I have to finish this boring project.
a) At top
b) At the top of
c) On top of it

1514. I don't see any … in arriving that early.
a) cause
b) aim
c) point

1515. His application was turned … by the consulate.
a) down
b) out
c) over

1516. This is a controlled environment which … concerns about the weather.
a) foster
b) necessitate
c) eliminate

1517. It is … impossible to tell the twins apart at this age.
a) virtually
b) closely
c) extremely

1518. Thomas claimed that he was the … heir to the throne.
a) due
b) rightful
c) correct

1519. This aspect in no way … from the beauty of the place.
a) protracts
b) attracts
c) detracts

1520. … no need to do it again.
a) There's
b) You're
c) It has

1521. Some colleagues only read the … lines in a newspaper.
a) top
b) head
c) main

1522. You should always check the sell … date of the products you buy.
a) by
b) in
c) off

1523. When the project was completed, the workers were paid … .

a) out

b) over

c) off

1524. The manager was good enough to … our mistakes.

a) overlook

b) overtake

c) overdo

1525. It is … when you misunderstand something.

a) singular

b) attitude

c) embarrassing

1526. Magazines are … to their door every day.

a) taken

b) delivered

c) handed

1527. She expressed her … for all the help.

a) thanking

b) gratitude

c) gratefulness

1528. In … nothing happened at the meeting.

a) short

b) quick

c) briefly

1529. The assembly gave the speaker a standing … .

a) applause

b) support

c) ovation

1530. Local politicians pretend to ignore opinion … .

a) votes

b) polls

c) numbers

1531. Start reading the story from page 20 and then go on until you … the end of the book.

a) arrive

b) touch

c) reach

1532. Make … that you check your ideas carefully.

a) definite

b) sure

c) clear

1533. The purpose of these exercises is to … your knowledge and enhance it.

a) prone

b) interpret

c) test

1534. A useful way to … your vocabulary is to read more.

a) increase

b) amass

c) gather

1535. You can also read novels so that you can see examples of … language.

a) automatic

b) axiomatic

c) idiomatic

1536. An important activity is to … your spoken language.

a) train

b) practise
c) exercise
1537. It's very good if you can
… the cost of travelling to that
country.
a) afford
b) spend
c) expend
1538. Try to … a native speaker
to talk to you. I challenge you!
a) influence
b) impress
c) persuade
1539. Play the recording and …
everything she said.
a) hold
b) repeat
c) take

1540. It won't be long before
you find yourself speaking the
language … .
a) fluently
b) frequently
c) flowingly
1541. You have to … a form
and send it to my secretary.
a) fill out
b) fill up
c) fill into
1542. We'll have to wait a little
longer because I'm sure he will
… soon.
a) turn in
b) turn down
c) turn up

1543. Last week I … that
perfume you wanted in a
boutique.
a) came up
b) came across
c) came into
1544. I have to … a new idea
that will enable me to make
more money.
a) think up
b) think about
c) think over
1545. I need to find a chemical
product that will … the weeds in
my garden.
a) keep off
b) keep down
c) keep out
1546. In spring, people feel
inclined to … their houses.
a) do over
b) do in
c) do up
1547. It will be necessary to …
making a better plan.
a) see about
b) see over
c) see into
1548. It's easy to see from the
way the forest is looking that
winter has … .
a) set out

b) set in
c) set off
1549. I will always … you
darling.

a) stand to
b) stand from
c) stand by

1550. By the way she talks and behaves it's clear that she … her mother.
a) takes after
b) takes to
c) takes back

1551. There's no need to worry. We have … of time.
a) parcels
b) bags
c) sacks

1552. The movie doesn't start at least an hour so I have time to … .
a) kill
b) murder
c) remove

1553. The station isn't far away. We have time to … .
a) save
b) store
c) spare

1554. With time on his … he is likely to get into trouble.
a) feet
b) hands
c) fingers

1555. I told her time and … not to do it.
a) often
b) already
c) again

1556. I like to get to an appointment in … time.

a) best
b) good
c) fine

1557. It's … time she learnt to cook.
a) of
b) in
c) about

1558. I'm not living here for good; just for the time … .
a) being
b) seeing
c) trying

1559. Time … ; it's difficult to believe that I've been here all day.
a) flows
b) flees
c) files

1560. Time will … whether I have made the right decision.
a) say
b) find
c) tell

1561. Our business has lost a lot of orders and is going through a … time.
a) thin
b) slender
c) poor

1562. The trains always arrive … time in this country.
a) for
b) at
c) on

1563. I think they are merely
playing … time.
a) at
b) for
c) in
1564. This company is well …
the times.
a) behind
b) across
c) under
1565. Her invention proved she
was … of her time.
a) before

b) forward
c) ahead
1566. You can tell Tom has hit
the … time because of the car
he drives.
a) high
b) large
c) big
1567. It's … time you went to
the post office.
a) quick
b) high
c) proper
1568. The artists are meant to
… time with the conductor.
a) take
b) keep
c) show
1569. If you want to grow your
business you must … with the
times.
a) move
b) hold

c) follow
1570. The parcel arrived two
weeks later and not … time.
a) after
b) for
c) before
1571. Before applying for a job
you should be sure that you
have the right
paper … .
a) qualities
b) qualifiers
c) qualifications
1572. You should work out the
… you have in mind for the
ideal employee.
a) picture
b) profile
c) sketch
1573. As soon as the … arrive
for the interview it will be your
job to show
them around.
a) candidates

b) chosen
c) appliers
1574. The company is doing an
advertising campaign with a
view to …
new staff.
a) taking
b) recruiting
c) reaching
1575. After you've read the
details of the job … your
application.

a) pursue

b) submit

c) undertake

1576. Do you expect her to …
with a cost cutting scheme?

a) come over

b) come by

c) come up

1577. You've chosen a good
industry to seek employment in
because I've
heard that jobs are … there.

a) many

b) frequent

c) plenty

1578. It can be a time …
process but it's worth in the end.

a) lasting

b) consuming

c) taking

1579. It's relevant to discuss a
candidate's … at previous jobs.

a) deeds

b) doings

c) accomplishments

1580. I can offer you a salary
that will be … with the
responsibilities.

a) equal

b) level

c) commensurate

1581. He was able to … the
cause of her headaches.

a) decide

b) diagnose

c) define

1582. It was beyond my
capability and I … the patient to
a specialist.

a) referred

b) reduced

c) returned

1583. The doctor reassured
Steve that his condition was not
… .

a) clear

b) possible

c) serious

1584. The dentist took out of
her bag an unusual … but
promised her
patient that it wouldn't hurt.

a) utensil

b) instrument

c) control

1585. The prescribed
medication has been … .

a) effective

b) effects

c) effecting

1586. If you cancel your … and
don't notify the clinic you will
be fined.

a) meeting

b) rendezvous

c) appointment

1587. A specialist had to … the
extent of her mobility.

a) assess

b) assume

c) accept

1588. The treatment has proved successful but he has to arrange to visit the doctor's … .
a) always
b) annually
c) usually
1589. It's much easier to … an illness than to cure it.
a) prevent

b) prepare
c) prefer
1590. We had to write to the previous hospital so as to obtain his … .
a) writings
b) recordings
c) records
1591. Perhaps you could start by telling me why you've … .
a) obtained for this job
b) applied for this job
c) asked for this job
1592. Steve likes working in …
.
a) the free air
b) the pure air
c) the open air
1593. Do you like the idea of an office with …?
a) air control
b) air condition
c) air conditioning
1594. I don't understand what you're … .
a) on about

b) in about
c) for about
1595. I thought this was … obvious.
a) pretty
b) mostly
c) clear
1596. To me, … obvious at all.
a) it can't be
b) it won't be
c) it isn't
1597. I think there must be a mistake. I … .
a) put it you're Mr. Smith
b) take it you're Mr. Smith
c) place it you're Mr. Smith

1598. I'm afraid it was a case of mistaken … .
a) personality
b) character
c) identity
1599. You're not after the job of police officer … .
a) I presume
b) I pretend
c) I preview
1600. I want to be a security guard … .
a) if you don't care
b) if you don't mind
c) if you don't see
1601. I am writing this e-mail to describe the … I've been having with this product.
a) incidents

b) instances

c) problems

1602. I am talking about your latest laptop … in the January catalogue.

a) deferred

b) considered

c) described

1603. I want to take … over the name itself this time.

a) issue

b) trouble

c) pains

1604. "Shrewd" to my mind suggests …, which she doesn't possess.

a) wonderful

b) excellence

c) outstanding

1605. You should have thought it was an essential … of this system.

a) require

b) requirement

c) requires

1606. Unfortunately, this doesn't … to your product.

a) concern

b) attribute

c) apply

1607. One day, the lawnmower simply … over the grass but didn't cut it.

a) walked

b) tripped

c) strode

1608. …, I was wrong about it.

a) Confessing

b) Admitted

c) Admittedly

1609. I want you to pay me … my money!

a) return

b) again

c) back

1610. I someone to come and repair my laptop at your … .

a) expense

b) expenditure

c) expending

1611. I thought it was … time I called you.

a) at

b) about

c) in

1612. She has at long last … to marry Mike.

a) concerted

b) consented

c) convened

1613. We will be able to make an … man of him.

a) honest

b) honour

c) honestly

1614. I want to ask of you a very important … .

a) favouring

b) favourite

c) favour

1615. Putting it … I am delighted!

a) easily
b) simply
c) fairly
1616. I can … you that the duties are not in any way intricate.
a) assure
b) affirm
c) assert
1617. She is an … supporter.
a) arduous
b) ardent
c) articulate
1618. Why aren't you tying the …?
a) knot
b) rope
c) string
1619. I don't understand why I have to give up my … .
a) latitude
b) scope
c) liberty
1620. I wait for your … as soon as possible.
a) recur
b) respect
c) response
1621. I would like to … this application for the job.
a) deliver
b) submit
c) return
1622. As you can see from my … C.V. I have relevant experience.
a) attached

b) appeared
c) included
1623. This is a … job for someone who has been a manager.
a) stranger
b) unusually
c) peculiar
1624. You should explain the … reason for what you've done.
a) underlying
b) undercover
c) understanding
1625. It's the job of a sales consultant to … the clients into choosing from the catalogue.
a) push
b) tempt
c) pervade
1626. I'm sure I could easily … all the requirements.
a) fulfill
b) commit
c) completed
1627. She cannot decide whether to have … fruit or tiramisu.
a) picked
b) wet
c) fresh
1628. Make sure you … the one we have most of.
a) decide
b) select
c) effect

1629. I am sure you can … your skills to the new employee.
a) transfer
b) translate
c) transverse

1630. I look forward to … from your company.
a) hear
b) hearing
c) heard

1631. We reached our … after a dramatic journey.
a) destination
b) end
c) aim

1632. She could say that she is having a wonderful time but that would be
… from the truth.
a) distant
b) long
c) far

1633. The airport had a problem because of the industrial …
taken by the
baggage handlers.
a) acts
b) action
c) acting

1634. They decided they didn't want to … my case on to the helicopter.
a) lode
b) lead
c) load

1635. Sorry! I was held … for one hour.
a) up
b) by
c) on

1636. As you can … I was tired, hungry and miserable.
a) anticipate
b) think
c) imagine

1637. When I arrived at the motel I had to … my luggage.
a) sort out
b) sort in
c) sort of

1638. She wasn't there any mote. She had simply … .
a) distorted
b) dislodged
c) disappeared

1639. My first day was spent in local shops … for gifts.
a) finding
b) searching
c) purchasing

1640. The manager greeted us … from ear to ear.
a) streaming
b) screaming
c) beaming

1641. Do you have any idea what this …?
a) means
b) tells
c) says

1642. Apparently, it is an … .
So the letters in the word are the
first letters
of a group of words.
a) addition
b) anomaly
c) acronym
1643. This acronym … the
central building.
a) stands by
b) stands for
c) stands up
1644. The soldier jumped out of
a plane 6.000 meters … the
river.
a) up
b) higher
c) above
1645. She intended to … across
the channel.
a) flee
b) flow
c) fly
1646. The pilot started early in
the morning so that he was able
to …
commercial flights.
a) avoid
b) evict
c) eject
1647. During the race my
supporters … that I reached 220
km/h.
a) attained
b) argued
c) claimed

1648. The fact remains that the
terrorist … and managed to
escape.
a) survived
b) lived
c) continued
1649. Wilma has created a new
… by beating him.
a) recorder
b) record
c) recording
1650. The … is about 30
minutes.
a) duration
b) lasting
c) during
1651. Teaching someone to fly a
plane is one of the …
experiences you can
have.
a) scariest
b) latest
c) cruelest
1652. I'm here to … you in
driving a car.
a) learn
b) instruct
c) perform
1653. Be careful when you
drive. You can end up in the … .
a) side
b) floor
c) ditch
1654. This is more … if the
partner is a member of your
family.
a) complicated

b) confused

c) confirmed

1655. The situation between you and your wife could end in … .

a) distance

b) diversion

c) divorce

1656. The secret of being a good teacher is never to lose your temper or your … .

a) brain

b) head

c) idea

1657. She might lose … of the car.

a) break

b) stop

c) control

1658. In my … none of what you've told happened.

a) case

b) example

c) instance

1659. I was proud of them because they all … the exam first time.

a) past

b) passing

c) passed

1660. The only … to me is where she is.

a) confusion

b) mystery

c) intrigue

1661. Those companies find themselves in a … situation.

a) precarious

b) pertinent

c) pretentious

1662. Whenever there is a meeting between them rumours … .

a) abut

b) about

c) abound

1663. They were judged for … the documents.

a) mistaking

b) misfiring

c) mishandling

1664. We want to … the concerns of our borrowers.

a) assert

b) assuage

c) assent

1665. Negotiations will eventually be … .

a) retaken

b) resumed

c) returned

1666. The government tries to convince everyone that it is … of all people.

a) supported

b) supportive

c) supporting

1667. Measures are due to come into … on Friday.

a) force

b) law

c) forcing

1668. Do you know when these laws will be …?

a) rating

b) ratified

c) rated

1669. This is very disappointing for the … car buyer.

a) would-see

b) would-go

c) would-be

1670. I have nothing of … to report.

a) notice

b) noted

c) note

1671. Suppose an … public figure attacked by press and public.

a) embattled

b) engrossed

c) empowered

1672. Any arguments he put up were regarded as a … .

a) cloud

b) fog

c) smokescreen

1673. Her protestations of innocence were wearing a bit …

.

a) bare

b) thin

c) scarce

1674. Police forces were determined to … this kind of crime.

a) curb

b) manage

c) restrain

1675. This media trust was … to make publicity about the candidate.

a) picked

b) proposed

c) prompted

1676. Mary spent a lot of time … the press on this subject.

a) briefing

b) training

c) showing

1677. Views … from utter conviction that she was guilty to wild support for her innocence.

a) started

b) ranged

c) began

1678. Even his supporters were beginning to … him.

a) despair

b) destroy

c) desert

1679. New evidence came to … proving she was innocent.

a) light

b) see

c) show

1680. The incident … everything he did for the rest of his life.

a) overlook

b) overcome

c) overshadowed

1681. Such a piece of information cannot be released into the public … .
a) domain
b) domestic
c) dominion

1682. They run the risk of facing a … if they break the official secrets act.
a) back store
b) back strike
c) backlash

1683. There is a … inquiry into specific information.
a) high profile
b) high brow
c) high drama

1684. The more you try to conceal information about an event, the more it fuels … about it.
a) spectacle
b) speculation
c) speculative

1685. You will get … by authorities if you dare reveal this report.
a) rave
b) savaged
c) wild

1686. The officer will … what can be disclosed.
a) sign
b) seal
c) signal

1687. Once the disclosure is … it's her job to analyze the facts.
a) hightailed
b) heightened
c) highlighted

1688. The public can see through the … of a weak argument.
a) clarity
b) clearness
c) transparency

1689. This is likely to … a threat to the safety of the community.
a) start
b) pose
c) place

1690. This small country is a … for troublemakers.
a) heaven
b) location
c) port

1691. Today the government is … plans for a new highway.
a) unveiling
b) opening
c) showing

1692. The plan is about trying to … stealing in the country.
a) kill
b) curb
c) confuse

1693. The new conference system will be … next academic year.
a) introduced

b) welcomed
c) enforced
1694. They should be taught to respect other people's property and … .
a) added
b) additions
c) belongings
1695. She will have to stand up in front of her colleagues and … to being a
thief.
a) confess
b) conduce
c) conform
1696. The … said the Prime Minister was sick.
a) spoken person
b) spokesperson
c) speaking person
1697. Last month we had to give an important address to an international …
.
a) assembled
b) assembly
c) assembling
1698. … of the speech she told funny stories.
a) In case
b) Intend
c) Instead
1699. The audience didn't see the funny … of her stories.
a) edge
b) part

c) line
1700. The presenter cannot continue with the news because someone has …
the next page.
a) misread
b) mistaken
c) misappropriated

Second set of items
1701. I take my hat … to the new manager for avoiding bankruptcy.
a) to
b) off
c) on
1702. She's not thinking straight. She's talking … her hat.
a) at
b) under
c) up
1703. This is a society wedding where men wear … hats and tails.
a) tall
b) full
c) long
1704. I'd like you to keep this information … your hat.
a) under
b) by
c) over
1705. She decided to throw her hat in the … and become a candidate.
a) circle

b) ring

c) middle

1706. If he wins I'll … my hat.

a) eat

b) consume

c) bite

1707. Steve changes his mind at the … of a hat.

a) jump

b) fall

c) drop

1708. That suit is … hat now.

a) gone

b) late

c) old

1709. I think it would be nice to … round the hat for him.

a) offer

b) hand

c) place

1710. There are so many responsibilities involved that she has to … several hats.

a) wear

b) take

c) put

1711. A salesperson should … potential customers of the usefulness of a product.

a) consider

b) confirm

c) convince

1712. You must believe in the product and be … enough to promote it.

a) included

b) indebted

c) inspired

1713. A … customer will return to the same firm and buy again.

a) satisfied

b) interested

c) encouraged

1714. That style of dress was once considered to be a … .

a) fuss

b) fad

c) fun

1715. We need to … a new product this year.

a) market

b) muster

c) maintain

1716. They watch the supermarkets … for the same clientele.

a) contrasting

b) confusing

c) competing

1717. Weekly meetings were not considered to be … enough.

a) produced

b) productive

c) products

1718. She is able to … facts and figures quickly.

a) consumer

b) consume

c) consuming

1719. On this website customers can … different prices for the same article.
a) continue
b) confer
c) compare

1720. If you want to keep … with the latest developments you have to read a lot.
a) current
b) currant
c) currents

1721. … every student passed the exam.
a) Near to
b) Next to
c) Nearly

1722. I can look back on my career with great … .
a) satisfied
b) satisfaction
c) satisfactory

1723. The captain, as well as the passengers, … frightened.
a) been
b) were
c) was

1724. Both of these girls … married.
a) are
b) have
c) has

1725. Each learner of a foreign language … a good dictionary.
a) need

b) is
c) needs

1726. Money, nor fame … brought happiness to everybody.
a) has
b) have
c) is

1727. I … at this university before I became an interpreter.
a) taught
b) had taught
c) were taught

1728. The salary of a truck driver is higher … .
a) than a teacher
b) than that of a teacher
c) to compare as a teacher

1729. Professionals expect you to call them when it is necessary … an appointment.
a) cancel
b) to cancel
c) canceled

1730. I have chosen this laptop because of its operation simplicity … its capacity to store information.
a) the same as
b) the same
c) as well as

1731. Many embarrassing situations occur … a misunderstanding.
a) for
b) because

c) because of

1732. This is an extremely cold planet and … .

a) so is Uranus

b) so does Neptune

c) so has Uranus

1733. … when gold was discovered in this area.

a) Because in 1850

b) It was in 1850

c) In 1850 it was

1734. This job has no … .

a) prospector

b) prospects

c) prospective

1735. Frost occurs in valleys … on adjacent hills.

a) more frequently than

b) as frequently than

c) frequently than

1736. The mountain can be … from more than 200 kilometers away.

a) see

b) saw

c) seen

1737. I'd like you … her family.

a) to meet

b) meet

c) meeting

1738. Mr. Smith along with his friends … arriving here tonight.

a) are

b) will

c) were

1739. You must listen very … in order to understand it.

a) care

b) careful

c) carefully

1740. Cold objects emit … hot ones.

a) fewer than infrared rays as

b) fewer infrared rays than

c) as fewer infrared rays

1741. Gunpowder … a mixture of potassium nitrate, charcoal and sulfur.

a) were

b) was

c) is

1742. This city has played a vital role in the industrial … .

a) developing

b) develop

c) development

1743. They … forced to make smaller cars to compete in the market.

a) will

b) are

c) should

1744. Jennifer has … the conditions for entry.

a) satisfied

b) satisfaction

c) satisfactory

1745. The person … was recommended by the manager to replace him is Marry.

a) whose
b) who
c) which
1746. His fame rested on the breadth of his range, which was … any other
tenor.
a) greater than that of
b) as large as
c) more greater
1747. Words are constantly being invented … new objects and concepts.
a) describe
b) describing
c) to describe
1748. You can't … to learn a foreign language in a month.
a) expect
b) expectant
c) expected
1749. … rain or snow there are always fans at these football games.
a) In spite with
b) Despite of
c) Despite

1750. The prices are … high in urban areas that I can't afford a house.
a) as
b) so as
c) so
1751. To see the church and … pictures of it are two reasons for visiting

this city.
a) taken
b) to take
c) taking
1752. I can't see the … of sitting there all day.
a) attract
b) attractive
c) attractiveness
1753. This product is equal … to none.
a) as
b) to
c) with
1754. These bricks are much harder … that are dried in the sun.
a) those
b) ones
c) than those
1755. Since infection can cause … fever … pain, you must avoid it.
a) both/as well as
b) both/with
c) both/and
1756. Schizophrenia … by genetic predisposition, stress, drugs or infections.
a) may be triggered
b) may triggered
c) may trigger
1757. They asked us, Olivia and … about it.
a) I
b) me

c) my

1758. She was guilty … racial discrimination.
a) of
b) with
c) for

1759. It is important … it on because it is an expensive coat.
a) of trying
b) try
c) to try

1760. What happened in this city … a reaction from outskirts workers.
a) were
b) was
c) is

1761. The result of the drug experiment was … .
a) satisfactory
b) satisfied
c) satisfaction

1762. A number of … submitted their manuscripts under pseudonyms.
a) novel
b) novelists
c) novels

1763. I require that the secretary … responsible for writing all reports.
a) was
b) been
c) be

1764. Although a medical doctor may be able to diagnose a problem … he may not be able to find a treatment.
a) perfect
b) perfectly
c) perfection

1765. This law is purely … .
a) prospective
b) prospect
c) prospector

1766. The number of days in a week … seven.
a) is
b) are
c) needs

1767. The nurses will not … you donate blood if you have just had a cold.
a) want
b) need
c) let

1768. This item has two parts: one made up of dust … made up of electrically charged particles.
a) the other
b) one another
c) each other

1769. There were over fifty boats on the river, … were quire luxurious.
a) many of them
b) many of which
c) many that

1770. Columbus thought that he … the East Indies.
a) had reached
b) has reached
c) had been reached
1771. Most university leavers have the … to go to work.
a) keen
b) keenly
c) keenness
1772. It's good that … objections to the plan haven't happened.
a) expected
b) expectant
c) expect
1773. Many students are afraid … failing an exam.
a) about
b) of
c) to
1774. It is important that the office … your registration.
a) confirms
b) will confirm
c) need confirm

1775. Please state your name, age and … .
a) occupy
b) occupied
c) occupation
1776. Deserts are often formed … surrounding mountain ranges.
a) because
b) in spite of

c) so
1777. … that they settled in this area.
a) It was in 1000
b) That in 1000
c) In 1000 that it was
1778. Staying in a hotel costs … renting a room.
a) twice more than
b) twice as much as
c) as much twice as
1779. When friends insist on … expensive gifts it makes most people uncomfortable.
a) them to accept
b) they accept
c) their accepting
1780. Do any of these designs … you?
a) attractive
b) attract
c) attractively
1781. These flowers usually smell … .
a) sweet
b) sweetly
c) sweetness
1782. Having … the topic for my essay, I began working on it.
a) chose
b) chosen
c) choose
1783. She is considered the … portrait painter.
a) greeting

b) greatest

c) grander

1784. The detonator for a nuclear device may be made of … .

a) two equipment

b) two equipment pieces

c) two pieces of equipment

1785. An equilateral triangle is a triangle … .

a) that has three sides of equal length

b) it has three sides equally long

c) that have three sides of equal length

1786. Some students are confused … about these exams.

a) about

b) with

c) in

1787. … are found on the surface of the moon.

a) Craters and waterless seas that

b) Craters and waterless seas

c) Since craters and waterless seas

1788. Her … made her cry.

a) fearful

b) fearless

c) fearfulness

1789. … two waves pass a point simultaneously they will have no effect.

a) That

b) If

c) So that

1790. A child in the first grade tends to have … other children in the class.

a) the old like

b) the same as

c) the same age as

1791. I'm very … to succeed.

a) determine

b) determinant

c) determined

1792. This structure is so strong … difficult for anyone to penetrate it.

a) that it is

b) that is

c) and is

1793. I hoped … the game.

a) Brian to win

b) Brian's win

c) Brian would win

1794. This item is … that it's completely damaged.

a) oldest

b) so old

c) such an old

1795. Many Americans … a bowl of cereals every day.

a) are used to eating

b) used to eating

c) use to eat

1796. I will keep you safe … the crowd.

a) on

b) of

c) from

1797. The best form of treatment ... mass inoculation.
a) it is
b) is
c) are
1798. I became bored ... this work.
a) in
b) with
c) of
1799. We don't require that the students ... a thesis in order to graduate.
a) write
b) will write
c) would write
1800. The oxygen of this planet is not ... to support life.
a) too sufficient

b) sufficient
c) much sufficient
1801. He supported himself by ... taxicabs.
a) driving
b) drive
c) to drive
1802. The kid viewed the ... of a week alone without much enthusiasm.
a) prospective
b) prospector
c) prospects
1803. If you have a family history of heart disease you should make yearly appointments with ... doctor.

a) his
b) your
c) yourself
1804. Support for research programs ... much less than it was last year.
a) is
b) will
c) being
1805. Here, apartments cost more to rent than they ... in other smaller cities.
a) did
b) will
c) do
1806. This model not only saves time but also ... .
a) to save energy
b) saves energy
c) save energy
1807. The government requires that a census be taken every five years ... accurate statistics may be compiled.
a) so that
b) such
c) such that
1808. The main ... of economics success is out ability to forecast indicators.

a) determinant
b) determine
c) determined

1809. Who is responsible … the project?
a) to
b) with
c) for
1810. TV has little … for me.
a) attract
b) attraction
c) attractive
1811. The average life expectancy for people born during that year … 68 years.
a) have been
b) was
c) are
1812. A … mountaineer reached the top of the mountain last week.
a) fearless
b) fearful
c) fearfulness
1813. The flag is … in the morning and taken down at night.
a) risen
b) raised
c) raise
1814. One way to inform the public about this problem is through … programs on TV.
a) industrial
b) agricultural
c) educational
1815. That book wasn't very …
.
a) well written
b) well typed
c) good written
1816. These species can be divided into three groups, two of which …
extinct.

a) is
b) are
c) was
1817. Without alphabetical order dictionaries would be … to use.
a) possible
b) impossible
c) possibility
1818. I was shocked … the news of the accident.
a) from
b) being
c) with
1819. He was awarded the Nobel … for peace.
a) award
b) gift
c) prize
1820. The extent to which an individual is a product of either heredity or environment … .
a) cannot be proved
b) cannot proved
c) cannot prove
1821. Every country … a national flag.
a) is

b) have

c) has

1822. Optical fibers ... to deliver laser light.

a) can also use

b) can used

c) can also be used

1823. This project may or may not have been ... by her.

a) make

b) made

c) making

1824. Laptops for sale at ... prices.

a) attractive

b) attraction

c) attractively

1825. Your mistakes are similar ... his.

a) by

b) to

c) with

1826. A team of engineers is often ... .

a) working on one project

b) no one project work

c) work on one project

1827. A vacuum will neither conduct hear nor ... .

a) sound waves are transmitted

b) transmitting sound waves

c) transmit sound waves

1828. To relieve pain cause by burns ... .

a) take immediate steps

b) to take immediate steps

c) taking immediate steps

1829. All cereal grains ... grow on the prairies and plains of this country.

a) excepting rice

b) expect the rice

c) but rice

1830. They are freshmen , ... whom come from countryside.

a) most

b) most of

c) most of the

1831. ... food is as nutritious for a baby as its mother's milk.

a) No

b) Not

c) None

1832. Civil engineers had better ... to use steel supports in this structure.

a) plans

b) to plan

c) plan

1833. Several criminals escaped ... prison yesterday.

a) out

b) for

c) from

1834. The exam results could ... your career.

a) determined

b) determine

c) determination

1835. If the oxygen supply ... replenished by plants, we would soon be

dead.
a) wasn't
b) weren't
c) hadn't been
1836. I used to earn … money.
a) many
b) lot
c) a lot of
1837. The legal implications of euthanasia are so controversial … it is
illegal in most countries.
a) as
b) that
c) since
1838. Understanding lightning might help us … life itself.
a) understand
b) understood
c) to understanding
1839. These species are particularly … because of their unusual structures.
a) interest
b) interested
c) interesting
1840. … poetry is enjoyable when it is read aloud.
a) Most
b) Almost
c) Many

1841. It is essential that cancer … diagnosed early.
a) was
b) is
c) be

1842. Products in this shop are … arranged.
a) attract
b) attraction
c) attractively
1843. The battlefield was a … sight.
a) fearsome
b) fear
c) fearless
1844. This plant supports itself even when the original supporting tree is … longer alive.
a) not
b) no
c) any more
1845. Parents have great … for their children's future.
a) expectant
b) expects
c) expectancies
1846. The consistency of this substance and that of glue … .
a) the same
b) are similar
c) they are alike
1847. The appliances in most homes use alternating current … .
a) instead direct current
b) for direct current instead
c) instead of direct current
1848. When Marry decided to run for another term, the opposition said she was … .

a) so old
b) too old
c) oldest

1849. This process results in an accumulation of … in porous rocks.
a) the oil
b) oil
c) oils

1850. We discussed the matter calmly and … .
a) reasonably
b) reason
c) reasoned

1851. I saw a sample … their work and it was impressing.
a) on
b) in
c) of

Set 6

1852. It requires that two pieces of identification … .
a) presented
b) must present
c) be presented

1853. Nerve impulses … to the brain.
a) sending sensations
b) send sensations
c) be send sensations

1854. More than one hundred separate nation … are included.
a) counties
b) states
c) continents

1855. … owe much of their success to migration.
a) The bird
b) That birds
c) Birds

1856. I believe … things openly.
a) of discussing
b) for discussing
c) in discussing

1857. People work for many reasons … .
a) besides money
b) beside money
c) money beside

1858. Seals can … .
a) keeps themselves warm
b) keep them warm
c) keep their warm

1859. Liquids flow freely from a container because they have … .
a) no definite shape
b) none definite shape
c) not definite shape

1860. One of hers … was stolen.
a) greatest work
b) greatest works
c) the greatest work

1861. They hoped that the field of transplantation … .
a) would progress
b) had progressed
c) progressing

1862. We can do this … .

a) efficient more
b) more efficiently
c) most efficient
1863. We are amenable …
discipline.
a) at
b) with
c) to
1864. … unknown quantities is
the task of algebra.
a) Find
b) To found
c) Finding
1865. I read two volumes but
neither book … interesting.
a) was
b) were
c) had been

1866. The path of the sun
around the heavens … .
a) is known as the ecliptic
b) known as the ecliptic
c) knowing as the ecliptic
1867. This table is already … .
a) occupy
b) occupied
c) occupation
1868. A man … a woman in so
many respects.
a) differs
b) different
c) differs from
1869. The … I'm late is that I
missed the flight.
a) reasoned
b) reason

c) reasonable
1870. … have used franchising
to extend their sales.
a) Chains restaurants
b) Chain restaurant
c) Chain restaurants
1871. A baby is under parental
… .
a) guide
b) guidance
c) guiding
1872. Uranus is … to be seen on
a clear night.
a) bright enough
b) brightly enough
c) enough brightly
1873. Before penicillin was
discovered, many people had
died … .
a) infected with bacteria
b) from infected bacteria
c) from simple bacterial
infections
1874. That most natural time
units are not simple multiples of
each other …
in constructing a calendar.
a) is a primary problem

b) is the primary problem
c) it is a primary problem
1875. The plow is being
displaced by new techniques
that promise more
crops.
a) abundant
b) scarce

c) sparse

1876. 60 percent of the budget is used … the development.

a) supporting

b) supportive

c) to support

1877. The bacteria in milk is destroyed when … to at least 65 Celsius

degrees.

a) it is heated

b) it will be heated

c) may be heated

1878. In order for people who spoke different languages to engage in trade

… they developed a simplified language.

a) with each another

b) with each the other

c) with each other

1879. There are two … :

permanent magnets and electromagnets.

a) kind of magnets

b) kinds of magnets

c) kind magnets

1880. You can't rely … a hotel room.

a) on finding

b) in finding

c) of finding

1881. … doctors do not have a personal physician.

a) A large number

b) A large number of

c) Large number of

1882. There are many beautifully preserved historic buildings … .

a) in this cities

b) in these city

c) in this city

1883. The prime rate is the rate of interest that a bank will charge when it

… money.

a) lends

b) borrows

c) borrowed

1884. The area where a microchip is manufactured must be the …

environment possible.

a) cleaner

b) cleanest

c) most cleanest

1885. Mathematics is … that it is a prerequisite for studying every scientific

discipline.

a) such important field

b) so an important field

c) such an important field

1886. Studies of this kind are unreliable because there … so many

variables.

a) are being

b) are

c) may being

1887. I knew I could rely … them to get the job done.

a) on

b) with

c) in

1888. He founded a military base there and … a fort two years later.

a) had built

b) built

c) might had built

1889. Natural gas often occurs together … petroleum.

a) in

b) along

c) with

1890. There is no limit to the diversity to be … in the people's cultures.

a) found

b) finding

c) find

1891. They were very proud of his …

a) fearlessness

b) fearful

c) fearless

1892. They spend most of … time playing.

a) theirs

b) they're

c) their

1893. They were called Americas according to the … at the time.

a) belief

b) believe

c) believed

1894. … missile was used in the war between America and Iraq.

a) Guided

b) Guidance

c) Guide

1895. This is a device with a sealed metal chamber designed … the changes in the pressure.

a) read

b) to read

c) to reading

1896. Cotton fiber, like other fibers, … composed of cellulose.

a) is

b) are

c) has

1897. All life depends … chemical reactions with oxygen to produce energy.

a) to

b) with

c) on

1898. Modern presidents have far … responsibilities than their predecessors did.

a) greater

b) more great

c) most great

1899. They put a well-… case for increasing the fees.

a) reason

b) reasoned

c) reasonable

1900. Grasshoppers can produce sounds by ... their hind legs against heir wings.

a) rub

b) rubbed

c) rubbing

1901. She was not only a poet but ... a successful businesswoman.

a) so well

b) also

c) so

1902. It is an ... advice organization.

a) occupy

b) occupation

c) occupational

1903. This is a powerful ... of both light and shade.

a) useful

b) useless

c) use

1904. I've succeeded ... hold of the telephone number.

a) in getting

b) on getting

c) upon getting

1905. Application fees are waived in cases of economic ... like this pandemic.

a) hard

b) hardship

c) hardware

1906. The elevator ... and I had to walk up to ninth floor.

a) stopped functioning

b) exploded

c) spread

1907. Three boys ... me and demanded some money.

a) came down to

b) came up to

c) came on to

1908. The secretaries report to the president, give him advice and ... him make decisions.

a) to help

b) helping

c) help

1909. The jury isn't satisfied ... the answer.

a) with

b) to

c) of

1910. The satellite ... in a fixed position from which it sends radio signals.

a) remain

b) remains

c) remaining

1911. The examiner must have been pleased ... my performance.

a) with

b) for

c) in

1912. Being grateful means ...

a) fed up with

b) proud of

c) thankful for

1913. That's the … I received!

a) inform

b) information

c) informs

1914. Mary said she … this race.

a) wants to win

b) want to win

c) wanted to win

1915. The thief was … to two years imprisonment.

a) given

b) allowed

c) sentenced

1916. There are some people that think the camel … water in its hump.

a) stores

b) stored

c) has stored

1917. Instead of … about the good news, she seemed quite upset.

a) being excited

b) exciting

c) exciting

1918. Women … to live longer than men.

a) tendency

b) tend

c) tending

1919. I finally finished … at 8 p.m.

a) cooking

b) cooked

c) being cooking

1920. Would you mind not … the radio?

a) turn on

b) turned on

c) turning on

1921. She hoped … to join the private club.

a) inviting

b) to be invited

c) being invited

1922. Many students tend … interest in literature.

a) to lose

b) lose

c) losing

1923. They complained … any sleep.

a) not getting

b) not get

c) about not getting

1924. Mary's perfectly … in her demands.

a) reason

b) reasonable

c) reasoned

1925. It's a plan worth … .

a) doing

b) being done

c) to be done

1926. There are many ways … that.

a) doing

b) to do

c) to be done

1927. Laptop prices continue to show an upward … .
a) tendency
b) tend
c) tendentious

1928. The quality of this photograph is not different … that one.
a) with
b) for
c) from

1929. You should get into the habit of … the news.
a) reading
b) read
c) being read

1930. It's important that you learn how … this tool.
a) using
b) used
c) to use

1931. They will never agree the effects of … the world's first atomic bomb
… the World War.
a) drop/to end

b) dropping/to end
c) drop/end

1932. She was unable to speak due to … .
a) fear
b) fearful
c) fearsome

1933. I felt ashamed … his action.
a) to

b) for
c) of

1934. A good schoolboy must know … .
a) how to study effectively
b) to be a good student
c) to study hard

1935. Radioactivity may … future generations.
a) develop
b) create
c) affect

1936. The pilot agreed to land only … the terrorist threatened to kill a passenger.
a) that
b) when
c) which

1937. I was delighted … you've won the first prize.
a) when
b) why
c) that

1938. You are responsible … this error.
a) to
b) on
c) for

1939. They were … to prevent it.
a) powerless
b) power
c) powering

1940. Either my plan or yours … wrong.

a) are

b) is

c) has

1941. She returned the money to the man who … it.

a) had lost

b) loose

c) have lost

1942. The movie didn't … to my expectations.

a) equally

b) give

c) equal

1943. There are two categories … answers you can choose from.

a) about

b) with

c) of

1944. Kids with … faces were waiting for the show to start.

a) expect

b) expectant

c) expected

1945. I want to get … of these items.

a) pant

b) rid

c) chance

1946. These are just some of the ways to increase your … awareness.

a) culture

b) culturally

c) cultural

1947. The guests … dinner by the time I got home.

a) finish

b) finished

c) had finished

1948. Humans express their thoughts by means … word.

a) of

b) in

c) to

1949. The witnesses' accounts were not … with the facts.

a) reliable

b) consistent

c) match

1950. It was not until she had arrived home … remembered her mistake.

a) when she

b) and she

c) that she

1951. Is this car capable … us all the way home?

a) of getting

b) in getting

c) for getting

1952. No one was aware … she had gone.

a) where that

b) of where

c) the place

1953. Mike didn't do well in the class because … .

a) he failed to study

b) he studied bad

c) he was a badly student

1954. They spoke during the … .

a) meet

b) meeting

c) met

1955. You should ask your mentor how to solve this problem … you can't find a solution.

a) because of

b) as long as

c) since

1956. Mrs. Brown will substitute … the history teacher.

a) at

b) on

c) for

1957. … you select reverse hear the car goes backwards.

a) If

b) Unless

c) In spite of

1958. … I get angry I try to take some deep breaths.

a) Until

b) Whenever

c) Therefore

1959. A … accident happened yesterday.

a) fearless

b) fearful

c) fearlessness

1960. A small animal needs camouflage to hide itself … its enemies cannot find it.

a) so

b) due to

c) so that

1961. I wouldn't give a … to a young child as a gift.

a) flowers

b) money

c) basket of fruit

1962. Did they … to that beach when they were in Greece?

a) went

b) go

c) to go

1963. Do you think … is a good gift for her?

a) money

b) cookies

c) gloves

1964. Her parents gave her some beautiful … when she finished university.

a) necklace

b) jewelry

c) ring

1965. Theoretically, a comedy is a movie … you laugh.

a) who makes

b) that makes

c) in that makes

1966. If you cross your fingers they … that way.

a) stayed

b) won't stay

c) stayed

1967. He's good … jokes.

a) for telling

b) in telling

c) at telling

1968. I investigate the
possibility … spending a week
at the seashore.
a) of
b) on
c) for

1969. What will happen if you
… to loud music?
a) listen
b) listened
c) listening

1970. Huge areas have been …
because of the nuclear incident.
a) restrained
b) evacuated
c) transmitted

1971. Tom was a very
unpopular man in that small
village. Nobody … him.
a) liked
b) hated
c) quarreled

1972. The country was in total
… after all those terrorist
attacks.
a) confusian
b) confusment
c) confusion

1973. In order to make a good
… at an interview, you should
prepare well.
a) impression
b) impressive
c) impressing

1974. When I go fishing for all
day I like to get an early … .

a) start
b) beginning
c) leaving

1975. If these TV series weren't
violent, they would not … in
increased
violence.
a) contribute
b) give
c) result

1976. … of the passengers were
reading.
a) Almost
b) Most
c) Mostly

1977. I was travelling home to
… Christmas with my family.
a) last
b) keep
c) spend

1978. Designing … for actors
requires a lot of creativity.
a) scripts
b) costumes
c) set

1979. The men were found
guilty … fraud.
a) with
b) by
c) of

1980. Every house in this
neighbour … the same.
a) is
b) has
c) were

1981. What is Mary so nervous
…?

a) about
b) for
c) to
1982. Such … statements are likely to provoke opposition.
a) tendency

b) tend
c) tendentious
1983. Mike was found guilty … from his employer.
a) of stealing
b) in stealing
c) for stealing
1984. We went on our work with an air of … .
a) determine
b) determined
c) determination
1985. He … that if we started at dawn we would be there by night.
a) reason
b) reasoned
c) reasonable
1986. The patient is getting on … .
a) satisfied
b) satisfaction
c) satisfactorily
1987. My cousin and my sister … engineers.
a) have
b) are
c) was
1988. She answered that question … .

a) fearfully
b) fearful
c) fearless
1989. This planet, … is so big, is the fifth planet from the sun.
a) who
b) whom
c) which
1990. The students took part in school's activities … .
a) keen
b) keener
c) keenly

1991. She went to meet me with an air of … .
a) expectancy
b) expectant
c) expect
1992. The telephone … by the time I was born.
a) had already been invent
b) had already been invented
c) had already finished
1993. The army … the enemy's capital.
a) occupation
b) occupied
c) occupational
1994. We objected … to wait so long.
a) with having
b) to having
c) for having
1995. Is Friday the day … not Thursday.
a) when you arrived

b) you'll arrive then

c) on that you arrive

1996. The drought … occurred last year ruined the crops.

a) that is

b) which it

c) that

1997. This city … the Ghost City attracts many tourists every year.

a) known as

b) is knows as

c) that is known

1998. The shopping mall is advertised as a place … you can find anything.

a) which

b) where

c) in where

1999. She is marrying to a man … .

a) that she hardly knows him

b) whom she hardly knows

c) whose she hardly knows

2000. Men who exercise regularly have greater physical endurance than those … .

a) who doesn't

b) who don't

c) which don't

2001. Is this the city to … you want the package sent?

a) where

b) that

c) which

2002. His latest book is about the people from a small island … for three years.

a) among whom he lived

b) that he lived

c) that he lived among them

2003. By the time he arrived to help, we … moving the furniture.

a) already finished

b) had already finished

c) has already finished

2004. It was hot when I got home, so I … the ventilation system.

a) turned on

b) turn on

c) would turn on

2005. I engaged a … to show me the way.

a) guided

b) guidance

c) guide

2006. By the time the fire fighters arrived, the building … to the ground.

a) burned

b) had burned

c) was burned

2007. I … so much on one outfit.

a) have never spent

b) never have spent

c) was never spent

2008. Two days ago a hornet … me under my arm.
a) was stung
b) had stung
c) stung

2009. Our girl is keen … to art college.
a) in going
b) on going
c) at going

2010. If any of your questions are still … you can call me.
a) unanswered
b) inasnwered
c) answered

2011. I was not happy with the plans … the architect showed me.
a) in that
b) that
c) in which

2012. When I saw that she was having trouble, I … her.
a) was helping
b) help
c) helped

2013. Prior to last year, we … to such a big city.
a) had never been
b) have never been
c) were never

2014. Two years ago I experienced … .
a) how tedious long plane trips can be
b) how can tedious long plane trips be
c) how tedious can long plane trips be

2015. I don't want you … that aspect.
a) mention
b) to mention
c) mentioning

2016. If you can't unscrew it, try … it with a hammer.
a) to hit
b) hit
c) hitting

2017. I remember hearing her say the grass needed … two days ago.
a) to cut
b) cutting
c) cut

2018. I advise you to wait before deciding … the job.
a) to accept
b) accepting
c) accept

2019. The lecture was dull and wasn't worth … .
a) listen
b) listening to
c) listened

2020. I couldn't resist asking her why she was trying … meeting me.
a) avoiding
b) avoid
c) to avoid

2021. Did Mary say she … me?
a) would telephone

b) will telephone

c) have telephoned

2022. The ... of coming next week is small.

a) possible

b) possibly

c) possibility

2023. There was a nasty ... at this crossroad yesterday.

a) happening

b) emergency

c) accident

2024. Some of the passengers were badly ... .

a) pained

b) injured

c) hurted

2025. Several ... helped to pull people out of the damaged car.

a) audience

b) supporters

c) bystanders

2026. Most of them were found to be suffering from severe ... .

a) surprise

b) worry

c) shock

2027. The truck crashed into a car and had completely ... it.

a) hit

b) wrecked

c) crashed

2028. The officers took the names and addresses of as many ... as possible.

a) suspects

b) viewers

c) witnesses

2029. Injured passengers have the right to claim ... .

a) rewards

b) refund

c) compensation

2030. This hat looks ... on you.

a) nice

b) well

c) beautifully

2031. I never expected that ... find the lost ring.

a) I would

b) I shall

c) I am going to

2032. The car was easy to recognize, ... it was easy to find the thieves.

a) because

b) that

c) so

2033. By the end of 2022, they ... the building.

a) will finish

b) finish

c) will have finished

2034. The news of his death ... the world.

a) astonished

b) announced

c) heard

2035. Select the proper word for: "a multitude of people".

a) large

b) huge crowd

c) small number

2036. Select the proper word for: "Steve has arrived to find his wife in tears".
a) crying
b) panicky
c) confused

2037. People have a … for special occasions.
a) meal
b) festival
c) ceremony

2038. … work is the work that is always done the same way.
a) Manual
b) Routine
c) Mental

2039. To … means to help someone remember something.
a) memorize
b) suggest
c) remind

2040. I … my money because I want it to grow in value.
a) save
b) invest
c) put away

2041. She … to attend the meeting tonight.
a) couldn't

b) shouldn't
c) will not be able

2042. The poor woman has not … .
a) lived lonely

b) lived alone
c) been living lone

2043. The emergency committee has met and … .
a) they have reached a decision
b) it has reached decision
c) its decision reached

2044. Mary's score on last test is the highest in class.
a) She should study
b) She must have studied hard
c) She must have to study hard

2045. The manager requested that … .
a) the employees studied more carefully the problem
b) the problem was more careful studied
c) the employees study the problem more carefully

2046. This county relies on income from fruit crops and … .
a) also Toronto
b) Toronto too
c) so does Toronto

2047. I wanted to serve some wine to my guests. However, … .
a) I didn't have glasses
b) I hadn't glasses
c) I was lacking in glasses

2048. They … to the cemetery.
a) sent faith flowers
b) sent flowers faithfully
c) sent faithfully flowers

2049. The car and the house that you own are your … .

a) area

b) property

c) personal belongings

2050. A … is an object that help you remember a place you have visited.

a) souvenir

b) note

c) memory

2051. If someone commits a …, the police try to catch him.

a) mistake

b) divorce

c) crime

2052. The article contained a lot of … about how much petrol the car used.

a) information

b) news

c) fact

2053. The … crowd moved closer to the barricades.

a) irate

b) irating

c) angrily

2054. We … the validity of her remarks.

a) assisting

b) denied

c) hunted of

2055. Steve … while we watched the movie.

a) withdrew

b) got off

c) napped

2056. Sarah is very stubborn. Find the synonym:

a) patient

b) nice

c) obstinate

2057. They have a full schedule. Find the synonym:

a) busy day

b) project

c) programme of work

2058. Radioactivity causes cancer and affects future generations. Find the synonym:

a) kill

b) be bad for

c) pollute

2059. They evacuated the area as the enemy advanced. Find the synonym:

a) left (because of danger)

b) bombed

c) attacked

2060. Mary offered a silly excuse. Find the synonym:

a) took

b) gave

c) accepted

2061. It must be … more than $250.

a) cost

b) expensive

c) worth

2062. I wouldn't eat salad … I were starving.

a) unless

b) or
c) provided that
2063. Next year I ... this class
for five years.
a) teach
b) will teach
c) will have taught
2064. I invited them ... the
meeting.
a) attend
b) to attend
c) for attending
2065. To call up means:
a) criticize
b) visit
c) telephone
2066. To give up means:
a) to surrender
b) to give all
c) to give a part of

2067. The professor ... several
words in my article.
a) corrected
b) added
c) cancelled
2068. To check out of a motel is
to ...
a) register it
b) leave it
c) ask for a room
2069. Children under the age of
five ... allowed to participate.
a) isn't
b) aren't
c) haven't

2070. Our company often
requires that candidates have not
only a degree ...
.
a) but two years experience
b) but also two-year experience
c) but more years experience
2071. I hope she ... to buy some
milk.
a) proposed
b) reminded
c) remembered
2072. If I were you I ... that suit.
a) would buy
b) will buy
c) am buying
2073. The vet decided that he
had to operate ... the dog.
a) to
b) on
c) with
2074. I ... like to apologize for
not being there.
a) might
b) must
c) would
2075. Many accidents in the
home could be ... .
a) excluded

b) protected
c) avoided
2076. Try to remember ... bring
your laptop.
a) himself to
b) to
c) yourself

2077. The bride looked … in her wedding dress.
a) pretty
b) lovely
c) handsome
2078. We didn't leave for the station until the very … moment.
a) last
b) latest
c) late
2079. When are you going to give back that money you … me?
a) lend
b) debt
c) owe
2080. These politicians were … by terrorists.
a) destroyed
b) murdered
c) collapsed
2081. Each … of the team had to take it in turns to do the washing up.
a) individual
b) person
c) member
2082. The little girl performs beautifully … the piano.
a) on
b) in
c) at
2083. The tour … about two hours to complete.
a) has
b) takes

c) spends

2084. The airport was temporarily … .
a) stormed
b) delayed
c) closed
2085. You will soon buy a house. …
a) What wonderful news!
b) How wonderful news!
c) What a wonderful news!
2086. If my documents had been found last week, I … to come.
a) would have been able
b) would be able
c) will have been able
2087. The buses are so dirty. … they are never on time.
a) Instead
b) For example
c) In addition
2088. You were warned never … with this extremist group.
a) to assign
b) to associate
c) to assume
2089. If your firm wants to attract workers it must … the pay.
a) raise
b) lower
c) rise
2090. I'm afraid this laptop is totally … for your needs.
a) undeniable
b) unspeakable

c) unsuitable

2091. I regretted my mistake. It was one that I … .
a) hadn't to make
b) shouldn't have made
c) mustn't make

2092. Members of a Parliament are … by the people.
a) represented

b) polled
c) voted

2093. Tom is Sarah's father, so Sarah is Tom's … .
a) daughter
b) niece
c) wife

2094. Her job was so tiring that she felt absolutely … .
a) sharpened
b) shattered
c) scattered

2095. I can sell you some apples but only … .
a) a little
b) little
c) a few

2096. I can't repay you this week. I'm completely … .
a) damaged
b) broken
c) destroyed

2097. I often … money from my parents.
a) borrow
b) lend
c) save

2098. She is said … our country next year.
a) to have visited
b) to be visiting
c) to visit

2099. These students … to Madrid tomorrow.
a) are going
b) have gone
c) will going

2100. Thank you for letting me … your car for a ride.
a) taken
b) taking
c) take

2101. Can you put me … for some days?
a) down
b) away
c) up

2102. Coal is still … in this county.
a) built
b) mined
c) manufactured

2103. The manager's presentation will be … by tomorrow night.
a) ready
b) soon
c) nearly

2104. You certainly wouldn't like … in such bad entourage.
a) to see
b) to be seen
c) to have seen

2105. There isn't … salt on the table.
a) some
b) the
c) any
2106. I tried to call last night you but your line was … .
a) occupied
b) taken
c) engaged
2107. Come to my party … Friday night.
a) the
b) at
c) on
2108. Nobody can fool her. She's never … in.
a) taken
b) giving
c) taking
2109. I will tell you if I … the answer.
a) knew

b) know
c) has known
2110. Are you able to drink something while you …?
a) were whistling
b) whistled
c) whistle
2111. I'll choose another strategy in case it … .
a) happen
b) happens
c) happening

2112. We'll go our if the weather … .
a) improve
b) will improve
c) improves
2113. The food … awful.
a) tastes
b) is tasting
c) have tasted
2114. Your support ... a lot now.
a) is meaning
b) meant
c) means
2115. This report … of four parts now.
a) consisted
b) consists
c) is consisting
2116. Where … you found it?
a) has
b) did
c) have
2117. She's just … it on the desk.
a) put
b) putting
c) putted

2118. When I came home, my wife … dinner.
a) already cooked
b) had already cooked
c) was already cooked
2119. They discovered she … it correctly.
a) hasn't done
b) hadn't done

c) didn't do

2120. Mary told me they … on this building project for two years.

a) were working

b) did working

c) had been working

2121. Why … produced now?

a) is it

b) it is

c) is it being

2122. The Moon … round.

a) is

b) could be

c) will be

2123. How long … German?

a) have you been learning

b) did you learn

c) do you learnt

2124. … criticized?

a) Was she ever

b) Has she ever been

c) Did she ever been

2125. It's high time … .

a) you go home

b) you gone home

c) you went home

2126. I'm fond … jogging.

a) at

b) in

c) of

2127. People were amazed … his progress.

a) with

b) at

c) in

2128. I'm not content … my income.

a) with

b) about

c) on

2129. I was absolutely delighted … my new flat.

a) for

b) at

c) in

2130. Don't worry! I strongly believe … .

a) for you

b) you

c) to you

2131. The committee weren't surprised by the approval … your decision.

a) of

b) to

c) on

2132. Mary's under … pressure.

a) a

b) on

c) –

2133. We use to talk on the phone from time … time.

a) to

b) a

c) with

2134. He said: "The method doesn't work.".

a) He said that the method doesn't work

b) He said that hadn't worked

c) He said that the method didn't work

2135. The secretary said: "They have already notified Steve.".
a) She said that they have already notified him
b) She said that they had already notified him
c) She said that Steve was notified

2136. Tim said: "She had forgiven me.".
a) Tim said that she had forgiven him.
b) Tim said that she has forgiven.
c) Tim said that she would have forgiven him.

2137. The assistant manager asked me: "Do you like your job?".
a) She asked me I liked my job.
b) She has asked me I liked my job.
c) She asked me whether I liked my job.

2138. She asked me: "Did they inform John?".
a) She asked me if they informed him.
b) She asked me if they had informed him.
c) She asked me if they have informed him.

2139. My girlfriend asked me: "Where did you do yesterday?".
a) She asked me where I had gone yesterday.
b) She asked me where have I gone yesterday.
c) She asked me where I had gone the day before.

2140. The manager asked me: "What will change?".
a) The manager asked me what would change.
b) The manager asked me what would have changed.
c) The manager asked me what will change.

2141. Mary asked me: "What information will Jane send?".
a) Mary asked me what information Jane would send.
b) Jane asked me what information Mary will send
c) Mary asked me what information Jane will send.

2142. I … well in the exam.
a) made
b) did
c) solved

2143. We were … by her results.
a) amazing
b) amaze
c) amazed

2144. Her husband is so … .
a) irresponsible
b) irresponsibly
c) disresponsible

2145. There are many people who are … in this country.
a) inliterate

b) unliterate

c) illiterate

2146. These details are … .

a) innecessary

b) unnecessary

c) overnecessary

2147. They won at last. They were so … .

a) lucky

b) luckily

c) unlucky

2148. It's … to think so. Most colleagues think so.

a) unnatural

b) innatural

c) natural

2149. Where is the stadium …?

a) situation

b) situating

c) situated

2150. I really can't figure it … . (understand)

a) with

b) out

c) in

2151. The company decided to take … three more employees. (employ)

a) on

b) in

c) about

2152. The woman was taken … . (deceived)

a) about

b) in

c) on

2153. Hang … a second! (wait)

a) up

b) about

c) on

2154. I will do it in spite … .

a) I'm busy

b) mine busy

c) of being busy

2155. She learns German intensively … of having little free time.

a) in spite

b) despite

c) despite in

2156. I'd rather you … it.

a) haven't done

b) don't do

c) didn't do

2157. I'd prefer … everything about her.

a) forget

b) to forget

c) forgetting

2158. This report must … .

a) receive

b) have been received

c) had been received

2159. That day it was … freezing.

a) absolutely

b) very

c) utter

2160. It's … ridiculous.

a) very

b) intense

c) absolutely

2161. Look! They … .
a) are returning
b) return
c) being returning
2162. This thing … us now.
a) concerned
b) concerns
c) is concerning
2163. … she playing the piano
professionally?
a) Were
b) Did
c) Was
2164. Choose the right sentence:
a) She has never lied to me. She
will lie me again.
b) She never lied. She is truly
constant.
c) She never lied. She had
always lied.
2165. It has … to enormous
problems.
a) leaded
b) lead
c) led

Set 9

2166. I'm afraid I … the details.
a) misheared
b) misheart
c) misheard
2167. The professor … Russian
since last year.
a) hasn't being teaching
b) hasn't been teaching
c) hadn't been teaching
2168. … analyzed now?
a) Are their reports
b) Are their reports being
c) Were their reports being

2169. This method … yet.
a) hasn't been verified
b) hasn't verified
c) hasn't being verified
2170. She inform us the
decision … .
a) had already been made
b) was already been made
c) has already been made
2171. We came to the
conclusion we … .
a) were been informed
b) had been misinformed
c) have been uninformed
2172. When …?
a) had it happened
b) has it being happened
c) did it happen
2173. I … you for ages. How
are you?
a) haven't being seen
b) hadn't seen
c) haven't seen
2174. The weather was good.
We were walking and talking
about future
plans. The sun … brightly.
a) shone
b) shining
c) was shining

2175. It was written that the stadium … .
a) was destroyed
b) had already been destroyed
c) has been destroyed
2176. If she … it much earlier, she would have left that building.
a) had known
b) knew
c) might have known
2177. Sarah … speak English without any mistakes. (it's her desire)
a) has to

b) couldn't
c) must
2178. Kim … to school tomorrow.
a) must go
b) must gone
c) must have gone
2179. They were late … the annual meeting.
a) to
b) for
c) about
2180. I want to congratulate you … passing the final exam.
a) on
b) for
c) with
2181. I heard the most important thing about the mission … the end.
a) for

b) in
c) with
2182. She told him: "I'm so tired".
a) She told him that she was so tired.
b) She told him that she's so tired
c) She told him that she has been so tired
2183. She said: "I have been working on this project for 5 days.".
a) She said that she has been working on this project for 5 days.
b) She said that she's working on that project for 5 days.
c) She said that she had been working on that project for 5 days.
2184. The employee said: "I'll be working more intensively.".
a) He said that he'll be working more intensively.
b) He said that he would be working more intensively.
c) He said that he will being working more intensively.
2185. John said: "I saw her yesterday.".
a) John said that he had seen her yesterday.
b) John said that he had seen her the day before.
c) John said that he has seen her the day before.

2186. She asked me: "Was he irritated?".
a) She asked me if he was irritated.
b) She asked me if he had been irritated.
c) She asked me if he has been irritated.
2187. … my article?
a) Don't you see
b) Haven't you see
c) Couldn't you seen
2188. … this method work?
a) Isn't
b) Doesn't
c) Hadn't
2189. … like our idea?
a) Didn't she not
b) Hasn't she
c) Did she not
2190. … improve his performance?
a) Didn't he
b) Hasn't he
c) Hadn't he
2191. … they join us?
a) Aren't
b) Won't
c) Hadn't
2192. Steve, why are you so …?
a) impatient
b) unpatient
c) ipatient
2193. I totally … of this plan.
a) unapprove
b) approved
c) disapprove
2194. Does this treatment make any …?
a) difference
b) different
c) differenting
2195. It's a very strange way of …, but I like it!
a) thought
b) thinking
c) be thinking
2196. Don't worry! You can share your … with us.
a) thinks
b) thinkings
c) thoughts
2197. It's an … situation.
a) imagine
b) imaginative
c) imaginary
2198. Will this management team be …, too?
a) unefficient
b) inefficient
c) effectively
2199. It's because of their … .
a) disobedience
b) unobedience
c) ilobedience
2200. I checked … at 9 o'clock in the morning at the best hotel.
a) on
b) in
c) within
2201. Today's lesson is … .
a) done

b) gone

c) over

2202. The terrorists wanted to blow … the building but they were arrested.

a) up

b) in

c) at

2203. Samuel owned up … making a mistake.

a) of

b) to

c) about

2204. We'll try to find … all the truth.

a) out

b) over

c) in

2205. I'd rather … at home than go there. It's a pandemic out there.

a) to stay

b) staying

c) stay

2206. This woman might … .

a) be invited

b) has invited

c) have been invited

2207. They may … .

a) accused

b) accusing

c) be accused

2208. Mark … .

a) should have been congratulated

b) should has been congratulated

c) should had been congratulated

2209. Their manager … .

a) could being informed

b) could have been informed

c) could to be informed

2210. I … understand you. Don't worry about it.

a) am

b) do

c) had

2211. I'll prepare for the exam as soon as I … free time.

a) will have

b) would have

c) have

2212. … it right now.

a) He does

b) He did

c) He is doing

2213. It started raining when I … .

a) was jogging

b) were jogging

c) jogged

2214. They … the managers about that problem.

a) didn't consulted

b) weren't consulting

c) being consulted

2215. … it bringing you enough money?

a) Were

b) Was

c) Did

2216. Why … they complaining all the time?

a) was

b) did

c) were

2217. It … five days ago.

a) happened

b) happening

c) had happened

2218. … congratulated me. I'm so happy!

a) He already

b) He has already

c) He had already

2219. The thief hasn't … .

a) shooted

b) shoot

c) shot

2220. My girlfriend … fashionable clothes.

a) wear

b) weared

c) wore

2221. I … Megan for a long time.

a) haven't been seeing

b) haven't seen

c) didn't seen

2222. The detectives found out they … it.

a) already stole

b) stolen

c) had already stolen

2223. What …?

a) has being changing

b) has been changed

c) was being changing

2224. We ... next month.

a) meet

b) will meet

c) couldn't meet

2225. I wish I … it two years ago.

a) had bought

b) bought

c) would buy

2226. I wish Mary … the test last month.

a) had passed

b) passed

c) has passed

2227. She's quite confused … the results.

a) by

b) in

c) about

2228. Our marriage ended … divorce.

a) up

b) in

c) about

2229. I'll pay … debit card.

a) by

b) on

c) about

2230. Olivia said: "My work is so boring.".

a) Olivia said that her work is so boring.

b) Olivia said that her work would be so boring.

c) Olivia said that her work was so boring.

2231. The reporter said: "The game will last for two hours.".
a) He said that the game would last for two hours.
b) He said that the game lasts for two hours.
c) He said that the game will last for two hours.

2232. She said: "My brother has been swimming.".
a) She said that her brother had been swimming.
b) She said that her brother was swimming.
c) She said that her brother have been swimming.

2233. I … for your reply.
a) will wait
b) waiting
c) will be waiting

2234. I … this book by December 2020.
a) will be finish
b) will finish
c) will have finished

2235. The manager asked me: "Did you solve the problem?".
a) She asked me if I solved the problem.
b) She asked me if I had solved that problem.
c) She asked me if I was solving the problem.

2236. They asked me: "Will he be in charge of this department?".
a) They asked me if he would be in charge of that department.
b) They asked me if he is in charge of the department.
c) They asked me if he would be in charge of this department.

2237. My wife asked me: "Was it getting more and more expensive?".
a) My wife asked me if it was getting more and more expensive.
b) My wife asked me if it had been getting more and more expensive.
c) My wife asked me if it has been getting more and more expensive.

2238. The teacher asked me: "Have you shown excellent results?".
a) The teacher asked me if you had shown excellent results.
b) The teacher asked me if I had shown excellent results.
c) The teacher asked me if I have shown excellent results.

2239. To my surprise, she asked me: "What are you doing tonight?".
a) She asked me what I was doing tonight.

b) She asked me what have I been doing tonight.

c) She asked me what I was doing that night.

2240. … happy?

a) Hasn't she

b) Isn't she

c) Haven't she

2241. … not return home?

a) Did they

b) Didn't they

c) Weren't they

2242. Are they not meeting …?

a) then

b) when

c) now

2243. Your experience is truly … .

a) amazed

b) amazing

c) been amazed

2244. These instructions are really … .

a) confusing

b) confused

c) confundant

2245. Sarah mostly wears … clothes.

a) unformal

b) deformal

c) informal

2246. Maria wears … clothes.

a) fashion

b) fashioning

c) fashionable

2247. There were … changes in this organization.

a) really

b) real

c) reality

2248. This cancer vaccine has changed our life for ever. It's a real … .

a) break

b) breaking

c) breakthrough

2249. Her remark left me … . I was utterly shocked.

a) speaking

b) speechless

c) speech

2250. She gently took … her dress. (removed)

a) off

b) of

c) about

2251. … the system more thoroughly.

a) You'd better check

b) You had better to check

c) You would better to check

2252. Maria you … better hurry up.

a) would

b) can

c) had

2253. This documentary was worth … .

a) to watch

b) watching

c) been watch

2254. It's no use ... now.
a) to cry
b) cried
c) crying
2255. Our team shouldn't ... .
a) be divided
b) division
c) divided
2256. It can't ... right now.
a) known
b) be known
c) knowing
2257. I'm sorry, but it needed
... .
a) to be done
b) to do
c) be done
2258. ... you spend on clothes,
the more money you have.
a) Less
b) Least
c) The less
2259. The little girl was ...
terrified.
a) very
b) absolutely
c) absolute
2260. ... here I feel satisfied.
a) Working
b) Worked
c) To working
2261. No truly one ... it.
a) expected
b) expecting
c) didn't expect
2262. I won't help him unless
he ... his point of view.

a) change
b) will change
c) changes
2263. I'll fix everything before
she ... .
a) returns
b) will return
c) will be return
2264. I'll call you as soon as I
... back.
a) will get
b) had got
c) get
2265. ... a party tonight.
a) Tom is giving
b) Tom gives
c) Tom will given
2266. ... this problem.
a) They often mention
b) They are often mentioning
c) They had often mentioning
2267. She ... them a request.
a) hadn't send
b) hadn't have
c) wasn't sending
2268. ... she leading a new
lifestyle after they had broken
off?
a) Were
b) Was
c) Had
2269. Choose the correct
sentence:
a) Sarah has just remembered it.
b) Sarah has just remembering
it.

c) Sarah has just remembered it two days ago.

2270. All of a sudden, the bell … .

a) rung

b) rang

c) ringing

2271. We know you … Russian for many year.

a) teach

b) had been teaching

c) have been teaching

2272. She … this problem with the car for many years.

a) has been having

b) having had

c) has had

2273. We all realized that she … to us.

a) hasn't lied

b) hadn't lied

c) having lied

2274. The child … very professionally now.

a) is taught

b) be teaching

c) is being taught

2275. What … yesterday?

a) had been deleted

b) were deleted

c) has been deleted

2276. We … for half a year.

a) have been dating

b) being dating

c) had dated

2277. By the time I got the letter I … that minor issue.

a) have already solving

b) had already solved

c) had already had solving

2278. The report … yet.

a) wasn't written

b) hasn't been written

c) hadn't been writing

2279. I wish I … another car last year.

a) has found

b) would find

c) had found

2280. It's high time Tim … them all the money.

a) paying

b) paid

c) had paid

2281. I … find a new car.

a) must

b) might can

c) have to had

2282. The managers let her … out.

a) to go

b) go

c) went

2283. I'm fully satisfied … your project. Congrats!

a) about

b) within

c) with

2284. The man said: "She never helps us.".

a) The man said that she never was helping them.
b) The man said she never helped them.
c) The man said she never helped us.
2285. Mark said: "I will be sleeping all night.".
a) Mark said that he would be sleeping all night.
b) Mark said that he will be sleeping all night.
c) Mark said that he would sleep all night.
2286. My girlfriend asked me: "How are you?".
a) She asked me how were you.
b) She asked me how I was.
c) She asked me how I would be.
2287. The thief asked me: "Why did she remain calm?".
a) The thief asked me why she remained calm.
b) The thief asked me why she was remaining calm.
c) The thief asked me why she had remained calm.

2288. The customer asked me: "Why was it a unique offer?".
a) The customer asked me why it had been a unique offer.
b) The customer asked me why had it been a unique offer.
c) The customer asked me why was it a unique offer.

2289. Choose the correct sentence:
a) What are you waiting?
b) What are you waiting for?
c) What are you wait for?
2290. They work … .
a) effective
b) effectiving
c) effectively
2291. Your wife sings so … .
a) beautiful
b) beautifully
c) beauty
2292. The professor really likes their … .
a) creativity
b) creative
c) creating
2293. The event was absolutely … .
a) fantasy
b) fantastic
c) fanatic
2294. Why can't she buy … things sometimes?
a) expensive
b) expensively
c) inexpensive
2295. The child has a vivid … .
a) imagination
b) imaginary
c) imagine
2296. Do you think that our … will change after the pandemic?
a) sociable

b) society

c) social

2297. In that area the ground was … .

a) uneven

b) ineven

c) unevenly

2298. Please, calm …! There's nothing to worry about.

a) in

b) over

c) down

2299. Does your laptop often break …?

a) off

b) in

c) down

2300. She really takes care … our child.

a) after

b) of

c) on

2301. We got … trouble during that mission.

a) into

b) on

c) within

2302. They ended up … about the budget.

a) argue

b) arguing

c) arguably

2303. I think they'll call … soon. (visit you)

a) back

b) over

c) round

2304. I would prefer … at home.

a) to stay

b) stay

c) to staying

2305. I have trouble … with this business partner.

a) to deal

b) dealing

c) on dealt

2306. We're supposed … the leaders in this organization.

a) to become

b) become

c) to becoming

2307. The text might … partially.

a) translate

b) translating

c) be translated

2308. I'm sure the employees … more.

a) could have be motivated

b) could have been motivated

c) could have being motivated

2309. Either Mark … John will do it.

a) nor

b) also

c) or

2310. Don't panic. I … see it. It's over there.

a) am

b) are

c) do

2311. We'll stay at home if the weather … .
a) don't improve
b) doesn't improve
c) won't improve
2312. … the trainers asking about that thing?
a) Had
b) Were
c) Have
2313. What … the professor saying about that problem?
a) was

b) has
c) had
2314. Is the following sentence correct? "I was wanting it with all my
heart."
a) correct
b) incorrect
2315. Is the following sentence correct? "They were fighting very bravely
at that moment."
a) correct
b) incorrect
2316. I … there for a few times.
a) had been
b) had be
c) have been
2317. … all the companies gone bankrupt? I can't believe it!
a) Have
b) Has
c) Having

2318. What things … they said?
a) had have
b) have
c) has had
2319. Have you ever been … the Netherlands?
a) in
b) at
c) to
2320. The lady has … the floor.
a) sweeped
b) sweeping
c) swept
2321. The little girl has … the cats.
a) feeded
b) fed
c) feeding

2322. I … more than enough.
a) sleeped
b) sleeping
c) slept
2323. It was said they … another choice regarding the product.
a) hadn't made
b) haven't made
c) didn't made
2324. These problems … yet.
a) weren't discussed
b) haven't been discussed
c) hadn't been discussed
2325. If she … my advice yesterday, Mary wouldn't be in trouble now.
a) heard

b) had heard

c) have minded

2326. You needn't … about this.

a) worrying

b) be worried

c) worry

2327. They … him about a preliminary result.

a) mustn't have informed

b) mustn't to inform

c) mustn't informing

2328. You … here so early.

a) needn't have come

b) needn't had come

c) needn't be come

2329. I won't let you … so much.

a) to risk

b) risk

c) risking

2330. We are engaged … this project.

a) at

b) for

c) in

2331. It's far … belief.

a) behind

b) beyond

c) beware

2332. The secretary said: "I will read the documents.".

a) The secretary said that she would read the documents.

b) The secretary said that she will read the documents.

c) The secretary said the she would have read the documents.

2333. Steve said: "I will be learning German all day.".

a) Steve said he will be learning German all day.

b) Steve said he would be all day German learning.

c) Steve said he would be learning German all day.

2334. I … this website for three weeks by next month.

a) will had used

b) will have been using

c) will have been used

2335. Susan asked me: "Do you live there?".

a) She asked me if I live there.

b) She asked me if I lived there.

c) She asked me if I would live there.

2336. The teacher asked me: "Are you proud of her?".

a) The teacher asked me if I was proud of her.

b) The teacher asked me if I am proud of her.

c) The teacher asked me if I have been proud of her.

2337. My girlfriend asked me: "Is it a popular resort?".

a) She asked me whether was it a popular resort.

b) She asked me if it had been a popular resort.

c) She asked me if it was a popular resort.

2338. They asked me: "Where do you live?".
a) They asked me where I live.
b) They asked me where I lived.
c) They asked me where I had lived.

2339. The manager asked me: "How will you manage to solve this problem?".
a) The manager asked me how I would manage to solve that problem.
b) The manager asked me how would I manage to solve that problem.
c) The manager asked me how I would manage to solve this problem.

2340. The detective asked me: "Why are they looking for it?".
a) The detective asked me why they are looking for it.
b) The detective asked me why would they be looking for it.
c) The detective asked me why they were looking for it.

2341. … agree with me?
a) Not you
b) Haven't
c) Don't you

2342. … a remarkable achievement?
a) Isn't it
b) Hasn't it
c) Hadn't it

2343. … him?
a) Didn't it interest
b) Didn't it interesting for
c) Hadn't it interesting

2344. This handwriting is totally … .
a) illegible
b) unlegible
c) alegible

2345. We prepared an annual … .
a) reporter
b) report
c) reporting

2346. It's really a matter of … . Let's hope that you'll do better next time.
a) lucky
b) luckily
c) luck

2347. Jessica speaks Russian … . She needs to learn more.
a) unnaturally
b) inaturally
c) unnatural

2348. I feel safe and … now. Thank you!
a) unprotected
b) protective
c) protected

2349. Our world is clearly … .
a) unperfect
b) imperfect
c) aperfect

2350. He … the door using a stolen key.

a) dislocked

b) unlocked

c) locking

2351. The teenager threw … his old clothes. (get rid of)

a) off

b) about

c) away

2352. You'd better … it.

a) not do

b) not doing

c) not to do

2353. I repaired my laptop.

a) myself

b) not myself

c) about myself

2354. … no point in asking her help.

a) There

b) There's

c) This

2355. This report … .

a) must spreading

b) must be spread

c) must be spreaded

2356. Can my perfumes … earlier?

a) deliver

b) delivered

c) be delivered

2357. The officers … .

a) should have been warned

b) should be warn

c) should had been warned

2358. Their mistakes … .

a) should have be correcting

b) should have been corrected

c) should corrected

2359. The book … last month.

a) could have been read

b) could has been read

c) could had been read

2360. The laptop … .

a) could to have sold

b) could had been sold

c) could have been sold

2361. Nobody … remember your mistake.

a) won't

b) will

c) wouldn't

2362. … next Saturday.

a) I work

b) I'm working

c) I'd worked

2363. Honestly, … now.

a) I doubt

b) I doubted

c) I'm doubting

2364. When the bell rang, we … the figures down.

a) was writing

b) had writing

c) were writing

2365. When I … an intricate book, my sister came in.

a) was reading

b) had reading

c) have been reading

2366. I … in that competition.

a) hadn't been participated

b) wasn't participating

c) hasn't been participating

2367. My girlfriend … German.

a) weren't spoken

b) wasn't speaking

c) didn't spoke

2368. … your commander saying it very clearly?

a) Did

b) Had

c) Was

2369. Is the following sentence correct? "The success was depending on me."

a) correct

b) incorrect

2370. … your colleague told you about it?

a) Did

b) Has

c) Had

2371. Where … your sisters seen it?

a) have

b) did

c) were

2372. What thing … the child heard before?

a) have

b) did

c) has

2373. We have … up a new revolutionary program.

a) setted

b) setting

c) set

2374. The evaluation … my strong and weak points.

a) shown

b) showed

c) showing

2375. We … the video system since last week.

a) have been testing

b) had been testing

c) would be testing

2376. … off the computer before she left home?

a) Had she turned

b) Has she turned

c) Did she turned

2377. Choose the correct sentence:

a) The food is cooked at the moment.

b) The food is being cooked at the moment.

c) The food is cooking at the moment.

2378. Choose the correct sentence:

a) Sarah still has problems.

b) Sarah has still having problems.

c) Sarah is still having problems.

2379. When they noticed it we … it.

a) already did

b) had already done

c) have already done

2380. They … us next month.

a) may have visited

b) could have visited

c) may visit

2381. I'm pleased … such amazing results.
a) by
b) on
c) with

2382. Their approach differs … ours.
a) into
b) from
c) of

2383. The marketing assistant disapproves … the decision.
a) of
b) on
c) about

2384. The scientists are … the brink of discovering the truth.
a) in
b) about
c) on

2385. Steve said: "It's what I need.".
a) Steve said that it was what he needed.
b) Steve said that it was what I needed.
c) Steve said that it has been what he needed.

2386. The manager said: "It will remain the same.".
a) The manager said that it will remain the same.
b) The manager said that it would remain the same.

c) The manager said that it would be remaining the same.

2387. Krista said: "I will be waiting for his response.".
a) Krista said that she will wait for his response.
b) Krista said that he would be waiting for her response.
c) Krista said that she would be waiting for his response.

2388. The marketing specialist asked me: "Has it become a real success?".
a) The marketing specialist asked me if it had become a real success.
b) The marketing specialist asked me if it became a real success.
c) The marketing specialist asked me if it has become a real success.

2389. Choose the correct sentence:
a) Was no this treatment effective?

b) Wasn't this treatment effective?
c) Didn't this treatment be effective?

2390. … the latest news shock you?
a) Wasn't
b) Hadn't
c) Didn't

2391. Choose the correct sentence:
a) Will she not come back?
b) Will not she coming back?
c) Won't she be come back?
2392. Who does she agree …?
a) with
b) about
c) within
2393. It was an … town for me.
a) infamiliar
b) unfamiliar
c) ifamiliar
2394. These conclusions are so … .
a) unlogical
b) alogical
c) illogical
2395. My cousin is … . He can't find a job.
a) employed
b) employing
c) unemployed
2396. This thing is … . You don't need it.
a) unnecessary
b) necessary
c) inecessary
2397. It was a very … investment. They lost all their savings.
a) wise
b) unwise
c) wisely

2398. Don't let anybody …! It's a dangerous area.

a) in
b) on
c) about
2399. Please, turn … the TV.
a) about
b) off
c) in
2400. Sorry for interrupting. Please, go … talking!
a) in
b) after
c) on
2401. Sit …, please!
a) down
b) about
c) within
2402. Come …! Hurry up!
a) after
b) on
c) backwards
2403. Today we need to weigh … all the pros and cons.
a) after
b) up
c) on
2404. The student continued learning … of the noise.
a) despite
b) although
c) in spite
2405. She washed her car.
a) itself
b) herself
c) on his own
2406. A new villa can … .
a) be built

b) built
c) building
2407. They mustn't … .
a) punishing
b) be punished
c) had been punished
2408. Might they … by me?
a) be invited
b) invite
c) inviting
2409. She is to … here at four.
a) arriving
b) arrived
c) arrive
2410. No sooner … at the station than the night train left.
a) had I arrive
b) had I arrived
c) arrived had I
2411. While they were having a break, we … negotiations.
a) had been having
b) were having
c) have been having
2412. Where … your sister been?
a) was
b) has
c) will
2413. Choose the correct sentence:
a) We have never been friends. We have almost nothing in common.
b) We never were friends. We have almost nothing in common.
c) We had never been friend. We have almost nothing in common.
2414. His wife has … him and everything is fine between them.
a) forgived
b) forgotten
c) forgiven

2415. They have … me. I will explain it again.
a) misunderstood
b) misunderstand
c) misunderstanding
2416. She … the book because she had enjoyed it a long time ago.
a) reread
b) reading
c) had reread
2417. I … the heating system since last Monday.
a) haven't checked
b) haven't checking
c) didn't check
2418. How long … the institution?
a) have they be controlling
b) have they been controlling
c) had they been controlled
2419. He said he … for two hours.
a) was working
b) has been working
c) had been working
2020. I read they … the assassin.

a) punish
b) be punished
c) had punished
2021. Choose the correct
sentence:
a) It has already been said.
b) It was already said.
c) It will already be said.
2422. If I were you, I … choose
another team member.
a) will
b) would
c) would have chosen
2423. I … improve my German
as soon as possible.
a) must

b) must have
c) must be
2424. This capital is crowded …
tourists.
a) of
b) about
c) with
2425. The new colleague is full
… innovative ideas.
a) in
b) about
c) of
2426. I'm fed up … this job.
a) with
b) about
c) of
2427. I was impressed … her
beauty.
a) of
b) by

c) about
2428. I'm really serious …
everything.
a) at
b) of
c) about
2429. I'm so excited … the
vaccine news.
a) about
b) in
c) on
2430. I don't know why she is
so pessimistic … their future.
a) with
b) about
c) of
2431. It's very nice … you to
remember it.
a) to
b) of
c) with

2432. I have just arrived … the
airport.
a) in
b) about
c) at
2433. What's the difference …
these two laptops?
a) between
b) among
c) of
2434. See you … two months.
a) of
b) with
c) in

2435. Tim said: "I don't teach German.".
a) Tim said that he doesn't teach German.
b) Tim said that he didn't teach German.
c) Tim said that he haven't taught German.

2436. The patient said: "I'm experiencing a strange feeling.".
a) The patient said that he was experiencing a strange feeling.
b) The patient said that he has been experiencing a strange feeling.
c) The patient said that he had been experiencing a strange feeling.

2437. John said: "She has sung a beautiful song.".
a) John said that she has sung a beautiful song.
b) John said that she was singing a beautiful song.
c) John said that she had sung a beautiful song.

2438. We … Russian for an hour by the time she enters the room.
a) are speaking
b) will have been speaking
c) would have been speaking

2439. I … English for five years by next year.
a) will have been teaching
b) will teach
c) will be teaching

2440. They asked me: "Did they destroy that building?".
a) They asked me they had destroyed that building.
b) They asked me if they had destroyed that building.
c) They asked me if they destroyed that building.

2441. The journalist asked me: "Is he accusing her?".
a) The journalist asked me if he had been accusing her.
b) The journalist asked me if he has been accusing her.
c) The journalist asked me if he was accusing her.

2442. My wife asked me: "How long have you been dating with her?".
a) My wife asked me how long I'm dating with her.
b) My wife asked me how long I had been dating with her.
c) My wife asked me how long I was dating with her.

2443. Choose the correct sentence:
a) Doesn't she like this phone?
b) Not she like this phone?
c) Didn't she liked this phone?

2444. Choose the correct sentence:
a) Wasn't it not obvious?
b) Didn't it been obvious?
c) Was it not obvious?

2445. Choose the correct sentence:
a) Who are you talking?
b) Who are you talk to?
c) Who are you talking to?
2446. Choose the correct sentence:
a) Who is this gift for?
b) Whom does this gift for?
c) Who is this gift?
2447. It's the most … song.
a) fame
b) famous
c) famously
2448. What do you know about the world of …?
a) fashion
b) fashionable
c) fashioning

2449. It was a … experiment regarding new treatments.
a) science
b) sciencely
c) scientific
2450. …, what he is saying is true.
a) Actually
b) Recently
c) Actual
2451. Turn … the sound! It's way too loud.
a) up
b) away
c) down
2452. I switched … the laptop.
a) off
b) about
c) away
2453. Sarah showed … at the end of the party.
a) within
b) up
c) beyond
2454. Our plan fell … . We'll try again soon.
a) away
b) through
c) about
2455. Choose the correct sentence:
a) I'm trying to learn German in spite of not having enough free time.
b) I'm trying to learn German in spite to have enough free time.
c) I'm trying to learn German despite of having enough free time.
2456. I … sooner go abroad.
a) had
b) could
c) would
2457. There is no point …, so let's calm down.
a) argue
b) in arguing
c) to argue
2458. The mission … last week.
a) should be cancelled
b) should have been cancelled
c) should cancel

2459. Whatever you say, it …
change my life.
a) was
b) has
c) did

2460. Not only … but I also
work.
a) I study
b) do I study
c) had I study

2461. Choose the correct
sentence:
a) Do you work next Friday?
b) Are you working next
Friday?
c) Have you worked next
Friday?

2462. Choose the correct
sentence:
a) I'm tasting this dish now.
b) I taste the dish now.
c) I've been tasting this dish
now.

2463. Choose the correct
sentence:
a) She's owing me 300 dollars
now.
b) She's been owing me 300
dollars now.
c) She owes me 300 dollars
now.

2464. Is the following sentence
correct? "I was wanting to help
them."
a) correct
b) incorrect

2465. Is the following sentence
correct? "Were you knowing all
the truth at
that moment?"
a) correct
b) incorrect

2466. My old family friend …
invited me.
a) will

b) should
c) have

2467. She … brilliant results.
a) showed
b) shown
c) has showing

2468. The manager said he …
those employees.
a) hadn't fired
b) doesn't fires
c) will fire

2469. When she noticed me I …
the car for two hours.
a) was driving
b) had been driving
c) have been driving

2470. Necessary conditions …
now.
a) aren't being provided
b) haven't provided
c) hadn't been provided

2471. Why … to the list?
a) has it adding
b) has it been added
c) had it being added

2472. Don't worry. Your
knowledge … enough.

a) are
b) has
c) will be
2473. How long … together?
a) have you being worked
b) have you been working
c) had you been working
2474. She was exhausted. She … hard all morning.
a) had been working
b) had work
c) has been working

2475. If Mary had passed the test, her parents … much happier.
a) would had been
b) would have been
c) might had been
2476. If only I … more time!
a) have
b) did
c) had
2477. Choose the correct sentence:
a) You don't have to overwork.
b) You don't need be overwork.
c) You didn't needed overwork.
2478. It … much better.
a) would to be
b) would been
c) would have been
2479. This name is familiar … me.
a) to
b) about
c) with

2480. You need to be more polite … your customers.
a) of
b) to
c) on
2481. He couldn't hear her. She shouted … him again.
a) to
b) of
c) towards
2482. I agree with you … some extent.
a) of
b) on
c) to
2483. They … this place by ten.
a) will leave
b) will be left
c) will have left
2484. The manager said: "I'm busy now.".
a) The manager said that he was busy now.
b) The manager said that he has been busy then.
c) The manager said that he was busy then.
2485. She asked me: "Do you agree?".
a) She asked me if I agreed.
b) She asked me I agreed
c) She asked me if had I agreed.
2486. My friends asked me: "Where is this place?".
a) My friends asked me where was that place.

b) My friends asked me where that place was.
c) My friends asked me where that place has been.
2487. She asked me: "How are your parents doing?".
a) She asked me how my parents were doing.
b) She asked me how my parents are doing.
c) She asked me how have been doing.
2488. Choose the correct sentence:
a) Won't you hurrying up?
b) Didn't you hurried up?
c) Won't you hurry up?
2489. Choose the correct sentence:
a) Isn't it getting more and more expensive?
b) Is not it getting more and more expensive?
c) Doesn't it getting more and more expensively?
2490. I was ... by the latest news regarding the war.
a) shocking
b) shocked
c) shockingly
2491. I was surprised by her ... to do something correctly.
a) inability
b) unability
c) irability

2492. I consider it's ... .

a) unprobable
b) improbable
c) aprobable
2493. I felt so ... . I wanted to leave that place.
a) comfortable
b) comfy
c) uncomfortable
2494. It happened ... because of them.
a) largely
b) large
c) larging
2495. You should think twice. It's a unique ... .
a) possibly
b) possibility
c) possible
2496. Wow! This it's the best ... .
a) salvation
b) solution
c) solve
2497. The player was fined and ... .
a) disqualified
b) qualified
c) unqualifiedly
2498. The little girl likes listening to ... music.
a) classic
b) class
c) classical
2499. I've just turned ... the laptop. I need to write a report.
a) on
b) up

c) about

2500. We need to think this plan … .

a) away

b) over

c) towards

2501. My parents split … twelve years ago.

a) in

b) against

c) up

2502. We decided to bring … the price of some products.

a) down

b) against

c) amongst

2503. I can't work this problem … .

a) over

b) out

c) beyond

2504. I'd rather … it.

a) didn't say

b) not say

c) not saying

2505. I'd rather … with her.

a) to agree

b) agree

c) agreeing

2506. This goal can't … .

a) achieved

b) be achieving

c) be achieved

2507. This decision may … today.

a) be taken

b) take

c) be token

2508. The truth needed … .

a) be said

b) being say

c) to be said

2509. … friends you have, the better.

a) The more

b) More

c) The less

2510. She felt … exhausted.

a) such

b) absolutely

c) very

2511. Choose the correct sentence:

a) She behaves strangely these days.

b) She had behaved strangely these days.

c) She is behaving strangely these days.

2512. Choose the correct sentence:

a) You are overestimating our abilities now.

b) You overestimate our abilities now.

c) You have overestimated our abilities now.

2513. My superior … me.

a) has being informed

b) was informing

c) informing

2514. … she assisting him that night?
a) Had
b) Did
c) Was
2515. … the detectives experiencing big problems?
a) Were
b) Did
c) Had
2516. Is the following sentence correct? "Was it belonging to you?"
a) correct
b) incorrect
2517. We … Kate.
a) were seen
b) have seen
c) are seen

2518. … the manager understood it?
a) Have
b) Did
c) Has
2519. I have … it completely. I'm sorry!
a) forgot
b) forgetting
c) forgotten
2520. We … those difficulties and everything was fine in the end.
a) overcame
b) overcome
c) overcoming
2521. How long … about it?

a) have you think
b) have you been thinking
c) had you be thinking
2522. I … here for fifteen minutes.
a) have be
b) was
c) have been
2523. … him before they called you?
a) Had you informed
b) Did you inform
c) Have you informed
2524. How about them? … now?
a) Are they trained
b) Are they being trained
c) Have they trained
2525. She understood her friends … her.
a) was using
b) had used
c) have been used
2526. These global opportunities ... today.
a) are considering

b) are considered
c) are being considered
2527. This problem … .
a) has never been mentioned
b) never be mentioned
c) will never mentioning
2528. She would work there if she … a millionaire.
a) is
b) had

c) were

2529. Choose the correct sentence:

a) You don't have prepare these documents today.

b) You didn't have prepare these documents today.

c) You don't have to prepare these documents today.

2530. Tom is rude … her.

a) of

b) to

c) about

2531. I'm familiar … this problem and I'll solve it.

a) to

b) with

c) on

2532. The businessman was so generous … us!

a) of

b) for

c) to

2533. I'll pay … cash.

a) in

b) about

c) on

2534. She always calls me … Mondays.

a) at

b) in

c) on

2535. … instance, it can mean that she likes you.

a) To

b) For

c) With

2536. The girl asked me: "How often do you visit this place?".

a) The girl asked me how often I visited that place.

b) The girl asked me how often I had visited this place.

c) The girl asked me how often you visited that place.

2537. The reporter asked me: "Who was getting richer?".

a) The reporter asked me who had been getting richer.

b) The reporter asked me who was getting richer.

c) The reporter asked me who has got richer.

2538. The journalist asked me: "Why has she become a real star?".

a) The journalist asked me why had she become a real star.

b) The journalist asked me why she had become a real star.

c) The journalist asked me why she was becoming a real star.

Set 10

2539. She asked me: "How long have you been playing football?".

a) She asked me how long I had been playing football.

b) She asked me how long I have played football.

c) She asked me how long had I been playing football.

2540. Choose the correct sentence:

a) Hasn't it lead to lots of problems?

b) Didn't it led to lots of problems?

c) Hasn't it led to lots of problems?

2541. Choose the correct sentence:

a) What are you pointed about?

b) What are you pointing at?

c) What have you been point about?

2542. Why was she so …?

a) frighted

b) frightened

c) frightening

2543. I was … to help him.

a) inable

b) ireable

c) unable

2544. They were … of the threat.

a) unaware

b) disaware

c) inaware

2545. She would like to feel more … .

a) safe

b) saving

c) save

2546. She doesn't know what she wants. She's so … .

a) decisive

b) undecisive

c) indecisive

2547. You are a very professional … .

a) professor

b) teaching

c) teachers

2548. She experienced a feeling of … .

a) amazing

b) amazement

c) amazed

2549. The level of … is high.

a) competitive

b) competing

c) competition

2550. She's my … .

a) friendship

b) relationship

c) girlfriend

2551. Katherine is a famous … .

a) art

b) artist

c) actor

2552. Her husband is an … man. He's a simple person.

a) ordinary

b) ordinarily

c) ordinal

2553. To our surprise, he turned … at the party.

a) in

b) beyond

c) up

2554. I decided to ask her … .

a) out

b) for

c) about

2555. I burst … laughing.

a) into

b) out

c) away

2556. Choose the correct sentence:

a) My grandmother remembers everything despite being 85.

b) My grandmother remembers everything despite to be 85.

c) My grandmother remembers everything in spite of be 85.

2557. She is known … German professionally.

a) teaching

b) to teach

c) taught

2558. The manager ought to be … .

a) informed

b) informal

c) informing

2559. … a lot, she feels tired.

a) To work

b) Worked

c) Working

2560. The director ought not to be … .

a) interrupt

b) interrupted

c) interrupting

2561. My friend … TV.

a) were watching

b) were being watching

c) was watching

2562. Where … it going on?

a) were

b) have

c) was

2563. What … they looking for in the city?

a) were

b) have

c) was

2564. Is the following sentence correct? "They were overestimating its power at that moment."

a) correct

b) incorrect

2565. I'm happy! We … a new project.

a) have started

b) had been started

c) will have starting

2566. … these words influenced her?

a) Did

b) Have

c) Might have

2567. Choose the correct sentence:

a) Did you ever hear it?

b) Have you ever heard it?

c) Have you ever be hearing it?

2568. The boy has … a horse.

a) rode

b) riding

c) ridden

2569. I had no other solution. I
… them into groups.
a) split
b) splitted
c) splitting
2570. Jane … there for two
months.
a) had been working
b) has been working
c) was working
2571. I told him I … Mary.
a) already saw
b) have already seen
c) had already seen
2572. When I came there she …
for me for a long time.
a) had been waiting
b) has been waiting
c) was waiting
2573. All the project details …
yet.
a) weren't considered
b) haven't been considered
c) hadn't been considered
2574. Choose the correct
sentence:
a) Had the losses being
covered?
b) Have the losses been
covered?
c) Were the losses been
covered?
2575. I … Chinese for an hour
when she called me.
a) was learning

b) had been learning
c) did learnt
2576. Poor conditions … there.
You should avoid that place.
a) provide
b) providing
c) are provided
2577. I wish she … know about
it.
a) didn't

b) doesn't
c) wasn't
2578. If she hadn't shown such
bad results, her parents … so
angry now.
a) wouldn't be
b) wouldn't have been
c) hadn't been
2579. You … insist on it. I
won't forget!
a) needn't have
b) didn't need to
c) hadn't need to
2580. He's really worried … his
future.
a) in
b) about
c) regard
2581. I'm waiting … my wife.
a) for
b) to
c) on
2582. They blame him …
everything.
a) on
b) for

c) about
2583. My cousin is … .
a) on diet
b) in diet
c) on a diet
2584. My wife asked me: "Are you tired?".
a) My wife asked me if I was tired.
b) My wife asked me if I am tired.
c) My wife asked me if I have been tired.
2585. My cousin asked me: "Did Jane enter that university?".
a) My cousin asked me if Jane entered that university.
b) My cousin asked me if Jane have entered that university.
c) My cousin asked me whether Jane had entered that university.

2586. Megan asked me: "Was it getting dark?".
a) Megan asked me if it had been getting dark.
b) Megan asked me if had it ben getting dark.
c) Megan asked me if it was getting darker.
2587. She asked me: "Why were you so serious?".
a) She asked me why you have been so serious.
b) She asked me why I had been so serious.
c) She asked me why I have been so serious.
2588. Choose the correct sentence:
a) Won't you concentrate on the main problem?
b) Not will you concentrate on the main problem?
c) Didn't you concentrated on the main problem?
2589. Choose the correct sentence:
a) Isn't she waited for us?
b) Isn't she waiting for us?
c) Weren't she waiting for us?
2590. The child was … of the dark.
a) terrifying
b) terrified
c) terrifyingly
2591. This is totally … .
a) unacceptable
b) disacceptable
c) inacceptable
2592. She was … to my eyes.
a) unvisible
b) disvisible
c) invisible
2593. It's … that life on other planets exists.
a) indeniable
b) undeniable
c) disdeniable
2594. Suddenly, we were … .
a) inconnected

b) unconnected

c) disconnected

2595. I can't put … with all this injustice.

a) in

b) up

c) about

2596. She made … this story. Don't believe her!

a) up

b) in

c) within

2597. Can you please speak …? I can't hear you well enough.

a) over

b) about

c) up

2598. Tell her to slow …! I'm afraid of her driving style!

a) up

b) away

c) down

2599. When will you stop hanging …? You should do something useful.

a) around

b) off

c) within

2600. Choose the correct sentence:

a) I am used to do it.

b) I used to do it.

c) I have using to do it.

2601. Choose the correct sentence:

a) I'm used to think so about her.

b) I used to think so about her.

c) I had using to think so about her.

2602. You'd better … .

a) don't complain

b) didn't complain

c) not complain

2603. My father repaired his watch.

a) itself

b) himself

c) by itself

2604. These rules … last month.

a) should revise

b) should be revised

c) should have been revised

2605. The strategy … more thoroughly.

a) should been taught

b) should have been thought

c) should had been thought

2606. People were … starving.

a) absolutely

b) utter

c) very

2607. She became … furious after hearing the news.

a) bad

b) extreme

c) absolutely

2608. It's … unbelievable.

a) most

b) absolutely

c) good

2609. By … business you can be more independent.

a) doing

b) done
c) be done
2610. … school, I entered a famous university.
a) To finishing
b) Been finishing
c) Having finished
2611. Choose the correct sentence:
a) Why do you hesitate now?

b) Why have you been hesitating now?
c) Why are you hesitating now?
2612. When I noticed it, they … on the phone.
a) did talking
b) were talking
c) had been talking
2613. Her manager … her of stealing the documents.
a) was accusing
b) did accused
c) have accusing
2614. What … your uncle building there?
a) was
b) did
c) have
2615. Is the following sentence correct? "I was logging in when she
entered."
a) incorrect
b) correct
2616. My old friend … said it.
a) did

b) was
c) has
2617. … the experts opened your eyes?
a) Did
b) Have
c) Will
2618. … you visited this place?
a) Has
b) Did
c) Have
2619. I … Jennifer two days ago.
a) saw
b) seen
c) did

2620. She has … many problems lately.
a) having
b) had
c) be having
2621. I … Russian since last month.
a) hadn't learning
b) didn't learnt
c) haven't been learning
2622. How long … correspondence?
a) did you maintained
b) have you been maintaining
c) had you be maintaining
2623. How long … it?
a) had you been wanting
b) have you wanted
c) were you wanted

2624. The girl said she … it for three hours.
a) had been doing
b) has been doing
c) will be doing
2625. He … now by the police.
a) is being controlled
b) is controlled
c) has been controlled
2626. I knew he … her yet.
a) didn't reply
b) hadn't replied
c) hasn't replied
2627. If I had known it, my score … much higher.
a) will be
b) has been
c) would have been
2628. I wish my result … better.
a) could

b) might
c) were
2629. She … her mistakes yesterday.
a) should corrected
b) should have corrected
c) should had corrected
2630. The thief was forced … .
a) to surrender
b) surrender
c) surrendering
2631. The little boy is excellent … maths.
a) in
b) on
c) at

2632. She's annoyed … her boss.
a) about
b) with
c) around
2633. It's very kind … you to help me.
a) of
b) to
c) on
2634. They spend lots of money … food and waste it.
a) for
b) away
c) on
2635. This flat belongs … me.
a) on
b) to
c) of
2636. Steven said: "She has remembered it at last.".
a) Steven said that she had remembered it at last.
b) Steven said that she has remembered it at last.
c) Steven said that she would be remembering it at last.

2637. The boy said: "I will go there anyway.".
a) The boy said that he will go there anyway.
b) The boy said that he would be going there anyway.
c) They boy said that he would go there anyway.

2638. The director said: "She has been working here for all her life.".
a) The director said that she has been working there for all her life.
b) The director said that she had been working there for all her life.
c) The director said that she was working there for all her life.
2639. My partner asked me: "Do you find this idea interesting?".
a) My partner asked me if I found that idea interesting.
b) My partner asked me if I find that idea interesting.
c) My partner asked me if I did found that idea interesting.
2640. My mother asked me: "Are you talking on the phone?".
a) My mother asked me if you were talking on the phone.
b) My mother asked me if I was talking on the phone.
c) My mother asked me if I have been talking on the phone.
2641. Choose the correct sentence:
a) Not it a different method?
b) Didn't it be a different method?
c) Isn't it a different method?
2642. Choose the correct sentence:

a) Weren't you afraid?
b) Didn't you afraid?
c) Were you afraid not?
2643. I will … it clear for you.
a) do
b) make
c) made
2644. It can only lead to his … .
a) unagreement
b) disagreement
c) inagreement
2645. These people are … connected.
a) unseparably
b) diseparably
c) inseparably
2646. This place is … .
a) isafe
b) insafe
c) unsafe
2647. This food is … .
a) inedible
b) unedible
c) disedible
2648. She showed a slight … in her Russian.
a) improvement
b) improving
c) improved
2649. There was a … of clean water.
a) short
b) unshortage
c) shortage
2650. For me, it was a … night.
a) unsleepy

b) sleepless

c) slept

2651. I checked … before midday. I was sorry for leaving.

a) within

b) out

c) about

2652. I'll pick you … in an hour.

a) up

b) about

c) beyond

2653. The marketing assistant handed … the leaflets.

a) about

b) in

c) out

2654. I'd like to point … it's really worth buying.

a) out

b) for

c) about

2655. I … prefer to drop this subject.

a) had

b) can

c) would

2656. Her idea might not … .

a) approved

b) be approved

c) be approving

2657. This report … .

a) could to attach

b) could been attached

c) could have been attached

2658. It may … .

a) to discuss

b) been discuss

c) have been discussed

2659. That problem shouldn't … .

a) have been mentioned

b) been mentioned

c) have mentioned

2660. Neither her mother … her father can help you.

a) or

b) either

c) nor

2661. No one … accused.

a) were

b) wasn't

c) was

2662. We'll discuss the issue after she … .

a) comes back

b) come back

c) will come back

2663. I won't call them unless they … .

a) will apologize

b) apologize

c) would apologize

2664. Choose the correct sentence:

a) What do you do tomorrow?

b) What are you doing tomorrow?

c) What will you done tomorrow?

2665. Choose the correct sentence:

a) I don't recognize you now.
b) I'm not recognizing you now.
c) I didn't recognize you now.
2666. Choose the correct sentence:
a) We are needing it at the moment.
b) We aren't needed it at the moment.
c) We need it at the moment.
2667. Why … your manager following her advice?
a) did
b) was
c) had
2668. Is the following sentence correct? "Her words were sounding strange."
a) correct
b) incorrect
2669. The trainer … divided us.
a) didn't
b) won't
c) hasn't
2670. … the documents been received by your department?
a) Have
b) Did
c) Will

2671. How long … here?
a) have you being
b) have you been being
c) have you been
2672. I wish I … America last year.

a) visited
b) had visited
c) have visited
2673. Choose the correct sentence:
a) It's high time we visit this place.
b) It's high time we had visited this place.
c) It's high time we visited this place.
2674. You don't have … so early.
a) to get up
b) getting up
c) get up
2675. Choose the correct sentence:
a) You needn't to explaining it again.
b) You don't need to explain it again.
c) You didn't needed to explain it again.
2676. He ought to … the meeting last week.
a) attend
b) been attended
c) have attended
2677. She won't let you … it.
a) do
b) doing
c) to do
2678. Mary's quite good … German.
a) in
b) at

c) about

2679. I'm terrible … dancing.

a) at

b) about

c) in

2680. I was fascinated … that modern technology.

a) with

b) on

c) of

2681. I haven't seen you … ages.

a) from

b) about

c) for

2682. The girl learnt English … herself.

a) on

b) with

c) by

2683. John said: "The professor is explaining these rules.".

a) John said that the professor was explaining those rules.

b) John said that the professor had explained these rules.

c) John said that the professor is explaining these rules.

2684. The professor: "She will correct her mistakes.".

a) The professor said that she'll correct her mistakes.

b) The professor said that she would correct her mistakes.

c) The professor said that she has corrected her mistakes.

2685. She said: "When he arrived I had already prepared everything.".

a) She said that when he arrived she had already prepared everything.

b) She said that when he arrived she has already prepared everything.

c) She said that when he had arrived he had already prepared everything.

2686. Katherine said: "My parents knew that I had missed that lesson.".

a) Katherine said that her parents had known that she had missed that
lesson.

b) Katherine said that her parents knew that she missed that lesson.

c) Katherine said that her parents have known that she had missed
that lesson.

2687. He said: "They were criticizing her sharply.".

a) He said that they were criticized her sharply.

b) He said that they had been criticizing her sharply.

c) He said that they have criticized her sharply.

2688. She asked me: "Are they ignoring him?".

a) She asked me if they had been ignoring him.
b) She asked me if they were ignoring him.
c) She asked me if they have been ignoring him.
2689. My wife asked me: "What's in the box?".
a) My wife asked me what' in the box.
b) My wife asked me what has been in the box.
c) My wife asked me what was in the box.
2690. The lady asked me: "What kind of job is it?".
a) The lady asked me what kind of job it was.
b) The lady asked me what kind of job was it.
c) The lady asked me what kind of job it has been.
2691. Choose the correct sentence:
a) Who does this business belonging to?
b) Which does this business belong to?
c) Who does this business belong to?
2692. It was a very … situation.
a) embarrassed
b) embarrassing
c) embarrass
2693. We were really … .
a) luckily
b) unlucky

c) inlucky
2694. I appreciate you because your lessons are so … .
a) informing
b) informed
c) informative
2695. The new colleague is … .
a) unintelligent
b) inintelligent
c) disintelligent

2696. To my surprise, everything was in … .
a) misorder
b) disorder
c) unorder
2697. This power is … .
a) unlegitimate
b) illegitimate
c) dislegitimate
2698. Thieves broke … the bank.
a) into
b) onto
c) away
2699. Would you turn … the sound? I can't hear it.
a) down
b) away
c) up
2700. Get …! I don't want to see you!
a) through
b) out
c) in
2701. Choose the correct sentence:

a) She had better to call him one more time.

b) She'd better call him one more time.

c) She would have better call him one more time.

2702. I'd rather you ... it.

a) do

b) done

c) did

2703. I think this meeting must ... .

a) be postponed

b) postpone

c) had postponed

2704. This thing can ... .

a) sell

b) be selling

c) be sold

2705. They ought not ... .

a) to be notified

b) being notified

c) be notified

2706. Choose the correct sentence:

a) Should these laptops to be purchased?

b) Should these laptops have been purchased?

c) Should these laptops had been purchased?

2707. We are ... the city in an hour.

a) leave

b) to left

c) to leave

2708. That moment, she was just about ... .

a) to panic

b) panicking

c) panic

2709. ... known it, he changed his point of view.

a) Being

b) Hading

c) Having

2710. Hardly ... some money when he spent it.

a) he had got

b) had he got

c) did he got

2711. I'll inform her in case the price ... .

a) doesn't get lower

b) wouldn't get lower

c) won't get lower

2712. Choose the correct sentence:

a) I'm doing it quite frequently.

b) I do it quite frequently.

c) I had being do it quite frequently.

2713. While she was checking her e-mail, I ... her project.

a) had checked

b) have checked

c) was checking

2714. The detectives ... that crime.

a) weren't investigating

b) hadn't investigating

c) won't being investigated

2715. What … becoming uncontrollable?
a) were
b) did
c) was

2716. Is the following sentence correct? "The project wasn't seeming interesting."
a) correct
b) incorrect

2717. Is the following sentence correct? "She way carrying the baby."
a) correct
b) incorrect

2718. Mary … kept her promise.
a) didn't
b) won't
c) hasn't

2719. I have … a new car.
a) buyed
b) bought
c) buying

2720. When she got to work I … a report for 40 minutes.
a) was making
b) have been making
c) had been making

2721. The dog … today.
a) wasn't been
b) hasn't been
c) didn't been

2722. Choose the correct sentence:

a) It seems strange now.
b) It is seeming strange now.
c) It has been seemed strange now.

2723. I will do it after Mary … .
a) will come back
b) had come back
c) comes back

2724. I know she … it for a long time.
a) has wanted
b) had been wanting
c) has being wanted

2725. The students … for the final exam.
a) wasn't preparing
b) prepared
c) didn't prepared

2726. Choose the correct sentence:
a) They are always being thanked.
b) They are always thanked.
c) They had always being thanked.

2727. If I were you, I … think about it one more time.
a) would
b) will
c) would have

2728. I wish I … 5 apartments.
a) have
b) did had
c) had

2729. You … her one more time.
a) didn't needed criticize

b) hadn't needed criticize

c) needn't have criticized

2730. I worked there … a while, it's true.

a) in

b) for

c) so

2731. They will pay … advance.

a) in

b) about

c) for

2732. This project can be interesting only … theory.

a) at

b) for

c) in

2733. Mr. Brown said: "We were having a great time there.".

a) Mr. Brown said that they had a great time there.

b) Mr. Brown said that they had been having a great time there.

c) Mr. Brown said that they were having a great time there.

2734. I … this project by November.

a) will started

b) will have started

c) will be started

2735. My mother asked me: "Do you enjoy learning English there?".

a) My mother asked me whether I enjoyed learning English there.

b) My mother asked me if I enjoy learning English there.

c) My mother asked me if I have enjoyed learning English there.

2736. The officer asked me: "Did they persuade her to do it?".

a) The officer asked me if they persuaded her to do it.

b) The officer asked me if they had persuaded her to do it.

c) The officer asked me if they did persuaded herself to do it.

2737. The lady asked me: "Will it depend on him?".

a) The lady asked me if it will depend on him.

b) The lady asked me if it would depend on him.

c) The lady asked me if it depended on him.

2738. The policeman asked me: "Who was following her?".

a) The policeman asked me who is following her.

b) The policeman asked me who has been following her.

c) The policeman asked me who had been following her.

2739. Her speech was so … .

a) inspiring

b) inspired

c) disinspiring

2740. I think we … each other.

a) disunderstood

b) misunderstood

c) inunderstood

2741. I think your business partner is … .
a) inreliable
b) disreliable
c) unreliable

2742. It wasn't … that Steve was in the first place.
a) surprising
b) unsurprising
c) dissurprising

2743. They don't know the … state of affairs.
a) actually
b) currently
c) actual

2744. I feel … about this idea.
a) enjoyed
b) enthusiastic
c) enthusiasm

2745. It's a bad result … with her previous achievements.
a) compared
b) comparison
c) comparing

2746. The employees don't like his … .
a) stictment
b) striction
c) strictness

2747. We decided to set … a company.
a) on
b) away
c) up

2748. I stick … the idea it can take place.
a) at
b) about
c) to

2749. She burst … laughter.
a) out
b) into
c) about

2750. Little girls like dressing … .
a) up
b) away
c) within

2751. Yesterday I got the fence … .
a) painting
b) painted
c) paint

2752. This book may not … .
a) be recommended
b) recommending
c) being recommended

2753. It has … controlled.
a) being
b) be
c) to be

2754. These men shouldn't be … .
a) trust
b) trusted
c) trusting

2755. May the final report … tomorrow?
a) be finished
b) finish
c) to finish

2756. It … beforehand.

a) should has been written

b) should had been written

c) should have been written

2757. Could that outcome …
been predicted?

a) had

b) have

c) did

2758. … can get rich. Trust me!

a) The poor

b) Poor

c) The poors

2759. This detail is … minor.

a) absolute

b) absoluting

c) absolutely

2760. The President is … China
next week.

a) to visit

b) visit

c) to visited

2761. Choose the correct
sentence:

a) It is seeming to me she's
making a terrible mistake now.

b) It seems to me she's making
a terrible mistake now.

c) It seems to me she's made a
terrible mistake now.

2762. While I was working, she
… a rest.

a) did having

b) has been having

c) was having

2763. … she thinking about it?

a) Did

b) Was

c) Has

2764. Is the following sentence
correct? "They were disagreeing
with us."

a) correct

b) incorrect

2765. Choose the correct
sentence:

a) I never wanted it. It didn't
interest me.

b) I have never wanted it. It
hadn't interest me.

c) I had never wanted it. It
wouldn't be interest me.

2766. I was … New York two
years ago.

a) to

b) about

c) in

2767. They … away yesterday.

a) flown

b) flew

c) had flown

2768. I … this text for an hour.

a) have been translating

b) had translated

c) was translating

2769. … to work before they
got the first call?

a) Did she already got

b) Had she already got

c) Have she already got

2770. Why …?

a) has it being said

b) has it been said

c) did it be saying

2771. Choose the correct sentence:
a) Mary is frequently visiting this place.
b) Mary is frequently being visited this place.
c) Mary frequently visits this place.

2772. Choose the correct sentence:
a) This laptop isn't belonging to me now.
b) This laptop doesn't belong to me now.
c) This laptop didn't belong to me now.

2773. The manager found out some employees … the money.
a) was stealing

b) had stolen
c) did stolen

2774. By the time she arrived I … for her for 10 minutes.
a) had been waiting
b) had waited
c) did been waiting

2775. … these days?
a) Are they watched
b) Are they being watched
c) Did they be watched

2776. Choose the correct sentence:
a) It's high time we will do it.
b) It's high time we did it.
c) It's high time we had do it.

2777. If your parents hadn't met, you … here now.
a) wouldn't have been
b) wouldn't been
c) wouldn't be

2778. Don't be afraid … this dog!
a) by
b) on
c) of

2779. The motel is suitable … me.
a) for
b) to
c) of

2780. … average, I get 50 dollars a month.
a) On
b) By
c) With

2781. We saw the laptop … TV.
a) in
b) on
c) about

2782. Many people are out … work these days.
a) off
b) away
c) of

2783. What's happening … reality? Can you tell me?
a) into
b) in
c) of

2784. Tom said: "I really hate it.".

a) Tom said that he is really hating it.

b) Tom said that he did really hate it.

c) Tom said that he really hated it.

2785. She … for you.

a) won't be waiting

b) haven't been waiting

c) didn't be waiting

2786. My mother asked me: "Is she at the station?".

a) My mother asked me whether she was at the station.

b) My mother asked me if she had been at the station.

c) My mother asked me whether she is at the station.

2787. Jane asked me: "Are you waiting for him?".

a) Jane asked me if I had been waiting for him.

b) Jane asked me if I was waiting for him.

c) Jane asked me if I have been waiting for him.

2788. The manager asked me: "When are they free?".

a) The manager asked me when were they free.

b) The manager asked me when they had been free.

c) The manager asked me when they were free.

2789. Kate asked me: "What did you stop doing?".

a) Kate asked me what I had stopped doing.

b) Kate asked me what had I stopped doing.

c) Kate asked me what I stopped doing.

2790. … it a good plan?

a) Isn't

b) Didn't

c) Doesn't

2791. Choose the correct sentence:

a) Will it hurt not your feelings?

b) Won't it hurt your feelings?

c) Wouldn't it hurting your feelings?

2792. Choose the correct sentence:

a) Haven't you be to Madrid?

b) Didn't you been to Madrid?

c) Haven't you been to Madrid?

2793. Her explanation was … .

a) unaccurate

b) inaccurate

c) disaccurate

2794. This speech is … .

a) inappropriate

b) unappropriate

c) disappropriate

2795. You will waste time reading it. This report is … .

a) useful

b) useless

c) uunuseful

2796. She drives so … . I feel safe with her.

a) carelessly
b) carefully
c) carefulness
2797. We were in a … situation.
a) dangerous
b) dangering
c) danger
2798. It's a … example.
a) classical
b) classically
c) classic

2799. The detectives managed to … the truth.
a) incover
b) uncover
c) recover
2800. This is a huge … .
a) misadvantage
b) disadvantage
c) inadvantage
2801. She turned … the TV after a while.
a) on
b) away
c) with
2802. I like working … at the gym.
a) away
b) in
c) out
2803. The team warmed … before the final game.
a) up
b) down
c) in

2804. Choose the correct sentence:
a) She's accustomed to work so much.
b) She's accustomed to being work so much.
c) She's accustomed to working so much.
2805. I have difficulty … English.
a) learn
b) in learnt
c) in learning
2806. She has difficulty … for her new car.
a) pay
b) paying
c) to paying
2807. This phrase mustn't … .
a) be repeated
b) repeat
c) repeating
2808. The problem might not … .
a) to solve
b) be solved
c) to solving
2809. Must it … during today's meeting?
a) mention
b) mentioning
c) be mentioned
2810. Mike's about … .
a) to return
b) returning
c) be returned

2811. Nothing … really difficult.
a) wasn't
b) didn't
c) was

2812. I'll give you this document after you … ready.
a) will be
b) are
c) had been

2813. Choose the correct sentence:
a) She is having two kids now.
b) She has two kids now.
c) She had two kids now.

2814. I … Chinese all day.
a) did learnt
b) had learnt
c) was learning

2815. We … TV at 7 o'clock yesterday evening.
a) were watching
b) did watched
c) had been watching

2816. Is the following sentence correct? "I was supposing it was right."
a) correct
b) incorrect

2817. John … missed the lesson.
a) didn't
b) hasn't
c) wasn't

2818. … they decided what to do?

a) Has
b) Did
c) Have

2819. What … the girl done?
a) would
b) have
c) have be

2820. Choose the correct sentence:
a) We knew it two days ago.
b) We have known it two days ago.
c) We had known it two days ago.

2821. Have you been … Moscow?
a) in
b) about
c) to

2822. She has … away.
a) went
b) gone
c) go

2823. She … me what to do.
a) told
b) asking
c) have asked

2824. The director … it perfectly.
a) known
b) knew
c) did knew

2825. The detective … pieces of information for two months.
a) has collecting
b) has been collecting

c) did collecting

2826. … now?

a) Is it spoilt

b) Is it being spoilt

c) Has it being spoilt

2827. Where … all this time?

a) have you been

b) did you being

c) have you been being

2828. I realized my keys … at home.

a) be left

b) had been left

c) did left

2829. I wouldn't say it if I … you now.

a) had been

b) was

c) were

2830. If only there … a way out!

a) was

b) has been

c) is

2831. Choose the correct sentence:

a) It's time for you say it.

b) It's time you said it.

c) It's time you had said it.

2832. As I have no choice, I … overwork.

a) have to

b) could

c) might

2833. I know she … win.

a) could to

b) did to

c) had to

2834. I'm disappointed … the results.

a) for

b) on

c) about

2835. The kid was absent … school.

a) from

b) at

c) in

2836. She's suspicious … her new manager.

a) in

b) of

c) with

2837. My grandfather is brilliant … chess.

a) in

b) with

c) at

2838. Jane is enthusiastic … this idea.

a) about

b) in

c) on

2839. It's very cruel … her to say such terrible things.

a) to

b) on

c) of

2840. It's very generous … you to give me this perfume.

a) to

b) of

c) with

2841. I … for the exam all day tomorrow.
a) will be preparing
b) would be preparing
c) will be prepared

2842. The secretary asked me: "Was this time convenient?".
a) The secretary asked me if that time had been convenient.
b) The secretary asked me if that time was convenient.
c) The secretary asked if that time was convenient for me.

2843. The customer asked me: "How much money does it cost?".
a) The customer asked me how much money did it cost.
b) The customer asked me how much money it had cost.
c) The customer asked me how much money it cost.

2844. She asked me: "How busy is the manager?".
a) She asked me how busy the manager was.
b) She asked me how busy was the manager.
c) She asked me how busy the manager had been.

2845. She asked me: "How much will it cost?".
a) She asked me how much will it cost.
b) She asked me how much it would cost.

c) She asked me how much did it cost.

2846. Choose the correct sentence:
a) Wasn't it a waste of time?
b) Wasn't it being a waste of time?
c) Didn't it be a waste of time?

2847. This approach is … .
a) imperfect
b) disperfect
c) unperfect

2848. What a … woman!
a) beautifully
b) beauty
c) beautiful

2849. I … like your YouTube channel.
a) real
b) really
c) reality

2850. … as it may seem, they won.
a) Incredible

b) Incredibly
c) Credible

2851. I'd like to get a good … .
a) educate
b) educational
c) education

2852. Her result was so … . It was a surprise.
a) unpredictable
b) predicting
c) predictable

2853. This mechanism is still …
.

a) inknown
b) unknown
c) unknowingly

2854. This perfume was sold …
. It was a real success.

a) out
b) in
c) about

2855. Choose the correct sentence:
a) They will never let you down!
b) They would never be let you down!
c) They will never let down you!

2856. These scenarios might not … .
a) be compare
b) comparing
c) be compared

2857. Can it …?
a) checking
b) be checked
c) being check

2858. I'm sorry but it had … .
a) to be said
b) be said
c) be saying

2859. The sooner, … .
a) better
b) the better
c) the best

2860. I … think so!

a) am
b) being
c) do

2861. We'll start reading the project as soon as she … .
a) arrives
b) will arrive
c) be arrived

2862. Some customers … refused to accept it.
a) would
b) be
c) have

2863. How … you done it?
a) has
b) did
c) have

2864. Choose the correct sentence:
a) I hadn't seen it yet.
b) I haven't seen it yet.
c) I didn't see it yet.

2865. Choose the correct sentence:
a) I have never met her.
b) I didn't never meet her.
c) I hadn't ever meet her.

2866. Choose the correct sentence:
a) I never did it in my childhood.
b) I never would done it in my childhood.
c) I never had did it in my childhood.

2867. It … more money than you think.

a) costed

b) costing

c) cost

2868. She has … her old car.

a) sold

b) sell

c) been sold

2869. My mother has … her finger.

a) cutted

b) cut

c) be cut

2870. The water was … .

a) frozen

b) freeze

c) freezed

2871. I … here since last year.

a) have live

b) have been living

c) had been living

2872. When I returned she … for about 2 hours.

a) had been sleeping

b) was sleeping

c) has been sleeping

2873. This project … now.

a) is discussed

b) has been discussing

c) is being discussed

2874. Those islands … now.

a) aren't attacked

b) aren't being attacked

c) haven't being attacked

2875. … 3000 dollars been paid?

a) Had

b) Have

c) Did

2876. I wish she … two hour ago.

a) came

b) had come

c) did come

2877. I think you … me tomorrow.

a) could help

b) helped

c) could been helping

2878. We'll be forced … with them.

a) agree

b) agreeing

c) to agree

2879. Megan is unaware … some possible threats.

a) about

b) on

c) of

2880. What's … the agenda for today?

a) on

b) in

c) about

2881. I went there … air.

a) by

b) with

c) among

2882. The family was … the verge of despair.

a) in

b) on

c) about

2883. They were out … sight.
a) from
b) with
c) of
2884. We'll see one another … Christmas. I promise!
a) on

b) at
c) in
2885. The student said: "It's really interesting.".
a) The student said that it's really interesting.
b) The student said that it has been really interesting.
c) The student said that it was really interesting.
2886. The marketing manager said: "It isn't the right choice.".
a) The marketing manager said it wasn't the right choice.
b) The marketing manager said that it isn't the right choice.
c) The marketing manager said it hasn't been the right choice.
2887. My cousin said: "We were there last year.".
a) My cousin said that they had been there last year.
b) My cousin said that they had been there the year before.
c) My cousin said that they have been there the year before.
2888. She asked me: "Why do you think so?".

a) She asked me why you thought so.
b) She asked me why I had thought so.
c) She asked me why I thought so.
2889. She asked me: "What time do you usually get up?".
a) She asked me what time I get usually up.
b) She asked me what time I usually got up.
c) She asked me what time I am usually getting up.
2890. The new employee asked me: "How did he create such a positive atmosphere?".
a) The new employee asked me how he had created such a positive atmosphere.
b) The new employee asked me how he created such a positive atmosphere.
c) The new employee asked me how has he created such a positive atmosphere.
2891. Choose the correct sentence:
a) Am not I the best professor?
b) Am I not the best professor?
c) Have I not being the best professor?

Set 11

2892. … you gain some experience during that months?
a) Wasn't
b) Didn't
c) Hadn't
2893. Who is she jealous …?
a) with
b) on
c) of
2894. I can't … away with money.
a) make
b) do
c) find
2895. You look really … .
a) worried
b) worrying
c) worry
2896. The 2019 pandemic was … .
a) avoidable
b) inavoidable
c) disavoidable
2897. Keep in mind that the … is different.
a) really
b) reality
c) real
2898. I felt there so … . I wanted to live there.
a) comfortable
b) uncomfortable
c) discomfortable

2899. It's … . There is only 1 per cent that you will win.
a) probable
b) improbable
c) disprobable
2900. Why is she so …?
a) unsincere
b) dissincere
c) insincere
2901. Her answers were … .
a) indefinite
b) undefinite
c) definitely
2902. The price went … suddenly.
a) wrong
b) up
c) away
2903. The kid grew … of his clothes.
a) out
b) off
c) behind
2904. She looks … her parents.
a) of
b) with
c) after
2905. She nodded … during the meeting.
a) out
b) in
c) off
2906. Choose the correct sentence:
a) Let's put off it.
b) Let's putting it off.

c) Let's put it off.

2907. I'd rather … them.

a) didn't compare

b) not compare

c) nor comparing

2908. She's supposed … that job.

a) to get

b) be got

c) get

2909. … often disagree with it.

a) The olds

b) Olds

c) The old

2910. It was … unimaginable that she would die.

a) over

b) absolutely

c) utter

2911. My wife … at 7 o'clock yesterday morning.

a) has been cooking

b) was cooking

c) had been cooking

2912. Is the following sentence correct? "I was owning a flat that time."

a) correct

b) incorrect

2913. Your plan … a tremendous success.

a) has been

b) had been

c) did be

2914. Steven … repaired his apartment.

a) hadn't

b) didn't

c) hasn't

2915. How … this book helped you?

a) has

b) did

c) had

2916. How long … it?

a) did you discussed

b) have you been discussing

c) would you being discussing

2917. This path … now.

a) isn't being chosen

b) isn't chosen

c) didn't be chosen

2918. Choose the correct sentence:

a) They are sometimes being helped.

b) They had sometimes been help.

c) They are sometimes helped.

2919. Her room … yet.

a) hasn't been decorated

b) wasn't decorated

c) didn't be decorated

2920. If it …, I'll stay at home.

a) won't stop raining

b) doesn't stop raining

c) hadn't stopped raining

2921. When I came back, she … a letter.

a) was writing

b) has been writing

c) had been writing

2922. When I called my girlfriend she … a shower for 5 minutes.
a) was taking
b) has been taking
c) had been taking
2923. The money … there.
a) aren't
b) isn't
c) didn't
2924. I knew the truth … yet.
a) hadn't been discovered
b) wasn't discovered
c) hasn't been discovered
2925. If they had caught him, they … him to prison.
a) would sent
b) would have sent
c) would had sent
2926. You don't need … .
a) say it

b) saying it
c) to say it
2927. The spy … her to do it during their conversation which took place
several weeks ago.
a) might not persuade
b) might not have persuaded
c) didn't have persuaded
2928. Mark is addicted …
smoking.
a) of
b) to
c) with

2929. What's your attitude … this method?
a) to
b) of
c) on
2930. Do you really believe in love … first sight?
a) with
b) to
c) at
2931. The members chose it … random.
a) for
b) at
c) in
2932. She said: "I'm talking on the phone.".
a) She said that she was talking on the phone.
b) She said that I'm talking on the phone.
c) She said that she has been talking on the phone.
2933. The financial advisor said: "It will be bringing him money all year.".
a) The financial advisor said that it would be bringing him money all
year.
b) The financial advisor said that it will be bringing him money all
year.
c) The financial advisor said that it might be bringing him money all

year.

2934. The girl asked me: "How old is your father?".
a) The girl asked me how old was my father.
b) The girl asked me how old my father had been.
c) The girl asked me how old my father was.
2935. Choose the correct sentence:
a) Weren't the presentations really boring?
b) Didn't the presentations been really boring?
c) Haven't the presentations being really boring?
2936. Choose the correct sentence:
a) What is he keen about?
b) What is he keen on?
c) What is he keen with?
2937. What are you accustomed …?
a) for
b) in
c) to
2938. The little boy is … in science.
a) interesting
b) interested
c) interest
2939. It was a … experience for her.
a) frightened
b) frightening

c) frighten
2940. This time is … .
a) disconvenient
b) inconvenient
c) unconvenient
2941. Maria is a very … woman.
a) unpractical
b) dispractical
c) impractical
2942. We were clearly in … .
a) danger
b) dangerous
c) dangering
2943. My best friend is a … person. I like his recommendations.
a) impractical
b) practical
c) dispractical
2944. This process is … . It will never stop.
a) ending
b) endless
c) endlessly
2945. We live … together.
a) happily
b) happiness
c) happy
2946. What's the … of Moscow?
a) populated
b) populating
c) population
2947. So? What are you …?
a) choice

b) choosing

c) chosen

2948. What's your …?

a) choice

b) choosing

c) chosen

2949. Hold … a second! I have something to tell you.

a) by

b) with

c) on

2950. Milton passed … last year.

a) out

b) away

c) in

2951. You bought a new flat. Have you already moved …?

a) out

b) with

c) in

2952. You … better stay there with your parents.

a) would

b) had

c) could

2953. I'd rather you … your sister.

a) didn't criticize

b) won't criticize

c) hadn't criticize

2954. These rules must … .

a) being follow

b) be followed

c) following

2955. This problem can't … .

a) foresee

b) be foresee

c) be foreseen

2956. Should the roof …?

a) be repaired

b) repaired

c) repairing

2957. … have lots of problems.

a) Unemployed

b) The unemployed

c) The employing

2958. We … to leave the party in ten minutes.

a) must

b) would

c) are

2959. They are due … at 20.

a) to arrive

b) arriving

c) to arrived

2960. She is due … the city at 10.

a) leaving

b) to leave

c) to left

2961. She'll buy a new laptop as soon as she … enough money for it.

a) will have

b) has

c) had

2962. Choose the correct sentence:

a) I'm flying tonight.

b) I fly tonight.

c) I will be fly tonight.

2963. Choose the correct sentence:
a) My wife's having a bath then.
b) My wife has a bath now.
c) My wife is having a bath now.

2964. His colleagues … him.
a) were criticizing
b) have criticizing
c) did criticizing

2965. … the companies getting richer?
a) Had
b) Did
c) Were

2966. How … the policy changing?
a) was
b) did
c) had

2967. Is the following sentence correct? "Mike was blaming her."
a) correct
b) incorrect

2968. Why … your partners changed their decision?
a) did

b) have
c) had

2969. This place has … several changes.
a) undergone
b) underwent
c) undergo

2970. The dog … a hole in the ground.
a) have dug
b) dugged
c) dug

2971. Her words … me.
a) misleaded
b) misled
c) misleading

2972. I knew he … the exam.
a) hadn't failed
b) hasn't failed
c) didn't failed

2973. The employees … now.
a) aren't controlled
b) aren't being controlled
c) didn't be controlled

2974. Her knowledge … .
a) has already been tested
b) have already been tested
c) had already been tested

2975. Choose the correct sentence:
a) We see each other rarely.
b) We are seeing each other rarely.
c) We did seeing each other rarely.

2976. If only I … speak Russian better!
a) can
b) couldn't
c) could

2977. She … something inappropriate last week.
a) may have said

b) may had said

c) may being said

2978. Mary's certain … her success.

a) with

b) on

c) about

2979. Why are they so rude … him?

a) of

b) to

c) with

2980. She was born … 25 July.

a) on

b) in

c) at

2981. Tom said: "I will achieve my aim this week.".

a) Tom said that he will achieve his aim this week.

b) Tom said that he would be achieving his aim that week.

c) Tom said that he would achieve his aim that week.

2982. Olivia asked me: "Will you join us?".

a) Olivia asked me if I would join them.

b) Olivia asked me if you would join us.

c) Olivia asked me if would I join us.

2983. The woman asked me: "Will it definitely happen?".

a) The woman asked me if it would definitely happen.

b) The woman asked me if it will definitely happen.

c) The woman asked me if it would be happening definitely.

2984. My business partner asked me: "Have they already invested their money?".

a) My business partner asked me if they already invested their money.

b) My business partner asked me if they had already invested their money.

c) My business partner asked me if had they been investing already their money.

2985. She asked me: "Have you been working here for more than two years?".

a) She asked me if I had been working there for more than two years.

b) She asked me if I had been worked there for more than two years.

c) She asked me if I have been working there for more than two years.

2986. She asked me: "Have you been teaching German for more than 3 years?".

a) She asked me if you have been teaching German for more than 3
years.
b) She asked me if I had been teaching German for more than 3
years.
c) She asked me if I had taught German for more than 3 years.
2987. The officer asked me: "When did she leave the city?".
a) The officer asked me when she left the city.
b) The officer asked me when she have left the city.
c) The officer asked me when she had left the city.
2988. She asked me: "What's happened there?".
a) She asked me what happened there.
b) She asked me what had happened there.
c) She asked me what did happened there.
2989. He asked me: "What has influenced her most of all?".
a) He asked me what influenced her most of all.
b) He asked me what has been influenced her most of all.
c) He asked me what had influenced her most of all.
2990. Choose the correct sentence:
a) Did she notice it not?
b) Didn't she notice it?
c) Hadn't she notice it?
2991. Choose the correct sentence:
a) Aren't you searching for a better car?
b) Didn't you searched for a better car?
c) Hadn't you been searched for a better car?

2992. Why do you consider it's an … word?
a) insulted
b) insulting
c) insult
2993. This laptop offer seems … .
a) unattractive
b) inattractive
c) disattractive
2994. That was so … for you.
a) inusual
b) unusual
c) disusual
2995. It's … to do this kind of things.
a) infair
b) disfair
c) unfair
2996. Not surprisingly, she has had so many accidents. She drives so … .
a) carefully
b) carelessly
c) careful

2997. The new colleague can't hide her … .
a) incompetence
b) uncompetence
c) discompetence

2998. Don't worry! I won't let you … .
a) off
b) away
c) down

2999. The officers clamped … on illegal protesters.
a) down
b) with
c) up

3000. You'd better … about it anymore.
a) not to think
b) not thinking
c) not think

3001. I'd rather you … with him.
a) not argue
b) won't argue
c) didn't argue

3002. I … prefer to keep this secret.
a) would
b) had
c) better

3003. I'd sooner … another model.
a) to buy
b) buy
c) buying

3004. It's no use … about it now.
a) to talk
b) talking
c) be talked

3005. She has difficulty … the exam.
a) passing
b) to passing
c) pass

3006. He can speak either German … Chinese.
a) nor
b) neither
c) or

3007. My wife is either at home … at work.
a) or
b) nor
c) neither

3008. His ideas are … brilliant.
a) utter
b) good
c) completely

3009. I was … amazed at her beauty.
a) utterly
b) intense
c) complete

3010. All students … this vaccine.
a) to take
b) are to take
c) are to taking

3011. We will go there in case Jane … us.

a) will join
b) joining
c) joins
3012. Choose the correct sentence:
a) I'm typing the letter now.
b) I have been typing the letter now.
c) I type the letter now.
3013. They … behaving strangely.
a) hadn't
b) weren't
c) didn't
3014. This employee … effectively.
a) hadn't be working
b) haven't been worked
c) wasn't working
3015. … the students making too many mistakes?
a) Were
b) Had
c) Did
3016. … she already returned?
a) Did
b) Had
c) Has
3017. What … your business partner decided?
a) did

b) has
c) had
3018. Choose the correct sentence:
a) I never visited this place.

b) I've never visited this place.
c) I had never visited this place.
3019. He has … about it many times.
a) think
b) thinking
c) thought
3020. I … it for the first time.
a) heard
b) heared
c) hearing
3021. My car … down.
a) breaked
b) broken
c) broke
3022. He … the town two days ago.
a) leaved
b) left
c) leaving
3023. They … for such a long time.
a) haven't been complaining
b) hadn't been complaining
c) didn't been complained
3024. I … in this place for more than 3 hours.
a) been
b) had been
c) have been
3025. The child's mistakes … now.
a) didn't been correcting
b) aren't being corrected
c) aren't correcting

3026. … now?

a) Is this thing being mentioned
b) Does this thing mention
c) Was this thing be mentioned
3027. Choose the correct
sentence:
a) It has usually checked.
b) It is being usually checked.
c) It is usually checked.
3028. The students said she …
the text by heart.
a) had already learnt
b) already learnt
c) did already learnt
3029. I wish I … it yesterday.
a) knew
b) knowing
c) had known
3030. I … finish the document
by 5.
a) might to
b) have to
c) could to
3031. I'm sure … our mutual
success.
a) in
b) on
c) about
3032. I'm aware … this specific
danger.
a) of
b) about
c) on
3033. She's looking … a new
job. She really wants to find it.
a) to
b) in
c) for

3034. Why are you laughing …
her?
a) on
b) at
c) with
3035. This house is for … .
a) sales
b) selling
c) sale
3036. I said it … the beginning.
a) in
b) at
c) on
3037. The professor said: "She
has failed her last exam.".
a) The professor said that she
has been failing her last exam.
b) The professor said that she
had failed her last exam.
c) The professor said that she
failed her last exam.
3038. My girlfriend told me: "I
have been extremely busy this
week.".
a) My girlfriend told me that she
had been extremely busy that
week.
b) My girlfriend told me that she
has been extremely busy that
week.
c) my girlfriend told me that she
was extremely busy that week.
3039. Mark said: "I want to see
her today.".
a) Mark said that he wanted to
see her today.

b) Mark said that he wanted to see her that day.

c) Mark said the he has wanted to see her today.

3040. The lady asked me: "Has he sent her all the money?".

a) The lady asked me if he would send her all the money.

b) The lady asked me if he has sent her all the money.

c) The lady asked me if he had sent her all the money.

3041. The detective asked me: "What did she teach there?".

a) The detective asked me what I had taught there.

b) The detective asked me what she had taught there.

c) The detective asked me what have she taught there.

3042. She asked me: "How was the party?".

a) She asked me how the party had been.

b) She asked me how had been the party.

c) She asked me how have the party been.

3043. My girlfriend asked me: "What are you doing now?".

a) My girlfriend asked me what I was doing now.

b) My girlfriend asked me what I was doing then.

c) My girlfriend asked me what I have been doing then.

3044. Choose the correct sentence:

a) Didn't you learnt English yesterday?

b) Didn't you learn English yesterday?

c) Hadn't you learn English yesterday?

3045. Choose the correct sentence:

a) Do they not providing all the necessary conditions?

b) Haven't they providing all the necessary conditions?

c) Are they not providing all the necessary conditions?

3046. She … badly in the exam.

a) made

b) did

c) could

3047. What made you feel so …?

a) frustrated

b) frustrating

c) frustrate

3048. I felt so … .

a) surprising

b) surprised

c) surprise

3049. This chair is so … .

a) uncomfortable

b) discomfortable

c) incomfortable

3050. What does he …?

a) prefering

b) preference

c) prefer

3051. Jennifer is so … . I always try to follow her advice.
a) unwise

b) wise
c) wisely

3052. I put … two proposals.
a) into
b) of
c) forward

3053. She dropped … school.
a) out of
b) away
c) within

3054. It's no use … .
a) to complain
b) complaining
c) to complaining

3055. There is no point … for it. It's lost!
a) in looking
b) looked
c) of looked

3056. I have difficulty … time for my hobbies.
a) to find
b) found
c) finding

3057. They might … .
a) be attack
b) be attacked
c) be attacking

3058. The soldiers must … more intensively.
a) be trained
b) training
c) trained

3059. I find you … gorgeous.
a) complete
b) absolutely
c) utter

3060. … my project, I went out.
a) Having finished
b) Hading finished
c) To finish

3061. Choose the right sentence:
a) They accuse him now.
b) They are accusing him now.
c) They had accusing him now.

3062. My wife … all night.
a) had been working
b) did working
c) was working

3063. … they using the right vaccine technique?
a) Were
b) Did
c) Had

3064. Is the following sentence correct? "She was wishing us good luck."
a) correct
b) incorrect

3065. You … achieved so much lately.
a) had
b) have
c) did

3066. The boat … sunk.
a) hasn't
b) didn't
c) couldn't had

3067. … your girlfriend changed her mind?
a) Did
b) Can
c) Has
3068. … your director paid her all the money?
a) Has
b) Did
c) Has been

3069. … the weather got worse?
a) Have
b) Did
c) Has
3070. Choose the correct sentence:
a) She just checked it.
b) She had just checked it.
c) She has just checked it.
3071. Choose the correct sentence:
a) I was there many times.
b) I have been there many times.
c) I did be there many times.
3072. Choose the correct sentence:
a) We achieved a lot this month and it's not over.
b) We had achieved a lot this month and it's not over.
c) We have achieved a lot this month and it's not over.
3073. I have … in the end.
a) winning
b) won
c) been won

3074. I read they … him in the end.
a) were arrested
b) had arrested
c) would be arrested
3075. He remembered he … there yet.
a) wasn't
b) haven't be
c) hadn't been
3076. This food … now.
a) isn't eaten
b) isn't being eaten
c) couldn't be eaten
3077. Why … now?
a) is she being ignored
b) has she be ignored
c) had she be ignored
3078. The truth … .
a) hadn't been revealed
b) hasn't been revealed
c) didn't be revealed
3079. What information …?
a) have been found
b) could being founded
c) has been found
3080. I … about that when I was a boy.
a) have never thought
b) never thought
c) didn't never think
3081. Looking back, this aspect … .
a) was never mentioned
b) has never be mentioning

c) would never being mentioning

3082. I … it during our last meeting.
a) wouldn't being said
b) wouldn't have said
c) wouldn't had said

3083. Brian won't be allowed … there until midnight.
a) stay
b) to stay
c) staying

3084. She's hopeless … foreign languages.
a) in
b) for
c) at

3085. I'm engaged … her.
a) to
b) in
c) on

3086. I was shocked … that accident.
a) with
b) by
c) on

3087. Listen … me!
a) to
b) about
c) with

3088. I feel … drinking a coffee.
a) like
b) how
c) about

3089. She reacted … it in a strange way.
a) on
b) about
c) to

3090. Don't worry! We're out … danger.
a) from
b) of
c) without

3091. She said: "Steve always tries to lead.".
a) She said that Steve always had tried to lead.
b) She said that Steve always tried to lead.
c) She said that Steve always trying to lead.

3092. John said: "I have never been there.".
a) John said that I have never been there.
b) John said that he had never been there.
c) John said that he would never be there.

3093. He said: "When Mary returned I had already done it.".
a) He said that when Mary had returned he had already done it.
b) He said that when Mary had returned I had already done it.
c) He said that when Mary returned he have already done it.

3094. She asked me: "Were the boys famous?".

a) She asked me if the boys were famous.

b) She asked me if the boys would be famous.

c) She asked me if the boys had been famous.

3095. She asked me: "Was she reading a book all day?".

a) She asked me if she had been reading a book all day.

b) She asked me if she was reading a book all day.

c) She asked me if she would be reading a book all day.

3096. Olivia asked me: "Have you been waiting for me for a long time?".

a) Olivia asked me if you had been waiting for me for a long time.

b) Olivia asked me if I had been waiting for her for a long time.

c) Olivia asked me if I had being waited for her for a long time.

3097. The professor asked me: "What things were interesting?".

a) The professor asked me what things had been interesting.

b) The professor asked me what things have been interested.

c) The professor asked me what things would be interested.

3098. My manager asked me: "Who will you inform?".

a) My manager asked me who you would inform.

b) My manager asked me who I would inform.

c) My manager asked me who I am going to be informed.

3099. The advisor asked me: "What was becoming real?".

a) The advisor asked me what was becoming real.

b) The advisor asked me what had been becoming real.

c) The advisor asked me what would be becoming real.

3100. The teacher asked me: "Who has already completed the project?".

a) The teacher asked me who already completed the project.

b) The teacher asked me who completed the project.

c) The teacher asked me who had already completed the project.

Set 12

3101. Choose the correct sentence:

a) Didn't you found out the truth?

b) Haven't you found out the truth?

c) Haven't you founded out the truth?

3102. Why is she so …?

a) inorganized

b) unorganzied

c) disorganized

Set 13

3103. The vaccine can have an … effect.

a) indirect

b) undirect

c) disdirect

3104. Of course we aren't … .

a) inmortal

b) immortal

c) amortal

3105. The sun went … and a new day was beginning.

a) up

b) down

c) with

3106. They broke … and stole more than 1 million dollars.

a) with

b) in

c) down

3107. They went … the rules.

a) for

b) without

c) against

3108. The group must … .

a) divided

b) be divided

c) dividing

3109. Should this be … down?

a) written

b) wrote

c) writing

3110. The document … two days ago.

a) had written

b) has been written

c) had to be written

3111. We … it at 10 o'clock yesterday.

a) were discussing

b) have being discussed

c) had being discussed

3112. The guests … Russian.

a) didn't spoken

b) weren't speaking

c) hadn't speaking

3113. … it becoming a success?

a) Had

b) Did

c) Was

3114. Is the following sentence correct? "Were you hearing her well?"

a) correct

b) incorrect

3115. The ship has … .

a) sunk

b) sinking

c) being sink

3116. What … now?

a) is delivered

b) is being delivered

c) is delivering

3117. This question … yet.

a) hasn't asked

b) hasn't been asked

c) wasn't been asked

3118. Listen! The young lady …
now.
a) sings
b) is singing
c) singed
3119. I … for you for one hour.
a) have been waiting
b) waiting
c) did waited
3120. It … now.
a) is checked

b) checking
c) is being checked
3121. I wish I … the city last
night.
a) had left
b) leaving
c) left
3122. If only she … another
way!
a) choosing
b) had chosen
c) has choosing
3123. If she had kept her word,
she … my wife now.
a) would have been
b) could have been
c) would be
3124. She's envious … her
manager.
a) to
b) of
c) with
3125. She apologized …
everything.
a) for

b) on
c) in
3126. I went to Turkey …
business.
a) in
b) on
c) with
3127. The commander said:
"They have trained
professionally.".
a) The commander said that
they have trained professionally.
b) The commander said that
they had trained professionally.
c) The commander said that
they be training professionally.
3128. My aunt told me: "He will
be staying with them.".
a) My aunt told me that he
would stay with them.
b) My aunt told me that he
would be staying with them.
c) My aunt told me that he will
be staying with them.

3129. I … English for 15 years
by next year.
a) will be learning
b) would be learning
c) will have been learning
3130. I … this report for two
hours by the time the director
gets to work.
a) have been making
b) will have been making
c) would be making

3131. I … German with her for six months by next year.
a) will have been speaking
b) will spoken
c) would be spoken
3132. The investigator asked me: "Was it happening there?".
a) The investigator asked me if it was happening there.
b) The investigator asked me if it has been happening there.
c) The investigator asked me if it had been happening there.
3133. Choose the correct sentence:
a) Is she not sincerely with you?
b) Isn't she sincere with you?
c) Didn't she be sincere with you?
3134. … she share your point of view?
a) Didn't
b) Hasn't
c) Doesn't
3135. Choose the correct sentence:
a) Didn't he worry about that?
b) Hasn't he worrying about that?
c) Hadn't he worrying about that?
3136. Choose the correct sentence:
a) Will not you train more intensively?
b) Won't you train more intensively?

c) Didn't you trained more intensively?
3137. Choose the correct sentence:
a) Are they not working on their mistakes?

b) Are they no worked on their mistakes?
c) Hadn't they been worked on their mistakes?
3138. Choose the correct sentence:
a) Didn't she apologized?
b) Hasn't she apologized?
c) Hadn't she be apologizing?
3139. Choose the correct sentence:
a) What are you talking?
b) What are you talking about?
c) What are you talk about?
3140. Choose the correct sentence:
a) Where are you from?
b) Didn't you been from?
c) Where from are you?
3141. Choose the correct sentence:
a) What are you interested?
b) Didn't you been interested?
c) What are you interested in?
3142. She … a purchase.
a) did
b) made
c) done
3143. These girls are … .
a) inemployed

b) unemployed
c) disemployed
3144. The scientists achieved international … .
a) famous
b) faming
c) fame
3145. I … agree with you on this matter.
a) utter
b) complete
c) absolutely

3146. It doesn't meet these … standards.
a) educational
b) education
c) educating
3147. It cost … 200 euros.
a) approximate
b) approximation
c) approximately
3148. This goal is … . It's impossible to achieve it.
a) achievable
b) achieving
c) unachievable
3149. I bumped … her near the shopping center.
a) into
b) with
c) about
3150. I hope we can count … your expertise.
a) in
b) on
c) with

3151. This report should … one more time.
a) check
b) be checked
c) checking
3152. Following this discovery, she should … .
a) be awarded
b) awarding
c) awarded
3153. The costs ought to … .
a) minimizing
b) be minimize
c) be minimized
3154. The most suitable candidate might … been missed.
a) had
b) have
c) having
3155. Her knowledge may … .
a) check
b) have been checked
c) been checking
3156. They may … yesterday.
a) have been examined
b) be examined
c) been examining
3157. … can't afford this car.
a) Poor
b) The poors
c) The poor
3158. They say that the more you pay, … quality you get.
a) better
b) the better
c) the best

3159. … discussed it, we signed
a new contract.
a) Having
b) Being
c) Hading
3160. In no way … it.
a) will I do
b) do I will
c) will do I
3161. Stay with us unless your
brother … .
a) return
b) returns
c) will return
3162. Choose the correct
sentence:
a) We are meeting two times a
week.
b) We were meet two times a
week.
c) We meet two times a week.

3163. Choose the correct
sentence:
a) It's getting hot today.
b) It gets hot today.
c) It has get hot today.
3164. Brian … encouraging us.
a) wasn't
b) didn't
c) hadn't
3165. Is the following sentence
correct? "They were needing
much more
money."
a) correct
b) incorrect

3166. Is the following sentence
correct? "She was signing the
contract
when I came in."
a) correct
b) incorrect
3167. I see you … laughed at
her.
a) didn't
b) weren't
c) haven't
3168. Her parents have … her
do that.
a) letting
b) let
c) letted
3169. They … thoroughly now.
a) are examined
b) are being examined
c) are be examining
3170. Their report … yet.
a) hasn't been read
b) weren't read
c) hasn't read
3171. The kids wish there …
only happiness in the world.
a) is

b) had
c) was
3172. If only I … about that
problem earlier!
a) had known
b) didn't know
c) have known
3173. She … her boyfriend
yesterday.

a) may not see
b) may not have seen
c) may didn't see
3174. We … them.
a) didn't need to warn
b) need not warned
c) did needed not warn
3175. This professor is very patient … his students.
a) about
b) on
c) with
3176. It's rude … them to push him.
a) to
b) of
c) on
3177. She said: "The baby is crying.".
a) She said that the baby is crying.
b) She said that the baby was crying
c) She said that the baby has been crying.
3178. The officer said: "The negotiations will be peaceful.".
a) The officer said that the negotiations would be peaceful.
b) The officer said that the negotiations would being peaceful.
c) The officer said that the negotiations will being peaceful.
3179. Steven said: "We'll talk about everything soon.".

a) Steven said that they would talk about everything soon.
b) Steven said that they'll talk about everything soon.
c) Steven said that they would be talking about everything soon.

3180. She asked me: "Do you see it?".
a) She asked me if I saw it.
b) She asked me if I see it.
c) She asked me if I did seen it.
3181. The manager asked me: "Was it the best offer?".
a) The manager asked me whether had it been the best offer.
b) The manager asked me if had it be the best offer.
c) The manager asked me if it had been the best offer.
3182. The customer asked me: "Have you already installed the program?".
a) The customer asked me if I have already installed that program.
b) The customer asked me if I had already installed that program.
c) The customer asked me if I installed the program.
3183. My girlfriend asked me: "Why is it becoming more and more expensive?".

a) She asked me why it is becoming more and more expensive.
b) She asked me why it would become more and more expensive.
c) She asked me why it was becoming more and more expensive.
3184. Jane asked me: "What has changed?".
a) Jane asked me what had changed.
b) Jane asked me what had had changed.
c) Jane asked me what would have changed.
3185. My wife asked me: "How long have you been waiting for me?".
a) My wife asked me how long I had been waiting for me.
b) My wife asked me how long I had been waiting for her.
c) My wife asked me how long had I been waited for her.
3186. The security advisor asked me: "How long have you been using this website?".
a) The security advisor asked me how long I was using that website.
b) The security advisor asked me how long I did being used that website.

c) The security advisor asked me how long I had been using that website.
3187. Choose the correct sentence:
a) You didn't understood?

b) Don't you understand?
c) Didn't you understood?
3188. Choose the correct sentence:
a) Doesn't she trust you?
b) Didn't she trusted you?
c) Haven't she trusting you?
3189. Choose the correct sentence:
a) Weren't they luckily?
b) Weren't they lucky?
c) Weren't they lucking?
3190. … it a rush hour?
a) Didn't
b) Haven't
c) Wasn't
3191. It was a … idea.
a) fascinating
b) fascinated
c) fascinate
3192. I was … with her reply.
a) insatisfied
b) dissatisfied
c) asatisfied
3193. This offer is so bad! It's really … .
a) unattractive
b) attractive
c) inattractive

3194. We reached … in the end. We started cooperating.
a) a disagreement
b) an agreement
c) a conclusive

3195. She's fond of … .
a) artist
b) actress
c) art

3196. I was … by his speech.
a) impressive
b) impressed
c) impressing

3197. Dave is his … relative.
a) distance
b) distantly
c) distant

3198. The poor woman came … against so many difficulties.
a) up
b) on
c) with

3199. Let's get … to business.
a) down
b) at
c) within

3200. Choose the correct sentence:
a) I used to be done it.
b) I am used to doing it.
c) I had used to be done it.

3201. Choose the correct sentence:
a) She used to getting up early.
b) She is used to getting up early.
c) She is using to getting up early.

3202. I would sooner … than play.
a) study
b) studying
c) to study

3203. I … sooner do it by myself.
a) had
b) should
c) would

3204. I'd rather you … him this information.
a) not tell
b) no telling
c) didn't tell

3205. The result may … .
a) have predict
b) be predicted
c) be predicting

3206. This misunderstanding could … .
a) have been avoided
b) had been avoided
c) have avoided

3207. You neither win … lose.
a) or
b) nor
c) either

3208. It was … hilarious.
a) absolutely
b) complete
c) utter

3209. … poor she lives in a small flat.

a) Be
b) To be
c) Being
3210. … stopped there, he asked her a question.
a) To
b) Hading
c) Having
3211. No one … against it.
a) isn't
b) hadn't
c) is
3212. Choose the correct sentence:
a) We meet this evening.
b) We are meeting this evening.
c) We have meeting this evening.

3213. Choose the correct sentence:
a) Listen! The girl is crying.
b) Listen! The girl cries.
c) Listen! The girl has crying.
3214. Choose the correct sentence:
a) They ignore Mary now.
b) They are ignoring Mary now.
c) They have ignored Mary now.
3215. It stopped raining when we … .
a) were eating
b) eaten
c) have been eating
3216. I know they disturbed you when you … .

a) was working
b) were working
c) have been working
3217. Is the following sentence correct? "I was preferring the first way."
a) correct
b) incorrect
3218. Choose the correct sentence:
a) Did you never done it?
b) Hadn't you never done it?
c) Have you ever done it?
3219. Choose the correct sentence:
a) We didn't get her answer yet.
b) We haven't got her answer yet.
c) We hadn't get her answer yet.
3220. She has … the door.
a) hitting
b) hitted
c) hit
3221. I see you … for the exam since Sunday.
a) haven't been preparing
b) haven't preparing
c) haven't prepare

3222. How long … him?
a) have you been knowing
b) had you known
c) have you known
3223. … when he came back?
a) Had she finished cooking
b) Have she finished cooking
c) Hadn't she finishing cooking

3224. It … now.
a) is checked
b) is being checked
c) have been checking
3225. Choose the correct
sentence:
a) The goods have been sold.
b) The goods have sold.
c) The good had be sold.
3226. The kids … football when
the professor arrived.
a) was playing
b) were playing
c) have been playing
3227. The meeting … by the
time I arrived.
a) already started
b) has already started
c) had already started
3228. When I joined that club
she … his member for two
years.
a) had been
b) have been
c) had been being
3229. It was said it … .
a) was already announced
b) had already been announced
c) have already be announce
3230. If I had one more chance,
I … show much better results.
a) will

b) would
c) would had

3231. If she … another man, her
parents would have criticized
her sharply.
a) married
b) have marry
c) had married
3232. Choose the correct
sentence:
a) It's high time the truth about
the pandemic was discovered.
b) It's high time we discover the
truth about the pandemic.
c) It's high time the truth about
the pandemic would be
discovered.
3233. I'm accustomed … it.
a) for
b) on
c) to
3234. She's keen … classical
music.
a) on
b) of
c) in
3235. She's sensitive …
criticism.
a) for
b) to
c) about
3236. I was amused … her
manners.
a) at
b) on
c) in
3237. The kid is allergic …
nuts.
a) with

b) to

c) about

3238. I understood everything … once.

a) for

b) in

c) at

3239. Don't take everything … granted!

a) on

b) for

c) at

3240. John said: "When she called me I was working.".

a) John said that when she had called him he had been working.

b) John said that when she called him he was working.

c) John said that when she would call him he would be working.

3241. Kate said: "I was learning English all day.".

a) Kate said that she had been learning English all day.

b) Kate said that she has been learning English all day.

c) Kate said that she was learning English all day.

3242. Jennifer said: "I have been watching his channel for more than a year.".

a) Jennifer said that she has been watched his channel for more than

a year.

b) Jennifer said that she was watching his channel for more than a

year.

c) Jennifer said that she had been watching his channel for more than

a year.

3243. My wife asked me: "Where is it happening?".

a) My wife asked me where it was happening.

b) My wife asked me where was it happening.

c) My wife asked me where had it happened.

3244. The detective asked me: "What things were happening there?".

a) The detective asked me what things were happening there.

b) The detective asked me what things had been happening there.

c) The detective asked me what things have been happening there.

3245. Choose the correct sentence:

a) What are you thinking?

b) What are you thinking about?

c) What have you thinking about?

3246. This function is … .

a) unactive

b) inactive

c) disasctive

3247. The results are … .

a) uncredible

b) discredible

c) incredible

3248. You can't … know it.

a) possibly

b) possible

c) impossible

3249. She feels … . She needs someone's help.

a) protected

b) protective

c) unprotected

3250. It's an … remark.

a) unrelevant

b) irrelevant

c) disrelevant

3251. Cheer …! Why are you so depressed?

a) down

b) up

c) again

3252. After some months she gave up … tennis.

a) play

b) playing

c) played

3253. Choose the correct sentence:

a) They called it off.

b) They called off it.

c) They had been calling it off.

3254. I'd rather you … with your boss.

a) not compete

b) not competing

c) didn't compete

3255. I … my car washed.

a) had have

b) having

c) got

3256. He is expected … .

a) to win

b) win

c) winning

3257. His question … .

a) had answered

b) had to be answered

c) had answering

3258. This interview … .

a) might already recorded

b) might have already been recorded

c) might had already be recording

3259. The artist must … .

a) have been inspired by her fans

b) have inspired by her fans

c) had be inspiring by her fans

3260. She's just about … herself to the committee.

a) introducing

b) introduce

c) to introduce

3261. The professor … those students.

a) hasn't been compared

b) wasn't comparing

c) hadn't be comparing

3262. What … your parents doing there?
a) did
b) were
c) had

3263. Mary … to convince him.
a) was trying
b) trying
c) has be trying

3264. Your child … enough yesterday.
a) eaten
b) has eaten
c) ate

3265. The man has … it at last.
a) founded
b) finded
c) found

3266. I have … him some money.
a) lent
b) lend
c) lended

3267. After receiving the treatment I … much better.
a) feeling
b) felt
c) had felt

3268. My wife has … back.
a) came
b) coming
c) come

3269. You … it brilliantly. Congrats!
a) did
b) has

c) done

3270. The dog … me yesterday.
a) bitted
b) bit
c) has bitten

3271. How long … for this competition?
a) has you be preparing
b) did you be preparing
c) have you been preparing

3272. … it when he came?
a) Has she already done
b) Did she already do
c) Had she already doing

3273. … the building by the time the police arrived?
a) Had they left
b) Have they left
c) Did they left

3274. Your brother … with murder now.
a) is charged
b) is being charged
c) has being charged

3275. Choose the correct sentence:
a) She currently works on this project.
b) She is currently working on this project.
c) She has currently being worked on this project.

3276. My sister … to Italy.
a) had been
b) was
c) has been

3277. I wish I … one more chance.
a) had had
b) have had
c) would had
3278. She needn't … it.
a) mentioning
b) mentioned
c) mention
3279. I'm ready … a change.
a) to
b) for
c) with
3280. The final decision depends … him.
a) on
b) from
c) about
3281. This mission plan can lead … big problems.
a) for
b) about
c) to
3282. What's the reason … doing it?
a) to
b) for
c) in
3283. We're … debt.
a) on
b) with
c) in
3284. The marketing specialist said: "My idea is brilliant.".
a) The marketing specialist said that his idea was brilliant.
b) The marketing specialist said that his idea had been brilliant.
c) The marketing specialist said that my idea was brilliant.
3285. She said: "When I saw him he was walking in the park.".
a) She said that when she had seen him he had been walking in the park.
b) She said that when she had seen him he would be walking in the park.
c) She said that when she has seen him he was walking in the park.
3286. John said: "I have been waiting for you for such a long time.".
a) John said that he was waiting for me for such a long time.
b) John said that he had been waiting for me for such a long time.
c) John said that he was waiting for me for such a long time.
3287. My wife asked me: "Did you decline their offer?".
a) My wife asked me if you had declined their offer.
b) My wife asked me if I would decline their offer.
c) My wife asked me if I had declined their offer.

3288. The professor asked me: "Have you already guessed the right
answer?".
a) The professor asked me if I had already guessed the right answer.

b) The professor asked me if you were already guessing the right
answer.
c) The professor asked me if I would already be guessing the right
answer.
3289. The examiner asked me: "Have you been learning Russian
intensively for the last three months?".
a) The examiner asked me whether I had been learning Russian
intensively for the previous three months.
b) The examiner asked me if I have been learning Russian intensively for the last three months.
c) The examiner asked me if I had learnt Russian intensively for the
last three months.
3290. The mentor asked me: "Why has she already known everything?".

a) The mentor asked me why she has already known everything.
b) The mentor asked me why she had already known everything.
c) The mentor asked me why she was already knowing everything.
3291. Choose the correct sentence:
a) Aren't you satisfied with her answer?
b) Hadn't you being satisfied with her answer?
c) Weren't you be satisfied with her answer?
3292. Choose the correct sentence:
a) Who is this document?
b) Who was this document about?
c) Who is this document for?
3293. How are you going to … a living in that country?
a) do
b) make
c) had
3294. They were … with the exams.
a) bored
b) boring
c) bore
3295. I was … by their presentation.
a) inspiring

b) inspire

c) inspired

3296. It's an … situation.

a) unsane

b) insane

c) insanely

3297. I'm for … methods.

a) traditional

b) tradition

c) traditionally

3298. She … so unexpectedly.

a) disappeared

b) unappeared

c) inappeared

3299. This step is … . It's the only right way.

a) unnecessary

b) necessary

c) necessarily

3300. These exercises will … your body.

a) strength

b) strengthing

c) strengthen

3301. The woman felt so … .

a) insecure

b) securing

c) asecure

3302. The detectives will look … the crime.

a) in

b) with

c) into

3303. My wife often shows … . She likes attracting other people's attention.

a) off

b) in

c) about

3304. … no use doing it.

a) How's

b) There's

c) What's

3305. There is no point … it again.

a) to check

b) about check

c) in checking

3306. I have difficulty … for this exam.

a) to prepare

b) preparing

c) prepared

3307. This competitor is expected … .

a) to lose

b) losing

c) lose

3308. It should … .

a) be say

b) be said

c) being said

3309. These conditions should … .

a) be provided

b) providing

c) provide

3310. The more practice, … .

a) better

b) the best

c) the better

3311. She won't change unless her parents … to her.

a) talk
b) will talk
c) had talked
3312. When his mother arrived, he … .
a) has been sleeping

b) would be sleeping
c) was still sleeping
3313. … the manager explaining it?
a) Had
b) Was
c) Did
3314. Is the following sentence correct? "What was she wanting?"
a) correct
b) incorrect
3315. Is the following sentence correct? "The girls were commenting."
a) correct
b) incorrect
3316. Is the following sentence correct? "I was parking there."
a) correct
b) incorrect
3317. Is the following sentence correct? "Brian was having a rest."
a) correct
b) incorrect
3318. Choose the correct sentence:
a) I was never to China.
b) I've never been to China.

c) I'd never been to China.
3319. You brother has … the last place.
a) be taken
b) been taken
c) taken
3320. Olivia … it for six years.
a) had been doing
b) has been doing
c) would be done
3321. … her since you finished university?
a) Have you known
b) Have you been knowing
c) Did you known

3322. Choose the correct sentence:
a) Did it ever been controlled?
b) Had it ever being controlled?
c) Has it ever been controlled?
3323. Her mistakes … .
a) did be spotted
b) have been spotted
c) had being spotted
3324. I observed that his mistakes … yet.
a) weren't corrected
b) didn't be correct
c) hadn't been corrected
3325. I … it two months ago.
a) have done
b) done
c) did
3326. How long … there?
a) are you staying
b) have you been staying

c) did you being stay

3327. My sister … Russian for three years.

a) has been learning

b) had been learning

c) did learning

3328. Choose the correct sentence:

a) It is currently monitored.

b) It had currently be monitored.

c) It is currently being monitored.

3329. I found out that some things … .

a) had been stolen

b) were stolen

c) did be stolen

3330. The students is frightened … her words.

a) of

b) with

c) on

Set 14

3331. She's ashamed … her poor skills.

a) by

b) on

c) of

3332. This text was translated from Russian … German.

a) into

b) with

c) on

3333. Why is he staring … her?

a) on

b) at

c) to

3334. I'm working here … the time being.

a) for

b) at

c) in

3335. The analyst said: "The situation isn't getting better.".

a) The analyst said that the situation isn't getting better.

b) The analyst said that the situation wasn't getting better.

c) The analyst said that the situation wouldn't get better.

3336. The manager said: "They were discussing it.".

a) The manager said that they had been discussing it.

b) The manager said that they were discussing it.

c) The manager said that they would be discussing it.

3337. The secretary asked me: "Did he apologize for it?".

a) The secretary asked me if he apologized for it.

b) The secretary asked me if he has apologized for it.

c) The secretary asked me if he had apologized for it.

3338. Mary asked me: "Has she already introduced him?".

a) Mary asked me if she had already introduced him.
b) Mary asked me if she already introduced him.
c) Mary asked me if she would already introduce him.

3339. Kate asked me: "What time do you usually get up?".
a) Kate asked me what time did I usually get up.
b) Kate asked me what time had I usually got up.
c) Kate asked me what time I usually got up.
3340. The manager asked me: "Who was responsible for it?".
a) The manager asked me who had been responsible for it.
b) The manager asked me who was responsible for it.
c) The manager asked me who has be responsible for it.
3341. The girl asked me: "How often will you go to the gym?".
a) The girl asked me how often I will go to the gym.
b) The girl asked me how often I would go to the gym.
c) The girl asked me how often I used to go to the gym.
3342. My neighbour asked me: "Why were you doing it all night?".
a) My neighbour asked me why you had been doing it all night.

b) My neighbour asked me why I had been doing it all night.
c) My neighbour asked me why have I been doing it all night.
3343. Choose the correct sentence:
a) Hadn't it improve your English?
b) Doesn't it improve your English?
c) Haven't it improving your English?
3344. ... she trust you?
a) Doesn't
b) Isn't
c) Hadn't
3345. ... she lose control?
a) Wasn't
b) Hadn't
c) Didn't
3346. Choose the correct answer:
a) Hasn't Dave become a rich man?
b) Didn't Dave became a rich man?
c) Hadn't Dave been became a rich man?
3347. ..., it ruined all our hopes.
a) Luck

b) Iluckily
c) Unluckily
3348. Maria feels so ... . Something bad must have happened to her.
a) unhappy

b) unhappily
c) happily
3349. This … isn't enough to enter our organization.
a) unknown
b) knowledge
c) knowing
3350. He's an … person. He's so special!
a) ordinarily
b) ordinary
c) extraordinary
3351. Her father ran … when she was a small kid.
a) off
b) in
c) out
3352. We'll sort … this problem quite easily.
a) in
b) about
c) out
3353. I can't get rid … my headache.
a) on
b) of
c) out
3354. She always stands … in a crowd.
a) within
b) out
c) about
3355. We broke … all the relations.
a) off
b) out
c) to

3356. You … better change your mind.
a) can
b) had
c) would
3357. I … my hair cut.
a) can
b) should
c) had
3358. This thing can be … .
a) proved
b) proving
c) prove
3359. The team shouldn't … .
a) divide
b) be divided
c) diving
3360. It's … fantastic what you've done.
a) completely
b) utter
c) such a
3361. We won't go there in case she … buy a ticket.
a) won't
b) doesn't
c) wouldn't
3362. How … it changing?
a) did
b) have
c) was
3363. It … an effect on me.
a) won't have
b) hadn't have
c) wouldn't had

3364. The police … suspected Mary.

a) have

b) has

c) did

3365. They … broken the law. I guarantee.

a) didn't

b) haven't

c) won't

3366. The customer … responded.

a) won't

b) didn't

c) hasn't

3367. She … the money.

a) withdrew

b) withdrawed

c) withdraw

3368. She realized she … inappropriate words.

a) was used

b) had used

c) did used

3369. They … now.

a) be criticized

b) are criticize

c) are being criticized

3370. What … now?

a) is being said

b) has being said

c) does been said

3371. Who … about this situation?

a) did been warned

b) has been warned

c) would being warned

3372. How long … this movie?

a) did you watched

b) hadn't you watch

c) have you been watching

3373. Jennifer confessed she … him all the truth.

a) didn't told

b) won't tell

c) hadn't told

3374. I wish I … a better job.

a) had

b) would had

c) have

3375. I … be in best shape because it's my desire to be so.

a) must

b) have to

c) had to

3376. I … to finish this report today.

a) have to

b) had to

c) would have

3377. The professor told me: "We'll support her.".

a) The professor told me that they will support her.

b) The professor told me that they would support her.

c) The professor told me that they would be supporting her.

3378. I … my final exam by December.

a) will completed

b) will be completing

c) will have completed

3379. We … for two hours by the time they arrive.
a) will have been talking
b) will had been talked
c) will had been talking

3380. The assistant asked me: "Will you compare their results?".
a) The assistant asked me whether I would compare their results.
b) The assistant asked me if I will compare their results.
c) The assistant asked me if I would be comparing their results.

3381. The professor asked me: "Have you been learning Russian for three years?".
a) The professor asked me if you had been learning Russian for three

years.
b) The professor asked me if I had been learning Russian for three
years.
c) The professor asked me if I have learnt Russian for three years.

3382. My cousin asked me: "How was your trip?".
a) My cousin asked me how my trip was.

b) My cousin asked me how my trip had been.
c) My cousin asked me how my trip would be.

3383. What does Jane insist …?
a) of
b) with
c) on

3384. Her colleagues … her.
a) disrespect
b) inrespect
c) arespect

3385. He's my … .
a) competition
b) competitive
c) competitor

3386. The coronavirus can't be cured … .
a) traditional
b) traditionally
c) tradition

3387. She improved her Chinese only … .
a) unsignificantly
b) insignificantly
c) dissignificantly

3388. We lead an … lifestyle.
a) inhealthy
b) dishealthy
c) unhealthy

3389. They are very … to him.
a) unkind

b) inkind
c) rekind

3390. Brian dozed ... during the lecture.

a) down
b) in
c) off
3391. Choose the correct
sentence:
a) Get out it your head!
b) Get it out of your head!
c) Get out of your head it!
3392. Choose the correct
sentence:
a) I'm accustomed to staying at
home all day.
b) I'm accustomed to stay at
home all day.
c) I'm accustom to staying at
home all day.
3393. I'd rather … cycling than
play computer games.
a) going
b) gone
c) go
3394. I'd rather … a little bit.
a) wait
b) waiting
c) to wait
3395. She's supposed … the
first place.
a) take
b) to take
c) to have take
3396. Are we supposed … there
on time?
a) arrive
b) arriving
c) to arrive
3397. These risk factors should
… .

a) minimize
b) minimizing
c) be minimized

3398. This subject shouldn't …
at university.
a) teach
b) be taught
c) teaching
3399. They mustn't … .
a) punished
b) punishing
c) be punished
3400. …, the better.
a) The shorter
b) Shorter
c) The shortest

Answers
1.a 2.a 3.c 4.c 5.b 6.c 7.c 8.a 9.c
10.b
11.c 12.c 13.a 14.b 15.c 16.c
17.a 18.c 19.b 20.c
21.a 22.c 23.b 24.c 25.a 26.c
27.a 28.b 29.c 30.a
31.c 32.a 33.b 34.b 35.c 36.a
37.a 38.c 39.c 40.b
41.a 42.c 43.b 44.a 45.c 46.c
47.c 48.b 49.a 50.b
51.b 52.c 53.b 54.a 55.c 56.b
57.b 58.c 59.c 60.a
61.b 62.c 63.a 64.b 65.c 66.c
67.a 68.b 69.c 70.a
71.b 72.b 73.c 74.b 75.a 76.a
77.c 78.c 79.b 80.a

81.c 82.c 83.a 84.b 85.c 86.c
87.b 88.a 89.b 90.c
91.b 92.a 93.c 94.b 95.c 96.b
97.a 98.c 99.b 100.a

101.c 102.c 103.a 104.b 105.c
106.c 107.a 108.b 109.a
110.c 111.b 112.c 113.c 114.a
115.b 116.c 117.a 118.b
119.c 120.a 121.b 122.a 123.c
124.b 125.c 126.b 127.a
128.c 129.c 130.a 131.b 132.c
133.a 134.a 135.c 136.b
137.a 138.b 139.c 140.c 141.c
142.a 143.b 144.c 145.c
146.a 147.a 148.b 149.c 150.b
151.a 152.c 153.c 154.b
155.c 156.a 157.b 158.b 159.c
160.a 161.b 162.c 163.c
164.b 165.a 166.b 167.c 168.a
169.b 170.c 171.c 172.b
173.b 174.c 175.a 176.b 177.a
178.c 179.a 180.b 181.a
182.c 183.b 184.c 185.b 186.c
187.a 188.a 189.c 190.b
191.a 192.c 193.c 194.b 195.c
196.a 197.c 198.b 199.a
200.c 201.b 202.a 203.c 204.b
205.c 206.a 207.c 208.b
209.a 210.c 211.c 212.a 213.b
214.a 215.c 216.b 217.c
218.b 219.b 220.b 221.a 222.c
223.c 224.b 225.c 226.a
227.b 228.c 229.b 230.a 231.c
232.b 233.c 234.a 235.c
236.b 237.c 238.c 239.b 240.a
241.b 242.a 243.c 244.b

245.b 246.b 247.a 248.c 249.b
250.a 251.b 252.c 253.c
254.c 255.a 256.c 257.b 258.c
259.c 260.c 261.b 262.a
263.c 264.a 265.b 266.c 267.a
268.c 269.a 270.b 271.b
272.a 273.b 274.c 275.c 276.a
277.b 278.a 279.c 280.b
281.c 282.c 283.c 284.a 285.c
286.b 287.c 288.b 289.c
290.a 291.a 292.b 293.c 294.c
295.c 296.a 297.b 298.a
299.b 300.a 301.a 302.c 303.c
304.b 305.b 306.b 307.c
308.b 309.a 310.c 311.c 312.c
313.a 314.b 315.c 316.b
317.c 318.a 319.c 320.c 321.a
322.b 323.c 324.c 325.b
326.a 327.c 328.b 329.a 330.c
331.c 332.c 333.a 334.b
335.b 336.a 337.b 338.c 339.a
340.c 341.b 342.a 343.c
344.b 345.b 346.c 347.c 348.b
349.a 350.c 351.b 352.a
353.c 354.a 355.c 356.b 357.b
358.a 359.c 360.b 361.c
362.a 363.c 364.b 365.a 366.c
367.c 368.a 369.b 370.c
371.b 372.a 373.c 374.a 375.b
376.c 377.c 378.a 379.a
380.c 381.a 382.c 383.b 384.b
385.c 386.c 387.a 388.b
389.c 390.c 391.b 392.c 393.a
394.c 395.a 396.c 397.b
398.c 399.a 400.b 401.a 402.b
403.b 404.c 405.c 406.b

407.a 408.a 409.c 410.a 411.c
412.a 413.b 414.b 415.c
416.a 417.c 418.b 419.c 420.a
421.b 422.a 423.c 424.b
425.b 426.a 427.c 428.b 429.b
430.a 431.c 432.c 433.b
434.c 435.c 436.b 437.a 438.c
439.c 440.a 441.b 442.c
443.a 444.b 445.c 446.c 447.b
448.a 449.c 450.b 451.b

452.a 453.c 454.a 455.b 456.c
457.c 458.a 459.c 460.b
461.c 462.b 463.c 464.a 465.c
466.b 467.b 468.c 469.c
470.a 471.a 472.c 473.b 474.b
475.c 476.a 477.b 478.a
479.c 480.b 481.c 482.a 483.b
484.c 485.b 486.c 487.b
488.c 489.a 490.a 491.b 492.c
493.a 494.b 495.a 496.c
497.a 498.c 499.b 500.a 501.a
502.b 503.c 504.a 505.b
506.c 507.a 508.c 509.b 510.a
511.c 512.b 513.a 514.c
515.a 516.c 517.b 518.a 519.b
520.c 521.a 522.c 523.b
524.a 525.c 526.a 527.b 528.a
529.c 530.c 531.b 532.a
533.c 534.b 535.a 536.b 537.b
538.a 539.c 540.a 541.c
542.a 543.c 544.b 545.b 546.c
547.c 548.a 549.c 550.b
551.b 552.b 553.a 554.c 555.c
556.c 557.b 558.b 559.a
560.b 561.c 562.b 563.c 564.a
565.b 566.c 567.b 568.c

569.c 570.a 571.b 572.c 573.b
574.a 575.a 576.c 577.b
578.b 579.c 580.b 581.c 582.a
583.b 584.b 585.a 586.c
587.b 588.c 589.b 590.c 591.b
592.c 593.a 594.b 595.a
596.a 597.c 598.b 599.c 600.a
601.b 602.a 603.c 604.a
605.a 606.c 607.b 608.a 609.c
610.b 611.c 612.c 613.a
614.b 615.a 616.c 617.b 618.c
619.a 620.b 621.c 622.b
623.a 624.b 625.b 626.b 627.a
628.c 629.c 630.a 631.b
632.a 633.c 634.c 635.b 636.b
637.c 638.a 639.a 640.c
641.c 642.a 643.c 644.b 645.b
646.a 647.b 648.b 649.c
650.a 651.b 652.a 653.c 654.c
655.a 656.a 657.b 658.c
659.b 660.c 661.c 662.a 663.c
664.c 665.a 666.b 667.c
668.b 669.a 670.c 671.b 672.a
673.c 674.c 675.a 676.b
677.c 678.c 679.b 680.a 681.a
682.c 683.b 684.b 685.c
686.b 687.c 688.b 689.c 690.c
691.a 692.c 693.b 694.c
695.a 696.b 697.c 698.b 699.c
700.b 701.a 702.c 703.c
704.b 705.a 706.b 707.a 708.b
709.c 710.b 711.b 712.c
713.a 714.c 715.a 716.c 717.a
718.c 719.c 720.b 721.a
722.c 723.b 724.a 725.c 726.c
727.b 728.a 729.c 730.b

731.a 732.b 733.a 734.c 735.b
736.c 737.b 738.a 739.c
740.b 741.b 742.c 743.a 744.b
745.a 746.c 747.b 748.a
749.c 750.b 751.a 752.b 753.c
754.c 755.a 756.b 757.a
758.c 759.c 760.a 761.a 762.c
763.c 764.b 765.b 766.c
767.b 768.c 769.a 770.b 771.b
772.a 773.c 774.b 775.c
776.a 777.c 778.b 779.a 780.c
781.c 782.b 783.a 784.c
785.b 786.c 787.c 788.c 789.a
790.b 791.c 792.b 793.c

794.b 795.c 796.b 797.a 798.b
799.a 800.c 801.b 802.b
803.a 804.c 805.a 806.c 807.b
808.c 809.c 810.b 811.a
812.c 813.b 814.a 815.b 816.a
817.c 818.a 819.b 820.a
821.b 822.b 823.c 824.c 825.a
826.b 827.c 828.a 829.a
830.b 831.a 832.c 833.b 834.a
835.a 836.c 837.b 838.c
839.b 840.b 841.c 842.c 843.a
844.b 845.b 846.a 847.c
848.c 849.b 850.a 851.a 852.b
853.c 854.b 855.c 856.a
857.c 858.c 859.b 860.a 861.c
862.a 863.c 864.c 865.b
866.b 867.c 868.c 869.a 870.b
871.a 872.b 873.b 874.c
875.a 876.b 877.c 878.b 879.c
880.a 881.c 882.b 883.a
884.c 885.b 886.c 887.b 888.a
889.b 890.b 891.b 892.a

893.c 894.c 895.a 896.b 897.c
898.b 899.a 900.c 901.b
902.a 903.c 904.a 905.a 906.c
907.b 908.b 909.c 910.b
911.c 912.a 913.b 914.c 915.a
916.c 917.c 918.a 919.c
920.c 921.c 922.a 923.c 924.b
925.a 926.c 927.b 928.a
929.b 930.c 931.a 932.b 933.c
934.b 935.a 936.a 937.c
938.c 939.b 940.a 941.c 942.c
943.a 944.b 945.b 946.c
947.a 948.b 949.c 950.b 951.a
952.c 953.b 954.c 955.a
956.c 957.a 958.a 959.a 960.b
961.c 962.c 963.b 964.c
965.a 966.c 967.b 968.b 969.c
970.a 971.b 972.c 973.a
974.b 975.c 976.a 977.b 978.a
979.b 980.c 981.c 982.a
983.b 984.b 985.c 986.a 987.b
988.c 989.a 990.b 991.c
992.c 993.b 994.c 995.a 996.c
997.b 998.c 999.a 1000.a
1001.b 1002.c 1003.a 1004.c
1005.b 1006.b 1007.a 1008.c
1009.a
1010.b 1011.b 1012.b 1013.a
1014.a 1015.a 1016.c 1017.b
1018.b
1019.a 1020.b 1021.a 1022.c
1023.a 1024.b 1025.c 1026.a
1027.c
1028.b 1029.b 1030.a 1031.a
1032.c 1033.a 1034.b 1035.b
1036.a

1037.c 1038.b 1039.a 1040.a
1041.b 1042.c 1043.b 1044.b
1045.a
1046.c 1047.b 1048.c 1049.a
1050.a 1051.b 1052.c 1053.b
1054.a
1055.c 1056.a 1057.b 1058.c
1059.b 1060.c 1061.b 1062.c
1063.b
1064.a 1065.b 1066.a 1067.c
1068.c 1069.c 1070.a 1071.a
1072.a
1073.b 1074.c 1075.b 1076.c
1077.b 1078.b 1079.b 1080.a
1081.b
1082.a 1083.c 1084.a 1085.b
1086.b 1087.a 1088.c 1089.b
1090.c
1091.b 1092.c 1093.a 1094.c
1095.a 1096.b 1097.c 1098.b
1099.b
1100.a 1101.b 1102.c 1103.a
1104.b 1105.c 1106.c 1107.a
1108.b
1109.a 1110.c 1111.a 1112.c
1113.b 1114.a 1115.b 1116.c
1117.a
1118.a 1119.b 1120.c 1121.c
1122.a 1123.b 1124.a 1125.a
1126.c
1127.b 1128.a 1129.b 1130.c
1131.a 1132.b 1133.c 1134.b
1135.c

1136.b 1137.b 1138.c 1139.a
1140.b 1141.c 1142.a 1143.b
1144.a

1145.c 1146.b 1147.b 1148.a
1149.c 1150.b 1151.b 1152.a
1153.c
1154.c 1155.a 1156.b 1157.c
1158.a 1159.c 1160.c 1161.b
1162.b
1163.c 1164.a 1165.a 1166.b
1167.c 1168.a 1169.a 1170.b
1171.b
1172.a 1173.b 1174.c 1175.a
1176.a 1177.b 1178.c 1179.b
1180.b
1181.b 1182.a 1183.c 1184.c
1185.c 1186.c 1187.a 1188.b
1189.b
1190.c 1191.a 1192.c 1193.b
1194.c 1195.c 1196.a 1197.a
1198.b
1199.c 1200.b 1201.a 1202.c
1203.b 1204.c 1205.c 1206.b
1207.a
1208.c 1209.c 1210.b 1211.b
1212.a 1213.c 1214.a 1215.c
1216.a
1217.a 1218.b 1219.b 1220.c
1221.b 1222.b 1223.a 1224.c
1225.b
1226.a 1227.c 1228.c 1229.c
1230.a 1231.b 1232.c 1233.a
1234.a
1235.c 1236.b 1237.c 1238.b
1239.a 1240.c 1241.a 1242.b
1243.c
1244.b 1245.c 1246.a 1247.b
1248.a 1249.c 1250.c 1251.a
1252.c

1253.b 1254.a 1255.c 1256.c
1257.a 1258.c 1259.b 1260.c
1261.a
1262.c 1263.b 1264.a 1265.c
1266.a 1267.a 1268.c 1269.b
1270.a
1271.a 1272.c 1273.b 1274.a
1275.c 1276.b 1277.c 1278.b
1279.a
1280.b 1281.b 1282.c 1283.a
1284.c 1285.c 1286.b 1287.a
1288.a
1289.b 1290.c 1291.a 1292.b
1293.c 1294.a 1295.c 1296.b
1297.b
1298.a 1299.b 1300.c 1301.c
1302.a 1303.b 1304.a 1305.c
1306.c
1307.a 1308.b 1309.c 1310.c
1311.a 1312.c 1313.b 1314.c
1315.a
1316.a 1317.c 1318.c 1319.b
1320.b 1321.b 1322.c 1323.a
1324.b
1325.c 1326.b 1327.c 1328.a
1329.b 1330.b 1331.a 1332.c
1333.a
1334.b 1335.c 1336.b 1337.a
1338.b 1339.a 1340.c 1341.a
1342.b
1343.c 1344.c 1345.a 1346.c
1347.b 1348.b 1349.a 1350.c
1351.a
1352.c 1353.b 1354.c 1355.a
1356.c 1357.b 1358.c 1359.c
1360.a

1361.c 1362.b 1363.a 1364.c
1365.a 1366.b 1367.c 1368.a
1369.c
1370.b 1371.c 1372.c 1373.a
1374.b 1375.c 1376.a 1377.c
1378.b
1379.a 1380.c 1381.b 1382.c
1383.b 1384.a 1385.b 1386.c
1387.c
1388.c 1389.a 1390.b 1391.c
1392.a 1393.c 1394.a 1395.c
1396.a
1397.a 1398.c 1399.b 1400.c
1401.b 1402.a 1403.c 1404.b
1405.a
1406.c 1407.c 1408.b 1409.a
1410.c 1411.b 1412.a 1413.c
1414.c
1415.a 1416.b 1417.a 1418.b
1419.a 1420.c 1421.c 1422.a
1423.b
1424.b 1425.c 1426.a 1427.b
1428.c 1429.b 1430.b 1431.a
1432.c
1433.b 1434.c 1435.b 1436.c
1437.a 1438.c 1439.c 1440.b
1441.b
1442.a 1443.c 1444.b 1445.a
1446.a 1447.c 1448.b 1449.a
1450.c
1451.b 1452.a 1453.a 1454.b
1455.c 1456.a 1457.c 1458.b
1459.c
1460.b 1461.b 1462.a 1463.c
1464.c 1465.b 1466.c 1467.b
1468.c

1469.a 1470.b 1471.a 1472.c
1473.c 1474.b 1475.b 1476.a
1477.b

1478.c 1479.a 1480.c 1481.a
1482.b 1483.c 1484.b 1485.a
1486.b
1487.c 1488.a 1489.c 1490.b
1491.a 1492.c 1493.b 1494.a
1495.c
1496.a 1497.b 1498.b 1499.c
1500.a 1501.b 1502.c 1503.a
1504.a
1505.b 1506.a 1507.c 1508.b
1509.b 1510.a 1511.a 1512.b
1513.c
1514.c 1515.a 1516.c 1517.a
1518.b 1519.c 1520.a 1521.b
1522.a
1523.c 1524.a 1525.c 1526.b
1527.b 1528.a 1529.c 1530.b
1531.c
1532.b 1533.c 1534.a 1535.c
1536.b 1537.a 1538.c 1539.b
1540.a
1541.a 1542.c 1543.b 1544.a
1545.b 1546.c 1547.a 1548.b
1549.c
1550.a 1551.b 1552.a 1553.c
1554.b 1555.c 1556.b 1557.c
1558.a
1559.b 1560.c 1561.a 1562.c
1563.b 1564.a 1565.c 1566.c
1567.b
1568.b 1569.a 1570.c 1571.c
1572.b 1573.a 1574.b 1575.b
1576.c

1577.c 1578.b 1579.c 1580.c
1581.b 1582.a 1583.c 1584.b
1585.a
1586.c 1587.a 1588.b 1589.a
1590.c 1591.b 1592.c 1593.c
1594.a
1595.a 1596.c 1597.b 1598.c
1599.a 1600.b 1601.c 1602.c
1603.a
1604.b 1605.b 1606.c 1607.b
1608.c 1609.c 1610.a 1611.b
1612.b
1613.a 1614.c 1615.b 1616.a
1617.b 1618.a 1619.c 1620.c
1621.b
1622.a 1623.c 1624.a 1625.b
1626.a 1627.c 1628.b 1629.a
1630.b
1631.a 1632.c 1633.b 1634.c
1635.a 1636.c 1637.a 1638.c
1639.b
1640.c 1641.a 1642.c 1643.b
1644.c 1645.c 1646.a 1647.c
1648.a
1649.b 1650.a 1651.a 1652.b
1653.c 1654.a 1655.c 1656.b
1657.c
1658.a 1659.c 1660.b 1661.a
1662.c 1663.c 1664.b 1665.b
1666.b
1667.a 1668.b 1669.c 1670.c
1671.a 1672.c 1673.b 1674.a
1675.c
1676.a 1677.b 1678.c 1679.a
1680.c 1681.a 1682.c 1683.a
1684.b

1685.b 1686.c 1687.c 1688.c 1689.b 1690.a 1691.a 1692.b 1693.a

1694.c 1695.a 1696.b 1697.b 1698.c 1699.c 1700.c 1701.b 1702.a

1703.c 1704.a 1705.b 1706.a 1707.c 1708.c 1709.b 1710.a 1711.c

1712.c 1713.a 1714.b 1715.a 1716.c 1717.b 1718.b 1719.c 1720.a

1721.c 1722.b 1723.c 1724.a 1725.c 1726.a 1727.b 1728.b 1729.b

1730.c 1731.c 1732.a 1733.b 1734.b 1735.a 1736.c 1737.a 1738.a

1739.c 1740.b 1741.c 1742.c 1743.b 1744.a 1745.b 1746.a 1747.c

1748.a 1749.c 1750.c 1751.b 1752.c 1753.b 1754.c 1755.c 1756.a

1757.b 1758.a 1759.c 1760.b 1761.a 1762.b 1763.c 1764.b 1765.a

1766.a 1767.c 1768.a 1769.b 1770.a 1771.c 1772.a 1773.b 1774.a

1775.c 1776.a 1777.a 1778.b 1779.c 1780.b 1781.a 1782.b 1783.b

1784.c 1785.a 1786.a 1787.b 1788.c 1789.b 1790.c 1791.c 1792.a

1793.c 1794.b 1795.a 1796.c 1797.b 1798.b 1799.a 1800.b 1801.a

1802.c 1803.b 1804.a 1805.c 1806.b 1807.a 1808.a 1809.c 1810.b

1811.b 1812.a 1813.b 1814.c 1815.a 1816.b 1817.b 1818.c 1819.c

1820.a 1821.c 1822.c 1823.b 1824.a 1825.b 1826.a 1827.c 1828.a

1829.c 1830.b 1831.a 1832.c 1833.c 1834.b 1835.b 1836.c 1837.b

1838.a 1839.c 1840.a 1841.c 1842.c 1843.a 1844.b 1845.c 1846.b

1847.c 1848.b 1849.b 1850.a 1851.c 1852.c 1853.b 1854.b 1855.c

1856.c 1857.a 1858.a 1859.a 1860.b 1861.a 1862.b 1863.c 1864.c

1865.a 1866.a 1867.b 1868.c 1869.b 1870.c 1871.b 1872.a 1873.c

1874.b 1875.a 1876.c 1877.a 1878.c 1879.b 1880.a 1881.b 1882.c

1883.a 1884.b 1885.c 1886.b 1887.a 1888.b 1889.c 1890.a 1891.a

1892.c 1893.a 1894.a 1895.b 1896.a 1897.c 1898.a 1899.b 1900.c

1901.b 1902.c 1903.c 1904.a
1905.b 1906.a 1907.b 1908.c
1909.a
1910.b 1911.a 1912.c 1913.b
1914.c 1915.c 1916.a 1917.a
1918.b
1919.a 1920.c 1921.b 1922.a
1923.c 1924.b 1925.a 1926.b
1927.a
1928.c 1929.a 1930.c 1931.b
1932.a 1933.c 1934.a 1935.c
1936.b
1937.c 1938.c 1939.a 1940.b
1941.a 1942.c 1943.c 1944.b
1945.b
1946.c 1947.c 1948.a 1949.b
1950.c 1951.a 1952.b 1953.a
1954.b
1955.c 1956.c 1957.a 1958.b
1959.b 1960.c 1961.c 1962.b
1963.a
1964.b 1965.b 1966.b 1967.c
1968.a 1969.a 1970.b 1971.a
1972.c
1973.a 1974.b 1975.c 1976.b
1977.c 1978.b 1979.c 1980.a
1981.a
1982.c 1983.a 1984.c 1985.b
1986.c 1987.b 1988.a 1989.c
1990.c
1991.a 1992.b 1993.b 1994.b
1995.a 1996.c 1997.a 1998.b
1999.b
2000.b 2001.c 2002.a 2003.b
2004.a 2005.c 2006.b 2007.a
2008.c

2009.b 2010.a 2011.b 2012.c
2013.a 2014.a 2015.b 2016.c
2017.b
2018.a 2019.b 2020.c 2021.a
2022.c 2023.c 2024.b 2025.c
2026.c
2027.b 2028.c 2029.c 2030.a
2031.c 2032.c 2033.c 2034.a
2035.b
2036.a 2037.c 2038.b 2039.c
2040.b 2041.c 2042.b 2043.a
2044.b
2045.c 2046.c 2047.a 2048.b
2049.b 2050.a 2051.c 2052.a
2053.a
2054.b 2055.c 2056.c 2057.c
2058.b 2059.a 2060.b 2061.c
2062.a
2063.c 2064.b 2065.c 2066.a
2067.a 2068.b 2069.b 2070.b
2071.c
2072.a 2073.b 2074.c 2075.c
2076.b 2077.b 2078.a 2079.c
2080.b
2081.c 2082.a 2083.b 2084.c
2085.a 2086.a 2087.c 2088.b
2089.a
2090.c 2091.b 2092.c 2093.a
2094.b 2095.c 2096.b 2097.a
2098.b
2099.a 2100.c 2101.c 2102.b
2103.a 2104.b 2105.c 2106.c
2107.c
2108.a 2109.b 2110.c 2111.b
2112.c 2113.a 2114.c 2115.b
2116.c

2117.a 2118.b 2119.b 2120.c
2121.c 2122.a 2123.a 2124.b
2125.c
2126.c 2127.b 2128.a 2129.b
2130.b 2131.a 2132.c 2133.a
2134.c
2135.b 2136.a 2137.c 2138.b
2139.c 2140.a 2141.a 2142.b
2143.c
2144.a 2145.c 2146.b 2147.a
2148.c 2149.c 2150.b 2151.a
2152.b
2153.c 2154.c 2155.a 2156.c
2157.b 2158.b 2159.a 2160.c
2161.a

2162.b 2163.c 2164.b 2165.c
2166.c 2167.b 2168.b 2169.a
2170.a
2171.b 2172.c 2173.c 2174.c
2175.b 2176.a 2177.c 2178.a
2179.b
2180.a 2181.b 2182.a 2183.c
2184.b 2185.b 2186.b 2187.a
2188.b
2189.c 2190.a 2191.b 2192.a
2193.c 2194.a 2195.b 2196.c
2197.c
2198.b 2199.a 2200.b 2201.c
2202.a 2203.b 2204.a 2205.c
2206.a
2207.c 2208.a 2209.b 2210.b
2211.c 2212.c 2213.a 2214.b
2215.b
2216.c 2217.a 2218.b 2219.c
2220.c 2221.b 2222.c 2223.b
2224.b

2225.a 2226.a 2227.c 2228.b
2229.a 2230.c 2231.a 2232.a
2233.c
2234.c 2235.b 2236.a 2237.b
2238.b 2239.c 2240.b 2241.a
2242.c
2243.b 2244.a 2245.c 2246.c
2247.b 2248.c 2249.b 2250.a
2251.a
2252.c 2253.b 2254.c 2255.a
2256.b 2257.a 2258.c 2259.b
2260.a
2261.a 2262.c 2263.a 2264.c
2265.a 2266.a 2267.c 2268.b
2269.a
2270.b 2271.c 2272.c 2273.b
2274.c 2275.c 2276.a 2277.b
2278.b
2279.c 2280.b 2281.a 2282.b
2283.c 2284.b 2285.a 2286.b
2287.c
2288.a 2289.b 2290.c 2291.b
2292.a 2293.b 2294.c 2295.a
2296.b
2297.a 2298.c 2299.c 2300.b
2301.a 2302.b 2303.c 2304.a
2305.b
2306.a 2307.c 2308.b 2309.c
2310.c 2311.b 2312.b 2313.a
2314.b
2315.a 2316.c 2317.a 2318.b
2319.c 2320.c 2321.b 2322.c
2323.a
2324.b 2325.b 2326.c 2327.a
2328.a 2329.b 2330.c 2331.b
2332.a

2333.c 2334.b 2335.b 2336.a
2337.c 2338.b 2339.a 2340.c
2341.c
2342.a 2343.a 2344.a 2345.b
2346.c 2347.a 2348.c 2349.b
2350.b
2351.c 2352.a 2353.a 2354.b
2355.b 2356.c 2357.a 2358.b
2359.a
2360.c 2361.b 2362.b 2363.a
2364.c 2365.a 2366.b 2367.b
2368.c
2369.b 2370.b 2371.a 2372.c
2373.c 2374.b 2375.a 2376.a
2377.b
2378.c 2379.b 2380.c 2381.c
2382.b 2383.a 2384.c 2385.a
2386.b
2387.c 2388.a 2389.b 2390.c
2391.a 2392.a 2393.b 2394.c
2395.c
2396.a 2397.b 2398.a 2399.b
2400.c 2401.a 2402.b 2403.b
2404.c
2405.b 2406.a 2407.b 2408.a
2409.c 2410.b 2411.b 2412.b
2413.a
2414.c 2415.a 2416.a 2417.a
2418.b 2419.c 2420.c 2421.a
2422.b
2423.a 2424.c 2425.c 2426.a
2427.b 2428.c 2429.a 2430.b
2431.b
2432.c 2433.a 2434.c 2435.b
2436.a 2437.c 2438.b 2439.a
2440.b

2441.c 2442.b 2443.a 2444.c
2445.c 2446.a 2447.b 2448.a
2449.c
2450.a 2451.c 2452.a 2453.b
2454.b 2455.a 2456.c 2457.b
2458.b
2459.c 2460.b 2461.b 2462.a
2463.c 2464.b 2465.b 2466.c
2467.a
2468.a 2469.b 2470.a 2471.b
2472.c 2473.b 2474.a 2475.b
2476.c
2477.a 2478.c 2479.a 2480.b
2481.a 2482.c 2483.c 2484.c
2485.a
2486.b 2487.a 2488.c 2489.a
2490.b 2491.a 2492.b 2493.c
2494.a
2495.b 2496.b 2497.a 2498.c
2499.a 2500.b 2501.c 2502.a
2503.b
2504.b 2505.b 2506.c 2507.a
2508.c 2509.a 2510.b 2511.c
2512.a

2513.b 2514.c 2515.a 2516.b
2517.b 2518.c 2519.c 2520.a
2521.b
2522.c 2523.a 2524.b 2525.b
2526.c 2527.a 2528.c 2529.c
2530.b
2531.b 2532.c 2533.a 2534.c
2535.b 2536.a 2537.a 2538.b
2539.a
2540.c 2541.b 2542.b 2543.c
2544.a 2545.a 2546.c 2547.a
2548.b

2549.c 2550.c 2551.b 2552.a
2553.c 2554.a 2555.b 2556.a
2557.b
2558.a 2559.c 2560.b 2561.c
2562.c 2563.a 2564.a 2565.a
2566.b
2567.b 2568.c 2569.a 2570.b
2571.c 2572.a 2573.b 2574.b
2575.b
2576.c 2577.a 2578.a 2579.b
2580.b 2581.a 2582.b 2583.c
2584.a
2585.c 2586.a 2587.b 2588.a
2589.b 2590.b 2591.a 2592.c
2593.b
2594.c 2595.b 2596.a 2597.c
2598.c 2599.a 2600.b 2601.b
2602.c
2603.b 2604.c 2605.b 2606.a
2607.c 2608.b 2609.a 2610.c
2611.c
2612.b 2613.a 2614.a 2615.b
2616.c 2617.b 2618.c 2619.a
2620.b
2621.c 2622.b 2623.b 2624.a
2625.a 2626.b 2627.c 2628.c
2629.b
2630.a 2631.c 2632.b 2633.a
2634.c 2635.b 2636.a 2637.c
2638.b
2639.a 2640.b 2641.c 2642.a
2643.b 2644.b 2645.c 2646.c
2647.a
2648.a 2649.c 2650.b 2651.b
2652.a 2653.c 2654.a 2655.c
2656.b

2657.c 2658.c 2659.a 2660.c
2661.c 2662.a 2663.b 2664.b
2665.a
2666.c 2667.b 2668.b 2669.c
2670.a 2671.c 2672.b 2673.c
2674.a
2675.b 2676.c 2677.a 2678.b
2679.a 2680.a 2681.c 2682.c
2683.a
2684.b 2685.c 2686.a 2687.b
2688.b 2689.c 2690.a 2691.c
2692.b
2693.b 2694.c 2695.a 2696.b
2697.b 2698.a 2699.c 2700.b
2701.b
2702.c 2703.a 2704.c 2705.a
2706.b 2707.c 2708.a 2709.c
2710.b
2711.a 2712.b 2713.c 2714.a
2715.c 2716.b 2717.a 2718.c
2719.b
2720.c 2721.b 2722.a 2723.c
2724.a 2725.b 2726.b 2727.a
2728.c
2729.c 2730.b 2731.a 2732.c
2733.b 2734.b 2735.a 2736.b
2737.b
2738.c 2739.a 2740.b 2741.c
2742.a 2743.c 2744.b 2745.a
2746.c
2747.c 2748.c 2749.b 2750.a
2751.b 2752.a 2753.c 2754.b
2755.a
2756.c 2757.b 2758.a 2759.c
2760.a 2761.b 2762.c 2763.b
2764.b

2765.a 2766.c 2767.b 2768.a
2769.b 2770.b 2771.c 2772.b
2773.b
2774.a 2775.b 2776.b 2777.c
2778.c 2779.a 2780.a 2781.b
2782.c
2783.b 2784.c 2785.a 2786.a
2787.b 2788.c 2789.a 2790.a
2791.b
2792.c 2793.b 2794.a 2795.b
2796.b 2797.a 2798.c 2799.b
2800.b
2801.a 2802.c 2803.a 2804.c
2805.c 2806.b 2807.a 2808.b
2809.c
2810.a 2811.c 2812.b 2813.b
2814.c 2815.a 2816.b 2817.b
2818.c
2819.b 2820.a 2821.c 2822.b
2823.a 2824.b 2825.b 2826.b
2827.a
2828.b 2829.c 2830.a 2831.b
2832.a 2833.c 2834.c 2835.a
2836.b
2837.c 2838.a 2839.c 2840.b
2841.a 2842.a 2843.c 2844.a
2845.b
2846.a 2847.a 2848.c 2849.b
2850.a 2851.c 2852.a 2853.b
2854.a

2855.a 2856.c 2857.b 2858.a
2859.b 2860.c 2861.a 2862.c
2863.c
2864.b 2865.a 2866.a 2867.c
2868.a 2869.b 2870.a 2871.b
2872.a

2873.c 2874.b 2875.b 2876.b
2877.a 2878.c 2879.c 2880.a
2881.a
2882.b 2883.c 2884.b 2885.c
2886.a 2887.b 2888.c 2889.b
2890.a
2891.b 2892.b 2893.c 2894.b
2895.a 2896.a 2897.b 2898.a
2899.b
2900.c 2901.a 2902.b 2903.a
2904.c 2905.c 2906.c 2907.b
2908.a
2909.c 2910.b 2911.b 2912.b
2913.a 2914.c 2915.a 2916.b
2917.a
2918.c 2919.a 2920.b 2921.a
2922.c 2923.b 2924.a 2925.b
2926.c
2927.b 2928.b 2929.a 2930.c
2931.b 2932.a 2933.a 2934.c
2935.a
2936.b 2937.c 2938.b 2939.b
2940.b 2941.c 2942.a 2943.b
2944.b
2945.a 2946.c 2947.b 2948.a
2949.c 2950.b 2951.c 2952.b
2953.a
2954.b 2955.c 2956.a 2957.b
2958.c 2959.a 2960.b 2961.b
2962.a
2963.c 2964.a 2965.c 2966.a
2967.a 2968.b 2969.a 2970.c
2971.b
2972.a 2973.b 2974.a 2975.a
2976.c 2977.a 2978.c 2979.b
2980.a

2981.c 2982.a 2983.a 2984.b
2985.a 2986.b 2987.c 2988.b
2989.c
2990.b 2991.a 2992.b 2993.a
2994.b 2995.c 2996.b 2997.a
2998.c
2999.a 3000.c 3001.c 3002.a
3003.b 3004.b 3005.a 3006.c
3007.a
3008.c 3009.a 3010.b 3011.c
3012.a 3013.b 3014.c 3015.a
3016.c
3017.b 3018.b 3019.c 3020.a
3021.c 3022.b 3023.a 3024.c
3025.b
3026.a 3027.c 3028.a 3029.c
3030.b 3031.c 3032.a 3033.c
3034.b
3035.c 3036.a 3037.b 3038.a
3039.b 3040.c 3041.b 3042.a
3043.b
3044.b 3045.c 3046.b 3047.a
3048.b 3049.a 3050.c 3051.b
3052.c
3053.a 3054.b 3055.a 3056.c
3057.b 3058.a 3059.b 3060.a
3061.b
3062.c 3063.a 3064.b 3065.b
3066.a 3067.c 3068.a 3069.c
3070.c
3071.b 3072.c 3073.b 3074.b
3075.c 3076.b 3077.a 3078.b
3079.c
3080.b 3081.a 3082.b 3083.b
3084.c 3085.a 3086.b 3087.a
3088.a

3089.c 3090.b 3091.b 3092.b
3093.a 3094.c 3095.a 3096.b
3097.a
3098.b 3099.b 3100.c 3101.b
3102.c 3103.a 3104.b 3105.a
3106.b
3107.c 3108.b 3109.a 3110.c
3111.a 3112.b 3113.c 3114.b
3115.a
3116.b 3117.b 3118.b 3119.a
3120.c 3121.a 3122.b 3123.c
3124.b
3125.a 3126.b 3127.b 3128.b
3129.c 3130.b 3131.a 3132.c
3133.b
3134.c 3135.a 3136.b 3137.a
3138.b 3139.b 3140.a 3141.c
3142.b
3143.b 3144.c 3145.c 3146.a
3147.c 3148.c 3149.a 3150.b
3151.b
3152.a 3153.c 3154.b 3155.b
3156.a 3157.c 3158.b 3159.a
3160.a
3161.b 3162.c 3163.a 3164.a
3165.b 3166.a 3167.c 3168.b
3169.b
3170.a 3171.c 3172.a 3173.b
3174.a 3175.c 3176.b 3177.b
3178.a
3179.a 3180.a 3181.c 3182.b
3183.c 3184.a 3185.b 3186.c
3187.b
3188.a 3189.b 3190.c 3191.a
3192.b 3193.a 3194.b 3195.c
3196.b

3197.c 3198.a 3199.a 3200.b
3201.b 3202.a 3203.c 3204.c
3205.b
3206.a 3207.b 3208.a 3209.c
3210.c 3211.c 3212.b 3213.a
3214.b
3215.a 3216.b 3217.b 3218.c
3219.b 3220.c 3221.a 3222.c
3223.a
3224.b 3225.a 3226.b 3227.c
3228.a 3229.b 3230.b 3231.c
3232.a
3233.c 3234.a 3235.b 3236.a
3237.b 3238.c 3239.b 3240.a
3241.a
3242.c 3243.a 3244.b 3245.b
3246.b 3247.c 3248.a 3249.c
3250.b
3251.b 3252.b 3253.a 3254.c
3255.c 3256.a 3257.b 3258.b
3259.a
3260.c 3261.b 3262.b 3263.a
3264.c 3265.c 3266.a 3267.b
3268.c
3269.a 3270.b 3271.c 3272.a
3273.a 3274.b 3275.b 3276.c
3277.a
3278.c 3279.b 3280.a 3281.c
3282.b 3283.c 3284.a 3285.a
3286.b
3287.c 3288.a 3289.a 3290.b
3291.a 3292.c 3293.b 3294.a
3295.c
3296.b 3297.a 3298.a 3299.b
3300.c 3301.a 3302.c 3303.a
3304.b

3305.c 3306.b 3307.a 3308.b
3309.a 3310.c 3311.a 3312.c
3313.b
3314.b 3315.a 3316.a 3317.a
3318.b 3319.c 3320.b 3321.a
3322.c
3323.b 3324.c 3325.c 3326.b
3327.a 3328.c 3329.a 3330.a
3331.c
3332.a 3333.b 3334.a 3335.b
3336.a 3337.c 3338.a 3339.c
3340.a
3341.b 3342.b 3343.b 3344.a
3345.c 3346.a 3347.c 3348.a
3349.b
3350.c 3351.a 3352.c 3353.b
3354.b 3355.a 3356.b 3357.c
3358.a
3359.b 3360.a 3361.b 3362.c
3363.a 3364.a 3365.b 3366.c
3367.a
3368.b 3369.c 3370.a 3371.b
3372.c 3373.c 3374.a 3375.a
3376.a
3377.b 3378.c 3379.a 3380.a
3381.b 3382.b 3383.c 3384.a
3385.c
3386.b 3387.b 3388.c 3389.a
3390.c 3391.b 3392.a 3393.c
3394.a
3395.b 3396.c 3397.c 3398.b
3399.c 3400.a